THE
New Ontario
Gardener

W9-CJT-134

THE
New Ontario
Gardener

Trevor Cole

WHITECAP BOOKS
Vancouver · Toronto

Edited by Linda Ostrowalker
Revised edition edited by Elaine Jones
Proofread by Kathy Evans
Cover and interior photographs by Trevor Cole
Interior illustrations by Robert Hart
Interior design by Lisa Eng-Lodge
Cover design by Roberta Batchelor
Production Assistant Felicia Lo
Printed and bound in Canada

National Library of Canada Cataloguing in Publication Data

Cole, Trevor J.
  The new Ontario gardener

  Originally published under title: The Ontario Gardener.
  Includes bibliographical references and index.
  ISBN 1-55285-086-2

  1. Gardening—Ontario. I. Title. II. Title: Ontario gardener.
  SB453.3.C2C64 2001   635'.09713   C2001-910112-0

This book
is dedicated to
the students of my home
landscaping courses.
They asked the questions
which prompted this book,
and I hope I have
answered them here.

Contents

Contents

LIST OF COLOURED PLATES

INTRODUCTION

The genuine green thumb needs no help, so this is a book for the brown thumb, the khaki thumb, and the potential green thumb. It is an introduction to gardening in the city and suburb, where lots are small and the time for gardening is short.

This book is the result of a chance meeting between Nick Rundall of Whitecap Books and myself, when the need for a book like this came up in conversation. After almost 20 years of teaching home landscaping to adult students in the Ottawa area, I jumped at the chance to put my lectures into print.

As a professional horticulturist, I found that sitting down to actually write a book was a very humbling experience. Things that I thought I knew all about needed hours of research, and facts that I had taken for granted were questioned and had to prove themselves again. I have tried to combine the latest trends and findings in ornamental horticulture with a basic instruction in the elements of gardening, always keeping in mind the trials and tribulations which our climate brings us.

Modern environmental concerns have greatly altered the way in which we garden. This has affected me both in my previous employment as curator of the Dominion Arboretum in Ottawa and as an avid home gardener. The current leanings towards good soil practices and composting can only have beneficial long-term effects. While I am not a dyed-in-the-wool organic gardener, I only use chemical sprays when all else has failed and it's a case of them or my plants. This, I hope, is reflected in my recommendations for plant care and pest control throughout the book.

Gardening is always evolving and, while in the past ten years techniques have only changed a little, the list of available plants has changed a lot. In updating this book, I have tried to peer into the future and include some of the new plants that I think we will be growing in our gardens in the next few years. More and more people are living in row housing and in apartment buildings, with only a few square metres to grow plants in, so I have added a chapter on container gardening. I have always been fascinated by rock gardens as they enable me to grow a lot of different plants in a small space. Judging by the growth of The Ontario Rock Garden Society and the Ottawa Valley Rock Garden Society, others share my interest. Read this new chapter on rock gardening and perhaps you will too.

No book of this scope could possibly be done unaided and my thanks go chiefly to my wife, Brenda, who is almost as big a garden nut as myself, and whose initial comments and criticisms of every chapter often rescued it from the round file. I am also indebted to my colleagues at Agriculture Canada in Ottawa; especially to Marcel Beauchamp and Brian Douglas, who read and passed comments on every chapter, and to David Johnstone for his help with the chapter on roses. The sections on landscaping and perennials were greatly improved following suggestions from David Tomlinson, Landscape Architect of Aurora, who also designed the garden plan on plate 2. I must also say a big thank you to Beverley Kennis of the West Carleton Garden Club who, as a beginning gardener, read each chapter with an uncluttered mind and made many valid comments. A special thank you also goes to Bob Hart for the wonderful job he did on the illustrations found throughout this book.

Finally, my thanks go to the staff at Whitecap Books in Vancouver for the help and advice they gave a novice author, and especially to my editor, Linda Ostrowalker, who polished my grammar and spelling without altering the contents.

PLANT HARDINESS ZONES

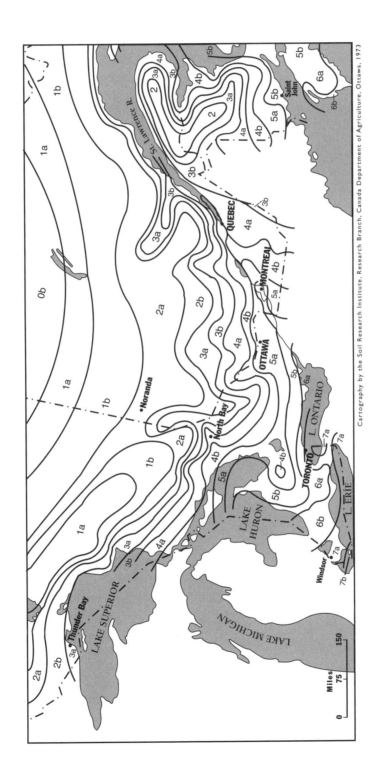

Cartography by the Soil Research Institute, Research Branch, Canada Department of Agriculture, Ottawa, 1973

Soils

1 chapter

When growing up in England, I would listen to a popular gardening radio program in which a team of experts answered questions sent in by listeners. Often, when the question was about the growth of a plant, one of the panel would remark in a broad country accent, "Oi think the aanswer lies in the soyul." The more plants I grow, and the more I learn about them, the more I think he was right. Very often the problems that occur with plants do have their answers "in the soil."

This first chapter is devoted to a brief look at soils—what they are, what they do, and how we can amend or improve them; at plant foods and their effect on plant growth; and at gardeners' black gold—compost. Read on a little before dismissing soil as a boring subject. A basic knowledge of how plants grow and the role of soil in their lives is of great benefit when actually engaged in the craft of gardening.

 PARTICLES

Long ago, when the world was new, there was no soil. Rain fell on rocks and gradually wore them away. Water froze in crevices in the rock and broke pieces off. Rivers rushing towards the newly formed seas tumbled the pieces together and turned them into finer granules. Waves washing up on the shores ground these granules together and turned them into the fine particles that make up part of our soil. Plants emerged from the water to colonize the shores, and animals evolved to feed on these plants. As the plants and animals died, their remains were broken down by micro-organisms and enriched the rock particles, forming a very simple soil.

To discover for yourself that soil is not just dirt, go into your garden and collect about a trowelful of soil. Let the soil sample dry out enough that you can crumble it into a fine powder, breaking up all the lumps. Get a straight-sided glass container such as an olive jar. Fill this about two-thirds full with water and add some of the crumbled soil, leaving room to shake. Put the lid on tightly and shake vigorously. Place on one side and allow to settle. In a few seconds the sand particles, being the heaviest, will have sunk to the bottom. Over that forms a layer of silt, while the clay particles will take several hours to settle (it may take a couple of days for the water to clear completely as the finest particles remain in suspension for a long time). On the surface of the water is a floating layer of the plant and animal remains, known as humus (Figure 1–1).

While there is no distinct boundary between the various layers, since one size of particle shades into the next, it is usually possible to make a fairly accurate measurement of the percentages of the different soil constituents and thus to determine your soil type. It is generally taken that sand particles average 1/50th of an inch, silt particles 1/500th, and clay particles 1/5000th; it might help to think of them as basketballs, large grapefruit, and grapes.

SANDY SOILS. These contain less than 15% clay, 50–75% sand and the rest silt. They are soils that can be worked early in the spring because the large particle size allows water to drain freely, but because the water leaches out the nutrients, they are poor growing soils for the rest of the year. Improve them with large helpings of organic matter.

SANDY LOAM. Not such a high sand content, generally between 35 and 50%, and thus more clay and silt. Because of their higher clay content they do not dry out as quickly as sandy soils. They are a good soil for the home gardener and can be worked soon after rain.

SILTY LOAM. Almost as good a soil as sandy loam but they tend to form lumps as they dry. Silty loam contains about 50% silt

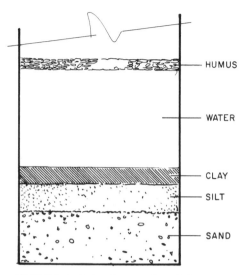

FIGURE 1–1 A simple experiment shows a cross-section of the basic components of soil.

and 15–25% clay. The addition of washed river sand to improve drainage make these ideal soils.

CLAY LOAM. Undoubtedly the worst type of soil for the home gardener to cope with and probably the cause of many a novice giving up in despair. These soils contain mostly silt and clay, are cold and wet in spring, and bake into hard lumps in the summer. And yet, if worked properly, clay soils are remarkably rich and produce wonderful flowers and vegetables. The clay particles are invaluable in any soil since they have the ability to form a chemical bond with plant nutrients and prevent them from being leached away by rain. If rough-dug in the fall and left to weather, the individual clay particles group themselves into little clusters, about the size of sand particles, and the soil then drains much better. Unfortunately, this crumb structure is easily destroyed, and walking on the soil will press the individual grains back into a sticky mass. To avoid having to walk on the cultivated soil and thus retain a good soil structure, make narrow beds that can be reached from either side in the vegetable garden, and put lots of stepping stones through flower beds. The best way to improve heavy clay soils is to work in large quantities of

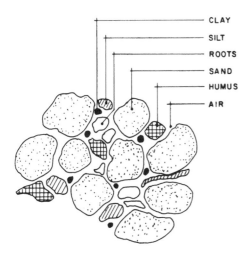

FIGURE 1-2 Component particles of soil are surrounded by pockets of air.

humus and sand. Both will improve the drainage—the major problem with fine-textured soil. The best form of sand is known as either horticultural sand or washed river sand. This has had the very fine particles, that tend to cake the soil, removed so you are only adding the coarser granules that do the best job of improving the drainage. There is one form of humus that is not very suitable for adding to clay soils, and that is the most readily available one, peat moss. While peat moss does a good job at separating the clay particles, it retains a large amount of water itself and does little to help the soil dry out. It is great on sandy soils, however.

It is interesting to compare the rate at which water passes through different soils as a way of bringing home the difference that particle size makes. In sand, water would move downwards at 230 m (750 ft.) per day, while in a clay soil the water would move only 15 cm (6 in.) in the same time.

ORGANIC OR MUCK SOILS. These are usually a dark brown or black in colour and contain 50–85% organic matter. They are quite rich in nutrients, but tend to hold a lot of water which makes them cold soils in the spring. They are often, but not always, acidic.

STRUCTURE

So, after all that, just what *is* soil, apart from various percentages of different-sized minerals? Many other very important ingredients contribute to a good garden soil: water, dissolved minerals, bacteria, insects, animals, and, most importantly, air. Remember, plants do not grow in soil—they grow in the spaces *between* the soil particles (Figure 1–2).

Unlike most animals, plants do not have a circulatory system that takes oxygen-rich fluids to all parts of the plant. Roots in particular have to take in their oxygen from the surrounding air. Every time a root makes new growth, the energy for cell division comes from turning some stored food into other chemicals, and this requires oxygen. This oxygen is absorbed through the cell wall from the air spaces between the soil particles.

This is why, when beavers build a dam and flood an area of woodland, the trees all die—not from an overdose of water but from a lack of oxygen. Certain plants have adapted to life in wet areas and are able to take in the necessary oxygen from the surrounding water, but they are in the minority.

When it rains, all the air spaces in the soil fill with water, but as the rain moves down through the soil it pulls new air in behind it, refilling the spaces with fresh oxygen. Each soil particle is left with a film of water around it that contains dissolved minerals. These minerals also diffuse into the cell and provide the raw materials for plant growth.

As the soil dries, this film of water gets thinner and thinner. In sandy soils the particles may dry out completely, but the microscopic clay particles retain their water through an electrical bond. This bonding is so strong that it forms the drying clay into a solid mass; eventually, if the drought continues, the bond fractures in places, causing the characteristic cracking of clay soils.

One final, very important, function of soil is to give mechanical support to the plant. Without soil to put its roots into, a plant would fall over. Those of you who have been to Epcot® at Walt Disney World in Florida, may have seen their hydroponic display. Some of the plants are growing suspended in air and are sprayed with dilute fertilizer solutions. They are, however, suspended, and could not stand up by themselves. Other hydroponic units have plants growing in rockwool, gravel, and similar soil substitutes, all designed to provide the mechanical support needed by the plant.

 # SWEET AND SOUR

To a new gardener, that mysterious soil factor, the pH, can seem akin to a cauldron of eye of toad and blood of dragon, but there is no great secret involved. A pH is simply a measure of the acidity or alkalinity of the soil measured on a scale of 1 to 14, with 7 being neutral and the lower numbers acidic. This, like the Richter scale used for measuring earthquakes, is a logarithmic scale, which means that each number is ten times the previous—thus a pH of 6 is 10 times as acidic as 7; a pH of 5 is 10 times as acidic as 6 but 100 times as acidic as 7.

All types of soil may be anywhere from very acidic to highly alkaline and, while it may not seem very important to know what your soil is, it does influence the type of plants you can grow. The pH has an effect on the availability of many of the nutrients in the soil—a particular mineral may be present in quite large quantities but because of the pH it is locked into the soil and is not available to the plant. Also, plants differ in the amount of a specific chemical they need. For example, as the pH increases, iron becomes less and less available to the plants. For most plants this is no big

deal since they only need minute quantities of iron. Rhododendrons, for some reason, need large amounts of iron and, if grown in a neutral or alkaline soil, they soon become discoloured with yellow areas between their leaf veins, a condition known as *chlorosis*. Iron is an essential mineral used by the plant in the manufacture and structure of the green chlorophyll. If given additional iron in a form that is readily available to the plant, this yellowing quickly disappears.

Most garden plants grow happily in the pH range of 6.5 to 7.2, but some like it sweeter or sourer than this. If the majority of the plants you grow look normal, then your soil is probably in this range. There are simple kits available in garden centres that you can use to determine the pH of your soil if you suspect it may be the source of poor growth or poor plant colour. Should the results show that your pH is way too high or low, then you will have to correct it. Acidic soils are relatively easy to adjust with lime, although the amount needed depends on the soil type. To raise the pH by one point, add the following quantities per 100 sq. m (1,000 sq. ft.).

Sandy soils . . . . 10 kg (25 lb.)
Medium loams . . . . 20 kg (50 lb.)
Clay soils . . . . 30 kg (75 lb.)

Note that on clay soils the addition of lime helps to form a good crumb structure as discussed earlier, but it should not be added to soils that are already alkaline. When lime is needed, use dolomitic limestone, which can be applied by hand or through a regular fertilizer spreader.

Alkaline soils are much harder to acidify. Peat moss is often touted as a good additive that will lower the pH, but the pH of the peat itself can vary from 8.0 to 2.5. Aluminum sulphate is also recommended for quick results, but if used very often it can lead to an aluminum toxicity in the soil that is almost impossible to cure. On a small scale—for example, if you want to try one blueberry bush, which has a preferred pH of 4.5—water the soil regularly with a solution of 5 mL (1 tsp.) vinegar per litre of water. For larger areas use powdered sulphur at about 125 mL (¹/₂ cup) per square metre (square yard) to lower the pH by one point. Again, the quantity needed varies with the soil type, so start with this and retest after a few weeks to see what the effect has been.

Whenever you need to change the reading by more than a single point, make haste slowly. Change the value one number at a time and watch your plants carefully to make sure there are no adverse reactions such as leaf fall or colour change, or dieback of the growing tips.

Remember, everything you do to the soil has some effect on pH. Many commercial fertilizers are alkaline. Adding peat moss will usually lower the reading; even digging opens the soil up so that chemicals leach through faster, affecting the pH. Acid rain will certainly play a large part in the near future in changing the pH readings in our gardens and influencing the types of plants we are able to grow. If the present warmer temperatures continue and are not just a blip in the statistics, we may see drastic changes in the weather with an increase in precipitation. More rain means cooler clay soils and nutrients washed out of the soil faster, possibly leading to a change in pH. We may have to check the pH more frequently to continue growing the plants we like. We may yet all end up growing rhododendrons and blueberries.

 # FERTILIZERS

Whenever you go into a store to buy some plant food, whether it be a bag of lawn feed or a bottle of something to perk up your house plants, you may notice that the container is marked with three numbers. It matters not if you live in Toronto or Tuktoyaktuk (or probably even Timbuktu), there should always be three numbers in the same order, and they always mean the same things: **Nitrogen** (N), **Phosphorus** (P), and **Potassium** (K). The numbers indicate the percentages of that specific ingredient in the mix and may be high (10-52-10), as in a plant starter, or very low (0-0-1), as in liquid seaweed. N, P, and K are known as the major nutrients and they are essential to good plant growth.

NITROGEN is the major factor in plant growth. Without it plants become stunted and growth eventually stops. Many fertilizers will have their nitrogen content in different forms that become available to the plant at different rates. Nitrates are available immediately, nitrogen in the form of ammonia becomes converted into nitrates fairly quickly, while nitrogen in the form of urea takes longer to become usable by the plant.

Just to confuse the issue still further, some fertilizers are called *slow release*. Here, the urea portion is treated to delay its breakdown still longer. In sulphur-coated urea (SCU), the beads of urea are given various thicknesses of sulphur coating. These are gradually dissolved by rain, releasing the urea over a longer period. In urea formaldehyde (UF), the urea is given a coating that needs to be broken down by bacteria in the soil before it becomes available. These special forms of fertilizer are used mainly on lawns and will be covered further in Chapter 3.

Nitrogen is soluble and leaches out of the soil with rain so it must be replaced frequently. It is also part of every cell of every plant and animal, so decaying plant remains are continually adding more nitrogen to the soil in a form which the plant can easily use.

Certain bacteria in the soil have the ability to fix nitrogen from the air (in its pure state nitrogen is a gas) and turn it into nitrites. These bacteria live in the roots of plants of the pea family and cause characteristic nodules on the plant roots. They gain other nutrients from the plants but give nitrogen in return, and, without doubt, infected plants crop better. This is the basis of the legume inoculant sold by many seed companies. HINT: Any time you grow peas and beans, when cropping is finished break the plants off at the base, leaving the roots in the ground to decay and release their nitrogen for the next crop.

PHOSPHORUS is not soluble and does not move readily through the soil, so it must be placed in the root zone where it is needed. The phosphoric acid in liquid plant foods breaks down to give insoluble forms of phosphate once it is added to the soil. Phosphorus is needed by growing tips—both shoots and roots—so fertilizers with a high middle number are listed as plant starters since they promote root growth. It is important for flower and fruit production and is most readily available to the plant in soils with a neutral pH.

POTASSIUM, commonly known as potash, is essential for the formation of starch and sugars and for the movement of foodstuffs within the plant. During the day, in sunlight, leaves manufacture sugars. These are changed into insoluble starches and stored within the leaf. After dark they are converted back into sugars again and moved through the plant to the growing tips or the storage areas. Potash plays a vital role in this conversion and is essential for healthy growth. A good source of potash is wood ash but this is very alkaline and on soils with a high pH its use would only make matters worse. The use of wood ash should be restricted to bare soil. It is so highly alkaline that, until leached by rain, it can seriously burn roots if used around growing plants.

In the normal course of events, the area just behind the rootcap is the major intake region, supplying nutrients to the rest of the plant as a

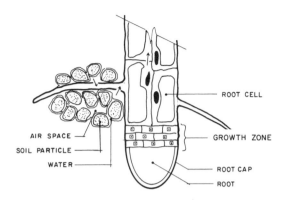

FIGURE 1-3 Plant roots absorb nutrients from the film of water that clings to soil particles.

root moves down through the soil. The cells contain a fluid called cell sap which is similar to a sugar syrup. The root hairs push out into the film of water surrounding each soil particle which, while it contains dissolved minerals, is a much weaker solution than the cell sap. This water diffuses through the cell wall, trying to dilute the sap and bring things to a state of equilibrium. When an excess of fertilizer is added to the soil (in this case, wood ash), the strength of the soil water becomes more than the cell sap. Instead of the diffusion being inward, it is outward and the cell dries out. This kills that particular root tip and, if enough roots are affected, it may kill the entire plant.

As a landscaping friend of mine put it, nitrogen for tops, phosphates for bottoms, and potash for all-round well-being.

If you have followed this so far, you may have one question unanswered. If the numbers on a fertilizer bag are the percentages of the ingredients, then why don't they add up to 100? On a bag of 10-6-4, what is the other 80%? As mentioned earlier, nitrogen in its natural state is a gas and so it has to be changed into a form that is both stable and non-toxic to plant life. This is also the case for the other ingredients. While it is theoretically possible to make a fertilizer whose analysis would add up to close to 100%, it would be so strong that application would be difficult; the slightest overlap when applying it would result in root burn. Chalk is the most common filler used in fertilizers, and as a result most are alkaline. Some brands use different fillers and are advertised as acid-based, specially made for acid-loving plants such as rhododendrons.

In addition to the three major nutrients, calcium is needed for cell formation and magnesium for chlorophyll, both in fairly large quantities. Then there are the minor (or trace) elements that are essential for healthy plant growth but are needed in very small amounts. These elements include iron, zinc, boron, sulphur, copper, and molybdenum. For example, molybdenum is needed at one part in 100 000 000; about equivalent to one drop of vermouth in a tanker truck of gin. A very, very dry martini, but without the vermouth it is not a martini and without the molybdenum, the plant will not grow properly.

A deficiency in any of these trace elements does funny things to a plant. It may cause yellow areas between the veins, a purple margin on the leaf, red lines along the veins, or give other strange effects. These deficiencies are usually found in container-grown plants and rarely occur in plants growing in the garden. They can happen on new sites where the developer has scraped away all the topsoil and the plants are trying to grow in a nutrient-poor subsoil.

If you suspect that a lack of trace elements is causing your plant problems, spray with a solution of fish emulsion or liquid seaweed. Both of these are very rich in the minor nutrients, which can be absorbed through the leaves. The results are almost miraculous and the plants regain their proper colour very quickly—not overnight, but in a matter of days. If this spraying gives a temporary cure, water the root area with more of the fertilizer immediately and repeat every spring.

As well as the pH test kits mentioned earlier, you can also buy more extensive kits that will tell you the levels of nitrogen, phosphorus and potassium in your soil, in addition to the pH. While these kits are not 100% accurate, using these kits over a period of time does indicate nutrient depletion and give a guide to the fertilizer you should apply. In addition, you can get a complete soil analysis done by a commercial company—look under Soil Testing in the Yellow Pages. However these are generally intended for commercial operations growing a specific crop, and I was very confused by the results the one time I had this done. I felt they had little relevance for my eclectic garden.

From a plant's point of view, there is no difference between the nitrates that come from a farmyard and those from a chemical factory. They are still just molecules that diffuse through the cell wall and are then built into other complex chemicals inside the plant. There is, however, a difference in the effects of the fertilizer on the soil. Soil that is given regular additions of some form of humus is in much better condition. It drains better but also retains moisture in dry periods, and the humus helps to "buffer" the plant foods; that is, it holds them in the soil and releases them slowly over a longer time, rather than all at once. The chances of overfertilizing are much less in soils with a high humus content.

Unfortunately, with many natural fertilizers, such as stable manure or homemade compost, you have no idea of the analysis. For example, adding old stable manure will work wonders on the soil texture but may do little to cure problems caused by a lack of nitrogen. The sterilized bags of sheep and cattle manure one can buy in garden centres in the spring are different, but you could hardly afford to add large quantities of these to the garden. Also, many natural manures contain large quantities of weed seeds—with free-range chicken manure being about the worst. If possible, add these to the compost heap, so the heat can sterilize the seeds.

While the analysis of many of the readily

available organic manures is known (for example, bone meal is 2-25-0, hardwood ash about 0-2-5, blood meal 9 to 14-0-0), these all have to be broken down by bacteria in the soil, and there is a delay between their application and their availability to the plant. With artificial fertilizers, particularly the water soluble ones, the plant can start to use them almost immediately.

Until a good soil structure is achieved, you will either have to use a limited amount of chemical fertilizer or have poor crops. Once you have improved your soil, then your plants will tell you their needs if you watch for signs of stunted growth, yellowing, or flowers and fruit failing to develop properly. While I add lots of compost to my own garden, I still use some inorganic fertilizer to give a boost to certain crops (such as asparagus) in the spring when the soil is still cold and the bacteria not active, and on the lawn areas.

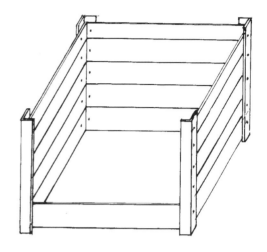

FIGURE 1–4 A homemade compost bin made of secondhand lumber and angle irons.

 ## COMPOSTING

I cannot understand why anybody who gardens would not have a compost bin. It may be a trace of Scottish blood, but I like the idea of something for nothing, of saving money by not having to buy soil amendments, and saving tax dollars by doing my bit to lessen the need for landfill sites.

Note that I said a compost *bin*. A pile of garden refuse thrown untidily into the corner is a pile of refuse—it is not a compost heap. Besides, piles need turning, an added chore that I can do without. You will read all sorts of information on the benefits of commercial composters, on how to make compost in six weeks, or on the miracles of this or that additive. No doubt they have merit, but they are not necessary.

When we bought our first house in Canada

we didn't have much money but we needed a compost pile because the garden was pure sand over rock. I managed to find some scrap sheets of rigid insulation 2.5 cm (1 in.) thick. Four old hockey sticks hammered into the ground to support the middle of each sheet and a length of clothesline top and bottom to stop the corners from spreading and we were in business. It didn't look very fancy (it wasn't) but it worked as long as we were careful shoveling out the finished product, and it lasted about three years.

If you are really desperate for humus in the garden, follow one of the rapid methods, wherein you turn the contents every few days. This will greatly speed up the decomposition, but you really need two containers: one that you are turning and another that you are putting your waste materials into.

A heap is probably the least satisfactory. It is difficult to construct properly and usually ends up as a domed pile that sheds water rather than a neat tapering heap with a concave top. Because it loses a lot of heat through the sides, the materials are slow to break down and the outside layer does not decompose, so at least one turning is required.

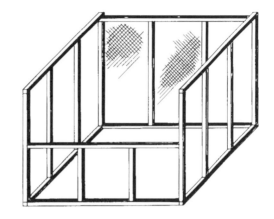

FIGURE 1-7 A wood frame covered with wire netting
is particularly good for composting leaves.

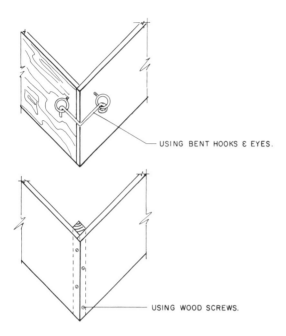

— USING BENT HOOKS & EYES.

— USING WOOD SCREWS.

FIGURE 1-5 Securing the corners of a homemade
plywood compost bin.

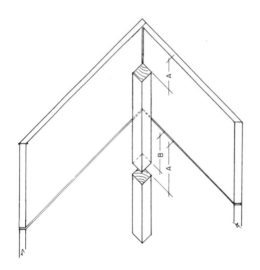

FIGURE 1-6 An extendible compost bin can be
constructed using short posts and plywood boards.

Commercial composters, while expensive initially, are efficient, long-lasting and ideal for compact townhouse gardens or apartment balconies. If properly made, homemade containers are cheap and durable. A container about 1 cubic m (1 cubic yd.) will be large enough for the average family on a regular suburban lot. You can make it of almost anything that will stand the weight of the compost. Use whatever is readily available at a reasonable cost.

If you can get some demolition lumber or old barn-boards about 3 x 15 cm (1 x 6 in.), drive angle irons in at each corner of the site and cut the boards to fit inside (Figure 1–4).

Exterior grade plywood, at least 1 cm (1/2 in.) thick, can either be held together with hooks and eyes bent around the corners or can be screwed onto corner posts (Figure 1–5). One other way, if you are cutting your own plywood boards, is to screw them onto individual short corner posts which project on one side, allowing the sides to be increased in layers (Figure 1–6). Whenever possible, make the front in sections that you can add as the contents build up and remove gradually when shoveling out. Treat all wood except cedar with a wood preservative that is non-toxic to plants when dry.

A method I find particularly good for leaves, although it will also work for regular compost, is to build a wood frame and cover it with wire netting (Figure 1–7). If lined with heavy-duty polyethylene sheeting (such as old peat moss bags) the contents don't dry out.

If your composter is built of logs or rough boards, there will be enough gaps between them to allow the necessary air flow into the pile. If you have built it of plywood sheets or with other solid sides, drill 3-cm (1-in.) holes about 15 cm (6 in.) apart to allow air circulation. In theory, decomposition without enough oxygen can create terrible smells (as in marsh gas).

While a single box is normally sufficient, a double container allows you to leave the contents for longer and get a better breakdown.

 # WHAT TO COMPOST

Virtually any vegetable material can be put into the compost, although diseased plants and weed seeds are best put in the garbage. Most kitchen waste is suitable—cabbage leaves, potato peelings, tea bags, coffee filters—plus hair, contents of vacuum cleaner bags (although fluff from nylon carpets does not decompose), and floor sweepings. Don't add meat or dairy products as they may attract vermin (or raccoons) and, unless you have a very acid soil, don't add eggshells. Your soil doesn't need the calcium, and they do not break down. (If needed, crush them finely first.) Pet litter should also be placed in the garbage since cat feces may contain two parasites that can affect humans, possibly causing blindness in children.

From the garden you can add grass clippings (except for the first two mowings after treating the lawn with a weed killer), weeds, flower heads, and, in the fall, all the frosted annuals. Try to mix lawn clippings in with other materials. If you put them on more than a few centimetres (inches) thick, they pack down and give off an unpleasant smell. If this happens, a layer of soil spread over the clippings will cure it in a few hours.

More difficult, because they take longer to break down, are clippings with woody stems, cabbage stalks, wood shavings, etc. If you add these to the heap, they will probably still be recognizable when you shovel out and you will have to throw them back in for a second season.

If you have access to a shredder, either by borrowing from a friend, or by renting, it is worth the effort. They are a big help in fall while cleaning up the annuals and cutting down perennials, and they chop corn and cabbage stalks into tiny pieces that decompose rapidly. I was amazed the first time I used one at the way it turned a bulky pile of old plants into a small pile of chop, and equaly amazed at the speed with which this chop heated and started to decompose in the compost bin. Within two days it was almost too hot to push my hand into. Shredders also do a good job of mixing carbon-rich (woody) and nitrogen-rich (green) plant wastes together.

If you only have a couple of trees and shrubs, add their leaves to the regular compost pile, but if you have several trees and large quantities of leaves, it is better to deal with them separately. Since leaves all fall in a short time, it is easy to give them their own home, which can be in a less convenient location. Pile the leaves inside the container and tread them down. To speed up decomposition, add a thin layer of soil to every 20- to 30-cm (8- to 10-in.) layer. Cover the top of the pile with netting to stop the leaves from blowing away over the winter.

In the spring, when the snow has melted, add a few handfuls of high-nitrogen fertilizer and a layer of soil. Cover with heavy-duty plastic sheeting and weight it down. During the summer, check occasionally to make sure the pile is moist, watering if needed. The leaves should be decomposed and ready to dig into the soil before the next lot falls. This marvelous soil amendment is known as leaf mould.

HOW TO COMPOST

Ideally a composter should be situated in semi-shade and protected from the coldest winds. Much more important is convenience. No one is going to trudge to the end of the garden with the potato peelings when the garbage can is much handier. Be sure the location is well drained and, if necessary, cover the area with paving slabs, leaving drainage channels between them.

If possible, the best time to start a compost pile is in the fall. You can then add all the dead annuals and clippings from non-woody perennials and have your container half-full in no time. The weather is still mild enough for decomposition to start, and the bacteria will multiply and be ready to do their job as soon as the frost melts in the spring. The next best time is any other season.

It is all too easy when adding material to a compost bin to pile it in the centre. Try to remember to spread the waste in even layers and fill the corners before the middle. About every 20–25 cm (8–10 in.) sprinkle a few shovelfuls of soil over the surface (Figure 1–8). This contains the bacteria and micro-organisms needed to break down the vegetable matter. If your soil is very poor, then one of the compost accelerators should be used. These are dried or liquid extracts of the fungi and bacteria that turn your garden waste into black gold for you. They are available at many garden centres.

Continue to build up alternate thick layers of compostables and thin layers of soil. Water during dry periods or, better still, water with a high-nitrogen liquid feed. The bacteria are simple organisms and need nitrogen to thrive and multiply. You will get it back later in the compost as they themselves decompose. If you don't have liquid feed, a couple of handfuls of lawn food will do the same trick—but *not* one that contains a herbicide.

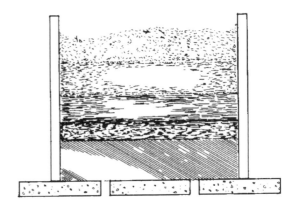

FIGURE 1–8 Alternating layers of waste and soil should be spread across the compost bin.

As you are adding to the top of the heap, the lower levels are breaking down. During the summer this action is rapid, and a few days away from home with nothing being added will make a big difference in the level. During winter, when the temperature in the heap drops below about 5°C (40°F), all decomposition stops until the spring. This is well into the winter, since a considerable heat is produced inside the heap during decomposition—enough to kill many weed seeds. I cover the top of my composter in the fall with a few planks. This keeps the snow out so that I can continue to add my household waste all winter.

Once your container has been filled and has composted down a few times, it will probably be late in the year. This is the time when most people spread their compost on the garden (although, of course, it can be used at any time), ready to dig in with fall clean-up. The top layer that has been added only recently will not have broken down yet and should be lifted off and put on one side. The resulting compost will look rather like a dark-brown or black soil. It can either be dug into the garden or spread round permanent plants as a mulch.

It is very rich in humus, and the worms will pull it into the soil during the coming summer.

The top layer that you lifted off, plus any woody stems that have not fully decomposed, are put back into the container afterwards, as the start of the next heap.

If you are using a commercial compost maker with sliding panels or a "door" in the bottom, you can dig out a little compost at any time. I must admit that with the one I use, once you have dug some out from inside the bottom opening it is very difficult to reach much more. Sliding panels, so you could work your way all round, would probably be more practical.

 # GREEN MANURING

There is one way in which you can improve the texture of your soil without composting or spending a lot of money on ready-made humus. This is by the process known as green manuring. It is particularly useful if you are not quite sure of what you want to do, but would like to make some sort of start on the garden while you decide on the details. Any area that will not be formally cultivated for a couple of months can be improved by green manuring.

Dig the area over enough to break up any hard surface and remove the large weeds. Then sow with clover, alfalfa, cow peas, lupins, or beans. These are all members of the pea family with the ability to fix atmospheric nitrogen and are great for improving very poor soils. Use a legume inoculant the first time you grow them; these are sold as powders or granules in garden stores and seed catalogues. Non-legumes used as green manure crops include buckwheat, ryegrass, millet, and most of the cereals. These add considerable amounts of vegetation to the soil and also break

down swiftly.

Grow the seedlings until they start to flower, then dig them under before they have set seed. With some of the rapid growers, like buckwheat, you can get three crops dug under in one summer. On sloping sites green manures have the added advantage of stopping erosion, and those that will overwinter, like winter rye, can be sown in the fall to give control until spring.

Seeds of most of these are not available from the average garden centre, but you will find them at farm supply stores and in some seed catalogues. The quantities of seed that you will need per 100 sq. m (1,000 sq. ft.) are:

alfalfa	250 g	(¹/₂ lb.)
beans	2 kg	(4 lb.)
buckwheat	1 kg	(2–3 lb.)
clover	250 g	(¹/₂ lb.)
cow peas	2 kg	(4 lb.)
lupins	1.5 kg	(3 lb.)
millet	500 g	(1 lb.)
oats	2 kg	(4 lb.)
rye	2–3 kg	(4–6 lb.)

The addition of green manures is beneficial to both sandy and heavy clay soils, improving the water retention of one and the drainage of the other. They are particularly good for smothering weed seedlings and helping to reduce the number of weeds you will get in the future. The more crops you can get, the better the weed control, since every time you dig, you bring fresh seeds to the surface to start growing.

If you have a vegetable garden, it is worthwhile green manuring after early crops such as peas, even in quite small areas. It improves the soil, prevents weeds taking over and helps to cut down on wind erosion. In fact, green manure any time you expect to have bare soil for more than a month during the growing season.

DIGGING

Having just told you that you have to dig in the green manure, this would seem a good spot to write a little about digging. As a sport, I must admit, digging leaves much to be desired; it is, however, not an unpleasant occupation on a cool autumn day providing you are not "greedy." Do not be tempted to try and dig great spadefuls of soil that strain your back muscles when you try to lift them. It is faster, healthier, and more efficient to dig small slices of soil.

If possible, especially on the vegetable garden, do your digging in the fall, turning the soil over in lumps and making no attempt to break it down. This is known as rough digging and will expose the maximum area of the soil to the frosts and snows of winter, which kill many of the pests that hibernate in the soil. It also has an effect on the soil structure of heavy clay soils, making them more manageable in the spring.

With spring or summer digging, such as preparing for green manuring, the clumps should be broken down to such a degree that the soil can be raked level, ready for seeding.

For most people, digging consists simply of turning the soil over in place, but you will actually find it much easier if you remove the first "spit" of soil across the width of the bed, leaving a shallow trench. (A spit of soil is either the amount removed by a spade, as in "Keep your spits narrow and you won't get backache," or the depth of the spade, as in "Make sure you dig that a full spit deep!"). Take this to the other end of the bed ready to fill in the last trench. You then work down the bed, turning the soil into the trench you have just made, until you reach the end. Digging is easier and the results more level using this method. If the plot to be dug is wide, divide it down the centre and move the first spit from

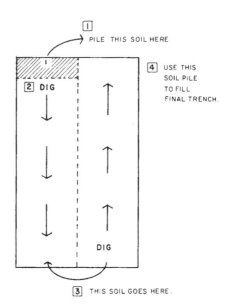

FIGURE 1–9 A systematic approach to turning over the soil using parallel trenches.

one side to the other half as in Figure 1-9. One of the advantages of growing your vegetables in narrow beds is that the soil from the trench at the start of the first bed can be taken to the end of the last one. You just change direction at the end of each bed and use the soil from the next bed to fill the trench you left. Think of it as multiples of Figure 1–9 with paths down the middle.

There are a couple of variations on this that are worth remembering. The first is to make the trench wide enough that you can put humus (compost, manure, grass clippings) as a layer in the bottom of the trench to provide a nutrient-rich zone for the plant roots next summer. The second is to take this a stage further and actually dig this humus into the bottom of the trench (double digging). This breaks up the subsoil and enriches it, encouraging the plants to put their roots down deep, which helps them during dry periods. The only problem with this is that it takes a lot of time. I try to double-dig a couple of the beds in my vegetable garden each fall, digging the rest one spit deep.

I do not recommend the use of a rototiller as a substitute for digging. Unless you have a really large machine, they do not go deep enough; you end up with a shallowly worked soil, and a compacted layer develops over time just below the rotors. When this happens the plant roots will not penetrate beyond this layer. Rototillers are great for working up seedbeds on light soils, but on heavy clays they destroy the soil structure.

 # TOPSOIL

One of the most frequent questions I am asked is, "Should I get a load of topsoil?" My answer is always, "Why?" The questioners can rarely give me a good reason but they seem to think that topsoil is the answer to all garden problems.

If you have a garden where the soil is very shallow or where it consists of builder's sand used to backfill around the house, then yes, you probably do need topsoil. If you have a very heavy clay soil, you are better to buy a load of washed river sand (the gritty one with all the fine particles removed) as this will work wonders to improve the drainage.

Remember that topsoil is what it says, the soil from the top of some farmer's field. You are buying weed seed and possibly herbicide residues along with the soil. Some of the new "supersoils" that are mixed with compost and sand are listed as being pasteurized. If possible, get a small sample of the soil and spread it about 5 cm (2 in.) thick on an area of the garden. Water it and see what germinates after a few days. Then, providing there is no danger of frost, sow some tomato seed on it. The seedlings should germinate in a few days and grow normally. Tomatoes are very sensitive to herbicides and will react with stunted growth or deformed foliage if there is a high level of residues.

Generally, a load of topsoil is 7 cubic m (9 cubic yd.), which looks like a tremendous pile when it is dumped on the end of your laneway. It also means about 80 wheelbarrows full when you come to wheel it away with the small barrow most homeowners use. But it is not a great deal once it is spread on the garden. To add a 10-cm (4-in.) layer to a sandy site—about the minimum to be able to grow grass—a load will only cover 90 sq. m (970 sq. ft.), about $^2/_5$ of an average city backyard.

Keep in mind that the soil itself is very cheap. It is the transport that costs the money; so order from a supplier close by, not from the other side of the city. The more you order the cheaper it becomes per cubic measure. It is worth scouting the neighbourhood, especially in new developments, to see if anyone else is wanting soil. If you can combine several orders in the same locality, you will be able to get a better price. But make sure the supplier will split the load into several drops. If not, phone a different firm.

 # SUGGESTED READING

The Rodale Book of Composting. Deborah L. Martin and Grace Gershuny (editors). Rodale Press, 1992.

Let It Rot. Stu Campbell. Storey Communications, 1998.

Two good books that will tell you everything you need about composting. The first goes into greater detail and is more scientific.

Landscaping

2 chapter

What do we mean when we talk about landscaping? To many municipalities, a landscaped lot is simply one that is covered with sod. To real estate agents it can mean whatever their imaginations want. I will always remember a property I looked at that was advertised as a "large treed lot." Sure enough there were three large trees on a regular size lot—not quite the picture I had in mind from the ad.

To many homeowners, landscaping begins and ends with some foundation planting. I have a theory about this obsessive use of evergreens around the base of a building. I think it dates from the Victorian era when the air was clean and sex was dirty. The time when tablecloths reached to the floor to cover up the legs of the table in case they gave rise to prurient thoughts. In the same way, the footings of the house were considered legs and every effort was made to cover them up. I have no objection to foundation planting as such, just to the

tedium of perpetual evergreens.

From an energy conservation point of view, it makes more sense to use deciduous plants whose leaves protect the walls from the summer sun but when they drop in the fall allow the sunlight through in the winter to warm the concrete slightly.

The fact that you are reading this book at all shows that you have ambitions to do more than just grow a few junipers and yews. You are probably interested in increasing the value of your property, in raising the tone of the neighbourhood, and in enjoying the satisfaction that glows within when someone praises your garden. Mind you, it is possible to go too far. In our last house we turned all the front yard into rock garden and I know that this put off some prospective buyers.

I should point out that my background is English (just in case you skipped Chapter 1). To me, the area surrounding the house is the garden, not the yard. It can grow anything, not just vegetables. It took me several years to learn what my North American friends meant when they asked, "Got your garden in yet?" Did they think I dug all my trees up for the winter and put them in the basement?

LANDSCAPE AND LIFESTYLE

The area around your home should be an expression of your personality. If you enjoy your garden it should reflect your interests and lifestyle. It is not something that can be copied piecemeal out of a book. There are dozens of books on the market on landscaping and they can all give you some ideas of features that you may want to include in your own home garden. But none of these books have a site like yours, in a climate like yours, to serve a family like yours.

As your family changes, you will find your interest in gardening changes, and your need for certain features in the landscape will alter. When the family is very young, you need sand boxes and paddling pools. Then comes the time of swing sets and playground equipment. Once they are old enough to be taught not to eat everything in sight, and that certain areas are off limits, you can start having some flowers and vegetables. (But not too many—it's amazing how often a ball ends up in the middle of a flower bed.)

Later still comes the era of bicycles left everywhere and of basketball hoops. Just pray they don't get bitten with a croquet bug and start bugging you to improve the lawn. At least by this time they are old enough to help mow.

Like most professional gardeners, I have been asked to give advice on how to landscape a property. First I ask a few questions. How much time do you want to give to the garden? What are your outside interests? What do you want to grow? Anyone who wants a garden full of roses in half an hour a week gets short shift!

Before you devote a lot of time to reading landscaping books and drawing up fancy plans, ask yourself seriously how much time you are going to have to look after it. *There is no such thing as a labour-free garden*, although proper planning and the use of landscape fabric and mulches can do much to keep certain plantings weed-free.

If you are off to the cottage every weekend, then make your main garden there. If you sail every time there is a puff of wind, keep your garden simple. If your idea of heaven is to lie in a hammock in the shade, then buy a home with two suitable trees and pay a teenager to mow the lawn. Try to form some realistic estimate of the amount of time you will be willing to devote to mowing, weeding, tying, and all the other jobs—and plan your plot accordingly. It is much better to start small; you can always add another flower bed or more shrubs later, when you have more time to tend them.

Live in a house for at least a year before you start any actual construction work. This way you will get to know the traffic patterns—where you want to go and how to get there, where the sun is at various times of the year, where the winds come from in winter, and where the snowdrifts occur. All these factors influence where you put paths and plants, and which plants you choose.

MAKING A PLAN

Unless you have very definite ideas on what you want to do with your lot, the first step will be to make a plan.

Begin by making a sketch of the lot, the house, and any other fixtures. If you are living in a new subdivision you quite likely have a site plan provided by the builder. This is a good start, although the scale is much too small to be of use in planning. Get a large sheet of squared paper, about 50 x 65 cm (20 x 25 in.),

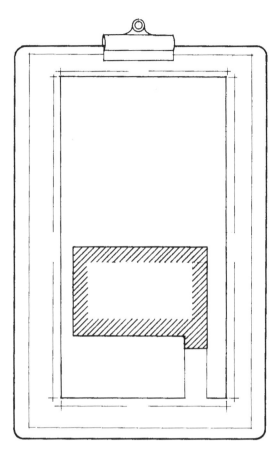

FIGURE 2-1 Preparing a scaled site plan from
an outline of your garden.

you can't find any reference point, you can still produce a rough plan of your site. Hammer in a picket at what seems to be one corner of your property and work from that. On a single sheet of your squared paper, sketch the outline of the garden ready to mark down the measurements (Figure 2–1).

Starting from one corner, measure all four sides of the site. If the two long sides and the two short sides are the same lengths, and the corners look like right angles, then they probably are. If you want to check, and in this instance you will only need to check one corner, measure 6 m (15 ft.) one way from the corner and 8 m (20 ft.) the other way. A line linking these two points should be 10 m (25 ft.).

Start by measuring the house and marking all the dimensions on your sketch. In most cases the walls of the house are built at right angles and are parallel to the property lines, so you can use this to measure the site. By lining up your tape with the sides of the house, and moving out to the boundary, you can reasonably accurately fix the lot lines around the house as in Figure 2–2. Once this is done you can use the house and lot corners to measure distances to other fixed objects, such as existing trees, hydro poles, entrance lights, etc., measuring from two fixed points. This method works equally well if the lot is not square. The distances from the sides of the house to the lot line will not be equal, but the principle is still the same (Figure 2–3).

All this sounds complicated, but it will all become clear as you take it step by step. With a willing helper to hold the end of a measuring tape it should only take about half an hour on an average city lot.

To transfer your rough sketch onto a good copy, you need to decide on a scale. One square equaling 10 cm (or 6 in. if you are using imperial units) is a good one and will usually fit on the large sheet mentioned earlier. Use double this scale when you are doing detailed planning of things like flower beds.

with 5-mm or ¼-inch squares, from an art supply store. This will be for your final plan. You will need a pad of squared paper from an office supply store for rough sketches.

Professional landscapers may use precisely accurate measurements when planning a garden, but we all know nature is not precise when it comes to plant sizes—for most of us a close estimate of our property and its major features will give an adequate framework for planning our garden.

If you don't have a site plan, then see if you can find any of the survey pins left from when the house was built. Even if you can find only one, this makes a good starting (and finishing) point when you are doing your measuring. If

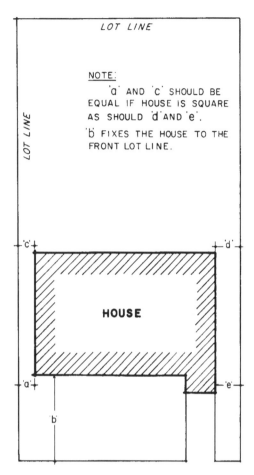

FIGURE 2-2 Lot lines are drawn to scale by measuring the site using house dimensions.

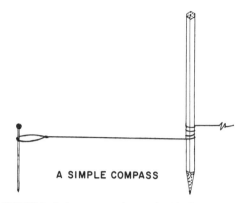

A SIMPLE COMPASS

FIGURE 2-4 A compass is needed to fix locations measured from two points.

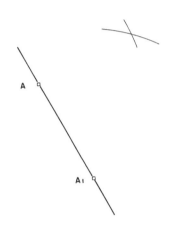

FIGURE 2-5 Pinpointing an object's location using a compass.

HINT: Use a soft pencil first; it is easier to erase if you make a mistake.

To fix the location of objects that you measured from two points you will need a compass (the kind to make circles, not to find north) or a long pin, a pencil, and a piece of thin string. Lacking a compass, you can make one as shown in Figure 2–4, but this is not as accurate since it is hard to hold the pencil vertical every time. Open your compass to the scale distance you measured from one point. With the point of the compass on that point, draw an arc in about the right place. Reset the compass to the distance from the other fixed point and repeat the arc from there. Where the two arcs cross is the location of that tree or whatever (Figure 2–5).

If you have large trees on the property, it is useful to note the spread of the canopy, as well as the size of the trunk. Also mark down which way is north, as this influences the choice of plants that you can grow.

Take your rough sketch and stand in the window of the kitchen and living room (and any other rooms where you will be spending a lot of time inside looking out). Note what you see. It may be the backs of other houses, but do they have nice gardens? Are they full of old cars or piles of junk? Do you have an apartment or office block looming over the garden?

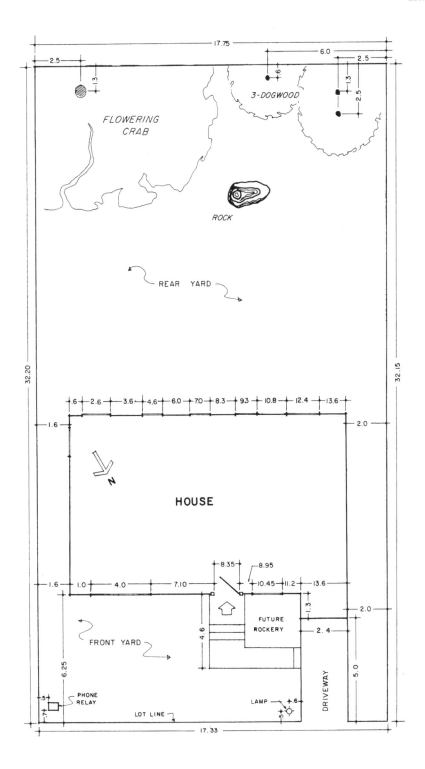

FIGURE 2-3 In this sketch, all measurements are based on house and corner lot dimensions.

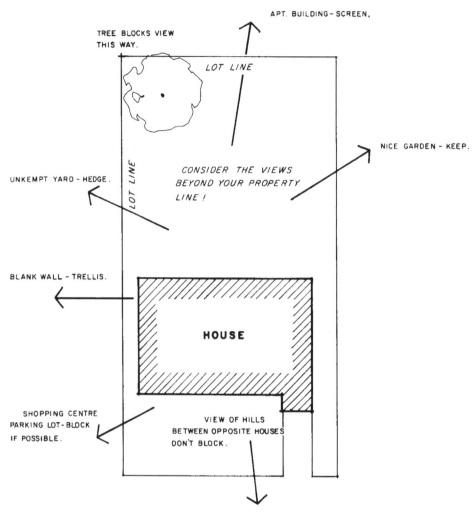

FIGURE 2-6 When planning your garden, take note of views from inside the house.

Is there a nice view towards the river? Is there a freeway close by? After you have done this from inside the house, both front and back, go outside into the bottom corners of the garden, look back towards the house and note what you see from there. Your sketch should now look something like Figure 2–6.

The views that you get can be used or hidden, depending on their type. Yes, I know you can't really hide an office block, but you can plant something in front of it that will attract the eye first. Freeways and other sources of noise can be minimized by plantings of evergreens. These findings may not shape the way you landscape your property, but they should influence you when you are considering whether to put a certain feature here or there.

 DESIGN PROCESS

Make a list of what features you would like to see in your garden. What are your plant interests? Roses? Dahlias? Flower arranging? If

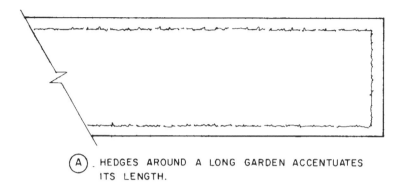

(A) HEDGES AROUND A LONG GARDEN ACCENTUATES ITS LENGTH.

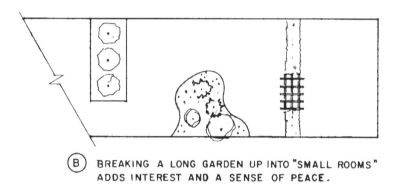

(B) BREAKING A LONG GARDEN UP INTO "SMALL ROOMS" ADDS INTEREST AND A SENSE OF PEACE.

FIGURE 2-7 Garden design should take into account the shape of the lot.

you have any special plants, they will need to be taken into account. Do you want a pool or waterfall? Do you have young children who need a swing set or a sand box? Do you want fresh vegetables and, if so, how much room are you willing to devote to them? Trees, shrubs, annuals, perennials—in single beds or in mixed borders? Trying to fit the things you would like in the space available is a cross between a jigsaw puzzle and a juggling act. As mentioned earlier, keep in mind the amount of time you are willing to devote to your garden.

What shape is your garden? The average 50 x 100 foot lot, with the house on the front half, gives a roughly square back yard. This is a restful place—although you may not think so for the first few summers as you make beds,

put in plants, and lay paths. Gardens that are pie-shaped can also be interesting and restful as the remaining area is vaguely circular.

Many condominiums and row houses have tiny, roughly square, gardens that, at first glance, can seem a challenge to improve. These provide an ideal opportunity to garden vertically, growing a selection of annual and perennial vines on trellises, and to grow an assortment of plants in containers (see Chapter 12, beginning on page 193). Changing the plants and moving the containers around renews the garden area in a different form each spring, something that is impossible to achieve in a regular garden.

Modern in-filling is giving rise to some very long, narrow sites and these gardens are a special problem. Narrow spaces have a corridor effect and they impart a feeling of restlessness, a feeling that you have to be up-and-away. Fortunately, the solution gives rise to some very interesting and pleasing gardens.

The worst thing you can do is to enclose this style of garden with hedges around the outside, no matter how unsightly the neighbours' gardens. This will only intensify the corridor effect. What you can do is to break the garden up into a series of small, squarish gardens by means of hedges, shrub plantings, fences or perennial borders with tall plants, to give inward-looking linked gardens as in Figure 2–7. If there are good surrounding gardens or views, you can utilize these in your design and make one large outward-looking garden. Think of your property in terms of three areas:

1. *The welcome area* is what passersby on the street and your visitors see. This is where you make a first impression, where you tell the rest of the world that you are proud of your neighbourhood or that you think gardening is for the birds.

2. *The utilities area* is where you keep garbage cans, tent trailers, bikes, tool shed, and the other things that we all need but don't want to look at.

3. *The living area* is where you personally spend your free time and where you grow your special plants (although this may also be in the welcome area). This is your outdoor living room where visitors come only by invitation.

The first thing to plan is what is known as the *hard landscape*; the paths, walks, patios, and standing ground for the garbage cans, bikes, etc. Think long and hard about paths. They need to go where people walk, and generally they should be in the most direct line. A path that is used only occasionally can detour around an object that provides a focal point, but a major path, like the one to your front door, must be direct. You have only to look at any school to see the truth of this. No matter where the architect put the paths, the students will take the most direct route from A to B. Many a home built in the thirties and early forties has its front path coming straight down to the sidewalk. Then, most people in cities traveled by public transport and walked along the street and up the front path. These days most people travel by car, and the front walk often leads from the driveway to the front door.

When designing paths, think about what they will be used for. The front path that brings visitors into the house should be wide enough for two people to walk side by side. In the wintertime elderly visitors may be glad of a helping hand and this is hard to give when you are behind them. A single row of patio slabs is not wide enough for a front path. Conversely, a path to the bottom of the garden may only be used once or twice a day, and need only be a series of 50-cm (18-in.) square or circular slabs set flush in the lawn. One advantage of this type of path is that it can go in a direct line over the lawn and through flower beds, providing the plants are low ones.

All the English, and many American, gardening books show pictures of brick paths and patios done in a variety of patterns. These are fine in the mild British climate but in our part of the world only glazed bricks are suitable. Unglazed bricks absorb water from the ground; the water then freezes and causes them to crack and flake.

Where funds permit, the material of choice for paths these days is interlocking bricks. This manufactured, weatherproof surface is now available in a wide range of styles from pseudo cobbles and bricks to shapes that can be combined to give intricate and pleasing patterns in a range of colours. They are best installed by a professional since they need deep footings and a base built up with layers of different-sized aggregates, each properly compacted and leveled, something easier to do with a machine than by hand. One of their better features is the ability to make curving or free-form paths and patios; you are no longer limited to right-angled corners. Matching stone for walls is often available—making colour-coordinated steps or raised beds easy to construct. If you live in an area with frequent winter snowfalls, steer clear of some of the more sculptured forms, especially on major walks, as they are difficult to shovel clean.

Railroad ties cut into short lengths and set into gravel can make an unusual path, as can large, 15-cm (6-in.) thick rounds cut from trees. If you plan on using these, try to get them in time to give the underside several coats of wood preservative before building the path. Both of these are very good on sloping sites where shallow steps are needed. Coarse gravel is also good providing it is used where high heels are unlikely to be worn; it has the advantage of perfect drainage.

Do you *need* a patio? This is not a silly question. If your home has a deck large enough to take lawn chairs and barbecue, then why do you need a patio as well? If you do need one, where is the best place to put it? Patios do not have to be tacked on to the house like an outside doormat, but should be linked to the house by a wide path. If you have an existing tree to give shade during the heat of summer, why put the patio in full sun? What shape of patio do you want? With modern interlock brick, the shape can be anything you desire. You might not be able to afford an interlock patio to start with, but put it on the plan as you really want it and make do with an approximation of patio slabs for the time being.

Having thought through the hard landscaping, it is time to start getting some of this down on paper. Find the list of favoured features you made earlier and try to give them a priority number. Most garden designs end up as a compromise between what we really want and what we will settle for. Then, on your final plan, lightly pencil in the paths, patios, etc. (The compromise may include moving or

changing the shape, so don't draw them in permanently yet.)

Then get a pad or sheets of cheap tracing paper (try an art supply store), lay one over your plan and start to doodle. "Now, we need a hedge down that side to block out the gas station on the corner and to cut the winter winds. It will have to be 2 m (6 ft.) tall, and should be easy to keep under control—I don't want to have to clip it every week. Let me make a note of that. If I put the kids' swing set here, and some flowers here, it will look good from the kitchen and I will be able to keep half an eye on them. No, won't do. Every time they run indoors they are going to cut across the flower bed." Rip! Wad, wad, wad. Throw. "Try again. Now the hedge goes here . . ." You get the idea.

As you get parts of the garden that look good to you, keep those tracings. Eventually you will have all of the areas done. Then review them, to make sure you didn't leave out any of your top priority features, and transfer them onto the final plan. You will end up with a garden that has the things you want and is an expression of your personality, something like Figure 2–8.

Now that you have the general outline of the garden done, it is time to design some parts in greater detail. If you have areas designated as mixed border or shrubs, fill in the details so that when planting time comes you can go to the garden centre with a shopping list. You can feel confident that the final result will be a harmonious blending of plants and not a "Well, I just bought one of everything." The descriptions of trees, shrubs and flowers in the following chapters will help you decide which plants to include in your own scheme.

When you are doing the detailed planting plans, remember that *plants grow* and space your plants accordingly. The small plant that you bring home from the garden centre bears little relationship to the final size of the mature plant. Look up the eventual height and spread

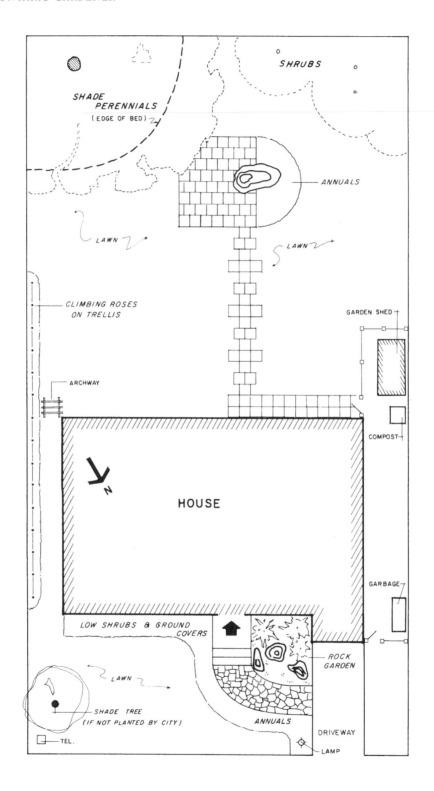

FIGURE 2–8 A custom-made landscape design is developed.

of the plants as you make your plans and space them far enough so the tips of the branches will just touch a few years down the road. They will look sparse for a year or two, but that is better than having to rip everything out in five years' time because you didn't realize they would get so big.

Keep in mind during this planning phase that, although you use the garden for only seven or eight months of the year, you look at it year-round. When you are choosing plants to include, take into consideration the winter effect. Does a tree or shrub have coloured bark that will show up against the snow in winter? Is there fruit that will persist and entice birds into the garden? Will the seed pods hang on for the winter months to add interest? Could you plant some early spring bulbs in a spot where you have noticed the snow melts first? You can't rush the seasons, but you can help them along a bit.

Consider that while evergreens are often planted with winter colour in mind, the winter effect is lost if they have to be wrapped in burlap to keep their shape. Some garden centres carry a coarsely woven burlap that holds the branches in place but allows the colour to show through. Better still, if you can find it, is a nylon mesh that comes in a stretchy tube. You need help to get it over the top of the tree and down to the base, but then you just expand it upwards to hold all the branches in place. Obviously, this is not suitable for very big trees.

If you have a home computer, there is one other avenue for design open to you, using a CAD (Computer Assisted Design) program. These are available in various degrees of complexity, at appropriate prices. Inexpensive programs are easy to learn but don't have very much flexibility. With the better programs, you will not be able to bring one back from the store and design your garden in one afternoon; it takes time and practice to learn all that it is capable of. The number of plants listed usually increases with the price of the program. You still need to do the initial survey to know what measurements to input. Most programs will be able to provide a list of plants suitable for your hardiness zone, but remember that most of these programs originated in the U.S. and use U.S. Department of Agriculture hardiness ratings. If they ask you for a zip code to determine your hardiness rating, choose somewhere in the U.S. with a similar climate. I use Green Bay, Wisconsin, for Ottawa.

The more expensive programs will be able to show you views from various locations in the garden, show how the garden will look at different times of the year, and can peek into the future to show how it will look in 5 or 10 years' time as the plants grow. In addition to the basic plan, you can zoom in and enlarge specific areas to plan individual beds in detail. They will also print a plan (in colour or black and white), a list of construction materials needed (with prices), and a list of plants that you can take with you to the garden centre. If you have a particular plant you simply must grow that is not on the list, many programs allow you to add plants; if not, simply substitute a plant you don't like and keep a note of the change.

POINTS TO PONDER

To fence or to hedge? Let us consider the pros and cons. Hedges are cheaper initially, but if you cost out the time they take to maintain, they may well be more expensive in the long run. They are definitely more work when you take into account at least one annual clipping. Hedges are not "instant," and nowadays this is probably their biggest fault. Fences have a limited life, and eventually part is going to blow down. There is a great temptation to paint them, whereupon their maintenance becomes greater than a hedge. Fences are the

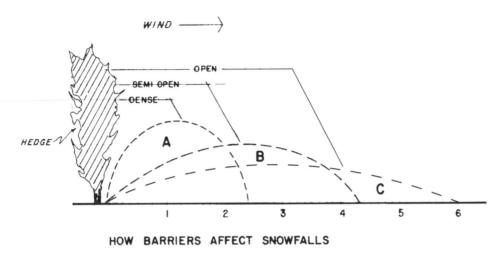

HOW BARRIERS AFFECT SNOWFALLS

(DISTANCE AS MULTIPLES OF BARRIER HEIGHT)

FIGURE 2–9 A solid fence may cause deep snowdrifts; a deciduous hedge will not.

same year-round, whereas a hedge changes in character with the seasons. They have a high wind resistance compared to an evergreen hedge and a very high one compared to a deciduous hedge in winter. This affects the snow patterns on the lee side.

As wind passes over a solid barrier, you get turbulence on the lee side. In a snow storm, this causes the snow to settle faster. The denser the barrier, the closer to it the snow settles and the less spread out it is (Figure 2–9). Thus a solid fence will cause the snow pattern A, an evergreen hedge, pattern B, and a deciduous hedge, pattern C. The units on the ground are multiples of the barrier height. This is well worth considering during the planning stage. If you put a permanent fence or solid hedge along a laneway it may well cause snowdrifts on your lane (depending on the prevailing wind direction) while a summer hedge of tall perennials or fast-growing annuals would serve the same purpose for much of the growing season without causing winter problems. A lattice fence may give enough of a visual block to fill the need, without causing any change in the snow patterns; if necessary, annual climbers could be grown on it.

If you are using arches or pergolas in your design, make sure that they lead somewhere. Nothing looks sillier than an archway—even if it is covered in roses—standing all on its own in the middle of a lawn. When used as an entrance into a small area of the garden it should be flanked on either side by a fence, hedge, or other planting that does not allow access except through the arch. Similarly, a pergola, which is just a succession of linked arches, should lead from somewhere to somewhere rather than starting and ending in an open space. By the same token, a structure that is designed to support plants should have plants growing on it. Obviously you are not going to be able to clothe it in the first year or two, but provision must be made at its base to grow plants that will climb.

Think about mowing when you are planning. Mowing is one of those chores that will need to be done on a weekly basis for most of the summer—unless you are going to cultivate the entire lot or lay indoor-outdoor carpet, there is no escaping it. If you use an electric mower remember that you have to start close to the power point and work out. If you fill your lawn area with small individual beds you will have a difficult time, and the cord will be continually dragging across them or snagging

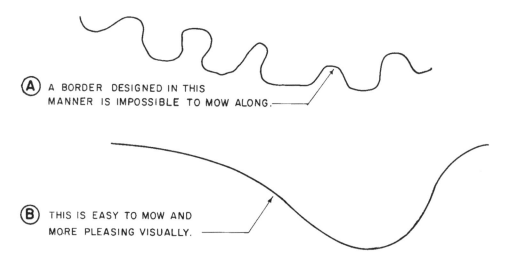

(A) A BORDER DESIGNED IN THIS
MANNER IS IMPOSSIBLE TO MOW ALONG.

(B) THIS IS EASY TO MOW AND
MORE PLEASING VISUALLY.

FIGURE 2-10 Some practical considerations are necessary during the design process.

on plants. If you design beds with sharp curves you will find it impossible to mow around them without stepping on the cultivated garden (Figure 2–10). At the same time, curved corners are easier to mow than square ones unless the curve is very sharp. If your mower has a grass catcher that mounts on the side, you should plan any narrow grass areas at least four cutting-widths across, since the catcher is over a width long. Otherwise you will either have to mow without the catcher or risk breaking down plants along the edge.

Earlier in this chapter, I said that it was a good idea to live in a home for a year before starting any serious landscaping. One of the reasons for this is so you can note where shadows fall throughout the year. The midday shade from the house during the summer does not extend as far as during the winter (Figure 2–11). Your local weather office may be able to tell you the relative angles of the sun so you can work it out for yourself. This matters when planting trees and shrubs for winter effect. Coloured bark loses much of its effect if it's in the shade.

When planning your permanent plantings, keep in mind the role that annuals and container plantings can play in the garden. A planter bright with annuals placed a distance away from the house will draw the eye to it. This can be useful when considering how to detract from a large building that obstructs the view. A spring-flowering tree—especially something like a crab apple that will have fall fruit—will act as a focal point early and late in the season, and a strategically placed planter can take over for the summer. Just remember that planters and window boxes need frequent attention if they are to remain bright and colourful. Hanging baskets need even more care and should not be used unless you are prepared to water almost daily during the summer heat. Planters in full sun get very hot, and the roots may cook if the walls are thin, although lots of trailing plants growing over the side look good and help to shade the planter. The average small plastic planter is neither large enough nor thick enough for this kind of task. To provide a good splash of colour you need something at least 60 cm (2 ft.) across, made of concrete or double-walled fibreglass. In one house I used a metal window box on a wall by the front door. All was well until July when the plants turned up their toes and died. It was a while before it occurred to me why, so the following year I cut

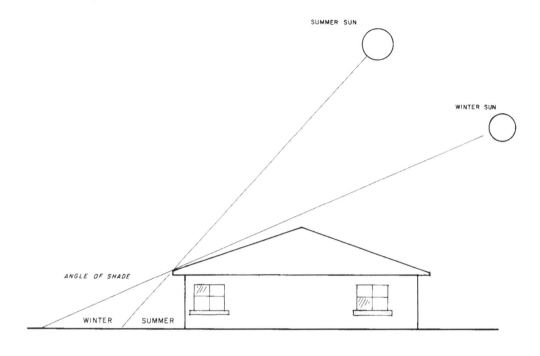

SHADE CONSIDERATIONS

FIGURE 2–11 Midday shade varies significantly from summer to winter.

a length of board to go in front and had no more problems. For more on container gardening see Chapter 12.

 # DREAMS INTO REALITIES

When you are ready to start the real work don't be overambitious. Unless you can afford to hire someone to help, be prepared to spread the work over several years. This way you will not get sick of it and throw the whole project out the window, and you will have some time to relax and consider the best ways to set about the next task.

The first place to start is the hard landscaping—walks, walls, fences, patio, decks, etc. These should go in first so you can wheel soil without damaging the planting areas too much. When making paths, the depth of the footings depends mainly on the soil type and the climate. In the Niagara region, where frost does not penetrate deeply, less digging will be required. Similarly, on a light sandy soil you will need far less backfill than on a heavy clay. Your local building codes may give an indication of the depth of footings required, or consult a local builder. To a lesser extent the amount of traffic and the use of the path also determines the excavation required. A summer path that will not be cleared in winter will not need as much preparation as a path leading to the front door that will be kept snow-free. If you have to dig out and replace soil, crushed stone or gravel is preferable to sand. Sand, being very fine-textured, tends to wash down into the underlying soil with time, causing the path to sink and become uneven.

If possible, trees and hedges should go in at the beginning, as these take some time to mature and give the desired effect. Once this is

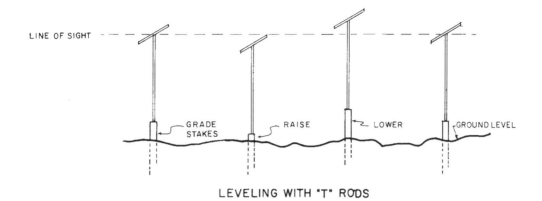

LINE OF SIGHT

GRADE STAKES RAISE LOWER GROUND LEVEL

LEVELING WITH "T" RODS

FIGURE 2–12 Site leveling can be done with a few basic tools.

done you can start in on the individual sections—a flower bed here, roses there, vegetables along the fence—as the mood, and need, dictates.

If you have to do major reconstruction, bring in a load or two of topsoil, or if working on a sloping site, you will probably need to do some surveying. This is not as terrible as it sounds and can be done quite simply by three people. There are two methods that are easy to understand, one for leveling a site and the other for making a regular slope.

Get three pieces of lumber, about 2 m (6 ft.) long and nail short cross-pieces on one end of each, making an elongated letter "T". Then clamp them all together with the tops level and saw the bases off evenly. You will also need a supply of small wooden pegs and a hammer. Starting with one side of the garden, hammer a peg into the ground in each corner, leaving them flush with the soil level. Stand one T-rod on each of these pegs and sight across the top of them. Put the remaining T-rod at intervals between them on hammered-in pegs so that this rod is level when seen across the tops of the outside two (Figure 2–12). Do the same thing across the other side of the garden. You then have two rows of level pegs and you can sight across these to give you a series of pegs between them. Rake the existing soil, or bring

in more soil, so that the final level is up to the tops of the pegs. Remove the pegs before you start to plant or lay sod.

On a sloping site use a variation of this method. Instead of T-rods, get a semi-transparent garden hose which allows you to see the water level inside. Mark off each end in equal graduations with a permanent marking pen and fasten each end down a 2-m (6-ft.) piece of lumber. Fill the hose with water and keep the ends upright. Since water always finds its own level, if you take this onto a sloping site, the water will overflow from the lower end, and the level will drop in the upper. If, for example, the water in the upper goes down three graduations on 1 m (3 ft.) of slope, then you can again use pegs to mark a three-unit difference in level on strings laid 1 m (3 ft.) apart across the slope (Figure 2–13). The actual units you use to mark the hose are immaterial, as long as they are the same at both ends. This works just as well on a flat site, but it is more awkward to use than the T-rods. It does ensure that the outside two pegs are level.

One method I have found useful when laying out new beds in a lawn is as follows. Mark out the edge of the proposed bed from the plan with small canes or sticks. Then lay a garden hose along the marked line and stand back to examine it. What looks good on paper does

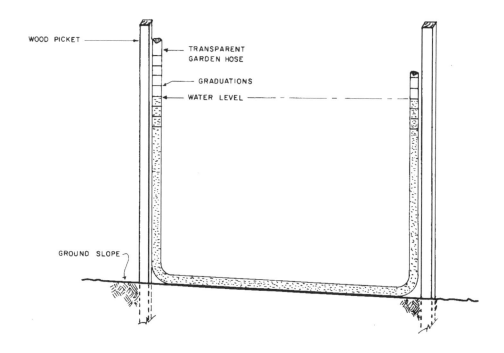

LEVELING WITH WATER

FIGURE 2-13 Another leveling method.

not always look right on the ground. (If you lay the hose in the sun or run hot water through it, it will be more flexible and easier to curve to the shape you need.) Move the canes if necessary and then leave them in place.

Next time the lawn needs mowing, mow along the line of the sticks, leaving the grass long on the part you want to dig up. This will tell you if the curves are gentle enough for the mower to follow or if you need to adjust even further. Don't mow inside the sticks. After a couple of mowings, when the grass is getting about 10 cm (4 in.) tall, you can either strip off the sod and add it to the compost or spray the whole area with glyphosate weed killer. This will kill the grass so that you can dig it in, adding valuable humus to the soil, without harming any future plantings.

Glyphosate is a very safe herbicide that kills only what it touches. It is absorbed through the foliage, travels down to the root and kills the plant from the bottom up. Any glyphosate that falls on bare soil is broken down into non-toxic compounds and will not travel sideways through the soil to affect plants outside the sprayed area. It is absorbed only through green foliage and can safely be applied to woody stems. Thus it is useful to kill off a circle of grass round the base of trees making mower damage to the bark less likely. Do not expect fast action—it will be several days before there is any sign of browning on the treated foliage. In fact, dandelions don't seem to be affected for so long you think they must be immune, but eventually they turn brown and die. Remember, this is a *total* plant killer, not just a weed killer. It is not selective. Any green foliage it touches will be killed. Take care also that you don't walk on the treated area before it dries and then walk onto the unsprayed lawn. You may end up with dead grass in the shape of footprints!

Having killed off all the weeds along with the grass, wouldn't it be nice if you could keep the new bed weed-free. In some instances you can. If you are planting trees or shrubs and don't want to interplant them with anything, you can cover the area with landscape fabric. This is a very fine cloth that allows rain and plant foods to pass through but stops weed seedlings coming up from below. If you are planting small shrubs, cover the area with landscape fabric first, make X-shaped slits in it where you need to plant, fold back the flaps and put your plants in (try not to get soil on the fabric or weeds will grow on top). Afterwards, fold the flaps back against the stems.

With trees or large shrubs, it is easier to plant them first and then lay the fabric down between them, cutting slits in the sides so that it can go around the trunk. Landscape fabric breaks down in sunlight but if covered with a mulch to keep the light away, it will last several years. What you use for a mulch depends on your tastes. The decorative bark chips or cedar bark sold in garden centres works well but is expensive if you need very much. If you have a woodyard making fence posts in your area, you may be able to pick up cedar bark at a considerable saving. Sawdust can also be used over landscape fabric where it will not come into contact with the soil. If sawdust is touching the soil it breaks down fairly rapidly and leads to a nitrogen deficiency, causing yellow foliage and stunted growth on the plants. Pine needles and cones look good under a planting of spruce, but out of place beneath deciduous shrubs. Compost is ideal since it acts as a slow feed, but few people have enough to spare to use it as thick mulch. A thin layer can be used to anchor the fabric, and grass clippings can be added if your mower has a grass catcher. They turn brown in a couple of days and look natural, but don't use more than about 5 cm (2 in.)

at a time or they will pack down, hindering water and air penetration.

The majority of houses have one side that faces approximately north and gets very little sun. The only exceptions may be row housing or one-half of a double when they run north to south. While many people look on shade as a problem, it is actually a blessing since it extends the range of plants you can grow. When we lived in the city with a small garden containing two very large trees, we had about five sq. m (6 sq. yd.) that were sunny enough to grow tomatoes; the rest was all shade. In this garden we grew about 50 different *kinds* of plants, and had around 200 different *varieties*. Many of these plants had to be left behind when we moved to a sunnier garden as they would not have survived without the shade. We have since worked hard to create shady areas in order to reintroduce some of these favourite plants into our new garden.

The plant lists in the following chapters identify those that require shade. Few sites get no sun at all and so by shade I mean sun until about 10 a.m. or from 6 p.m. in the middle of summer. Semi-shade means they get more sun than this but are shaded from direct sunlight from at least 11 a.m. to 4 p.m.

 # TOOLS

Before you can start working in the garden you need something to work with. There are certain basic gardening tools that should be hanging in everybody's garage or garden shed. First in importance is some means of digging, both for turning over the soil and for making holes to plant things. To me, the long-handled pointed shovels are used only by gravediggers; gardeners dig with a spade. But if you grew up using the pointed shovel and are comfortable with it, then who am I to argue. I must admit that for digging a round hole it is ideal, but I don't like it for digging a flower bed or vegetable plot.

Next in importance is the garden fork. In many ways the spade and fork are interchangeable. Both can be used to turn over soil, although the fork is not very good in dry, light, sandy soil. It is difficult to dig a neat hole with a fork, but it does a much better job of lightly turning over the soil between plants and it is indispensable for dividing perennials.

Every gardener needs a trowel, both for planting and for removing small weeds. The small hand forks that match a trowel in size are a nice addition, but not essential. They don't do anything that a trowel won't do. When shopping for all tools, but especially for trowels, buy the best you can afford. The cheap ones made of a piece of metal stamped out and folded to make the tongue that goes into the handle are a waste of money. After a few holes they bend at the back of the blade and eventually the handle snaps off. Look for trowels where the tongue is a separate piece, either riveted or, better still, welded onto the blade. If you can afford stainless steel it will not matter if, like a friend of mine, you leave your trowel stuck in the garden where you last used it instead of cleaning it and putting it away.

Weeds grow when nothing else will, and the best way to control them is with a hoe. There are two main types of hoe, and all the various shapes are really just variations on these two themes. The chop hoe, sometimes listed as swan-necked hoes, should be used for mounding-up round potatoes, taking out shallow trenches, and attacking large weeds. All too often, they are used for controlling small weeds, a task for which they are not well suited. They are used with a chop and pull motion and tend to turn the soil up in lumps. The other hoe is usually known as a scuffle or Dutch hoe. It is used for small weed control, being pushed through the soil just below the surface to cut the weeds off below ground level. If you can only afford one hoe, this is the

more useful of the two. Its shape may be square, triangular, or diamond, the handle may be joined on one side, on both sides, or centrally, and the blade may be fixed or hinged, but the basic use of the hoe is the same and they are all great for killing small weeds. There is a small hand-held hoe often called a Cape Cod weeder. This is a small version of the scuffle hoe with the handle attached to one side of the blade. It is very good for small spaces like rock gardens or along rows of small seedlings.

Lawnmowers are probably already part of your garden equipment. This is the one tool that just about every homeowner has. There are two distinct types of mower: reel and rotary. Most North Americans use rotary mowers, either gas- or electric-powered. Reel mowers for homeowners tend to be either small hand-pushed ones that are hard work in July (unless you only have a pocket-handkerchief lawn), or very expensive imported machines. In general, reel mowers do a better job since they actually cut the grass, rather than flailing the top off the plants. Their blades act like continuous scissors, cutting the grass along a fixed bottom blade. The better the quality, the more blades there are on the reel; some of the ones used on lawn-bowling greens have 16 blades—those sold for home lawns usually have four.

You will probably need a pair of shears, both to cut the grass in awkward corners where the mower won't reach, and to trim hedges. The electric nylon cord trimmers can replace shears for cutting grass along the house wall, but not for cutting hedges and they should *never* be used around trees. They will cut into the bark, even on large trees, and once a strip of bark is removed all the way around, the tree dies. As with trowels, there are a lot of poor-quality shears on the market. Cheap shears will not hold their edge and will soon start to work loose at the central bolt.

If you have any trees or shrubs, you will

have to do some pruning eventually. The best tool for this is pruning shears—also known as secateurs. There are two types. One cuts like scissors, with the blades moving past each other; the blades are usually curved. This type is often called parrot-bill. With the other kind, one blade cuts onto a flat platform on the other, and they are usually known as anvil type. Buy the best you can afford. Most professionals use a good brand of parrot-bill pruners with replaceable parts.

You will need two different kinds of rakes. The garden rake, with solid short teeth, is used to level out areas, rake off stones and prepare seed beds. The lawn rake is fan-shaped with long, flexible teeth. This is used to rake the lawn in the spring and rake up leaves in the fall. The kind with an adjustable fan that can be moved to different widths is very handy for working between shrubs, but the hollow aluminum handle is cold to use and echoes all the noise of the teeth. Don't try to use a garden rake on the lawn as it will tear the grass out in big lumps.

Try to get into the habit of bringing your tools back to the garage or garden shed and cleaning them when you have finished using them. I find an old ice scraper, as sold for windshields, is great for scraping off clods of dried-on soil, and a piece of burlap does a great job of cleaning off the rest. I rarely find it necessary to wash tools, unless they have been used on a wet soil and are really sticky. At the end of the season, clean your tools thoroughly and give them a thin coat of oil; old engine oil is good for this but WD40 is too thin and evaporates before winter is over. At the same time, give the handles a light rub with boiled linseed oil to stop the wood from drying and keep it springy. I have never found it necessary to sharpen tools, but this is a good time to file out any nicks or burrs on spades or hoes. It pays to care for good tools. We have had the same spade for more than 40 years, and it is still doing good service.

Watering equipment varies widely. If you plan to have pop-up irrigation installed, do this before you start your landscaping. Most of us just make do with hose and sprinklers. The turret type of sprinkler, which allows you to select the pattern of the area to be watered, is very handy if you have different-shaped beds, while the regular oscillating type is probably the best for lawn areas. On heavy clay soil, even the force of the droplets from these overhead sprinklers can break down the soil structure.

I am turning more and more to the use of soaker hoses, which I put in place at the beginning of the season and connect up to the water supply as required. With the holes pointing up, they give a fine mist that soaks without beating things down, but in the heat of summer, much of the water is lost through evaporation before it soaks into the soil—a point to consider with the likelihood of hotter summers and water rationing. If you turn them over, the water goes directly into the soil and spreads out in an inverted V to water a wide strip. This has the added advantage of forcing the plant roots to go down to find the water, making them better able to withstand drought conditions.

 # A BIT OF BOTANY

I use common names throughout this book, but also give the botanical or Latin name. When you shop for plants, check the Latin name against the plant tag, just to be sure you are getting the plant you actually want. There are some strange common names out there: one man's burning bush is another man's spindletree, and I can think of at least six plants called Star of Bethlehem.

Don't let the Latin names throw you. You don't have to actually pronounce them as long as you recognize them on sight. Actually, pronunciation is not difficult. Just break them up into syllables, and pronounce each part as it is written. And, since Latin is a dead language anyway, who is to say your way is wrong? If you can get your tongue around *chrysanthemum*, most of the names you meet will be child's play.

A **genus** is a group of plants that all have a similar characteristic, such as maples (*Acer*). It is always written in *italics* with a capital letter. A **species** is a distinct group of plants within the genus, that have some feature that makes them different from others in the group, such as leaf shape, flowering time, flower colour, or fruit structure. The species name is written in *italics* with a small letter. It is often descriptive (*Dictamnus albus*, the white gasplant), or is given in honour of a person (*Tiarella wherryi*, the foamflower named in honour of Dr. Wherry, its discoverer), or denotes where the plant is found (*Acer japonica*, a maple from Japan). An "x" in the scientific name is a multiplication sign and shows that this plant is a cross between two other species.

There are two different types of **variety**. Naturally occurring varieties differ in some small way from the species and are generally found in a localized area. Variety is abbreviated to var. and follows the species name (*Acer japonica* var. *aureum*). Cultivated varieties, usually abbreviated to **Cultivar** or **cv.**, are forms that have originated in the garden or nursery, by accident or design. They are shown enclosed in single quotes and start with a capital. *Acer rubrum* 'Morgan' is the Morgan red (*rubrum*) maple (*Acer*) that originated at the Morgan arboretum in Montreal.

One of the nice things about using Latin names is that they are the same the world over. I have been on a garden conference with people from Germany, Czechoslovakia, Japan, and Austria and when it came to plants we all talked the same language.

SUGGESTED READING

There is an abundance of landscaping books on the market, many of which may be very suitable, but the following are ones that I know and feel are a good guide for smaller gardens.

Successful Small Gardens. Roy Strong. Conran Octopus, 1999.

The Complete Home Landscape Designer. Joel M. Lerner. St. Martin's Press, 1991.

Landscaping Makes Cents. Frederick C. Campbell and Richard L. Dubé. Storey Publishing, 1997.

This is a very down-to-earth guide to landscaping written by two professional landscape contractors. Full of good ideas on the practicalities and mechanics of doing the job. It includes a guide to hiring a contractor if you don't want to do it yourself.

Creating Small Gardens. Roy Strong. Random House, 1987.

The Garden Design Sourcebook. David Stevens. Raincoast Books, 1995.

Crammed full of pictures and ideas on using materials in the garden: everything from concrete to canvas.

The City and Town Gardener. Linda Yang. Random House, 1990.

Written by the gardening correspondent of the *New York Times*, it contains a lot of information that applies equally well here.

Lawns

3
chapter

More time and money is spent on lawn care than on all other forms of gardening combined. What other part of the garden needs attention every week, raking in the spring, fertilizing regularly, gathering the autumn leaves and daring any dandelion to show its head?

Nevertheless, almost every home has its patch of lawn to set off the flower beds and act as a backdrop for the trees and shrubs. Even cottage owners, trying to get away from it all, often take some of it with them in the form of a lawn that needs weekly mowing.

If you want to grow good grass you must provide a good depth of soil for it to grow in. An absolute minimum of 10 cm (4 in.) is needed, and even at this your lawn will suffer considerable browning in summer drought periods. The deeper you can make your soil, the deeper the grass roots will go and the more drought resistant your lawn will be. If you are on a new development where the sod has not

become established, lift a corner in an out-of-the-way part of the garden and push a trowel straight down into the soil. By carefully sliding the sample off the trowel blade, you can see what depth of good soil you have. If the soil is shallow and the area not too large, you could lift and roll the sod, add more topsoil and then re-lay the sod.

In a more established garden, you will have to decide whether to add topsoil or not. If the grass is good, with not too many weeds, you are probably better off leaving it alone. If weeds predominate then you have a chance to kill off the existing cover, add more soil, and resod. It is possible to improve the soil depth by top-dressing the lawn. The only trouble is that you need only a few barrow loads of soil at a time, and having small quantities delivered is not economical. If you are able to bring in soil in small amounts, spread .5 to 1 cm ($^1/_4$ to $^1/_2$ in.) all over the lawn area each time and wait until the grass has grown through properly before you add more. Adding more soil than this may smother the grass and kill it.

HINT: Get a plank about 1 m x 15 cm (3 ft. x 6 in.) and lay it on the ground. Stand your garden rake on it and hammer a couple of large staples over the teeth and into the plank (Figure 3–1). This makes an ideal float for leveling soil and the rake can be knocked out of the staples for its proper use. Don't use a plank much bigger than this or it will gather so much soil you will never be able to pull it.

Grass grows best in a moist, fertile soil that is not waterlogged, so if you have light sandy soil or heavy clay, you will need to add humus to improve the texture. The lawn is going to be in place for many years and this is probably the only chance you will have to improve the soil texture; don't miss it. The pH should be above 6.0 so lime will be needed on very acidic soils. The ideal to strive for is between 6.5 and 7.2 and, luckily, this is where the pH of average garden soil lies.

If you are renovating an existing lawn or making a new one, you will be bringing fresh soil to the surface. This will contain weed seeds, so leave the area fallow for as long as possible. This allows a lot of the weed seeds to germinate so you can hoe them off and, providing you don't cultivate deeply, you will have a lot fewer weeds in your new lawn. You are going to get weeds germinating whatever you do but the majority of them will be killed by the mower. It takes a very special weed to stand up to repeatedly having its head cut off a few centimetres above the ground.

When you have finished improving the soil and leveling the site, add superphosphate at the rate of 10 kg per 100 sq. m (20 lb. per 1,000 sq. ft.) and work it lightly into the top 5–10 cm (2–4 in.). Phosphates are good for root growth and we want to stimulate the roots of the new lawn. If you intend to sod the area, you can ignore this step providing you water with a plant-starter fertilizer as soon as you have finished laying the sod.

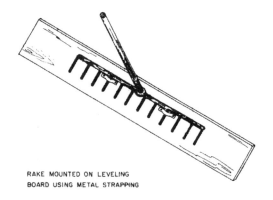

RAKE MOUNTED ON LEVELING
BOARD USING METAL STRAPPING

FIGURE 3–1 This device can be used to level new topsoil.

You now have the choice of sowing seed or laying sod. Seed should be sown only in early spring or from mid-August to mid-September—late August to late September in the Niagara region. It must germinate and put down a root system before the heat of summer or hard frost. Sod can be laid almost anytime as long as it is watered. I have seen sod being laid onto frozen ground in late November and it looked fine the following spring—but I don't recommend it. Seed is relatively low cost but it does not give the Instant Lawn one can achieve with sod.

One of the main benefits of sodding your lawn is that you do away with that couple of weeks between sowing and the first cut, when, no matter how carefully you rope off the area, the children and all their friends manage to walk across the new lawn and track mud into the house; when there is a perpetual gale blowing loose soil in through every window; and when every bird in the province comes to your lawn for three meals a day.

The advantage of seed, however, is that you can use a wide variety of grass species and cultivars and either custom-blend a mix for your conditions or buy a suitable ready-made blend. With sod, you are limited to what was sown at the sod farm, generally a mixture of named varieties of Kentucky bluegrass. Here are the most commonly available grasses you can grow from seed:

Kentucky bluegrass (*Poa pratensis*) is the mainstay of most lawns. It is a hard-wearing, drought-resistant grass and spreads by underground shoots known as tillers. It does best on open soils in full sun, but '**Nugget**' will take light shade. Other varieties to look for include '**Banff**', '**Fylking**', '**Harmony**', '**Adelphi**', '**Touchdown**' and '**Windsor**'.

Creeping red fescue (*Festuca rubra* var. *rubra*) is a good grass for poor, dry soils and shade. It has very fine leaves, as do many of the fescues. It also spreads by runners, making it good at filling the holes left where weeds have been killed. '**Pennlawn**' and '**Durlawn**' are the most commonly available varieties.

Chewings fescue (*Festuca rubra* var. *commutata*) is similar to creeping red fescue but it does not spread by runners. Look for '**Highlight**', '**Victory**', '**Luster**', and '**Jamestown II**'.

Tall fescue (*Festuca elatior*) is a hard-wearing grass that is becoming increasingly used by parks departments and public gardens. It does well in light shade and will make a good lawn in full sun except in the southern tip of Ontario. It has good disease resistance, low nutritional needs, and spreads by stolons to make a thick, dark green sod. It needs to be left a little longer than Kentucky bluegrass and should be cut to 9 to 10 cm (3.5 to 4 in.) high during the heat of summer. If you have to renew your lawn, this is a grass well worth considering, especially if you have young children. Look for '**Crossfire II**', '**Pixie**', and '**Mustang II**'.

Canada bluegrass (*Poa compressa*) is another grass that does well in shade, especially in damp areas, and requires minimum maintenance. It does not grow well in the sun.

Perennial ryegrass (*Lolium perenne*) is often added to lawn seed mixes because it germinates quickly and acts as a nurse grass,

shading the young Kentucky bluegrass plants and helping them to become established. It is not reliably hardy in colder zones, but once the bluegrass is established, this does not matter. '**Norlea**' is a Canadian introduction that is readily available while '**Manhattan**' and '**Pennant**' are U.S. varieties. '**Pennant**' has proven to have a built-in pest resistance.

Redtop (*Agrostis alba*) is a rapid-growing grass that is sometimes included because it makes a quick lawn from seed. It forms an open sod that allows weeds to gain a toe-hold but is useful for acidic or wet soils.

Bentgrass (*Agrostis palustris*) gives a perfect lawn, providing you are willing to mow it every two days with a reel mower and water and feed copiously. This grass is often used on golf course greens and, under the high maintenance that they receive, it works fine. In the real world, where lawns are mown once a week, it leaves brown patches and should be considered a weed. Look for '**Pencross**' and '**Prominent**' if you want to make your own putting green.

 # GROWING FROM SEED

To start a lawn from seed, buy the best lawn seed there is. Inexpensive seed is no bargain. As well as the grasses mentioned above, there are many more grass species which do not make good lawns. Many of these have large seed which is both cheaper to harvest and gives you fewer seeds per unit of weight. For example, Kentucky bluegrass has about 4.5 million seeds per kilogram (2.2 lb.); the native buffalo grass only 0.7 million. Whether you intend to blend your own mix or buy it ready-made, the following mixtures give the best results.

For light soils in full sun use 30% Kentucky bluegrass, 60% creeping red fescue, and 10% redtop sown at 1.5 kg per 100 sq. m (3 lb. per 1,000 sq. ft.).

On heavier soils, including clays, use 80% Kentucky bluegrass and 20% creeping red fescue at the beginning or end of the annual sowing seasons. If you are late sowing in spring, or early in fall, when temperatures are likely to be higher, use 60% Kentucky bluegrass, 30% creeping red fescue, and 10% perennial ryegrass. A similar mix to this is used by many sod nurseries, making this a good choice for patching small areas on newly sodded lawns. If you use a very different mix it will show up as a different colour.

In moist shade sow a mix of 30% Kentucky bluegrass, 10% creeping red fescue, 20% redtop, and 40% rough-stalked bluegrass. Sow this and the next mix at 2 kg per 100 sq. m (4 lb. per 1,000 sq. ft.).

In areas of dry shade use 20% Kentucky bluegrass, 65% creeping red fescue, and 15% redtop. For a tougher but slightly coarser lawn in sun (except in the warmest region) or shade, replace the creeping red fescue with tall fescue.

Remember to use 'Nugget' bluegrass in the shade mixes if you can find it.

Lawn seed can be put on in two ways, by hand or with a spreader. Applying it by hand will result in a lawn that germinates in swirls, thicker in some places, but in a few months' time it won't show. If you use a spreader you need one of the drop type, a long rectangular box with a wheel at each end and an adjustable slot underneath. The broadcast type, with a round drum hopper that drops the seed onto a spinning disk, will spread the seed all over the garden, not just on the desired area.

HINT: To calibrate the spreader, sweep off some of the garage floor or driveway and mark out an area the equivalent of one square metre (square yard), but the width of the spreader. If the spreader is 40 cm wide, this area would be 2.5 m long (at 15 in. wide you would need 2 yd. 15 in.). Then push the seeder along this strip, sweep up the seed and then weigh it. At 1.5 kg per 100 sq. m (3 lb. per 1,000 sq. ft.) you should have 15 g (just over ½ oz.).

When you are ready to sow your lawn, divide the seed into two equal portions. Put one half in the spreader and sow it from side to side. Then put the rest of the seed in and sow it from top to bottom. Sowing at right angles like this means you get a more even coverage and, if you didn't quite cover it all the first time, you can make sure you get that part with the second try. Rake the lawn with your spring-tine rake to scratch the grass seed into the soil surface, just resting the rake on the soil and pulling it towards you to leave a series of tiny furrows. If possible, try to sow the seed when rain is forecast.

As soon as you have finished sowing, it is a good idea to set out oscillating sprinklers to water the area. If it is larger than one sprinkler can cover, borrow one from a neighbour because you don't want to be walking on the young grass to move the sprinkler. Do not let the area dry out, but don't water to the point of runoff either or you will wash the seed away. The young plants are very delicate until they get their roots down into the ground, so plan on watering for 15 minutes every day, unless nature does it for you. When the grass is established, and you move the sprinklers, you will see the marks where they and the hoses were, but these will soon green over.

When the grass is about 5 cm (2 in.) high it is time to cut it. This first cut is very important. The grass plants are still small and are not well anchored in the soil. If you go in with a blunt mower blade you will uproot these young plants and all your hard work will be wasted. Please, have your mower sharpened first, and be careful when turning it and when mowing along the edges so that you do not allow the mower wheel to either gouge grooves in the soil or drop off the edge, allowing the blade to scalp the grass.

GROWING FROM SOD

Starting a lawn from sod is a lot easier than seeding in many ways, but there are a few things to keep in mind. Always buy your sod from a recognized sod farm (look in the Yellow Pages under Sod & Sodding Services); if you only need small quantities, your local garden centre will have their supply from a sod farm, but refuse any roll of sod that is crumbly and broken. As with lawn seed, there are a lot of pasture grasses that are fine for feeding cows, but not good in lawns. They are wide-bladed and form tufts that grow much faster than the surrounding grass so a couple of days after mowing, the lawn looks untidy again. Door-to-door sales of lawn sod should be avoided like the plague.

If you are willing to take the time, you can do a much better job of laying lawn sod than a commercial firm, for whom time is money. Ideally, sod should be laid the day it is delivered, but providing you keep it moist, waiting another day will not do any harm. Start in the area farthest away from where the sod was unloaded. The rolls get heavier as the day goes on so make the longest walks first.

Machine-cut sod is fairly regular in thickness but if, as you lay it, you find the occasional sod that is thinner or thicker, take the time to add or remove some soil so that your lawn is perfectly level. The sod comes in strips three or six feet long by eighteen inches wide, making one or two strips per square yard, and at the time of writing the sod growers had not gone metric. Start by laying a row of sod along the far edge. If there are any curves, lay the sod to overlap and cut it to fit later; don't try to bend it into shape (Figure 3–2). Start the next row in the centre of a previous row and so on. The joints should look like bricks in a wall when you are done.

Try to find planks to place in front of the row you are working on and to use a walkway

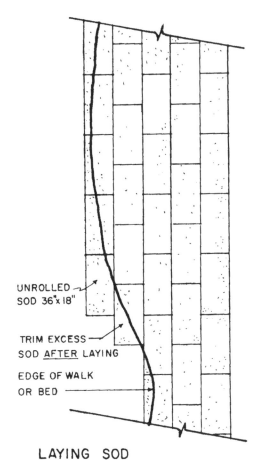

LAYING SOD

FIGURE 3–2 A bricklayer's design is best when laying strips of sod.

to bring the sod up. This saves having footprints all over the area you have so carefully leveled and is especially important on very light or very heavy soils. Keep a bucket of dryish soil close by as you work. Then, if you find a sod with an irregular edge or a torn-off corner you can fill the hole at once. Use sterilized soil from a garden centre, if possible, to avoid bringing in weed seeds. Butt the sods up close together but be careful that you don't push the new sod in so tight you lift the one in the previous row. Any sod that overlaps on curves can be cut with a lawn edger (also known as a half-moon) or an old knife. You can, of course, cut shorter lengths off a full sod to finish the ends of rows.

If you are laying sod on a bank, run the length of the sod up and down the slope, if possible, and peg the upper end in place with a small stick or cane to stop it sliding. Roll the flat areas with a garden roller filled no more than one-quarter full with water. This ensures a good contact between the soil and the sod. Then give the area a good watering (use a plant-starter fertilizer this first time if you didn't add superphosphate) and water daily for about two weeks—longer if you are laying sod in midsummer.

You can also use a combination of sodding and seeding, laying sod in a strip around the outside and as an edging to any garden beds and then seeding the central part. This gives you a good firm edge immediately but is more economical than sodding the entire area. Remember that you will have to sink the sod slightly so that the soil level on the individual strips is the same as the level of the area to be sown. Otherwise you will have a ridge when you start to mow.

 # FERTILIZING

The quality of the lawn you end up with a few years hence depends to a large extent on the fertilization schedule that you follow. The better the lawn you desire, the more often you should apply fertilizer, but the less you apply each time. The basic rate for fertilizer is 5 kg of nitrogen per 100 sq. m per season (10 lb. per 1,000 sq. ft.). Thinking back to Chapter 1, you may recall that the numbers on a fertilizer bag are percentages, so to apply 5 kg (10 lb.) of a 10-6-4 you would spread 50 kg (100 lb.) of the fertilizer on each 100 sq. m (1,000 sq. ft.). Even with a slow-release type, if you applied this all at once you would have problems with fertilizer burn, but in several applications it would be fine.

I know that many people don't apply anywhere near this quantity each summer and still have green lawns, but generally their lawns are not thick and lush—they are prone to burning badly in the summer and they are full of weeds. A well-fertilized lawn is so thick that weeds haven't much chance to become established, and the grass is deep-rooted so that droughts have less effect.

You want to apply fertilizer to give a spring flush of growth, and this can be accomplished in two ways. By fertilizing in late fall with a high-nitrogen fertilizer, the nitrogen is taken into the plant as cold weather arrives, and remains there ready to boost growth as soon as spring arrives. This application should be made in early October in zone 4, mid-October in zone 5, and late October to early November in zone 6, using something like a 12-3-3 fertilizer at 1 kg (2 lb.) nitrogen per 100 sq. m (1,000 sq. ft.). This equals 8 kg or 18 lb. of actual fertilizer. (See page 11 for the zone map if you are not sure in which zone you live.) Alternatively, you can use a regular lawn food as early as possible in the spring—as soon as you can walk on the lawn without leaving foot marks—and count this as part of your total nitrogen application.

In addition to the applications just described for an early spring boost, you should ideally feed four more times: in mid- and late spring and early and mid-fall; applying 1 kg (2 lb.) of actual nitrogen each time. Do not apply fertilizer during the heat of summer when the grass is not actively growing. Many homeowners give just two feedings a year, in the spring and early fall, but their lawns would improve greatly with more frequent applications. If you want a really tiptop lawn, put on only half a kilogram (1 lb.) of fertilizer twice as often as outlined above—a total of 10 applications each year! This is also kinder on the environment since more of the nitrogen is used by the grass, rather than leaching into the groundwater.

One way to cut down on the number of times you need to walk round the garden pushing a fertilizer spreader is to use one of the slow-release forms of fertilizer mentioned in Chapter 1, sulphur-coated urea or urea formaldehyde. You would still give the very early or very late application but the other four could be replaced by two, using a slow-release formulation. This also helps to eliminate the sudden flush of growth that you get soon after applying regular fertilizer, when you have to mow about every five days. The higher the percentage of SCU or UF in the lawn feed, the better the spread on the feeding period. If you buy a fertilizer with 50% SCU and put it on at 2 kg (4 lb.) nitrogen per 100 sq. m (1,000 sq. ft.), 1 kg (2 lb.) is still available immediately—the same amount you would apply with a regular fertilizer.

There are other types of fertilizer that are advertised as winterizer blends. These have a lower nitrogen content and much more potash—somewhere in the range of 4-8-15. They are intended to be applied in late summer or early fall to improve the general health of the grass (remember, potash is for all-round well-being) so that the lawn does not suffer from winter kill. But tests done at the University of Guelph indicate that the late application of high-nitrogen fertilizer is more beneficial.

A fairly recent introduction for the homeowner is liquid lawn fertilizer, very often in a special container that you attach to the end of the hose for automatic dilution. Being in a liquid form, this type of fertilizer is available to the plant faster than granular forms, but it is harder to see where you have just applied the fertilizer (with a spreader you can normally see the wheelmarks), and so the risk of overfeeding is greater.

 # WEED CONTROL

To many people, feeding and weeding are the same thing, and they use a fertilizer that contains a herbicide whether the lawn has any weed or not. If you are feeding your lawn properly, young weeds don't stand a chance. True, existing weeds need to be dealt with to get the lawn weed-free in the beginning, but after this you should not need to kill weeds for several years.

There are two main types of lawn weed killer on the market: 2,4-D on its own and 2,4-D plus either mecoprop, dicamba, fenoprop, or dichlorprop, or a combination of these. Each of these weed killers will control a certain group of weeds, so you need to identify your weeds and then read the labels on the herbicides in the garden centre. The most common weed in lawns is dandelion and this is killed by 2,4-D. If, however, you have bad infestations of the white-flowered chickweed in mid-summer, then you need a weed killer containing 2,4-D plus mecoprop or dicamba.

The Ontario Ministry of Agriculture, Food and Rural Affairs has an excellent inexpensive publication (number 529), *Weed Control in Lawns and Gardens*, which, as well as listing the major weeds and their controls, has very good line drawings of the weeds, making identification quite easy.

These are selective weed killers. That does not mean they select only the plants that you want them to kill, just that they don't kill grass and grasslike plants when used at the recommended rates. If you spray all over your shrubs and flowers, they will die, just the same as the dandelions. Because very small quantities of most weed killers can do so much damage, don't ever spray on a windy day when spray drift will be carried onto other plants. Test your sprayer first with clean water and adjust the nozzle to give as large a droplet size as possible—large drops drift least. Don't wave the spray wand around all over the place, but keep it pointing down to the grass. Most of these chemicals are very difficult to wash out of sprayers and if you spray 2,4-D and then use the sprayer for an insecticide, you will have, at the very least, distorted growth, and probably dead plants. A friend of mine used his sprayer to treat his lawn for weeds, washed it out with soapy water and then with clear water, and then sprayed his roses for aphids. He used to have a good rose garden. Out of 35 plants, only one survived.

Remember, these are poisons and should be treated the same as you would any other toxic chemical, such as toilet bowl cleaner. Wear rubber gloves while spraying, don't inhale the fumes from the concentrate, and wash all exposed skin after using. In other words, use common sense. Used properly, these are very safe products, but anything ending in "cide" is meant to kill something, and they can cause problems if the directions on the label are not followed.

The weed killers are absorbed by the broad leaves of most plants, but run off the narrow, smooth leaves of the grass. Once they are in the plant they react with the plant hormones that regulate the rate of growth. You will notice that the weeds start to elongate a few days after applying these weed killers. Eventually the weeds turn brown and die. Selective weed killers are also absorbed by the grass foliage to a degree and they do put the grass plants under stress. Using them at the wrong rate can kill the grass along with the weeds. Do not use on newly seeded lawns for the first season.

These herbicides work best in moderate temperatures. If you apply them with the first fertilizing in early spring, you are wasting your money. Wait until the average daytime temperature, not just the midday high, is above 20°C (70°F) before use. If you apply them in the heat of the summer you will kill the weeds, but you will put the grass under great stress and probably kill it as well. Since they have to be absorbed through the leaf surface, it should be obvious that you do not spray weed killers when rain is forecast within the next 12 hours.

There are many different ways of applying these herbicides. As mentioned, you can spray them on or apply them as granules with your fertilizer. If you have only a few weeds you can get a special see-through cane that you drop a tablet into and fill with water. This has a valve on the base and you put the cane on the weed and push down to release a small amount of the herbicide. I have found the Weed Bar to be very effective and foolproof. Here the herbicide is mixed with a wax and shaped into a bar. You simply drag it across the lawn with no danger to other plants and, because it is wax-based, rain shortly afterwards does not affect it. The only drawback I have found with the weed bar is that it is slower than spraying it. To get good coverage you need to drag the bar across the lawn twice at right angles and then repeat the process after two mowings.

If you are worried about your pets and children playing on a treated lawn, apply to the front and back lawns separately. Spray the lawn first thing in the morning and keep this lawn blocked off for the day. By evening the plants will have absorbed enough of the chemicals and you can spray the lawn with water to wash the herbicide off the foliage and into the soil where it will break down.

Always follow the directions on the container *exactly*. Don't add extra on the theory that if one spoonful is good, two will be twice as good. You waste money and may damage the grass as well. Wash all equipment out thoroughly, including spraying through the nozzle to wash the lines, and empty the rest of the wash onto some bare soil, not down the sink. Store out of the reach of children, preferably under lock and key, since the concentrate can make you quite sick in large doses. Finally, bring any concentrate indoors for the winter. Allowing 2,4-D to freeze destroys its effectiveness. It is a good practice to seal it in a plastic bag since any fumes given off may be toxic to house plants.

Crab grass is one type of weed that does not respond to selective weed killers. This is an annual grass with a coarse foliage which can make a lawn look very scruffy. As with broad-leaved weeds, if you have a really dense sod, you are not likely to have problems, but on a thin lawn crab grass will crowd out the desirable grasses and soon colonize a large area. Because it is an annual grass, you can control it by applying a pre-emergent weed killer (one that kills the seedlings as they emerge from the ground) early in the year before the seeds germinate. The best time for this is when the forsythia shrubs—the early, bright yellow ones—are in flower. There are also chemicals that can be used during the summer to kill the growing plants but they may also put your lawn under stress.

Weeds are incredibly tough. That is why they are weeds. In the lawn, they can stand up to being walked on, having their tops mown off at frequent intervals and still manage to thrive, flower and seed themselves into any small patch of bare soil. The secret to weed control is to have a lawn so thick and lush that there is no bare soil for the weeds to grow in. A dense sod will shade germinating weedlings and they will not grow into adult weeds.

Many people are worried about the effects of weed killers on the environment, and some municipalities have gone so far as to ban their use on city-owned properties at least. Weeds can be controlled by organic means, but it is more labour intensive than simply spraying with a chemical. In the home garden, hand-weeding, regular fertilization (with organic fertilizers if you wish), aeration, and correct mowing heights will ensure a thick swath of grass that will prevent weed seeds from reaching the soil and choke out any seedlings if they do manage to germinate.

The following are organic ways to deal with the most common lawn weeds.

Dandelion. This well-known perennial has a deep tap root and spreads by seed. Try to pull out young plants in early summer before they establish a deep root system. With established plants, cut them off with a sharp knife as deep as possible; at least 10 cm (4 in.) below the soil surface.

Plantain. These are rosette-forming perennials that have deep, fibrous roots and rat-tail-like flower spikes that never seem to open—but still set copious seed. Dig, or spray with a soap-based weed killer. This will also kill the grass, but on almost circular plants like plantain, it is not difficult to spray just the weed.

Creeping Charlie or **ground ivy** is an invasive perennial with a shallow root system. Frequent rakings with a fan-type rake will stop him creeping too far. Be sure to collect up the parts you rake off to stop any seeds from ripening.

Knotweed is an annual that thrives in sandy, compacted soils. Once the mower has cut the top off the plant, it spreads horizontally through the grass. Hand-weed as early in the summer as possible to stop the plants shedding even more seed, and aerate the area to reduce compaction. It is deep-rooted but just cutting the top off at the crown will kill it.

Clover, a perennial, may have white or pink flowers, depending on the species. Many people encourage clover in their lawn since it remains green during drought when grass goes dormant and turns brown, but it stains clothes green when it's rolled on. It is a sign of a soil lacking in nitrogen, so control by hand-weeding initially and then fertilizing more frequently.

Black medick is often mistaken for clover in its young stage, but it has yellow flowers later in the season. This annual gets its name from the colour of the seeds, which are edible if you have the patience to collect them. It thrives in poor, compacted soils, so aerate and increase the fertilization.

Mouse-eared chickweed, an annual, forms mats in the lawn as it twines itself round the grass stems. It is difficult to hand-weed for this reason and can sprout again from roots left in the soil. Try to spot it while it is young and treat it with organic soap. The grass will soon grow back in to fill any dead areas.

English daisies are perennial and can take over a lawn, although on my most recent trip to England, I hardly saw any. They should be hand-weeded, best done with a small, clawed tool called a daisy puller. Or you can move to zone 5 where they are not hardy.

Moss, an ancient plant, indicates poor growing conditions for the grass. The location is too wet, too shady, or too acidic, or a combination of these. Control it by improving the drainage, pruning trees or shrubs to let in more light, or by applying lime; but do a pH test first to be sure this is needed.

Crab grass is annual and best controlled by using a pre-emergent weed killer. Organic gardeners should avoid close mowing, fertilize regularly, and, if the crab grass still appears, mow with a grass catcher to remove the seed heads, rather than allow the seed to fall on the lawn.

Annual bluegrass is an upright species with pale green leaves. It usually has two generations a year, in spring and fall, dying during the heat of summer. Its form and colour make it easy to identify; it is equally easy to weed out, but time-consuming.

Nut sedge is a perennial with light green foliage that can be most invasive in moist soils. Sedges can be distinguished from grasses by the leaves, which are in three ranks rather than in two, and by the triangular stems. You can control sedges by improving the drainage.

 # MOWING

Lawns need a weekly mowing to keep them looking nice. In fact, in the spring when growth is rapid, they could often do with mowing every four or five days. While one is loath to give this much time to lawn care, it is only for a few weeks and it does make a difference to the subsequent growth of the lawn.

Mowing is a very unnatural process. Even in the wild, as grass was evolving, while it might get chewed back occasionally by a passing herd of ruminants, it was not subjected to a regular close trim. Every time you mow your grass, you deprive the plant of its major source of nutrients, the sugars that are manufactured by the leaves in sunlight. This reduction in sugars slows down the rate of root production and puts the plant under stress. The more you remove at any one time, the greater the shock to the plant. Most lawn experts say you shouldn't remove more than one-third of the leaf surface at any one time. In other words, if you keep your grass 5 cm (2 in.) long, you should mow it when it gets to 7.5 cm (3 in.). I know that I don't always follow this rule, especially during the spring growth flush, but my lawn would look better if I did.

Start the mowing season with the blade about 4 cm (1 ½ in.) high. When the hot days of late June arrive, raise the deck by a notch, and another notch in the really hot July–August period, although you probably won't have to mow very much then anyway. When cooler weather arrives gradually lower the cutting level until you are back at 4 cm (1 ½ in.) again. This low cutting in the fall is important since short grass is less liable to be attacked by snow-mould fungus disease. I said to raise the deck a notch because most of us use rotary mowers where the height of the cut is controlled by adjusting the wheels, either by means of a ratchet on the side or by unbolting them and moving them to a new hole on the frame. Actual heights of cut are governed by the spacings on the machine but aim for about 8 cm (3 in.) in the summer, longer if you are growing tall fescue.

When you mow, try not to follow the same pattern all the time. I always try to remember which way I mowed last time and mow at right angles the next. This serves two purposes: it stops the grass growing one way, with the direction of the mow, and it saves you getting a series of tiny ridges in the lawn from the wheels. Even with an electric mower you can usually manage to mow most of the lawn in different directions and still not have to cross the cord.

There was a time when all mowers were created equal, but now we have regular mowers and *mulching mowers*. In these, the blade usually has a longer sharp edge and is twisted slightly, like a propeller, and the delivery chute can be closed. The intent is to swirl the clippings under the deck so they are cut into small pieces and drop evenly onto the lawn. Some models do this better than others—mine still leaves a trail of grass down one side of each strip—so try to get a practical demonstration before you buy. The small pieces of grass break down more rapidly and you avoid the thatch build-up, to a large degree at any rate.

If you have a non-mulching mower with a grass catcher, you would be well advised to use it. Large clippings break down quite fast in a compost heap, but when left on the lawn they decompose more slowly. Even in one summer they will build up into a layer a centimetre (½ in.) or more thick. Until quite recent times, homes were roofed with a layer of dead grass stems called thatch. It worked very successfully to keep the rain out. The same thing happens in your lawn when the dead clippings build up, and the same name is given to it: *thatch*. New mulching mowers chop the clippings into short pieces that break down fairly quickly. Thatch is seldom a problem with these mowers, and clippings can be left on to fertilize the lawn.

If you have thatch problems—and you can soon tell by digging your fingers into the sod—you either have to rake with the fan rake to scratch it out (one of the hardest jobs I know) or use a mechanical de-thatcher. You can rent these machines as a self-contained unit or you can buy a special blade for gasoline-driven rotary mowers. This replaces the regular blade while you de-thatch and has small spring-mounted spikes on the end that scratch out the thatch. It is not recommended for electric mowers. Once the machine has brought the thatch to the surface, you must rake it up and dispose of it. It is too dry to compost well but can either be used as a mulch or dug into a bed where it will decompose in time.

Always keep your mower blade sharp. They get blunt far quicker than most of us realize—I was horrified last time I took my blade off to see just how blunt it had become. If the blade is blunt, instead of cutting the grass it flails the top off, leaving a ragged, bruised edge. After a few days this bruised area turns brown and the whole lawn takes on a strange tint. After you have sharpened your mower blade, balance it across the centre on a knife edge. If one end sinks, it means it is heavier and needs some more filing off to keep the blade in balance. Failure to balance the blade results in uneven wear on the bearings that support the spindle that the blade bolts onto.

Because mowing throws a lot of small particles of grass into the air, you should frequently check the air filter on a gas-powered engine and the screens allowing cooling air around an electric one. One final word of caution: wear proper footwear while mowing. Bare feet or loose sandals do not give you a proper grip on the grass and mower blades are no respecters of toes. Bare feet can slip under the edge of a mower deck so easily, but wearing shoes with toe caps will probably raise your feet high enough to protect them.

WATERING

Although grass will not grow well in wet soils, it does need a regular supply of water to thrive. During dry periods you will probably have to irrigate to keep your lawn looking green. On fertile, loamy soils, your lawn will need 2 to 3 cm (about 1 in.) of water each week throughout the growing season, probably double this on light, sandy soils. It is a good idea to have a rain gauge set up somewhere in the garden to give you some idea of how much water nature has provided and how much you need to add. Small plastic gauges are available at the larger garden centres, or you can mark off the scale on a straight-sided glass jar. Site the gauge where it will not get drips from the house or from plants, and, if you are using glass, where there is no danger of it being smashed.

The first time you irrigate, and any time you buy a new sprinkler, set a series of empty cans across your lawn. Turn on the water for 30 minutes and then check the depth of the water in the cans. Work out the average reading and from this you can calculate how long you need to leave the sprinkler on to give the desired amount of water.

It is much better to give the 3 cm (1 in.) of water all at one time and then not water for another week than to water less two or three times a week. When you water little and often, the moisture does not penetrate very far into the ground, but stays in the top couple of centimetres (1 inch). This encourages the grass to form roots close to the surface, which makes them even more susceptible to future droughts.

While rain is likely to fall at any time, try to water so that the lawn has time to dry before night. Grass that is wet late in the evening when the temperature drops seems more subject to fungus disease. Don't ask me why this should be, when grass gets wet every evening from dew anyway, but there does seem to be a link between artificially wet grass and disease.

AERATION

Like de-thatching, aerating is best done with a rented machine. It is most often needed on heavy soils where walking on the lawn compacts the soil surface until eventually rain cannot penetrate. Sandy soils seldom require aerating. The aeration machine has a drum fitted with hollow tubes (rather like apple corers); as it moves across the lawn it removes plugs of soil about 2 cm across and 10 cm long (³/₄ in. by 4 in.) and leaves them on the top of the lawn. They can either be raked up and added to the compost or be allowed to dry slightly and then be broken down to act as a top-dressing by raking or brushing them over the lawn.

Aerating the lawn allows air, water, and fertilizers back into the soil, which in turn has a marked effect on the growth of the grass. Several weeds, particularly knotweed, thrive on compacted soils, giving competition to the grass. Aerating helps to eliminate these.

PROBLEMS

The better your lawn, the less likely you are to have problems, since healthy plants are better able to fight off pest and disease attacks. However, there are a few things that may happen to even the best lawn. If brown patches appear in the spring or fall and when you tug on the dead grass it comes away in your hand, you have **white grubs**. These feed on the roots of the grass and are the larvae of several different species of insect, including both the June and Japanese beetles. When you dig into the dead area you will find a fat, white grub, up to 4 cm (1 ½ in.) long with a brown head. It usually curls into a semicircle when exposed to light. Skunks enjoy a feed of white grubs and may come into the garden at night to dig them out, which leaves your lawn looking like a battlefield with small craters everywhere. If you have a bad attack of white grubs, with large areas killed, you can water with an insecticide containing chlorpyrifos to kill them below ground level. This is a non-persistent insecticide, but it is highly toxic to fish so be extra careful if you have a garden pool. A mild attack can be tolerated, when the dead patches are small and easy to overseed, but they should not be ignored. The grubs can live in the soil for up to five years, growing each year. Small dead areas one year will be larger the next as the grubs grow and move out in search of new pastures.

If your lawn turns brown in summer and doesn't pull out in handfuls, then the pest is probably **chinch bugs**. Unlike white grubs, which are fairly slow to kill an area, chinch bugs can turn a patch of grass brown in a few days. They are quite small—4 mm (¹/₈ in.)—but are present in large numbers and they kill the grass by piercing the stem at ground level and sucking the sap. Lay a piece of white cloth on the live grass at the edge of the dead area and water it with warm water. If you lift the cloth after a few minutes you will see the dark adults on the underside. Control them by drenching the area with carbaryl, diazinon, or chlorpyrifos as soon as you see signs of an attack. They live in the thatch layer so keeping your lawn thatch-free will help prevent attacks.

If you don't want to treat your lawn with chemicals, there is an alternative. Nematodes are microscopic animals that live in the soil, in plants and in animals. Some are the cause of disease, but some are beneficial, from our point of view at least. Some nematodes are parasitic on insect grubs living in the soil and these can be used to control white grubs and chinch bugs. They are purchased by mail from organic supply houses as an inoculant that is mixed with water and watered onto the lawn. The nematodes feed on the pests and multiply in the soil, attacking any new pests that hatch. If this seems too good to be true, there is one catch; they do not survive over winter in our climate. If you apply them in spring, they will kill any existing pests and any new ones, giving, in effect, two years' protection.

There is one more cause of brown patches in lawns—female dogs using it as a bathroom. The size of the spots depends on the size of the dog. Toy poodles are preferable to Great Danes. The control is obvious but not likely to make you popular in the neighbourhood.

If your soil is very sandy you may have a problem with ants. Although they do not actually feed on the grass, their nests can leave an area of lawn too well drained, so it dies, and the mounds that they raise can swiftly blunt the mower blade. A mix of half borax and half sugar syrup, sheltered from the rain, but placed where the ants will find it and carry it back to their nest, will eradicate the nest in a couple of weeks.

Snow mould is a fungus disease associated with wet locations and long grass. It is most likely to occur on north slopes where the snow persists or where snow becomes extra deep—for instance, along the driveway where you dump the winter snowfalls. Try to spread the snow in these areas once spring arrives. If allowed to persist, the snow mould will kill the grass, but if you break up the threads with a fan rake as soon as you see them, the grass will usually recover. This problem goes away as soon as the weather warms up.

In both new and old subdivisions **toadstools** can be a problem but for different reasons. Scraps of lumber, buried in the soil when the house was being built or the lot graded, can give rise to **fairy rings** a couple of years later. This is a form of fungus that feeds on decaying wood and expands its growth area each year, forming the characteristic expanding ring. An enzyme excreted by the fungus causes the grass on the edge of the ring to become a darker green, which forms the actual "ring." Toadstools are produced in the fall. You have two choices to control this; you can dig in the centre of the circle and remove the wood that is fueling the growth or you can wait a few years until the ring grows off your property and becomes your neighbour's problem.

In older homes, the masses of dark brown fungi that appear in large clusters on the lawn are growing on the remains of tree roots, very often an elm that was taken down because of Dutch elm disease. The toadstools, which quickly turn black and slimy, are produced for much of the summer and for many years if the tree was a large one. Watering the area with benomyl will kill the fungus for a while, but it will probably return eventually when new spores colonize the decaying roots. Benomyl is also highly poisonous to earthworms, so using it over a large area is not a good idea.

In the hot, humid days of midsummer, particularly where the grass is under heavy shade, the lawn may turn almost white with **powdery mildew**. While there are several fungicides that will control this, powdery mildew seldom kills the grass and will disappear once cooler, drier weather returns. If the shade is from trees or large shrubs, removing some of the lower branches so more light can fall on the grass will often eliminate future problems.

There are several other fungus diseases that attack grass, but they are rarely fatal and generally disappear as soon as the weather warms up or cools down, depending on the season when they occur. Often, simply raking the area with a fan rake will allow more light and air down to the soil surface and cure the problem.

WILDFLOWER MEADOWS

This is a grandiose name for what need only be a small area given over to wildflowers. Their beauty lies not only in the flowers themselves, but also in the variety of wildlife they attract into the garden. It seems so simple: dig a piece of ground, rake it level, sprinkle on the seed, water and wait. This will work, but the results may not be all you were hoping for, so let us look at this in detail.

Preparation. Given good growing conditions, almost any exposed piece of soil will quickly green over with germinating weeds. These weed seeds will compete with the wildflower seeds you sow, crowding out many of them. After all, that's what makes a weed successful. It pays to take time and eliminate many of these weeds before you sow. If the area you want to turn into a wildflower garden is covered in vegetation, you will either have to dig out the large plants and hoe off the small ones or spray it first with a herbicide containing glyphosate, and wait a week. The existing plants will then be dying and you can safely turn them under as you dig, adding humus to the soil. Rake the area level after digging and wait again. As soon as the area has greened over with tiny weed seedlings, hoe it very shallowly with a Dutch (scuffle) hoe. Repeat this at least twice, more if you can possibly wait, being careful not to disturb the soil layers and bring fresh weed seeds up to the surface. Sow the wildflower mix and lightly rake it into the surface with a fan rake—just like you did for lawn seed (see page 50). If you start preparing your site in midsummer, you can control the weeds for the rest of the growing season and the soil will be all ready to sow early the following spring. Fall sowing is not recommended for this part of the country.

What to sow. There are a great number of mixtures of wildflower seeds available and you need to choose one suitable for your area but without too many aggressive species that will eventually choke out the rest. Try to avoid ox-eyed daisy (often just listed as daisy) or this is all you will have after about five years; and while purple coneflower is pretty, it is also most invasive and difficult to weed out. Look for a mix with a combination of annual and perennial species. This will give you a good display in the first couple of years from the annuals, then a mixed display from both types. Eventually the perennials may form a dense enough cover to prevent the annuals germinating. If you are buying from the U.S., you need a Northeast Mix for most of Ontario and a Prairie Mix for the western parts.

Aftercare. If the weather turns dry soon after sowing, you will have to irrigate. Just like any other seedling, wildflowers are vulnerable to drought while they are young. If you tried to skimp on site preparation, you may have weeds germinating with your wildflowers. To pull them out, you will have to step on the plot, which will squash several of the desirable plants. Even with good preparation, you may still get a few weeds appearing—dandelions that have blown in before the wildflowers have made a good cover, for example; these will have to be removed carefully. If necessary use spot application of glyphosate; this is preferable to disturbing the soil and bringing more weed seeds to the surface.

OTHER GROUND COVERS

In recent years there has been a great interest in alternatives to grass. This is very desirable, as an area with a different texture and colour adds greatly to the interest of a garden. Unfortunately, many books lead you to suppose that these areas are also less work than a lawn. Initially at least, this is definitely not the case.

In the following chapters, I note those plants that do well as ground covers, those that take considerable wear, and those that should be used only in places where they will not get heavy traffic. Some plants that are used for ground cover grow too tall to be walked on but, since they cover the ground and suppress weed growth, they do give an alternative to mowing. Other plants are annuals that seed themselves and come up anew each spring. Use these with caution in areas that get strong winter winds or where erosion can be a problem.

Many of the alternatives to grass are slow-growing. This means that while they may eventually make a marvelous cover, the area will need hand-weeding until the ground cover is well established.

While most ground cover plants are also used for other purposes (covered more fully in later chapters), there are a few that are almost exclusively lawn substitutes, or commonly grown on a rock garden. Those are dealt with in some detail here.

BARRENWORT. See Chapter 8.

BEARBERRY. See Chapter 5.

BUGLEWEED. See Chapter 8.

CHAMOMILE. I have had several people ask me about a chamomile lawn and how to go about making one. There is reputed to be a chamomile lawn at Buckingham Palace, and I guess people figure that what is good enough for Her Majesty is good enough for them. Unfortunately, the readily available form of chamomile, *Chamaemelum* (or *Anthemis*) *nobilis*, which is used to make chamomile tea, does not make a good lawn. There is a special dwarf, non-flowering strain called 'Treneague' that is used for lawns since it needs less cutting. This does not seem to be available in North America and, in any case, it is only satisfactory on light sandy soils and will not take heavy use.

COTONEASTER. See Chapter 5.

CROWN VETCH. Where it does well, this pretty clover relative makes an ideal ground cover. In many parts of the U.S. it is widely used on roadsides as an alternative to grass. I have seen good stands in the Ottawa area, but for some reason have never been able to get it to overwinter. It should be more persistent in warmer parts.

DAYLILY. See Chapter 8.

DEADNETTLE. See Chapter 8.

DOGWOOD. See Chapter 5.

FALSE SPIREA. See Chapter 5.

FERNS. Although we tend to think of ferns as woodland plants, many will take a surprising amount of sun. I have seen sensitive fern growing in the open with no shade at all, and even the ostrich fern (the source of fiddleheads) can get by with just a little protection from the midday sun. Once established, most species are drought-tolerant and are useful for filling the odd corner that is difficult or time-consuming to mow.

GOUTWEED, BISHOPS WEED. There is one suitable location for growing this plant— surrounded by concrete walls that go 2 m (6 ft.) into the ground. It takes being walked on, is hardy and grows in poor soil, all of which make it an excellent ground cover *providing* it cannot escape to invade the rest of your property. The variegated form is more attractive than the green and is slightly less invasive. Use either with extreme caution. *You have been warned!*

GERANIUM. See Chapter 8.

HEATHS AND HEATHERS. See Chapter 5.

HEN AND CHICKS. The Latin name for this plant, *Sempervivum*, means *live forever*, which it certainly seems to. It is a good choice for small areas in full sun but would not be very suitable for a mass planting as it cannot be walked on. The rosettes die after flowering, leaving the "chicks" to grow on, but they also leave a hole where weed seeds can get a start.

HOSTA. See Chapter 8.

JAPANESE SPURGE. See Chapter 5.

JUNIPER. See Chapter 5.

LILY-OF-THE-VALLEY. This also is an invasive plant but is not in the same league as goutweed. It can be kept in check by burying a wall of heavy-gauge plastic in the soil at the limit of the area you allow for it. Lily-of-the-valley grows well in light to medium shade and will thrive in poor soil, but flowering will be much better in good soil. The white, sweetly scented flowers appear in spring.

LILYTURF. This grass-like plant is only hardy in the warmer parts (zone 6) but where it will survive, it makes a good ground cover, with pale mauve flowers in late summer. The warmer your climate, the wider the range of lilyturf species and varieties you will be able to grow.

MOSS PHLOX. See Chapter 8.

OREGON GRAPE. See Chapter 5.

PERIWINKLE. See Chapter 5.

PINKS. There are many different pinks (*Dianthus*), both annual and perennial, that are easy to grow from seed and make good ground covers for sunny places with well-drained soil. The perennial types are spring-flowering and will often rebloom if the old flowers are sheared off when they fade. They will take some foot traffic but should not be used in areas of high wear.

RUSSIAN ARBORVITAE. A dwarf, bright green, spreading conifer that looks somewhat like a juniper. It is fast growing and very prostrate, reaching about 3 m (10 ft.) across by 30 cm (1 ft.) high. It takes on a bronzy tinge with cold weather and is hardy to zone 3. Don't be misled by the small plant you buy—give it lots of room or you'll be forever pruning.

SNOW IN SUMMER. This is a rock garden plant too invasive for use there, but it makes a good ground cover for light-use areas. The leaves are a grey-green and the white flowers appear in July. They seed themselves freely.

STONECROP. There are dozens of stonecrops and most make good ground covers. The showy stonecrop mentioned in Chapter 8 can be used but cannot be walked on. The golden stonecrop (*Sedum acre*) is very tough, but every piece that breaks off will root wherever it lands, even in the lawn.

SWEET WOODRUFF. A delightful, low, bright green plant with white starry flowers. This was one of the old strewing herbs that was dried and used to cover the floors of ye olde manor house where it gave off a pleasant scent to mask the household odours. It will withstand light foot traffic and grows in deep to mottled shade.

THYME. Thyme makes a good ground cover that will take quite a lot of wear, as long as you don't mind the smell. There are many different varieties, but the culinary thyme is too tall to be used in this way.

WINTERCREEPER. See Euonymus in Chapter 5.

YARROW. See Chapter 8.

YELLOW ARCHANGEL. See Deadnettle, Chapter 8.

 # SUGGESTED READING

Green Side Up: Growing a Perfect Lawn in Northern Climates. Wesley R. Porter. Fitzhenry and Whiteside Ltd., 1999.

Building a Healthy Lawn, A Safe and Natural Approach. Stuart Franklin. Storey Communications, 1988.

Both of these books are full of readable information.

Weed Control in Lawns and Gardens. J.F. Alex, C.G. Waywell, and C.M. Switzer. Ontario Ministry of Agriculture and Food, 1982.

My bible for common weed identification.

The Gardener's Guide to Groundcovers. Jennifer Bennett, ed. Firefly Books, 1996.

Rodale's Successful Organic Gardening: Lawns, Grasses and Groundcovers. Lewis and Nancy Hill. Rodale Press, 1995.

The Scotts Company, one of North America's largest lawn supply firms, has a website, *http://www.scottscompany.com*, where you can get help with lawn problems, etc.

Plate 1 Upper: *Small gardens may be just a square of lawn surrounded by flower beds. The lawn needs mowing every week and the plants also require attention. Lower: Here, although there was more work initially, the weekly maintenance is minimal.*

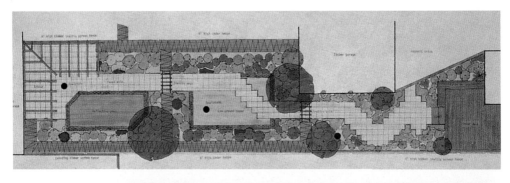

Plate 2 Upper: *This design for a long narrow garden breaks it into a series of individual areas with no direct view down the entire length.*
Lower: *If only a few plants are needed, be sure you select ones that make a bold statement.*

Plate 3 *This path of wood rounds and bark is edged with logs to prevent the soil from washing in.*

Plate 4 *Paths of fieldstone or small patio slabs can be brushed clean and don't need edging.*

Plate 5 Upper: *Periwinkle is slow to make a good cover, but, with time, will make an excellent groundcover for sun or shade.*
Lower: *Bugleweed is quick to colonize and spread—even into the lawn if you aren't careful.*

Plate 6 Upper: *Blue spruce will grow into large trees in time and are best suited to large properties.*
Lower: *Great care should be taken in choosing a site for this Red Jade crab apple, which may eventually have a greater spread than height.*

Plate 7 Upper: Most trees, like this redbud, flower in spring.
Lower: Japanese tree lilac flowers later, at the end of June, thus extending the season.

Plate 8 *Shrubs have a wide variety of forms and habits and subtle use can be made of their different textures.*

Trees

4 chapter

I was in a local garden centre last spring, watching the people coming in to buy their trees and shrubs. Most people had little idea of what they wanted, and many were buying trees that would eventually grow 10 m (30 ft.) or more across for a small city lot. Otherwise sane people, who would do their homework and compare specifications for a new kettle, seem to lose all sense when buying growing plants. There is nothing magical about live plants. They don't really cast a spell over you and compel you to buy them. Treat the purchase of plants for your garden the same way you would buy drapes or floor coverings—*research first*. In the public library system you will find all sorts of books on trees that will give you the detailed information you may need to find exactly the right tree for your garden.

DECISIONS, DECISIONS

When you sit down with the master plan you made in Chapter 2, you will probably find you have room for at least one tree—if not, read this chapter anyway; some of the information applies to shrubs as well. Now comes the interesting task of deciding just what tree you need. This is done on a sort of elimination process, ruling out those that don't fit certain criteria until you are left with a short list of suitable trees. Then you can allow your personal preference to make the final decision. So let us look at this list of decisions that have to be made.

HARDINESS: If a tree isn't hardy for you, all other considerations go by the board. In

Canada we use a hardiness system developed by Agriculture Canada in the mid-1960s. This divides Canada up into 10 zones based on certain indicator plants, with zone 0 being the coldest. Each of these zones is subdivided into a colder and warmer half, (a) and (b). Thus Canada is really divided into 20 zones— actually there are only 19 because there is no zone 9b.

If you live in Ottawa, Barrie, or Parry Sound you are in zone 5a; Montreal, Kingston, Peterborough, and Owen Sound are in 5b; Kitchener and Guelph are in 6a, while Toronto and Hamilton are in 6b (but North Toronto on the escarpment is probably in 6a); Niagara and Windsor are in a mild 7a and you have to go to the west coast to get warmer than this. Most of the Canadian nursery catalogues use this system and many of the larger ones include the map on page 11 showing the zone boundaries.

Many of the gardening books we buy are American, or British books aimed at the American market. These give hardiness on the American system, which is not the same as the Canadian system. Under the American zoning system most of the zone numbers are at least one number lower. Thus Kitchener, Guelph, Toronto, and Hamilton are all in U.S. zone 5. Keep this in mind while using these books. Many plants will not survive if the temperature is too high for a long period, so modern books from the U.S. also include the heat zone as well as the hardiness zone. This is rarely a limiting factor in Ontario and can be ignored.

The zone divisions on a hardiness map are averages. They are an indication only. If you live in zone 6a close to the 6b border and you have a sheltered garden, then, quite likely, you can grow some plants that would not survive in an exposed garden in 6b. To start with, stick to plants that are rated for your zone. As you gain experience, or learn from friends and neighbours, you may want to experiment with other plants that should be on the borderline of hardiness in your area.

Even within one garden there will be microclimates, and a plant that would not survive where the wind buffets round the corner of a building may be quite happy a little farther away, sheltered by a strip of fence. Remember that the warmest spot of all is against the house wall; the snow cover may not last as long, however, which can be important in northern areas.

The origins of the plant you buy and the time of year you plant it can make a difference to survival. Very few garden centres actually grow the plants they are selling. Even those associated with a large nursery may not be getting all their plants from the parent company. In this mobile society, where much of the food we eat comes from distant places, it is no problem to ship a container-load of plants from B.C. or Oregon if they are not available locally, or if it makes economic sense. Thus, the tree you buy in your local garden centre may have been grown half a continent away in a totally different hardiness zone.

If you plant this tree in the spring, it has all summer to acclimatize and to adjust its biological clock to the state of the seasons where you live. If you buy this plant in the fall, and it has come from a fresh shipment, then you could be in trouble. Plants grown in a place with a longer growing season are not as ready to go dormant. Their internal clock tells them that they still have several weeks before they need to sleep, and they may start putting out new leaves in late October. There is nothing wrong with fall planting providing you know the tree has been growing locally since spring.

SIZE AND SHAPE: Many of the older sections of the city have gardens that are almost unusable because of the trees that were planted 60 or 70 years ago. Trees such as sugar maples, where they have survived, have now grown out of all proportion to the size of garden they inhabit. They cast such a dense shade that grass will not survive, and their root system, just below the surface, prevents any other plants from becoming established. When they were planted the homeowner had no choice—there were no small trees suitable for the confines of a city lot. Now, however, things have changed.

Before making your decision on which tree to buy, go outside and look up. Are there any utility wires that will interfere with the tree's growth? Utility companies have the right to prune any tree that is growing into their wires and their pruning may ruin the form of your tree. If, on the other hand, all the utility wires are buried in your community, make sure you know the locations of these wires before you dig. Ma Bell does not take kindly to people who put a spade through her lines and it is your responsibility to avoid such accidents.

Low single-storey homes, tall, narrow row houses, and garden homes require trees of different sizes and shapes. Many new subdivisions have street trees provided by the city or the builder. Here you probably don't want an additional tree in the front. It may look fine now, but in a few years they will be crowding each other. Similarly, in the back, talk to your neighbours on either side and behind you. If you plan to put a tree in your east corner and the neighbours are going to put one in their west corner, one of you will have to give way.

Like people, trees come in different shapes and sizes. You may select from *columnar*, in which the branches grow upright close to the main trunk; *cylindrical*, similar to columnar but the branches grow outwards first, giving it a broader outline; *pyramidal*, broad at the base and tapering to a point; *globe*, which has an almost perfectly round head without clipping; *spreading*, in which the branches come out parallel to the ground and the tree is often wider than tall; *weeping,* in which the branches trail back towards the ground, usually from the top of a stem rather than having branches that grow up the stem. And finally there is *open habit*, which does not have a definable shape

and includes the majority of trees you will see. Several of these shapes may be available within the same species, and the one you decide on determines how far away it should be from another tree.

FLOWERING TIME: The majority of trees and shrubs flower in the spring so that they will have all summer to ripen and disburse their fruit, but it is possible to find a tree that will flower in almost any month of the growing season. If, however, you decide that you have to have a tree that flowers in September, you are severely limiting your choice. Trees that flower in midsummer tend to have shorter flowering periods than those that flower in cooler weather. The flowers don't stand up well in the heat, and often a summer storm will smash all the blooms to the ground.

FLOWER COLOUR: "Any colour you like as long as it's red, pink, or white," to paraphrase Mr. Ford. Actually, it is not quite that bad, but these are the predominant colours. There are a few trees with yellow or mauve blooms but the only blue I can think of that is hardy here is a vine—wisteria—and even that has a mauve tint.

FRUIT: Fruit can be an attractive feature, especially if it persists into the winter months to add colour to an otherwise drab garden. If selected with a little care it can also attract birds to brighten the dull winter days. It does have some drawbacks, however. Unless the birds eat all of it, it makes an additional clean-up job in the spring. Often the seeds within the fruit will pass through the bird undigested and will sprout all over the place in the spring (mountain ash is bad for this). As with flowers, the fruit may be in different colours and forms, from small yellow apples the size of your fingertip to slender brown pods up to half a metre (18 in.) long. If you prefer a flowering tree that doesn't set much fruit, try and get a double-flowered form. Usually the modification of the flower to give the extra petals makes the flower sterile. Many of the succulent fruits such as crab apples, hawthorns, and mountain ash can be used to make jellies and jams even if they are not palatable while raw.

FOLIAGE FORM: While all leaves perform the same function on the plant, they are not all the same shape and size, which makes identifying the various trees much easier. The larger the leaf, the denser the shade that it casts, the cooler it will be to sit under, and the harder it is to grow a good lawn underneath. A catalpa tree, which can have leaves up to 20 cm (8 in.) across, gives an entirely different effect from a honey-locust, which has leaves composed of many tiny leaflets.

Think also about raking up the leaves. Tiny leaves go between the teeth of the lawn rake when you are trying to tidy up in the fall, and larger leaves may stick to a patio (especially after rain) and have to be picked up one by one.

FOLIAGE COLOUR: Leaves are green, right? Well, maybe. They can also be red, copper, purple, yellow, green, and white—or splashed with an entire palette of colours. They can even be one colour and change to another as the summer goes on. Then you have the fall effect to take into consideration! Remember, too, that a pale tree at the end of the property will seem to be closer than it actually is—a useful way to shorten a long narrow garden.

BUYING THE TREE

Before you actually get to the garden centre you have a couple more decisions to make. Do you want an instant tree or the pleasure of watching a young one grow? You may have gathered that I am not altogether in favour of transplanting large trees. When a tree grows, it puts out a network of feeding roots close to the surface of the soil. These roots spread out up to twice the height of the tree and when the tree is dug, with even the largest tree spade, these roots are left behind. This also happens with a small tree, but it will recover much quicker and it doesn't have the same amount of foliage to support. A large tree will often sit in its new home for 5 or 10 years before it starts making normal amounts of new growth, during which time a smaller tree has almost equaled it in size.

If you have decided that you are going to plant a large tree (usually known as a caliper tree because the size is measured by the diameter of the trunk rather than the height), then you don't need to go to the garden centre at all. Look in the Yellow Pages under Tree Service and phone round for quotations, then visit the nursery to select the actual tree, but be sure to keep in mind the effect of soil type explained on page 14.

If you decide to get a small tree, you have three choices. You may find the tree either growing or heeled in (loosely planted) in a nursery, ready to be dug and sold bare-root. The roots of the plant will be wrapped in burlap or plastic for carrying it home. With certain specimens the roots will be balled-and-burlapped—dug with a ball of soil that is then wrapped in burlap.

The trend these days is towards containerized nursery stock. If you are lucky it will be container-grown. More commonly, it is freshly potted into a pot or basket. With plants in containers you are not limited to the traditional planting periods; with care you can plant from spring to fall.

When faced with a row of trees from which to choose only one, how do you make the decision? Look first at the top of the tree. With the possible exception of apple trees on a dwarf rootstock, trees should have a definite leader, a shoot that will continue the upward growth of the tree in a straight line. Even young crab apples, which will eventually have an open habit, should have a leader while small. If this leader is missing or broken, another shoot will have to be trained to take its place, resulting in a crooked trunk. Look next at the placement of the branches on the trunk. Are they evenly spaced down the trunk and do they radiate evenly round the trunk? If the branches when seen from above form an oval, rather than a circle, it indicates that the tree was crowded in the nursery row and it will take skillful pruning to bring the tree back to its proper shape. Mind you, in some small gardens, this flattened form may be a decided advantage. Lastly, look closely at the trunk and the branches for torn bark, broken or twisted limbs, and other evidence of damage. There is always going to be a little, but avoid trees which will require major surgery to make them presentable.

Try to find out where the trees were grown, not just that they came from "our own nursery," but where that nursery is located. This is particularly important with caliper trees and with balled and burlapped plants, but it also applies to bare-root trees. As well as the hardiness factor mentioned earlier, the growth and establishment of trees is influenced by the type of soil they are grown in. Trees grown in a sandy loam do not establish well if moved to a heavy clay and vice versa. If possible, try to get trees from the same soil type. "Our own nursery" may be on an acidic muck soil, while your garden is a light sand.

 **PLANTING**

At last the great moment has come. All the decisions have been made and you have the ideal tree just waiting to leap into growth. If you bought a caliper tree you have nothing to worry about. The location was decided in your master plan and the cost of the tree should have included digging the hole, planting, and fitting the guy wires. You will be expected to water it.

If you bought a smaller tree then each of the types mentioned above need slightly different treatment, but in each case you must start by digging a hole. The size of the hole depends on the type of root system (bare, balled, or potted) and on your soil type. As the old adage puts it, "Never put a $20 tree in a $5 hole." Time spent in preparing the site is well worth it.

Before you start, look at the plant you bought. If bare-root, remove the packing and examine the roots. If any are broken, trim them back to good root with a pair of pruning shears. If you have a container large enough to take the roots, fill it with water or, better yet, diluted plant starter, and leave the plant to soak while you dig the hole. If not, put the plant in the shade, spray the roots with water and cover again with the wrapping the plant came with. Do not leave the roots exposed to the sun and wind for any longer than you have to. If balled and burlapped, try to undo the burlap where it is tied round the neck of the plant and get your finger inside to feel the root ball. If it is dry, water it. Potted plants should be watered the evening before you intend to plant. Give enough water so that it runs out of the drainage holes in the bottom.

Dig the hole large enough to take the roots without crowding and without them curling up at the bottom of the hole. Ideally, there should be about 15 cm (6 in.) clear all around the roots in sandy soil and double this in a clay soil. *Do not* add things to the soil you take out, especially on clay soils. If you improve this soil with humus and make it fertile, when the roots start to grow and reach the surrounding cold clay they turn back into the good soil. Eventually either the tree blows over in a storm because it never made any anchor roots or it strangles itself in a tangled mass of roots. Try to break up the bottom of a hole in heavy soil so that water can drain away. Otherwise the hole may fill with water and drown the plant. Don't add gravel to the base of the hole either. While it would seem to improve drainage, it actually makes a layer that the surrounding water drains into.

You will probably need three hands to plant a tree, or someone to help you. Have at hand a 5 x 5 cm (2 x 2 in.) stake about 2 m (6 ft.) long. Hold the tree in the hole so that the roots are evenly spread and the soil-mark on the stem is just at ground level. Place a long plank across the hole to give you the soil level without getting on your hands and knees. Hammer the stake into the bottom of the hole about 30 cm (12 in.) away from the trunk of the tree. If placed closer it may shade the trunk, causing uneven growth. You put the stake in first so that there is no danger of driving it through a root after you have filled the hole with soil. Partly fill the hole with soil, working it underneath the roots so that you leave no large air pockets. On all but the heaviest soils, firm the soil in the hole with your foot at this stage, or better still, water the soil as you add it to wash it down between the roots. Fill the hole to ground level and firm again. This should leave a slight depression around the tree which will act as a saucer when you add water.

With balled and burlapped trees, dig the hole larger than the diameter of the ball and slightly deeper. Put the ball in the hole without removing the burlap and adjust the depth so that the soil mark on the stem is at ground level. Fill in the bottom half of the hole and then undo the burlap from the neck of the plant and fold it back over the soil. Fill the rest of the hole and firm. The reason for doing it this way is the burlap deflects the water away from the root ball if it is left over the top of it, but collects the water into the ball if it is spread out. Obviously you do not want to drive a stake

into the roots, so if the tree needs support, as in the case of a large evergreen, put in two stakes, one on either side of the ball, with a cross-brace to which you then fasten the tree.

The treatment of container-grown stock depends on the time of year and the nature of the container. If the plant is still dormant (the leaves haven't yet opened), knock it out of the container. If all the soil falls off, treat it like a bare-root tree. If the root ball seems full of roots, try to tease the basal ones out to break the circle of roots and again plant like a bare-root plant.

If the leaves are growing, and the plant is in a paper-fibre pot, break off the top of the pot down to the soil, make some slits down the sides of the pot and plant with the level of the soil inside and outside the pot equal. If you don't remove the pot rim it acts like a wick and draws all the moisture from the root ball, evaporating it into the air. The rest of the pot will break down during the summer. If the container is made of a non-degradable material such as plastic, metal, or rubber, you will have to very carefully slide the pot off the roots at the edge of the hole, and hope that the soil stays intact. If you see that there is a mass of roots, use a sharp knife and make three cuts down the root ball about 1 cm deep ($\frac{1}{2}$ in.). This encourages the formation of new roots into the fresh soil. Fill in around the root ball and firm gently.

After planting, water thoroughly, preferably with one of the plant-starter soluble fertilizers. Give enough water to wet the soil for the depth of the roots. The water should move freely through the disturbed soil, but on heavy clays you will have to spread the watering over several days. Thereafter, water as needed, remembering that the plant probably does not have a great number of roots at first. One of North America's foremost arborists who has researched tree growth suggests that you water every 7 to 10 days for the first season. HINT: It is often helpful to put two large juice cans into the hole as you plant. The bottom one should have some small holes punched in it with a nail and the top one have both ends removed. By putting these one above the other, you can pour water in the top and it will soak out at the bottom, down where the roots are.

It is now thought better not to add fertilizer at planting time—except for a liquid plant starter. This encourages the new roots to spread out into the surrounding soil seeking nutrients, rather than growing only in comparatively rich soil used to fill the hole. A handful of high-nitrogen, slow-release fertilizer should be sprinkled over the planting area in the fall and again the following spring. If you plant in the fall, don't fertilize until the following fall to allow time for new roots to develop.

Fasten the tree to the stake using either a special adjustable tree tie, available from many garden centres, or a length of coat hanger wire through a piece of old hose (Figure 4–1). Recent research suggests that the tie should not be too high up the stem. Fastening the stem high up restricts the amount of flexing that the tree can do and, apparently, flexing is necessary to give a tapered stem, without which the stem remains brittle and likely to snap in a wind. If the fastening can be put within a metre (yard) of the ground, saw off the top of the stake to stop any chance of it rubbing on the trunk and damaging the bark. Even if the tree will stand up without a stake,

it is a good practice to use a short one for the first year while the tree is putting down anchor roots.

Pruning trees at planting time is now thought to be harmful. Remove only broken branches, shoots growing into the centre of the tree, or branches that rub together. Don't be tempted to prune the lower branches off at first. Young trees should have two-thirds of their branch area in the base of the crown to keep the wind load down low. This helps to stop them blowing over while roots are produced to anchor the tree.

Young trees grow best if they are not in competition with the grass for the first few years. Leave a good circle of bare ground around the trunk of the tree after planting and don't allow the grass to grow back in. Research in commercial nurseries has shown that trees grown in clean rows grow much faster than in rows that are grassed over. To keep the weeds down during the summer you can mulch with wood chips, compost, or shredded bark in a layer up to 10 cm (4 in.) deep, but not in contact with the trunk. This circle of clear space around the tree also serves to keep mowers and weed-eaters away from the trunk, preventing damage.

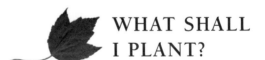

WHAT SHALL I PLANT?

The following is a list of readily available trees commonly recommended for city properties. I have used a "movie review" rating system of one to five stars to show my personal assessment of their suitability. Shade tolerance is given by the ● symbol; ●●●● denotes plants that will thrive in deep shade.

ALMOND—see Cherry.

ARBORVITAE—see Cedar, eastern white.

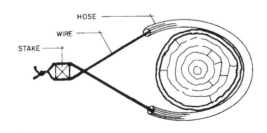

STAKING A NEW TREE

FIGURE 4-1 A coat hanger through a piece of old hose acts as a tree tie.

ASH *Fraxinus**
Height: 15 m (50 ft.) Spread: 10 m (33 ft.)
Zone 2

Ash trees are used so much for street plantings and in parking lots that they are in danger of being overplanted (a fate that befell littleleaf linden a few years ago). While they are tolerant of tough city conditions and good for planting in this type of location, I do not feel that most are a good choice for private gardens where the range of what will survive is much greater.

The one exception I would make to this is **'Fallgold'** black ash***. This is a good small tree (10.5 x 9 m/35 x 30 ft.), hardy to zone 2b, with an upright shape and good fall colour. It does well on wet soils but will also thrive on regular garden soil.

BEECH *Fagus*
European beech *F. sylvatica***
Height: 10 m (33 ft.) Spread: 15 m (50 ft.)
Zone 6

The European beech grows in many forms ranging from fairly slender, upright ones to wide-spreading, weeping ones. There are also many purple-leaved forms in various shapes. In general they are simply too large for urban gardens and can only be seen and appreciated properly in a park setting.

BIRCH *Betula*
Canoe birch, paper birch *B. papyrifera***
Height: 15 m (50 ft.) Spread: 10 m (33 ft.)
Zone 2

This is one tree that just about every nursery sells. It is also one of the few trees that often has several stems (normally a tree has one stem; a shrub has multiple stems). Birches are subject to several serious pest and disease problems, including leaf miner, bronze birch borer, and dieback. The leaf miner is preventable by painting a band of dimethoate on the trunk in the spring. A second application in early June will control the bronze borer. The chemical is absorbed into the sap stream and makes the plant toxic when the pests start to feed on the plant. The dieback is caused by a fungus and starts at the top of the tree, working downwards. Prune out infected branches as soon as they are seen. Both the dieback and the borer are more likely to occur on trees that are under stress from drought, poor growing conditions, or poor nutrition. Keeping the plant growing strongly is the best way to combat these problems.

European white birch *B. pendula***
Height: 18 m (60 ft.) Spread: 12 m (40 ft.)
Zone 2

This also tends to be overplanted and to grow too large for the site but it is such a graceful tree that their overuse is not surprising. **'Gracilis'***, a weeping form, has more divided leaves and does not grow quite as large as some. **'Youngii'*** (Young's weeping birch) has slender weeping branches. It is usually grafted onto a 3-m (8- to 9-ft.) stem so that the branches can cascade almost to the ground. It can reach 10 x 10 m (35 x 35 ft.) in time, so allow room for it to spread.

River birch *B. nigra***
Height: 15 m (50 ft.) Spread: 12 m (40 ft.)
Zone 3

A native birch, the species is rarely seen, but the cultivar **'Heritage'** makes a good garden subject with bark that flakes off in plates to reveal a paler inner bark. It is quite pest and disease resistant but needs a site where the soil is wet in spring, such as the bottom of a slight slope.

Whitebark Himalayan birch *B. utilis* var. *jacquemontii****
Height: 9 m (30 ft.) Spread: 6 m (20 ft.) Zone 4

This is the whitest of all birches, but when grown from seed the colour can be creamy. See them in a nursery to select the whitest form.

BOX ELDER—see Manitoba maple.

BUCKEYE—see Chestnut.

BUCKTHORN *Rhamnus cathartica*
Height: 6 m (20 ft.) Spread: 5 m (15 ft.) Zone 3

This is included only as a warning; it rates minus four stars in my estimation. This is a weedy small tree or large shrub that produces black berries in small clusters. Birds eat the fruit but don't digest the seeds, which then germinate wherever they fall. Areas around Ottawa have been completely taken over by this plant. If you find it in your garden, remove it immediately.

CATALPA *Catalpa*
Chinese catalpa *C. ovata****
Height: 8 m (26 ft.) Spread: 6 m (20 ft.) Zone 6

I am of two minds about catalpas in general. True, their flowers are lovely, even though they always seem to coincide with a summer storm, but they are the first trees to lose their leaves in fall and the last to leaf out in spring, and our season is short enough as it is! There is a lot of confusion between this and the umbrella catalpa, both of which form round heads, and I half suspect that they are one and the same plant in the nursery trade.

Northern catalpa *C. speciosa****
Height: 15 m (50 ft.) Spread: 8 m (26 ft.) Zone 5

This is the most popular of all the catalpas. It grows quickly and is tolerant of poor soils. The fruit is a bean up to 50 cm (20 in.) long which persists into winter and is an added attraction, but is an additional chore in the spring when the pods must be raked up. The leaves are very large, up to 30 cm long by 20 cm across (12 x 8 in.), and cast a dense shade. Since the crown is open, however, there is seldom any problem growing grass underneath this tree.

Umbrella catalpa *C. bignonioides* 'Nana'***
Height: 6 m (20 ft.) Spread: 4 m (13 ft.) Zone 5b

Try to plant this in a sheltered location, protected from strong winds, especially at the limit of its range. It forms an almost globular head if it is cut back hard (leaving only 10 cm [4 in.] of previous year's growth) each spring.

CEDAR *Thuja*
Eastern white cedar, Arborvitae *T. occidentalis*
Height: 5 m (16 ft.) Spread: 3 m (6–10 ft.) Zone 2 or 3 ●

This plant is commonly known as cedar, as in "Nice cedar hedge you've got there," but the true cedar (*Cedrus*) is hardy only on the west coast. At least we won't be confused. Apart from being the number-one choice for hedging, there are a number of good forms of arborvitae that make excellent specimen plants. These are propagated from cuttings and are nursery grown, so naturally they are considerably more expensive than native cedars dug from the wild.

'Brandon'**** is a selection from Brandon, Manitoba, that grows about 7 m (23 ft.) tall and is very upright. It has a dark green colour. 'Robusta'*** ('Wareana'), known as the Siberian cedar, is another very hardy selection that gets to be 5 m (16 ft.) tall. This is probably the most vigorous form.

'Techney'**** is a slow-growing selection that forms a dense, dark green column to 5 m (16 ft.) high.

CHERRY *Prunus*
Amur chokecherry *P. maackii****
Height: 12 m (40 ft.) Spread: 8 m (26 ft.) Zone 2b

There are several smallish cherry and plum trees that are suitable for city gardens. This is about the largest of them, but it's worth growing for the bark alone, which is a rusty red with white flecks, and it peels like the bark on birches. In addition, it has many small trusses of white flowers in spring with a faint almond scent. These are followed by black fruit that, as the common name suggests, are not nice to eat. Birds, however, think differently—they must have a different sense of taste.

European birdcherry *P. padus****
Height: 10 m (33 ft.) Spread: 8 m (26 ft.)
Zone 2

Similar to Amur chokecherry, except that the flower clusters are longer and more fragrant, the fruit ripens earlier, and the bark is not quite as nicely marked. *P. padus* var. *commutata*, the Mayday tree, flowers earlier.

Japanese flowering cherry, *P. subhirtella* 'Kanzan'**** (also listed as 'Kwanzan' and 'Hisakura')
Height: 8 m (26 ft.) Spread: 6 m (20 ft.) Zone 6

This is the most popular of all the Japanese flowering cherries. Its double pink flowers appear in early spring before the leaves and clothe the branches. The new leaves are a bronzy red, turning green as they age and then an orange-bronze in the fall. There are several other named forms in different shades of pink and in white, both single and double. The single forms may produce black fruit; the doubles seldom do.

Double-flowering almond *P. triloba* 'Multiplex'***
Height: 4 m (13 ft.) Spread: 2 m (6 ft.) Zone 2b

Most often grown as a shrub, this species makes a wonderful small tree, just smothered with pink buttons in spring. Prune the branches back in midsummer to keep it from becoming overlarge. If grown in a lawn, the mower will keep the inevitable suckers cut down.

Shubert chokecherry *P. virginiana* 'Shubert'***
Height: 8 m (26 ft.) Spread: 5 m (16 ft.) Zone 2

Forming a pyramidal small tree with purple leaves, Shubert chokecherry will survive in very inhospitable situations. I have seen it growing and thriving in a sunken windswept yard at the University of Alberta in a minuscule plot of land. The leaves open green and change colour later, the opposite of the flowering cherry. The fruit may be used for jams, jellies, or wine.

CHESTNUT *Aesculus*
Ohio buckeye *A. glabra****
Height: 10 m (33 ft.) Spread: 10 m (33 ft.)
Zone 2b

Flowers on this species are yellow and borne in clusters up to 20 cm (8 in.) long on the ends of the branches. The floral effect does not stop you in your tracks while walking by, but close up they are very attractive. The fruit are prickly and each usually contains one buckeye.

Ruby red horse-chestnut *A.* x *carnea* 'Briotii'****
Height: 12 m (40 ft.) Spread: 10 m (33 ft.)
Zone 5b

The flowers of this hybrid horse-chestnut appear in late spring and are followed by globular, prickly fruit. It does not seem to suffer from the chestnut blotch that attacks the common horse-chestnut, turning the leaves brown in late summer.

CRAB APPLE *Malus*
Zone 2b unless stated—see following text

There are dozens of named forms of crab apples available in the Canadian nursery trade and several hundred named worldwide. With all this selection it is very easy to fall into the trap of buying what the local nursery offers, because who can ever decide which is best? They must be good or they wouldn't have been named. Right? Wrong! There are several things to consider before you decide. Read back through the introduction to this chapter and apply the criteria for selection to crab apples—shape, flower, fruit, form—they are all to be taken into consideration. Then there is the problem of alternate bearing. Some varieties only flower and fruit well every other year; on the in-between years they produce just a few flowers. The third thing to check is disease resistance. Crab apples have three serious diseases—scab, fire blight, and powdery mildew. While it is possible to spray for two of these, this is a time-consuming and costly procedure, all right for commercial fruit production but not for the homeowner. The following list of crab apples covers those that are most readily available.

'Almey'* has purple flowers and red fruit. Very susceptible to disease. 8 x 7 m (26 x 23 ft.).

'Dolgo'**** has white flowers followed by bright red fruit in alternate years. Good for jelly. Upright shape. Mainly disease resistant. 12 x 10 m (40 x 33 ft.).

'Hopa'* has rose pink blooms that give bright red apples. Very susceptible. 9 x 7 m (29 x 23 ft.).

'Liset'*** has rose pink flowers and purple foliage. It is somewhat susceptible to mildew only. Zone 4; 5 x 5 m (16 x 16 ft.).

'Makamik'** has purple flowers and foliage and red fruit. Suffers badly from mildew. 12 x 12 m (40 x 40 ft.).

'Profusion'*** has purple-red flowers and dark red fruit. Closely related to 'Lizet', it shares that variety's disease resistance. Zone 4; 6 x 6 m (20 x 20 ft.).

'Radiant'** has deep pink flowers with bright red fruit. Gets scab badly. Zone 3b; 9 x 7 m (29 x 23 ft.).

'Red Jade'*** has white flowers on a weeping tree that gets its name from the fruit. Moderately disease resistant. Zone 5; 4 x 6 m (13 x 20 ft.).

'Royalty'* has purple flowers and leaves. Very susceptible to scab and fire blight. 5 x 3 m (16 x 10 ft.).

Here are some disease-resistant crab apples worth searching for.

'Baskatong'**** is a Canadian introduction that is resistant to all three diseases. It has rosy flowers and purple foliage. 8 x 8 m (26 x 26 ft.).

'Candied Apple'**** is a weeping tree with pink flowers and bright red fruit. It has good scab resistance and is not normally affected by other diseases. Zone 5; 5 x 5 m (16 x 16 ft.).

'Pink Spires'**** has salmon pink flowers and maroon fruit on an upright tree. Good to

moderate disease resistance. Zone 5; 5 x 4 m (16 x 13 ft.).

'Red Splendor'**** has rose pink blooms that stand out against the dark foliage. The red fruit last well into the winter. Good resistance to disease. 6 x 6 m (20 x 20 ft.).

'Snowdrift'*** has a rounded shape and bears white flowers and orange fruit. Susceptible only to fire blight. Zone 5; 6 x 6 m (20 x 20 ft.).

'White Angel'**** is another white selection but with red fruit. It is somewhat susceptible to fire blight. Zone 5; 6 x 6 m (20 x 20 ft.).

These are disease-resistant trees that are on all the lists of crab apples you should grow, but that don't seem to be available in Canada.

'Adams' has pink flowers and red fruit. Zone 5; 6 x 6 m (20 x 20 ft.).

'Henry Kohankie' has blush-white flowers and glossy red apples. Zone 5; 6 x 6 m (20 x 20 ft.).

'Professor Sprenger' has white flowers and orange fruit. Zone 5; size unknown.

'Robinson' has crimson flowers and fruit. Zone 5; 6 x 6 m (20 x 20 ft.).

DOGWOOD *Cornus*
Pagoda dogwood *C. alternifolia*****
Height: 6 m (20 ft.) Spread: 9 m (30 ft.) Zone 3b ●●

A wide-spreading small tree or large shrub with branches in layers. The flowers are a creamy white and very fragrant in late spring. The individual flowers are small but they are in clusters up to 6 cm (2 ½ in.) across. Fruits are black and attractive to birds.

Flowering dogwood *C. florida*****
Height: 6 m (20 ft.) Spread: 6 m (20 ft.) Zone 6b ●●

Flowering dogwood has a similar habit to the pagoda dogwood but is more effective in flower. The individual flowers are quite large, about 5 cm (2 in.) across and can be white, pink, or red. Actually the flowers are very small, but like the Christmas poinsettia, it is the modified leaves below them (bracts) that provide the display.

The Japanese kousa dogwood (*C. kousa*) is similar to the flowering dogwood but hardier (zone 6). The flowers are white and give rise to edible, strawberry-like fruit that adds interest in late summer.

GOLDENCHAIN TREE
Laburnum *Laburnum x watereri* 'Vossii'***
Height: 6 m (20 ft.) Spread: 4 m (13 ft.) Zone 6

Having grown up with a laburnum in the front garden, this tree symbolizes spring to me. I just wish we could grow it in Ottawa. This cultivar is the best form and has trusses of yellow flowers up to 60 cm (2 ft.) long. It is a fairly brittle tree so keep it away from windy locations. Best moved in spring as a balled and burlapped plant.

HAWTHORN *Crataegus*
Paul's Scarlet hawthorn *C. laevigata* 'Paul's Scarlet'***
Height: 6 m (20 ft.) Spread: 5 m (16 ft.) Zone 6

Bright red, double flowers in late spring make this the most popular form of the English hawthorn. It does, however, suffer from several diseases that many of the other hawthorns are immune to, and in wet years the trees may lose all their leaves by late summer.
Toba thorn *C. x mordenensis* 'Toba'****
Height: 5 m (16 ft.) Spread: 4 m (13 ft.) Zone 3

The flowers are not quite such a bright red, but the Toba thorn, developed at Morden, Manitoba, is an excellent substitute for the disease-prone 'Paul's Scarlet'. There is also a double white form called '**Snowbird**'.

HONEY LOCUST *Gleditsia triacanthos***
Height: 15 m (50 ft.) Spread: 12 m (40 ft.) Zone 4

A desirable tree, although eventually it will get rather large. The foliage is very fine and lets a lot of light through so grass grows well under

this tree. The cultivar '**Sunburst**' has foliage that starts yellow and greens up as it ages, but the ends of the branches are always bright. There are some green forms with different silhouettes; '**Skyline**' is fairly upright while '**Shademaster**' is wider. A very popular tree, probably overplanted in fact, with the result that serious pest and disease problems are starting to crop up, especially a midge that causes inflated galls (swellings) on the leaflets.

HORNBEAM *Carpinus*
American hornbeam *C. carolinianus***
Height: 9 m (30 ft.) Spread: 9 m (30 ft.) Zone 3b ●●●●

A native tree with smooth bark that grows well in sun or shade. In nature it is an understorey tree in woodlands. It has orange fall colour and makes a good hedge. Plant container-grown trees in spring for success.
Pyramidal European hornbeam *C. betulus* 'Fastigiata'****
Height: 10 m (33 ft.) Spread: 5 m (16 ft.) Zone 6b

A very much under-used upright tree. Not quite as cylindrical as some of the other species, it becomes almost egg-shaped in time. The closeness of the branches makes it an excellent choice for a windbreak, even in winter. Best transplanted in spring, balled and burlapped.

JUNIPER *Juniperus*
Zone and size—see individual descriptions

There are several junipers that make good specimens in a lawn, give a nice contrast to deciduous plants, and also provide winter interest. '**Fairview**'*** has a narrow, upright habit, growing 5 x 1.5 m (16 x 5 ft.). It is pale green and has silver berries in early winter. Hardy to zone 5. '**Mountbatten**'*** was introduced by Sheridan Nurseries in Toronto in 1948 and has become one of the most popular upright junipers. It is a silvery green, grows to 4 x 1 m (13 x 3 ft.), and is hardy to zone 4.

'Fairview' and 'Mountbatten' are both forms of the Chinese juniper.

Suitable forms of the western red cedar (*J. scopulorum*) include '**Greenspire**'*** which, as its name suggests, is a very columnar form growing 4 x 1 m (13 x 3 ft.). '**Springbank**'**** is a midgreen and it takes on a purple tint in the fall. This cultivar is the best one to choose if you have a light soil. It also grows to 4 x 1 m (13 x 3 ft.). '**Wichita Blue**'***** is a good blue shade all year but has a more open habit and grows to 4 x 1.5 m (13 x 5 ft.). All forms are hardy to zone 4, 'Springbank' to zone 3.

The eastern red cedar (*J. virginiana*) has only one commonly available upright form, '**Skyrocket**'***** (although some authors list this as a form of the western red cedar). This, again, is a good blue juniper but with a much slimmer habit than 'Wichita Blue'. A good specimen will grow 5 x 1 m (16 x 3 ft.) but they must be selected with care. This plant is so popular that nursery workers are not being as selective as they might be when taking cuttings. I have seen a large number of small plants that have a very loose habit, with the branchlets fanning outwards, rather than held close to the main stem. These will still make nice upright blue junipers, but they will never have the characteristic slim line of a good 'Skyrocket'. This is hardy to zone 3.

This is just a selection of the taller junipers that are readily available in most large garden centres. There are many others that you will find with a little effort. If you live in an area where ice storms occur in winter, all of these upright forms should be wrapped in late fall to hold the branches in place—the plastic mesh mentioned in Chapter 2 will do fine. Otherwise, the ice bends the branches down and they set in this position and don't spring back when the ice melts, even if it is only a few days later.

KATSURA TREE *Cercidiphyllum japonicum*****
Height: 12 m (40 ft.) Spread: 4 m (13 ft.)
Zone 5

The small grey-green leaves turning yellow, pinkish, or red in the fall and smelling of caramel are the chief attraction of this tree. Leaves are also reddish-purple when they unfurl. It is most commonly grown with several stems and is best planted in spring from container-grown plants. A good choice for city gardens.

LABURNUM—see Goldenchain tree.

LILAC *Syringa*
Japanese tree lilac *S. reticulata*****
Height: 8 m (26 ft.) Spread: 6 m (20 ft.) Zone 2

Later-blooming than the French hybrid lilacs, this species is often sold as a multi-stemmed plant. The creamy flowers have a strange scent, which I find attractive but some people cannot stand. When mature, the tree has a "bonsai" look about it and the bark has bronzy highlights that glow when wet. '**Ivory Silk**', introduced by Sheridan Nurseries, is smaller and has a less spreading habit.

LINDEN *Tilia*
Littleleaf linden *T. cordata***
Height: 20 m (66 ft.) Spread: 15 m (50 ft.)
Zone 3

As mentioned earlier, this tree suffered from serious overplanting problems in the 1970s because it was thought to be pest-free and pollution resistant. Unfortunately, once a tree is planted in large numbers, problems seem to pop up out of the cracks in the sidewalk, particularly the European bark borer and the linden mite that can almost defoliate a tree. To my mind—with one exception—this is still a "nothing" tree with no redeeming features other than its one-time lack of pests. It has neither attractive flowers, nor fruit, nor fall colour. Even the bark is nothing special.

'**Glenleven**' is a fast-growing upright selection from Sheridan Nurseries and '**Greenspire**' is a darker green and has a more rounded shape at maturity. '**June Bride**' has masses of fragrant white flowers in early summer.

MAGNOLIA *Magnolia*
Saucer magnolia *M.* x *soulangeana******
Height: 6 m (20 ft.) Spread: 6 m (20 ft.) Zone 5b

Another of the borderline trees that is often grown as a shrub, but even with multiple stems it makes an ideal specimen plant and should be on its own where it can be seen and appreciated, not stuck in a border with other shrubs. The hardiness on this should be zone 5a and a half. It will survive there with just a little bit of protection, or in a sheltered garden. One of the harbingers of spring, many magnolias flower early, before their leaves appear, with flowers up to 25 cm (10 in.) across. This should always be sold potted or balled and burlapped and is planted in early spring, often in full flower. Now that is real Instant Garden!

MAIDENHAIR TREE *Ginkgo biloba****
Height: 12 m (40 ft.) Spread: 3 m (10 ft.) Zone 4

The species itself will grow a lot wider than the size given above, but there are several upright selections, such as '**Princeton Sentry**' and '**Mayfield**', that have this slim outline. The maidenhair tree is slow-growing for the first two or three years, while it is establishing a good root system, then it grows rapidly. Fall colour is a bright yellow, and the fruit are produced at this time. The husks on the nuts have a very unpleasant odour as they rot, and for this reason, most of the trees sold are propagated by cuttings from male trees.

MAPLES *Acer*
Amur maple *A. ginnala******
Height: 9 m (30 ft.) Spread: 4 m (13 ft.) Zone 2

This plant is available either as a tree or a shrub, depending on how it was trained when young. The fragrant flowers are creamy white in late spring, the fruit (keys) is a pinkish red and can make the tree look as if it is in flower again. This tree is generally grown from seed and, unfortunately, the seedlings vary greatly in the colour of their fruit. In the fall the entire tree becomes a brilliant red. The bark has no special merit but the winter silhouette is interesting and vaguely Japanese-looking.

Manitoba maple, box elder *A. negundo**
Height: 15 m (50 ft.) Spread: 12 m (40 ft.) Zone 2 ◖

I was badmouthing the Manitoba maple to some city parks employees one day when they remarked, "but at least it will survive in a downtown situation." This is really a weed tree that grows where little else can survive. The wood is brittle and likely to come crashing down in an ice storm. It sets copious seed which does attract winter birds. What the birds leave falls in the early spring and germinates in the most awkward places—along the house wall, in cracks in the laneway. I swear every seed germinates three times. If nothing else will grow, try this.

Moosewood *A. pensylvanicum****
Height: 9 m (30 ft.) Spread: 4 m (13 ft.) Zone 2b ◖◖◖◖

This native tree is included for two reasons. It has attractive bark, which in the young plant is green with silvery stripes, and it is tolerant of shade. If you need a tree that will survive in the shadow of the building next door, this is one to consider.

Norway maple *A. platanoides*
Zone 5; see individual descriptions ◖

Norway maples are beginning to appear in native woodlands and are crowding out some of the native trees. If you live in the country, where seeds could blow into a native habitat, you should try to grow something other than this. This is a tough maple that comes in many forms, most of which are too large for urban gardens. The best known is probably '**Crimson King**'* which keeps its reddish hue all summer. Grows to 12 x 15 m (40 x 50 ft.). Also quite well-known, **'Schwedleri'***—the Schwedler maple—starts out red but turns green as the summer progresses. Grows to 15 x 18 m (50 x 60 ft.). Both of these are great when young but soon get too large unless you have an acreage to play with.

If you like this red colour, look for **'Crimson Sentry'*****, a new columnar form of 'Crimson King' that will reach 9 x 2 m (30 x 6 ft.). The same shape is found in the variety **'Columnare'****, which grows to 12 x 2 m (40 x 6 ft.), but it is green, not red. Either are good for situations where a narrow outline is required.

The smallest of the Norway maple group is also the most striking. **'Drummondii'******, known as the harlequin maple, has green leaves splashed with white. It grows to 9 x 6 m (30 x 20 ft.) and is a slow grower. Watch for any branches that revert to all-green and prune them out as they are more vigorous and will take over if left.

Red maple*, *A. rubrum*; **Silver maple***, *A. saccharinum*; and **Sugar maple***, *A. saccharum* are all too large to be considered for planting in small gardens. The red maple is the least objectionable of these three maples. The other two have invasive root systems just below the surface.

MOUNTAIN ASH *Sorbus*
Mountain ash *S. aucuparia***
Height: 10 m (33 ft.) Spread: 6 m (20 ft.) Zone 3

While mountain ash make very good trees for smaller properties, their use cannot be encouraged because of their susceptibility to fire blight.

Oak-leaved mountain ash *S. x thuringiaca* 'Fastigiata'****
Height: 8 m (26 ft.) Spread: 4 m (13 ft.) Zone 5

This hybrid seems to be much more resistant to fire blight than any of the forms of common mountain ash, even though that is one of the parents. The leaves are lobed and the gen-

eral shape of the tree is upright. The fruit is not as bright a colour as that of its parent.
Swedish mountain ash *S. intermedia*****
Height: 7.5 m (25 ft.) Spread: 6 m (20 ft.) Zone 3

An interesting tree with white-backed leaves that show their underside in the slightest breeze. The bright orange-red clusters of berries show up well against the silvery foliage and it seems to be resistant to fire blight.

MULBERRY *Morus*
White mulberry *M. alba***
Height: 9 m (30 ft.) Spread: 9 m (30 ft.) Zone 3

While the white mulberry itself is not particularly desirable, being somewhat weedy, it is tough and, like the Manitoba maple, will survive in very adverse locations. The weeping form, **'Pendula'******, does make an interesting small tree with cascading branches that will reach the ground. The trunk becomes very gnarled in time, which adds to the winter effect. It eventually reaches 4 x 5 m (13 x 16 ft.), so allow room when planting.

NANNYBERRY—see Viburnum.

OAK *Quercus*
Pin oak *Q. palustris*****
Height: 10 m (33 ft.) Spread: 8 m (26 ft.) Zone 4

One of the nicest of the oaks, it has very deeply lobed, pointed leaves that turn a coppery shade in autumn but remain on the tree for most of the winter. It transplants easily and is one of the fastest-growing oaks. This one you can plant for your own enjoyment, rather than for your grandchildren. Both this species and the next do best on an acidic soil and may become yellow and chlorotic if the pH is high. If this happens, spray and water the tree with chelated iron every spring.

Red oak *Q. rubra****
Height: 20 m (66 ft.) Spread: 15 m (50 ft.)
Zone 3

Although this eventually makes a large tree, it is very popular in new developments. Most people probably think that because it is an oak it is slow-growing, but once it is established it will grow up to half a metre (1 ½ ft.) a year. Like the pin oak, this species transplants readily.

Upright English oak *Q. robur* 'Fastigiata'***
Height: 15 m (50 ft.) Spread: 4 m (13 ft.)
Zone 5

This is the best selection of the English oak, forming a narrow column that is very suitable for small gardens, providing there are no overhead wires.

PEAR *Pyrus*

Bradford pear *P. calleryana* 'Bradford'****
Height: 10 m (33 ft.) Spread: 7 m (23 ft.)
Zone 5b

This ornamental pear is a most attractive tree, especially when young. White flowers cover the branches in spring just as the leaves unfurl. Transplant in the early spring as a balled and burlapped plant. It is hardy to zone 5a and a half. There are several trees in protected spots in Ottawa, but they suffer badly in colder than normal winters. Some of the new cultivars, such as 'Chanticleer', may prove hardier than this one.

PEASHRUB *Caragana*

Weeping peashrub *C. arborescens* 'Pendula'***
Height: 2 m (6 ft.) Spread: 2 m (6 ft.) Zone 2

A small tree that is ideal for gardens where space is limited. The weeping form is grafted on the top of a straight stem of the regular peashrub, so keep an eye open for suckers growing from below the graft and prune them off. A new form called **'Walker'******* has much finer leaves that are almost fernlike.

PINE *Pinus*

Black pine *P. nigra****
Height: 10 m (33 ft.) Spread: 5 m (16 ft.) (but can get much larger with time) Zone 4

While the dark green of its needles makes this a rather sombre pine, it is tolerant to salt and is the best choice if you need an evergreen close to a major road. As it ages the bark becomes very attractive.

Scots pine *P. sylvestris****
Height: 10 m (33 ft.) Spread: 6 m (20 ft.)
Zone 2

The Scots pine is the exact opposite of the Swiss stone pine and loses its lower branches with reckless abandon. A young Scots pine is just another evergreen, but as the tree matures and the bark starts to age, it becomes an orange colour, peeling in flakes. Trees that have had their leader damaged before they gain full height sometimes take on a particularly interesting "windswept" look.

Swiss stone pine *P. cembra*****
Height: 10 m (33 ft.) Spread: 4 m (13 ft.)
Zone 2

This is a personal favourite of mine. I like the way it keeps its lower branches right down to the ground and doesn't develop the bare stem that so many of the other pines do. It does best in an open situation and should not be used close to buildings.

POPLAR *Populus**
Zones 2b to 4

Poplars are very fast-growing and are of use in the country for temporary windbreaks if well away from septic systems—while something more desirable grows. In the city and suburbs, there is not really any place for them. They have invasive roots, are brittle, short-lived, and often produce an objectionable fluffy seed—hence the other common name—cottonwood.

REDBUD *Cercis canadensis*****
Height: 8 m (26 ft.) Spread: 8 m (26 ft.) Zone 6 ●●

If you live in the areas where redbud will survive, you have probably already noticed this tree. Flowers occur in small pink clusters all along the branches and also on the trunks. This native tree is a real tonic in the spring. It will survive in most soils, providing they are not wet, and will tolerate some shade. Try to get locally grown trees. Those grown further south from seed may not be hardy in your area.

RUSSIAN OLIVE *Elaeagnus angustifolia****
Height: 5 m (16 ft.) Spread: 5 m (16 ft.) Zone 2b

Another plant that can be a small tree or a large shrub. It is salt tolerant, which makes it useful for planting close to roadways with a high salt use. It makes a spreading tree that is fairly short-lived (about 20 years). The grey foliage serves as a foil for more colourful shrubs. Do not plant where it will grow to overhang your laneway, since the wood is brittle and it may shed branches in ice storms.

SPINDLETREE *Euonymus*
European spindletree *E. europaeus****
Height: 5 m (16 ft.) Spread: 5 m (16 ft.) Zone 4 ●

 Usually grown with several trunks, this is a plant for fall effect. The flowers are a lime-green and easily overlooked, but the fall colour is a glowing, dark red. Once the leaves have fallen, the red to pink fruit can be seen. These open to reveal bright orange seeds inside. They only last a short time, since the birds quickly make a meal of them and spoil the display for us.

SPRUCE *Picea*
Colorado spruce *P. pungens****
Height: up to 20 m (66 ft.) Spread: 10 m (33 ft.) Zone 2

 The Colorado spruce is one of the most popular conifers to use as a specimen on the front lawn. What a pity that many people don't do their homework and discover the eventual size before planting. Then, so many wouldn't get cut down because they are growing over the path or drive. The blue forms are the most popular, but the named varieties are expensive because they are very slow-growing. If you have a nursery near you that is actually growing these from seed, it may be possible to select a specific plant from the nursery row. The seedlings vary in colour and some are almost as blue as the named forms, at a fraction of the cost. '**Glauca**' is the name given to the blue form that can be grown from seed, while '**Hoopsii**', '**Koster**', and '**Moerheimi**' are the most readily available named forms that are grown by grafting. They differ mainly in the mature shape of the plant, and while 'Hoopsii' is the bluest it is not such a good shape as 'Koster'. '**Montgomery**', another selection that is commonly available, forms a slow-growing mound.

VIBURNUM *Viburnum*
Nannyberry *V. lentago****
Height: 6 m (20 ft.) Spread: 3 m (10 ft.) Zone 2 ●●●

This native plant can be a small tree or a shrub. It has white flowers in June, followed by fruit that change from green through yellow, red, and purple before becoming black. The different colours are often present at the same time, making the fruit clusters very attractive.

WILLOW *Salix*
Niobe willow *S. alba* 'Tristis'**
Height: 14 m (46 ft.) Spread: 7 m (23 ft.) Zone 4

 This golden weeping willow is a very spectacular tree when seen in a park setting. It is, however, almost as much of a problem in a small garden as a poplar. The roots are invasive, the wood is brittle, and the tree is continually dropping twigs and branchlets.

CARE OF MATURE TREES

While they are young, providing the soil is reasonably good, trees need little additional feeding. If they are growing in the lawn, they will obtain extra nutrition from the lawn food. In a border situation, a regular spring feeding with 6-9-6 or 7-7-7 fertilizer at 50 g/m^2 (2 oz./yd^2) or top-dressing in the fall with compost should supply all their requirements. As the trees mature, their nutritional needs increase and they are no longer happy with the lawn's leftovers. If you have an older tree, look for smaller leaves, yellowing foliage, and more-than-normal winter injury as signs that your tree is suffering from a lack of nutrition. In the wild, where the leaves remain on the ground, these break down to feed the trees, but in our manicured gardens, where we rake up every fallen leaf, starvation does occur.

As I mentioned earlier in this chapter, most trees have their feeding roots close to the surface and grow from the drip-line of the tree (the circle made by the ends of the branches) outwards. This is the area where extra feed should be applied in early spring, just as the buds begin to plump up. If you apply this to the lawn early in the spring before the grass is growing, it will be washed into the tree's root zone and the roots will get most of the benefit. Another method is to use an injector, which you push into the soil. Using water pressure, it injects soluble feed into the root zone. This method is short-term and needs repeating a couple of times each growing season. A more labour-intensive way is to dig holes in the ground and place a dry slow-release fertilizer in them. The holes can be punched with a crowbar, but this causes compaction. It can also be removed with an industrial-type electric drill and a large auger bit. Make the holes about 60 cm apart and 30 cm deep (2 ft. apart and 1 ft. deep) in circles up to one-fourth more

than the diameter of the spread. In other words, if the tree spread is 8 m (26 ft.), the feeding zone should reach to 10 m (33 ft.).

Use a fertilizer with a fairly high first number, something like a 10-8-4, although the fertilizer sold for lawns as 10-6-4 will work well. Make sure you use plain fertilizer, not Weed and Feed. Apply at $^1/_4$ to $^1/_2$ kg per cm of trunk diameter (8 to 16 oz. per $^1/_2$ in. diameter) measured at chest height, for trees up to 15 cm (6 in.) diameter. Double the rate over this size but, if part of the root zone is covered by a road or other solid material, reduce the total amount by this percentage. If you made holes, trickle the fertilizer down them, putting between 25 to 50 g (1 to 2 oz.) in each hole. Fill the holes with soil or sand, and water well. Use the lower rates in harsh climates (zone 4 and colder) and increase the rate as your climate gets milder. If you used a drill to make the holes, there is probably enough soil on the surface to refill the holes. If you use an aerator on your lawn in early spring, a trickle of fertilizer down each of the holes it leaves in the feeding zone will help the tree.

One further way to feed mature trees is by using fertilizer spikes. These are solid cones of fertilizer formulated to supply the needs of various plants. Use the ones for fruit trees if flowers are a big part of your tree's attraction, the ones for shade trees if not. The directions say to hammer them into the ground, but unless you have a very soft, sandy soil, it will be better to make the hole first with a crowbar or wooden stake. Follow the directions on the box as to the number of spikes to use.

Once the leaves are off your trees, it is time to give them an annual inspection. Choose a day when it is bright, so you can see fine details, and use a pair of binoculars if your trees are large. Look for some of the problems listed at the start of Chapter 6—rubbing branches, broken limbs, cankers or other fungi, etc. With the majority of trees, this pruning can be left until spring, as long as you deal with it before the leaves start to unfurl, but trees with a heavy sap flow, like birches and maples, should be done in late fall so the wounds have time to seal before spring.

If the trees are not too large, you can probably do any pruning needed, but once it involves anything higher than a pair of steps, call in an arborist. I have heard of people being seriously injured after being thrown off a ladder when the tree they were pruning whipped back as they removed a branch. Professional arborists know what precautions to take against such things happening, and they have insurance!

TREES LISTED BY ZONE

Select the zone where you live: these are the trees that will survive in your area. See page 11.

ZONE 2A:
Amur maple; ash; canoe birch; Colorado spruce; eastern white cedar; European birdcherry; European white birch; Japanese tree lilac; Manitoba maple; nannyberry; Scots pine; Shubert chokecherry; Swiss stone pine; weeping peashrub.

ZONE 2B:
The above, plus
Amur chokecherry; black ash; crab apple (many); moosewood; Ohio buckeye; poplar (many); Russian olive.

ZONE 3A:
All the above, plus
European mountain ash; junipers (some); littleleaf linden; red oak; river birch; Swedish mountain ash; Toba hawthorn; white mulberry.

ZONE 3B:
All the above, plus
American hornbeam; pagoda dogwood.

ZONE 4A:
All the above, plus
Black pine; European spindletree; honey locust; maidenhair tree; niobe willow; pin oak; whitebark Himalayan birch.

ZONE 5A:
All the above, plus
Katsura tree; northern catalpa; Norway maple; oak-leaved mountain ash; upright English oak.

ZONE 5B:
All the above, plus
Bradford pear; ruby red horse-chestnut; saucer magnolia; umbrella catalpa.

ZONE 6A:
All the above, plus
Chinese catalpa; European beech; goldenchain tree; Japanese flowering cherry; Japanese kousa dogwood; Paul's Scarlet hawthorn; redbud.

ZONE 6B:
All the above, plus
Flowering dogwood; pyramidal European hornbeam.

SUGGESTED READING

Manual of Woody Landscape Plants. Michael A. Dirr. Stipes Publishing Co. (4th edition), 1990.

Landscape Plants for Eastern North America. Harrison L. Flint. Wiley-Interscience (2nd edition), 1996.

These are the best two reference books, packed with information on woody plants.

The International Book of Trees. Hugh Johnson. Simon and Schuster, 1973.

A coffee-table book that covers the distribution, discovery and classification of trees. It adds interest and colour to the information of the first two.

Gardening with Trees and Shrubs. Trevor Cole. Whitecap Books, 1996.

This gives a lot more details of care and selection than I could fit in here.

Trees of North America and Europe. Roger Phillips. Random House, 1978.

A photographic book of trees, leaves, twigs, fruit, etc. Great for helping you decide between two choices.

Flowering Shrubs and Small Trees. Isabel Zucker. Michael Friedman, 1995.

A revised and updated edition of a book long out of print, now with coloured photos and modern hybrids included.

Tree Maintenance. Pascal P. Pirone. Oxford University Press (6th edition), 1988.

Arboriculture. Richard W. Harris. Prentice-Hall, 1999.

These two books will tell you all you need to know about the care of trees.

Conifers: The Illustrated Encyclopedia. D.M. van Gelderen and J.R.P. van Hoey Smith. Timber Press, 1996.

This is about the best book on conifers available, with lots of coloured pictures.

Shrubs
5 chapter

Much of what I wrote in the last chapter applies equally to shrubs. People are just as careless when it comes to choosing shrubs as they are with trees. Do your homework and know just what you want, because shrubs are often planted close to the house, and the variation in size within the same species is more important when the plant is placed underneath a window. Why would you plant a mock orange that grows 3 m (9 ft.) tall in front of a low window, especially when there are dwarf forms of the same shrub available? Yet many people do just that.

It makes good sense to know just what you want and go out with a shopping list. Don't allow yourself to be talked into buying a variety that is not on your list without checking it out first. In spring, shrubs are available as prepackaged plants at checkouts in all sorts of stores, not just garden centres. The temptation to pop one in your shopping cart is strong, but you could regret it in years to come if it grows out of control.

Use the same criteria when deciding on a shrub as you use when choosing a tree. Hardiness zones are the same, but some of the dwarf shrubs will survive outside their recommended zone if you can rely on a good snow cover (or are willing to take a chance).

There is a lot of variation in the size and shape of shrubs. They range from prostrate ground covers a few centimetres (inches) tall to plants that will reach 5 m (15 ft.) or more at maturity. They can be massed for use in a border or foundation planting, or planted as a specimen in the lawn where the individual plant can take on many of the attributes of a shade tree.

Because there is a greater selection of suitable plants, you have more choice when considering flowering, fruiting and foliage. There are several shrubs with blue flowers, for instance, and while the majority of shrubs bloom in the spring, there are a number that will extend the flowering season. Given a large enough garden, it is not difficult to have shrubs in flower from early spring until late October.

Like trees, shrubs are available bare-root, balled and burlapped, and in containers, but not generally in large sizes that have to be dug and moved with a tree spade. Varieties not available locally can be mail-ordered. These are either bare-root or in small pots. With bare-root plants, a little care is needed when selecting the one to take home with you. Most of the larger garden centres have either cold storage or a shaded outside display area where they keep their plants. Providing they are kept cool, prepackaged plants in plastic bags are a good buy, but when they are kept indoors in a heated store they should be selected with great care. There should be no problems if you buy the plants within a few days of when they are put on display, but if growth has started, be very cautious. A plant with several centimetres (an inch or more) of new growth has put a lot of its stored energy into making these new shoots, energy that should have gone into root production. Also, most stores have very low light levels so the shoots are spindly and drawn and, because they have grown in a hot place, they will be very susceptible to cold winds or a late frost.

If you decide to take a chance on one of these shrubs (and I must admit that I often see varieties that never seem to get into garden centres on sale at hardware stores), there are a few precautions you can take that will help the plant survive. Protect the plant from wind and direct sunlight for a couple of weeks and, if frost is forecast, give some extra protection. HINT: I have found that the large 20-kg (50-lb.) paper sacks that bird seed comes in do a great job of protecting small plants when opened top and bottom to form a sleeve. I push a bamboo cane into the ground behind the plant, put the bag over the cane and plant and then use two more canes to open the bag into a triangle. This cuts the wind and, if you use a full-height bag, it provides shade as well.

Additional insulation can be dropped over the sticks at night if needed. The bags stand up to the weather very well and don't get soggy in the rain. If mail-ordered plants arrive at a time when you cannot plant them, they should be heeled-in. See Chapter 7, Roses, for directions on doing this.

Planting a shrub needs the same care and attention as with a tree except that it is seldom necessary to give any form of support. Prune by removing a proportion of the branches, rather than by cutting them all back. If the plant is small and hasn't got many shoots anyway, don't worry about pruning at all.

Planting can take place in spring or fall and those that have a preferred season are noted in the list. Prepackaged plants are only available in spring and should be planted as soon as possible, while container-grown plants can be planted at any time—although the hot muggy days of July and August are best avoided since the inevitable root disturbance does give the plant a setback. Evergreens can be planted in the spring until about four weeks after bare-root deciduous plantings have leafed out, while in the fall they must be given time to make roots, and should not be planted later than six weeks before the average date of hard frost.

 # HEDGES

Hedges serve three functions in a garden. When used to break a long garden into smaller units, they define a space; as a screen to hide the service area they act as a visual barrier; and, if planted in the right location, they act as a windbreak. Often they combine these duties; a boundary hedge, for example, may be both a visual barrier, giving privacy, and a windbreak. As a privacy screen or windbreak, a hedge generally has to be fairly tall, 2 m (6 ft.) or more, but when planted to define a space it can be much smaller. A low hedge running across the front of a property can define the front lot-line and act as a barrier to dogs and children without spoiling the view or making the house feel boxed in.

It may come as a surprise to many people that there are plants other than cedar which can be used for hedges. In the plant list that follows, these are noted. Most nursery catalogues have a list of plants that are fast-growing and are sold in smaller sizes for hedging. The trouble with using fast-growing plants is that they don't stop being fast-growing when they reach the desired height and they need frequent clipping to keep them within bounds. One house I moved into had a front hedge of Chinese elm that I had to clip every two weeks to keep looking nice. I moved in during July and the hedge was replaced by the fall. I have better things to do with my time than trim elms.

Many of the plants suitable for hedging are not listed in the hedge section of nursery catalogues because they are not available as cheap bare-root plants. If the hedge is small, and only a few plants are involved, the cost factor may not be important. To see what sort of a hedge some of the more unusual plants will make, visit a hedge collection. You will actually see how the hedge you fancy will look as it matures. There are hedge collections at the University of Guelph arboretum; the Royal Botanical Gardens, Hamilton; the Central Experimental Farm, Ottawa; and the Jardins Botanic, Montreal.

To most people the word *hedge* is synonymous with a clipped green wall of formal plants. There are informal hedges, however, that use plants that are naturally small, and they grow almost unpruned. This type of hedge can take up more garden space than its clipped counterpart, but it can also be more attractive. Because you are not clipping each year, the flower buds are not removed and the hedge can be a riot of colour from flowers and

fruit in turn. The only pruning needed is an annual once-over to remove any shoots growing out of line.

You will need three plants per metre (yard) with dwarf formal hedges where the final height will be under a metre (yard); two plants per metre (yard) for hedges up to 2 m (6 ft.) tall and three per 2-m (6-ft.) run for formal hedges over this height. With cedars dug from the bush, planting slightly closer than this in a double, staggered row will give you a thick hedge faster than using a single row. For an informal hedge, place the plants at half the final height of the plant apart. In other words, if the plants will grow 1 m (3 ft.) tall, plant them 45 cm (18 in.) apart.

TRAINING A FORMAL HEDGE

Remember that a hedge will grow sideways as well as upwards, and plan the site accordingly. Allow for the eventual width to be half the chosen height. If the height will be 2.5 m (8 ft.), the width will be 1.2 m (4 ft.), and the hedge should be planted about 70 cm (2 ft.) inside your property line. If the plants are bare-root, dig a trench first and fork over the bottom of it before you start to plant. Keep the hedging plants wrapped and in the shade while this is going on. Run a taut string down the centre of the trench at soil level to act as a guide while you plant. With an assistant to hold them in place against the string, fill in around the plants, firm them into place and water them in with a plant-starter fertilizer.

The next step is the one that is most often overlooked, but it is essential if you want a good, even hedge in the years to come. Step back and look along the row of plants and select the shortest one. Prune about one-tenth the height of this plant off the top. Then prune all the other plants down to this height. Taking the top off a plant encourages it to produce side shoots, which results in a thicker hedge. Failure to make this cut will result in a thin hedge that is uneven for many years.

Once the hedge is planted and trimmed back to an even height, leave it alone except for watering as needed. There will probably be very little growth this first year, especially if you used bare-root plants. (If the hedge was short and you planted container-grown plants, then you may get appreciable growth, in which case some clipping will be required.) The second spring, or late the first summer, if the plants grew well, shear the sides lightly, removing enough of the growth to shorten back most of the side shoots. The idea is to remove the growing tip from each branch so the dormant buds down the branch start to grow. Where you had one shoot you will have five or six, and the hedge will thicken considerably. Keep the top cut back quite hard for the first year or two. It is easy to gain height but more important to get a thick hedge.

For the first few years, as soon as you think to yourself, "Mmm, I must cut that hedge in a week or so," it is time to do it. Once the hedge is well formed it is not so critical if the shoots get a bit overlong. With a cedar hedge you should prune in June, once the spring flush of growth is over, and again in August or early September to shorten back the new growth that developed from the first cut. In later years, one cut in the late summer will be enough.

With evergreen hedges, taper the sides slightly towards the top and either point or round the top of the hedge. This helps to prevent snow that settles on top of the hedge from breaking the branches or bending them outwards. As mentioned in the last chapter, boughs that bend in cold weather rarely recover their former shape. If the top becomes wider than the base, either through bad trimming or from snow damage, the bottom is shaded and loses its leaves or needles, the branchlets die, and you end up with a hedge that looks like a row of telephone poles with green fuzz on top.

With deciduous hedges where the snow will sift down through the branches, this taper is not as critical, but it is still a good idea.

CLIMBERS

Anywhere you have a wall or fence you can have a climber. They are great for covering blank spaces, making dull objects beautiful, and adding a third dimension to a flat plane. This chapter covers perennials; see Chapter 9 for annual climbers.

Climbers climb by various means, and the nature of the surface determines which ones are suitable in a given site. Some, like roses, are sprawlers rather than climbers. They push their way up through other plants and lean on them, using their recurved thorns to hook onto the host plant's branches and stop themselves sliding back down. Roses will seldom climb on their own in a garden situation and have to be tied to a trellis or some other support.

Most people think of climbers as twining plants, and this is probably the most common form of support. The twisting may be clockwise or anti-clockwise depending on the species (as fans of Flanders and Swann will know). Support for twining vines must be something that they can wrap around. Garden netting on a frame works well but is a devil to clean when you prune the plants. For annual climbers, I like a wooden frame with strings stretched top to bottom. It is so easy to clean in the fall—just cut the strings and compost the whole lot, providing you use natural string, not nylon twine.

Clematis, probably the most popular of all climbers, has leaf stalks that twist around anything they touch, a good reason to keep moving in the garden. I saw them growing on 2-m x 60-cm (6- x 2-ft.) wooden frames covered with chicken wire in the Minnesota Landscape Arboretum, an idea which I have borrowed with great success. Mount the frames on spacers in front of the fence or wall to give the tendrils room. The fan-shaped trellises you will find in garden centres are not much good for anything other than climbing roses, and if you have a vigorous plant, they are not tall enough for that.

Both Boston ivy and Virginia creeper climb by means of tendrils that can be either modified leaves or specialized shoots. The tendrils twine around even the smallest projection and can be very difficult to unfasten. If you allow Virginia creeper to climb on stucco, it will remove all the stones when you pull it off. The form known as Engelmann's ivy also has little suction cups on the ends of the tendrils by which it can climb on even smooth surfaces. Real ivy puts out fine roots along the stem, which work their way into tiny crevices, especially in brickwork. It looks pretty but can be very damaging to bricks in the long run.

WHAT SHALL I PLANT?

The following is a list of the shrubs you are likely to find in your local garden centre. These are the ones most nurseries propagate. They are not necessarily the best shrubs and it doesn't include several of my favourites, which have a very restricted availability. Sometimes, because nurseries carry many different cultivars (varieties) of the same plant, I have not given individual varietal names and you will have to take whichever one is available. In other cases, because just a few cultivars are available at most nurseries, I have given brief descriptions of each. As in the previous chapter, I have given my personal rating using a five-star system. The shade tolerance is noted by the ● symbol; plants rated ●●●● will grow best out of direct sunlight entirely. An "H" indicates shrubs that will form hedges if clipped or pruned.

ALMOND—see Cherry.

ANGELICA-TREE *Aralia*
Japanese angelica-tree*** *A. elata*
Height: 3 m (10 ft.) Spread: 10 m (30 ft.)
Zone 5

This is a good shrub for city conditions or gardens with poor soils. The most outstanding feature is the sharp recurved spines on the stems (wear good work gloves while planting this). The leaves are much-divided and up to 1.5 m (5 ft.) long. White flowers in summer turn into dark fruit that attracts the birds.

ARBORVITAE—see Cedar.

ARROWWOOD—see Viburnum.

AZALEA *Rhododendron****
Height: 1 m (3 ft.) Spread: 3 m (10 ft.) Zone 5 to 7 ●●●

Botanically, azalea is one section of the genus *Rhododendron*. They are mostly deciduous spring-flowering shrubs, although some of the more tender varieties are evergreen. The flowers are often bright in the white-yellow-orange-red range and many varieties are deliciously perfumed. I find them easier to grow than the more flamboyant rhododendron, especially on the edge of their hardiness range. They *must* have acidic soil to grow properly and do best in light shade.

The '**Lights Series**'*** of azaleas, developed in Minnesota, seem to be exceptionally tough (zone 3) and flower each spring without pampering. Look for varieties such as '**Orchid Lights**' and '**White Lights**'.

BEARBERRY *Arctostaphylos uva-ursi****
Height: 30 cm (1 ft.) Spread: 1 m (3–6 ft.)
Zone 2 ●●

A good ground cover for poor, sandy soils (although it will grow equally well on good soils) and in sun or shade. It is salt tolerant and can be planted near major roads. The glossy evergreen leaves show up the springtime clusters of white flowers and the red fruit in the fall. As the common name suggests, the fruit is a favourite food of bears. Buy container-grown plants for best results. '**Vancouver Jade**' is a good variety.

BEAUTYBUSH *Kolkwitzia amabilis***
Height: 3 m (10 ft.) Zone 5a

Beautybush is barely just hardy in zone 5 and should be planted in a sheltered location. Whether it is worth the pampering is debatable; although it is very attractive during its two-week flowering period, for the rest of the year it has little to commend it. The flowers are pale pink with a yellow throat and appear in early summer.

BOSTON IVY—see Virginia creeper.

BROOM *Cytissus*
Scotch broom, *C.* x *praecox* and *C. scoparius****
Height: 2 m (6 ft.) Zone 6

There are many hybrids grouped under these two names with pealike flowers of mauve, pink, red, yellow, or white. The plants also have attractive winter stems, do best in poor, sandy soil and will not thrive with wet feet. Plant pot-grown specimens.

BUTTERFLY BUSH *Buddleja davidii****
Height: 3–5 m (10–16 ft.) Zone 6

The rate of growth on an established butterfly bush has to be seen to be believed. We had an ancient plant close to the drive when I was a child, which my father used to cut almost to the ground each spring. By flowering time in August, it would be close to 4 m (13 ft.) tall again. The flowers are produced on the growth made each year. They are in trusses made up of hundreds of individual, sweetly scented blooms that are a magnet to butterflies. There are many named forms in pastel shades of mauve, pink, blue, and white.

CEDAR *Thuja*
Common cedar, Arborvitae *T. occidentalis*
Height: up to 6 m (20 ft.) Zone 3 H ●

The native cedar makes a valuable hedging plant and thousands are dug from the wild each year and successfully transplanted into gardens. This is one of the few evergreens that will survive being moved bare-root. There have been a considerable number of selections made from wild or nursery-grown plants that have been given names and are propagated from cuttings. These are usually too expensive to use for long hedges and are most often used as foundation plants or lawn specimens. Their shape varies from low, slow-growing globes to broad pyramids to narrow columns.

'**Fastigiata**'** is a narrow upright form reaching 5 m (16 ft.), too tall for most foundation plantings.

'**Holmstrup**'***, from Denmark, makes a broad pyramid, almost as wide as it is high in the young stages. It can reach 4 m (13 ft.).

'**Little Champion**' and '**Little Giant**'*** are similar slow-growing globes.

'**Woodwardii**'** is a similar shape but is larger eventually.

'**Nigra**'***, the black cedar, has very dark green foliage and upright growth.

There are also forms such as '**Golden Globe**', '**Rheingold**', and '**Sunkist**' which have new growth tipped with yellow. They make a good contrast to the rather somber green of some other selections.

CHERRY *Prunus*
Flowering almond *P. triloba*****
Height: up to 5 m (16 ft.) Zone 2b

There are single and double forms of this, the double being without fruit. Flowers of the double form ('Multiplex') look like miniatures of the pink rosettes people stick on bridal cars. It is also grafted onto a single stem to form a small tree.

Manchu or Nanking cherry

P. *tomentosa******

Height: 3 m (10 ft.) Zone 2 H

Even when grown as a hedge and clipped four times a year this shrub still produces its pale pink flowers in spring. If allowed to grow untrimmed it is a mass of blossoms. The fruit are small edible cherries that can be eaten out of hand or made into jam or wine. Unlike regular cherries, Manchu cherries do not have the dimple at the stalk.

Purple-leaved sand cherry, P. x *cistena******

Height: 3 m (10 ft.) Zone 4

This is one of the best purple shrubs, but it should be used with discretion—too many are overpowering. It is particularly effective against the brown-grey of exposed aggregate concrete walls. The flowers are light pink in spring, just as the leaves unfurl, so they tend to be lost against the foliage. Virginia bluebells or forget-me-nots look especially good under this shrub. I was never aware of its fruit until a few years ago when a flurry of activity from a robin family drew it to my attention. I don't know what they were getting excited over—it didn't taste good to me.

CINQUEFOIL *Potentilla fruticosa*

Height: 30 cm–1 m (1–3 ft.) Zone 3

The German common name for this, "fingerbush," describes the foliage exactly. This is a good, free-flowering shrub that will bloom for most of the summer. It is a native plant, in fact it is circumpolar, and several selections have been made in Scandinavia. There are many named forms including the following.

'Abbotswood'**** is a white variety that has a spreading habit of growth. This is one of my favourites.

'Coronation Triumph'*** makes a dense, rounded bush 1.5 m (5 ft.) high. The flowers are bright yellow and the leaves are a pale green.

'Goldfinger'*** is a shorter, dark green form that flowers well into the fall.

'Farreri' ('Gold Drop')*** This plant answers to either name. It is 60 cm (24 in.) tall and has masses of small, bright golden flowers.

'Daydawn'*** has interesting biscuit-coloured flowers that stand up to heat well.

'Jackman's Variety'*** is another yellow-flowered form with dark foliage and 3-cm (1-in.) flowers. It grows 1.5 m (5 ft.) tall.

'Red Ace'* This plant must be a big disappointment to a great number of people. It is widely advertised but does not live up to its promise. In the cool summers of England, where this plant originated, the flowers are red, but in hot Canadian summers they are as yellow as a buttercup. They do revert to the proper colour in the fall when the weather cools off.

'Tangerine'** This selection suffers from the same drawback as 'Red Ace'—the flowers are the correct colour only for a short time in the fall.

CLEMATIS *Clematis*

Virgin's bower, traveller's joy

Height: vine to 6 m (20 ft.) Zone 3b

Without doubt, this is the most popular of all climbers, and providing certain conditions are met, it is one of the easiest to grow. To thrive, clematis like warm tops and cool bottoms. Plant them where the shoots will be in the sun but the roots shaded. Either grow a low plant in front to shade the roots or cover the root area with stones, rocks, or patio slabs. Clematis don't have to be trained on a trellis; they will quite happily scramble up through a large shrub (a spring-flowering one is best so that the flower season is extended). You can also grow it up a tree if you use a loose cylinder of chicken netting to bridge the gap to the lower branches. Clematis seem to grow best in alkaline soil and I have had success in reviving ailing plants by mixing up a couple of cups of lime in a watering can and watering this round the roots. The lime does not dissolve, so stir it frequently to keep it in suspension.

Most of the large-flowered varieties that we grow are woody, although we tend to treat them more like herbaceous perennials and cut them back almost to the ground each spring. The more popular ones belong to two distinct groups, which should be pruned in different ways.

The following flower on the new wood. They should be cut back almost to ground level in early spring.

'Ernest Markham'**** has red-violet flowers 10 cm (4 in.) across.

'Jackmanii'**** has violet-purple flowers 13 cm (5 in.) wide.

'Ville de Lyon'*** has carmine-red flowers 10 cm (4 in.).

The next three all flower first on the old wood in late spring and then again on the new wood later in the season. They should not be cut back as hard. Wait until growth starts in the spring and just trim off the dead parts. At the edge of their hardiness range the old-wood buds may be winter-killed but they will still give a good display of late flowers on the new wood.

'Henryi'**** (often listed as 'Henry I') has white 13-cm (5-in.) flowers.

'Nelly Moser'**** has pale pink flowers with a darker stripe down each petal.

'Ramona'*** has lavender-blue flowers with darker centres.

As well as the large-flowered varieties listed above, there are some with smaller flowers that are well worth a place in any garden, especially as they bloom at different times. The **alpine clematis** (*C. alpina*) (zone 4), flowers in early spring. The individual blooms are bell-shaped and quite small, in shades of pink, white or blue. Good varieties include 'Willie'****, pale pink, and 'Francis Rivis'***, deep blue. The **big-petal clematis**, *C. macropetala*, (zone 2), has flowers that are like the large-flowered type but only half the size and often double. The bloom time is still early but later than the alpine group. 'Markham's Pink'*** is a good

variety. Do not cut either of these groups back in spring.

Commonly known as **Virgin's bower**, *C. viticella* (zone 3) flowers in late summer. The individual, star-shaped blooms are about half the size of a large-flowered clematis but are produced very freely and over a long period. My favourite is 'Polish Spirit'****, with wine-red, satiny petals. From midsummer until well into fall the **scarlet clematis**, *C. texensis*, (zone 4) are in flower. These produce a profusion of small bell-shaped flowers. Although it's called the scarlet clematis, some of the varieties are bright pink. I grow 'Duchess of Albany'*** into one side of an apple tree, with an alpine clematis on the other side to give a succession of blooms. The **Russian virgin's bower**, *C. tangutica*, (zone 1b) has bright yellow bells in late summer, followed by fluffy seed heads. This is a very vigorous climber that does well on a fence or arbour. It has naturalized itself on hillsides in Drumheller, Alberta, growing in a very sticky clay. These three groups should be cut back in spring, as they flower on new growth.

COTONEASTER *Cotoneaster*
Peking cotoneaster *C. acutifolius***
Height: 4 m (13 ft.) Zone 2 H

A plant used mainly for hedging. It does not make a good individual specimen.

Cranberry cotoneaster *C. apiculatus***
Height: 60 cm (24 ft.) Spread: 2 m (6 ft.)
Zone 4b

A creeping ground cover that is good for planting on top of a wall where it will cascade down. The flowers are in small pink clusters and the fruit look like cranberries but are not edible unless you have feathers.

Bearberry cotoneaster *C. dammeri***
Height: 50 cm (20 in.) Spread: 3 m (10 ft.)
Zone 4

An excellent evergreen ground cover for slopes, banks, or the flat. It is fast-growing but the foliage doesn't get thick enough to smother weeds. This is the sort of situation in which landscape fabric is most useful. The flowers are white and the fruit dull red. 'Coral Beauty' sets masses of brighter-coloured fruit that is loved by partridges.

CURRANT *Ribes*
Alpine currant *R. alpinum****
Height: 2 m (6 ft.) Zone 2 H ●●

This is used almost exclusively for hedging and can be kept as low as 60 cm (2 ft.) if you clip it three or four times a year. It does flower and fruit but the flowers are not very showy and the fruit is not edible.
Golden currant *R. aureum*****
Height: 3 m (10 ft.) Zone 2 ●●●

If you are planning a border of mixed shrubs, this is a good choice for the back. When it flowers in spring, it is showy and sweetly perfumed, but for the rest of the year it is a "nothing" plant. The only other good point is that it will take shade and thus is useful for planting under an overhanging tree.

DAPHNE *Daphne*
February daphne *D. mezereum*****
Height: 1.2 m (4 ft.) Spread: 1.2 m (4 ft.) Zone 4

Probably the first shrub to flower, but not in February in our climate. The rose-purple flowers are fragrant, and branches can be cut early to force indoors. It does best in light, sandy soils from container-grown plants.
Rose daphne *D. cneorum*****
Height: 15 cm (6 in.) Spread: 60 cm (24 in.) Zone 2b ●

A very fragrant evergreen shrub for the front of the border or rock garden. The branches disappear under the masses of rose-pink blooms in late spring. If grown in light shade it may rebloom in late summer. The foliage should be given a light winter protection of evergreen boughs to shade them from the winter sun. Plant container-grown plants only.

DEUTZIA *Deutzia*
Slender deutzia *D. gracilis****
Height: 1 m (3 ft.) Zone 6

Deutzias are similar to mock orange but are neither as fragrant nor as hardy. They are prone to considerable winter dieback if the winter is colder than normal.

DOGWOOD *Cornus*
Tatarian dogwood *C. alba*
Height: 3 m (10 ft.) Zone 2 ●●●

Dogwoods are one of the few shrubs whose variegated forms will not revert to green in shade. They are also good for the winter effect of their twigs, especially against snow. The various forms of the Tatarian dogwood grow better on dry soils than the native red osier dogwood, below.

'**Argenteo-marginata**'**** (sometimes listed as '**Elegantissima**') has green leaves with a white margin and dull red twigs.

'**Gouchaltii**' and '**Spaethii**'*** are similar, being yellow and green, but the former has a pink tinge as well.

'**Sibirica**'*** has plain green leaves but has the brightest coloured twigs.
Cornelian cherry *C. mas****
Height: 6 m (20 ft.) Zone 5b ●●●

A large spreading shrub that is useful as a background plant, especially in shade. It has bright yellow flowers in early spring, long before the forsythia have even thought about blooming.
Red osier dogwood *C. stolonifera**** (also called *C. sericea*)
Height: 3 m (10 ft.) Zone 3 H ●●●

A native shrub that thrives in wet or shady locations. It spreads by underground runners (stolons, hence the Latin name) and will form large thickets in time. It is grown mainly for its red twigs and is often used on cottage properties to stabilize slopes. '**Flavirama**'**** has bright yellow twigs. Both make good hedges but should be cut back almost to ground level every couple of years so the growth remains young and brightly coloured.

DUTCHMAN'S PIPE *Aristolochier macrophylla* (or *durior*)**
Height: vine to 10 m (33 ft.) Zone 5

This plant is often seen climbing over porches on rural properties, but it is equally at home in the city. The huge leaves huge give dense shade and the small brown flowers, which give the plant its common name, are hidden in the foliage.

ELDER *Sambucus*
Golden american elder *S. canadensis* 'Aurea'***
Height: 3 m (10 ft.) Zone 3

The leaves have seven leaflets and retain their yellow colour well into the summer. Flowers are white, in flat heads and with a peculiar smell that some people can't stand. Fruit is red when ripe but not very tasty.

Cutleaf golden European elder *S. nigra* 'Plumosa Aurea'****
Height: 3 m (10 ft.) Zone 3

This European counterpart of the native elder has five leaflets rather than seven, although in this cutleaf form it is hard to tell. Fruit are black when ripe and are good for pies, jellies, and wine. 'Sutherland Gold', from Sutherland, Saskatchewan, is an improved form that keeps its bright colour longer into the summer. Once the shrub is established, for the best foliage colour, cut the stems back almost to the ground each spring to promote new growth. HINT: Use discretion when eating elderberry pie and start with a small slice. Some people get the runs from the berries.

EUONYMUS, SPINDLETREE *Euonymus*
Winged euonymus *E. alatus****
Height: 5 m (16 ft.) Zone 3 H

This shrub has inconspicuous, small, greenish flowers and is grown for its fall and winter effect. The fall colour is a bright red, turning plum with age. When the leaves fall the fruit becomes visible; as the pods open, they reveal the bright orange seed inside. The bark has corky wings which stand out and add winter interest. The form 'Compactus' grows to only half the height given above and is the best choice for hedging. This plant will not grow well in either wet or very dry soils.

Wintercreeper *E. fortunei*
Zone 6 unless stated; prostrate or climbing

Originally introduced from China by the Scottish plant hunter Robert Fortune, in just over 80 years it has given rise to many different forms. The original plant was an evergreen with dark shiny foliage but modern forms come in many guises. They are often used as mound-forming ground covers, but some forms climb and can be trained into small trees in milder areas. Others grow well up house walls and will survive above the snowline in cold districts, providing they are shaded from the winter sun. These are the most common varieties.

'Coloratus'** Green, turning purple in the fall; a trailing ground cover.

'Emerald Gaiety'*** More upright, and the leaves are edged with white which turns pink in fall. Zone 5.

'Emerald 'n Gold'*** A low selection with the leaves edged yellow. Zone 5.

'Gold Tip'*** Another low form but the new leaves are splashed with gold, which loses intensity as they age.

'Sarcoxi'*** One of the hardiest climbing forms for zone 5; glossy green.

'Sunspot'*** This is the reverse of 'Emerald 'n Gold', the leaves having golden centres. It forms a low mound.

There are many other varieties listed in catalogues, but I sometimes suspect that half the names are inventions since they never appear anywhere else.

EUROPEAN HIGH BUSH-CRANBERRY—see Viburnum.

EUROPEAN SNOWBALL—see Viburnum.

FALSECYPRESS *Chamaecyparis*
Sawara falsecypress *C. pisifera*
Height: 2–3 m (6–10 ft.) Zone 4b

It's easy to confuse this with cedar, to which it is related. There are many other species and dozens and dozens of cultivars, many of which are dwarfs used in rock gardens. These are two forms you are most likely to find.

'Filifera'*** Mound-forming, with thin, drooping branches.

'Filifera Aurea'*** The golden form, which makes a good winter accent plant.

FALSE SPIREA *Sorbaria*
Ural false spirea *S. sorbifolia***
Height: 2 m (6 ft.) Zone 2 ●●●

A good plant for stabilizing banks since it spreads by underground runners. It will grow equally well in sun or shade and has plumes of creamy white flowers in late summer. Once it is growing strongly, it can be cut back to ground level in early spring, resulting in larger flowers. This also removes the need to trim out dead twigs and old flower heads.

FIRETHORN *Pyracantha*****
Height: 50 cm (20 in.) Zone 6 H

Firethorns are grown for their yellow or red fruit, which lasts well into winter. They are adaptable shrubs and can be trained against a wall as an espalier or used in a mixed border. Because of the thorns on the branches they make a good, impenetrable, informal hedge. Plant container-grown stock in full sun for the best fruit production.

FORSYTHIA *Forsythia*
Lynwood forsythia *F.* x *intermedia* 'Lynwood'**
Height: 3 m (10 ft.) Zone 6

Forsythia is probably the best-known of all spring shrubs—its bright yellow blossoms give a promise of warm summer evenings and an end to dirty snowbanks. They were named in honour of William Forsyth, one of the founders of the Royal Horticultural Society of London, and the plant name should be pronounced as such (with a long "i" sound).

'Lynwood' is a free-flowering selection of the border forsythia but suffers from the same drawback that many of its varieties have. While the plants are hardy to zone 3, the flower buds are killed in zone 5. Often the plants flower only below the snowline where the flower buds were protected. (The hardiness zones given here are for flower bud survival.)

Ottawa forsythia *F. ovata* 'Ottawa'***
Height: 1.5 m (5 ft.) Zone 4

This selection was made for the hardiness of its flower buds and the earliness of its blooms.

Northern Gold forsythia *F.* 'Northern Gold'****
Height: 2 m (6 ft.) Zone 3b

Another hybrid from Ottawa, this one was the result of a planned cross between two of the hardiest forms. It is later to flower than 'Ottawa' and is a slightly darker yellow. It has flowered at Morden, Manitoba, without protection. If you can't find 'Northern Gold', two other hardy forsythias to look for are 'Northern Sun'*** and 'Meadowlark'***, both developed in the northern U.S.

HAZEL *Corylus*
Harry Lauder's walking stick *C. avellana* 'Contorta'***
Height: 3 m (10 ft.) Zone 5

This shrub gets its common name from an old-time British music hall comedian who used a stick made of wood from this plant as part of his act. The stems grow in a twisted and contorted fashion, constantly changing direction. Young shoots are much used by flower arrangers.

HEATHS AND HEATHERS
Spring heath *Erica carnea*
Heather *Calluna vulgaris*
Height: 60 cm (24 in.) Spread: 20 cm (8 in.)
Zone 4 (3 with reliable snow cover) ●●

Strictly speaking, these are the correct common names for these two species, but they are often mixed up or used indiscriminately. There are many other species of heath, with varying degrees of hardiness, but the spring heath is the most common. Both need an acidic soil and grow well together; they make a good underplanting for rhododendrons and azaleas if you can grow these. Spring heath sets its flowers in fall and they overwinter to open in early spring (small branches force well in late winter). Heather flowers in summer but it is often grown for the foliage effect, which can range from copper to yellow depending on the variety. There are many cultivars of both, but the easiest spring heaths to find are 'Springwood Pink'**** and 'Springwood White'**** None of the heathers are as easy to find, but 'Aurea'***, with yellow foliage and purple flowers, and 'H.E. Beale'*** with greyish foliage and pink flowers, are worth searching for. The cross-leaved heath, E. tetralix, is summer blooming. It has woolly grey foliage and, in the variety 'Con Underwood'***, bright pink flowers. It flowers after the summer-blooming heathers, extending the season.

HIGH BUSH-
CRANBERRY—see Viburnum.

HONEYSUCKLE Lonicera
Dropmore Scarlet honeysuckle L. x brownii 'Dropmore Scarlet'***
Height: vine to 5 m (16 ft.) Zone 2

Listed under a variety of names in nurseries, including 'Dropmore', 'Dropmore Trumpet', 'Scarlet Trumpet', this is one of the most popular climbers—second only to clematis. It is slow to get established and, although it flowers from the first year, good growth does not occur until about the third summer. The flowers appear in July, are bright red and continue almost to frost. This plant climbs by twining and is a good choice for chain link fencing.

Goldflame honeysuckle L. x heckrottii***
Height: vine to 5 m (16 ft.) Zone 5

Similar in habit to the last listing, this variety has dull red flowers that fade to pink with age. As they open they reveal a yellow interior. They are a lot more colourful than they sound—honest!

Hall's honeysuckle L. japonica 'Halliana'**
Height: vine to 8 m (26 ft.) Zone 6

A very vigorous climber that has naturalized itself and become a weed in warmer parts of the U.S. The flowers are very sweetly scented. On a trip to North Carolina my wife was in heaven, surrounded by her favourite perfume. The flowers are white, turning yellow with age, and the plant is evergreen in warm regions, deciduous in cool. The variety 'Aureo-maculata'*** has leaves marked with yellow and is much more restrained, but doesn't flower as freely.

Zabel's honeysuckle L. korolkowii 'Zabelii'***
Height: 3 m (10 ft.) Zone 2b H ●●●

This may be listed in some nurseries as a variety of the Tatarian honeysuckle. It has dark green leaves on a well-shaped plant (honeysuckles tend to get bare at the base). The flowers are bright red and are followed by red berries. Like all the honeysuckles, the berries are edible but not palatable—you can eat 'em, but you wouldn't want to!

Tatarian honeysuckle L. tatarica**
Height: 4 m (13 ft.) Zone 2 ●●●

There are many named hybrids of this species with flowers in shades of white, pink, red, and maroon, and fruit of yellow, orange, or red. They are great for bringing birds into the garden in the fall but suffer from a very specific pest. The Russian aphid attacks the new shoots in early spring and as a result of its feeding, the shoots become stunted and take on a "tassel-like" appearance. Spray with dormant oil during the winter to kill the overwintering females, and then with insecticidal soap or pyrethrins as the leaves start to unfold, to get any you missed. This should do the trick.

The adults live inside the curled leaves and are difficult to control later in the season.

Clavey's dwarf honeysuckle *L.* x *xylosteoides* 'Clavey's Dwarf'***

Height: 1–2 m (3–6 ft.) Zone 2 H ●●

The flowers are cream, followed by dark red fruit. It is excellent as an informal hedge, but if clipped formally it loses most of the flower buds.

HYDRANGEA *Hydrangea*

Climbing hydrangea *H. anomala petiolaris*****

Height: vine to 20 m (65 ft.) Zone 5

Most probably listed in catalogues without the middle name. This plant climbs by holdfasts (aerial rootlets) and is good on brickwork or for covering an old tree stump. Growth is slow at first but quite rapid once the plant becomes established. In zone 5 it should be planted on the east side of the house where it will be shaded from winter sun. Any shoots that grow round the south side are most likely to be winter-killed by temperature fluctuations caused by the sun.

Annabelle hydrangea *H. arborescens* 'Annabelle'****

Height: 1 m (3 ft.) Zone 2b

Many hydrangeas are late-flowering because the blooms appear on the wood grown that summer. These should be cut back in early spring almost to ground level. When I lived in a half double, we had an Annabelle hydrangea next to the front door. In winter, once the ground was covered in snow, the mailman took a shortcut across the gardens, right over poor Annabelle. Come spring there was not a lot remaining, but within a few weeks up she would shoot and flower profusely in July with heads so large they would bow the branches to the ground. The flowers last for weeks, gradually turning brown. The variety 'Grandiflora'**, called hills of snow (and not to be confused with the next species) is similar but the flower heads are smaller and the plant is hardy only to zone 3b.

Peegee hydrangea *H. paniculata* 'Grandiflora'***

Height: 3 m (10 ft.) Zone 3b

This plant gets its common name from the initials of the species and variety names. It is the most common of all the hydrangeas and can also be found grown into a tree with a single stem. The flowers are in dense spikes, rather like ice cream cones. They open white, turn pink, and eventually brown. They can be cut and dried at any stage for winter use indoors. The plants grow from the base; to get good big flowers, thin out the number of shoots each spring.

JAPANESE SPURGE *Pachysandra terminalis****

Height: 30 cm (12 in.) Zone 3 ●●●●

An excellent ground cover for deep shade, this will survive where little else will grow. The leaves are dark green but the new foliage is pale, giving a nice contrast in spring. Growth is slow, so be prepared to weed for a few years. Eventually it will become thick enough to smother all opposition and can then survive being walked on.

JUNIPER *Juniperus*

Chinese juniper *J. chinensis*

Zone 5 (unless stated); various sizes; ●

There are many forms of Chinese juniper, ranging from ground-hugging forms to trees, but most are mound-forming in shades of green, blue-green, and yellow. There are more than 50 named forms in Canadian catalogues; these are the most popular.

'Blaauw'*** This is named for a Dutch nursery, hence the (to us) odd spelling. This plant is dark green and vase-shaped, growing to about 2 m (6 ft.).

'Gold Coast'*** One of the better slow-growing forms, making a hummock 1 m (3 ft.) tall in time.

'Gold Star'**** A Canadian introduction that is equally slow but more spreading. Hardy to zone 2.

'**Mint Julep**'*** Bright mint-green mounds grow to 1 m tall by 2 m across (3 ft. by 6 ft.).

'**Old Gold**'*** This is more yellow in colour than 'Gold Star' is and will spread to 1.5 m (5 ft.) wide.

'**Pfitzeriana**'* A very popular form, at least with nursery workers. It grows quite rapidly and can get 3 m wide by 1.5 m tall (10 ft. by 5 ft.) in time. This is the one that grabs your ankles as you walk up the front path in the dark. Hardy to zone 2b.

'**San Jose**'*** A very prostrate bright green selection.

Creeping juniper *J. horizontalis*
Zone 2; various sizes; ◗

This native species is mostly prostrate and spreading, making it ideal for rock gardens or as a ground cover.

'**Bar Harbor**'*** A bluish-green creeper that turns purple in the fall. It will reach 2.5 m across by 50 cm tall (8 ft. by 1 ½ ft.).

'**Blue Chip**'**** A prostrate blue form that will follow the contour of the ground and reach 3 m (10 ft.) across.

'**Plumosa Compacta**'*** (compact Andorra juniper). A grey-green selection that turns a bronzy shade with cold weather. This grows 1.5 m by 40 cm (5 ft. by 1 ½ ft.), while the regular Andorra juniper grows about half as much again.

'**Prince of Wales**'*** A variety from Morden, Manitoba, that is bright green with a blue sheen. It is very prostrate, growing only about 15 cm (6 in.) high.

'**Wiltoni**'**** (blue rug juniper). Not named for Wilton carpets but for the nursery that introduced it in Wilton, Connecticut. It is very similar in form to 'Prince of Wales' but is blue.

Savin juniper *J. sabina*
Height: up to 3 m (10 ft.) Zone 2

This is the most popular of all the species in spite of what I consider to be very prickly leaves and a poor habit of growth. Most of the named forms are a big improvement.

'**Arcadia**'*** A prostrate green form that grows 1 m across by 30 cm tall (3 ft. by 1 ft.).

'**Blue Danube**'**** Taller, to 2 m (6 ft.), and a good blue shade.

'**Broadmoor**'*** This is spreading while young but eventually gets to 3 m (10 ft.). Foliage is a grey-green.

'**Tamariscifolia**'** (tamarix juniper). Very rapid growth once it becomes established. It will need pruning annually unless you allow it 3 m (10 ft.) in the planning stages.

Blue star juniper *J. squamata* 'Blue Star'*****
Height: 1 m (3 ft.) Zone 5 ◗

A slow-growing form with an intense blue colour. This is ideal for small spaces and rock gardens.

Eastern red cedar *J. virginiana*
Zone 3; various sizes

There is much argument among botanists over the classification of some of the junipers, especially the older cultivars that have been around for many years and whose parentage is uncertain. A case in point is the next plant, which some claim to be a form of the Chinese juniper. Since the majority of catalogues list it as a form of the eastern red cedar, I describe it here.

'**Hetzii**'*** is a bluish form with spreading branches. Attractive while young, it can reach 3 to 4 m (10 to 13 ft.) high and wide at maturity.

All junipers should be transplanted either balled and burlapped or container-grown. Plant them in full sun. The blues will take part shade and the green types can get by on just a bit of sun each day but they tend to grow spindly as the light decreases. All of these junipers have many more cultivars than those listed here, and a visit to almost any nursery or garden centre will give you more names to research.

KERRIA *Kerria*
Double Japanese kerria *K. japonica* 'Pleni-flora'***
Height: 3 m (10 ft.) Zone 5b ●●●

A good shrub for shade where it produces

its ball-like yellow flowers in early summer. The single variety is not quite as showy but is hardy to zone 5. The twigs are green, giving a nice winter effect, but dieback is quite common and some pruning may be required in early spring to remove it.

KOLOMIKTA VINE *Actinidia kolomikta****
Height: vine to 6 m (20 ft.) Zone 4

Related to the kiwi fruit, this vine has leaves splashed with pink and white when grown in full sun. You need both male and female plants to get the small, sweet, edible fruit. The closely related **Tara vine***** (*A. arguta*) has larger fruit but plain green leaves. **'Issai'** is self-fertile so you only need one plant.

LILAC *Syringa*
American lilac *S.* x *hyacinthiflora****
Height: 3 m (10 ft.) Zone 2b

This is the earliest of the three groups of lilac. The flower shape, colour range, and perfume are similar to the common lilac, which is one of the parents.

Common lilac, French lilac *S. vulgaris*
Height: 4 m (13 ft.) Zone 2

Everyone knows lilac. Driving about the countryside you can often tell where there was once a home by the ever-spreading clump of lilac that remains long after the house has crumbled. There are several hundred named French hybrid lilacs (so-called because much of the early breeding work was done in France), with single or double flowers, in shades from white to dark mauve. A visit to the lilac collections at Hamilton, Ottawa, or Montreal at flowering time will show you just how wide the range of colours can be. Those commonly available or worth searching for include the following.

'Agincourt Beauty'**** Dark mauve but with the largest individual flowers of all.

'Belle de Nancy'*** Double rose pink.

'Charles Joly'*** Double purple.

'Dappled Dawn'**** The flowers are single

and light mauve but the foliage is variegated, which gives interest when not in flower.

'Frank Paterson'***** Single, just about the darkest purple of all.

'Ludwig Spaeth'*** Single, bright mauve. (Often listed as 'Souvenire of Ludwig Spaeth'.)

'Mme. Lemoine'**** Double white.

'President Grevy'*** Double light lilac.

'President Lincoln'**** The best single blue.

'Primrose'** Double white, creamy yellow buds. Whoever named it had a good imagination.

'Sensation'***** Single flowers of a light purple with a white edge to each petal.

Preston lilacs *S.* x *prestoniae****
Height: 3 m (10 ft.) Zone 2

Developed in Ottawa during the 1920s, these are late-flowering hybrids. The flower trusses are longer and more drooping and the individual flowers much smaller. The scent differs from the French hybrids and the colour range is more muted. Use them to extend the flowering season for lilacs. If you have room for only one lilac, plant a French hybrid. If you have room for two, add a Preston lilac and make the American hybrid your third choice.

Beautiful as lilacs are in flower, for the other 50 weeks of the year they are just large shrubs with little else to recommend them; they don't even have fall colour. They must be planted in full sun to bloom.

MAGNOLIA *Magnolia*
Star magnolia *M. stellata*****
Height: 5 m (16 ft.) Zone 5

This is usually given as a zone 5b plant but there are lots of them growing in Ottawa. I wouldn't suggest you try it on an open site subject to strong winter winds, however. Even with shelter there will be the occasional winter when the buds are killed, although the plant will survive. It makes a good specimen plant and can also be used for foundation planting, but note that it does grow to 5 m (16 ft.) tall and about 3 m (10 ft.) wide. The fragrant flowers are usually white but there are some pink forms that fade to white as the flowers age. It is very early-flowering and should be spring-planted only—usually while it is in bloom.

MAPLE *Acer*
Amur maple *A. ginnala.* See entry in tree listings (Chapter 4).
Cutleaf Japanese maple *A. palmatum*****
Height: 2–5 m (6–16 ft.) Zones 5–6b

This is the one plant that makes me wish I lived in a slightly warmer climate. It forms a small tree or shrub with lacy foliage in shades of green, red, or purple. The degree of laciness varies with the cultivar, of which there are probably well over 100, although only relatively few are available in Canada.

MOCK ORANGE *Philadelphus*
Height: 1–5 m (3–16 ft.) Zones 2b–5

This is also known as syringa in the U.K., which is the Latin name for lilac—just how confusing can common names get? Mock oranges are a very mixed bunch of plants with widely different hardiness and sizes. When choosing one for your garden, take great care that it fits the space you have. Don't accept substitutes without checking them out first. Though beautiful in flower, they have little to commend them for the rest of the year, except for the golden form.

'Aureus'*** The golden form has sweetly scented flowers but they are lost in the foliage. Zone 3; 5 m (16 ft.).

'Buckley's Quill'*** Named for my predecessor at the Dominion Arboretum in Ottawa, it has spikey flowers with a pleasing, but not strong, perfume. Zone 4; 2 m (6 ft.).

'Minnesota Snowflake'*** Often shortened to 'Min Snowflake', which is confusing since there is also a variety called 'Miniature Snowflake'. The description should help sort them out since one grows 3 m (10 ft.) tall, the

other only 1 m (3 ft.). Double flowers up to 5 cm (2 in.) across with a good scent. Zone 3b.

'Virginal'** Probably the most widely sold cultivar, but I can't think why because at 4 m (13 ft.) final height, it is far too large for most city gardens. Zone 3b.

'Waterton'*** Probably the hardiest of all the mock oranges (zone 2b); it was selected in Waterton National Park, Alberta. It grows to only 2 m (6 ft.) tall but has no perfume.

NINEBARK *Physocarpus opulifolius*
Height: 3 m (10 ft.) Zone 2b H

This native shrub has some good selections that are readily available.

'Dart's Gold'**** A dwarf form to 1 m (3 ft.) with bright yellow foliage, especially in spring.

'Luteus'*** This is twice the size of 'Dart's Gold' and not quite such a bright yellow.

'Nanus'*** The green counterpart of 'Dart's Gold'. Both are good for hedging, either clipped or informal.

OREGON GRAPE *Mahonia aquifolium******
Height: 1 m (3 ft.) Zone 5 ●●

An evergreen shrub with hollylike foliage that is a shiny green when young, turning a wine-purple in fall. In zone 5, foliage above the snowline may be killed and need pruning off in spring, but the new growth quickly hides the scars. The bright yellow flowers are in clusters and turn into edible black fruit resembling bunches of grapes. One of my personal favourites.

PEASHRUB *Caragana*
Siberian peashrub *C. arborescens***
Height: 5 m (16 ft.) Zone 2 H

A very hardy shrub much used on the prairies. It is good on poor soils and is a member of the pea family, using the symbiotic bacteria to provide extra nitrogen. It rapidly forms a hedge but, equally rapidly, gets bare at the base. When this happens, cut it back almost to ground level in early spring and new growth will soon appear. It is best used as a short-term windbreak in our region, while other, more desirable shrubs get established. The flowers are yellow in early summer. **'Lorbergii'***** has narrow, almost linear, leaves.

PERIWINKLE *Vinca minor****
Zone 3; ground cover; ●●●

A low, spreading plant that is good for shade. It is slow-growing and takes several years to form a dense-enough stand to prevent weed growth, but given time it makes an excellent ground cover.

PIERIS *Pieris*
Japanese pieris *P. japonica*****
Height: 3 m (10 ft.) Zone 5b ●●

A most attractive plant for acidic soils in light shade. The new foliage is tinged a bronze to red colour and the flowers are strings of white bells. There are many named forms, of which **'Mountain Fire'** is outstanding, with bright red new growth. Plant container-grown or balled and burlapped plants only.

PINE *Pinus*
Bristlecone pine *P. aristata****
Height: 3 m (10 ft.) Zone 3

While this will form a small tree eventually, it is very slow-growing, especially in exposed locations. This is the pine that has been dated at over 4,000 years old in the Rockies. The needles, which are in clusters of five, have small white resin dots on them. These are natural, not pests. A good choice for a rock garden or small area.

Mugho pine *P. mugo* var. *mugo****
Height: 1 m (3 ft.) Spread: 3 m (10 ft.) Zone 2b

A good dwarf pine for the rock garden or foundation planting. Make sure you get the mugho pine and not the mountain pine (*P. mugo*). That one will grow to 3 m (10 ft.) high by 10 m (33 ft.) across. These plants are often grown from seed and there is a tremendous difference in the rates of growth among the seedlings. When buying, check the length of the needles and the growth from the previous year to find (or avoid) the really dwarf forms.

QUINCE *Chaenomeles*
Flowering quince *C. speciosa* and *C. japonica*****
Height: 2–3.5 m (6–11 ft.) Zone 5b H

There are many named selections from these two species of quince and they vary in the colour of the flowers and the growth habit of the plant. They are all spiny, with sharp thorns up to 5 cm (2 in.) long. All flower in spring with orange to red blooms and the fruit can be used to make jams and chutneys. They can be trained against a wall as an espalier and the upright forms make an impenetrable hedge, which can be clipped formally or left informal where space allows. Grow them in sun for best bloom.

RHODO *Rhododendron*
Height: 50 cm–5 m (2–16 ft.) Zones 5–8 ●●●●

Most people with the slightest interest in gardening have heard of rhodos and seen pictures of them. The name brings to mind a large-leaved shrub with great big trusses of pink or red flowers. The colder the climate you live in, the less true this picture becomes. Yes, you can grow a wide range of rhodos in the Niagara region if you are willing to give them some extra care. In Toronto, the range of those that will survive is smaller but still considerable. If you live in Ottawa or Montreal, you are limited to a few of the so-called iron-clad rhodos. Wherever you live, you must have, or make a bed of, acidic soil for rhodos to thrive. They also do not like full sun, and light shade from distant trees for much of the day is desirable. The following large-flowered cultivars (which are all iron-clads) are quite readily available.

'America'*** Bright red.

'R. catawbiense'*** Three equally hardy forms—'Album', 'Boursault' and 'Grandiflorum'—have white or pink flowers.

'English Roseum'*** Bright pink.

'Nova Zembla'**** Dark red.

'Roseum Elegans' Mauvish-pink.

New large-flowered hybrids, originating in Finland, are now appearing in garden centres. They seem to be hardy to at least zone 4, although the exact lowest zone has yet to be determined. They have Scandinavian-sounding names like 'Hellikki' and 'Élviira'.

There is one other rhodo that is in a lot of nurseries, called 'P.J.M.'****. This is hardy to zone 4, but it doesn't have large trusses of flowers or big leaves. The foliage is a shiny green, turning a copper colour in the fall and greening up again in the spring. Flowers are quite small, about 5 cm (2 in.) across and, instead of being in clusters at the ends of the shoots, they are in small clumps all along the branches. The flowers vary slightly from plant to plant and are in shades from mauve to pink.

Don't forget that azaleas are really rhododendrons and like similar conditions. A mix of the two gives you a longer flowering period and a wider range of colours.

ROSE *Rosa*
Various hardiness and heights

There are a great number of hardy shrub roses that can be grown without a lot of fuss and bother. True, you may never win "Queen of the Show" at a rose show, but they will flower for you year after year, no matter how much you neglect them. Like most shrubs, many of these roses have a single period of bloom and, usually, attractive fruits (hips) in the fall. Some are recurrent bloomers and will give you several flushes of flowers through the summer. The hips are very rich in vitamin C and can be made into jam or wine—or you can just bring them indoors for winter decoration.

Some nurseries specialize in roses and have a wide selection of both the modern bush roses and the hardy types, which are commonly called shrub roses. (For advice on growing the modern hybrids see Chapter 7.) Most nurseries and large garden centres carry a few of the shrub roses. These are the most common.

Austrian copper*** (*R. foetida bicolor*) Zone 3; 2 m (6 ft.); bright copper; but flowers for a short time only.

'Blanc Double de Coubert'*** Zone 2; 2 m (6 ft.); white, very fragrant; recurrent; H.

'F.J. Grootendorst'*** Zone 2b; 2 m (6 ft.); red, recurrent; H.

'Hansa'*** Zone 2b; 1 m+ (3 ft.+); mid-red, fragrant, reblooming; H.

Harison's yellow*** (*R. harisonii*) Zone 2; 2 m (6 ft.); bright yellow, slight rebloom; H.

Persian yellow*** (*R. foetida persiana*) Zone 2; 2 m (6 ft.); the yellow form of Austrian copper.

'Pink Grootendorst'*** Zone 2b; 2 m (6 ft.); like F.J.G. but pink; H.

'Prairie Dawn'**** Zone 4; 1 m+ (3 ft.+); medium pink, reblooming.

Red-leaved rose*** (*R. glauca*) Zone 2b; 2 m (6 ft.); single, pink, non-recurrent but a good show of hips.

'Thérèse Bugnet'*** Zone 2b; 2 m (6 ft.); dark pink, reblooming.

There are two other groups of roses that have been developed especially for cold tolerance and disease resistance; these are the Explorer and Parkland roses. Both were introduced by Agriculture, AgriFoods Canada, the first from the Central Experimental Farm, Ottawa, and the second from Morden Research Station, Manitoba. Some of the best are:

Explorer roses

'Champlain'**** Zone 3; 60 cm (24 in.); bright red, recurrent; H.

'Frontenac'*** Zone 3; 1 m (3 ft.); upright and free flowering; bright pink with good recurrent bloom.

'John Cabot'**** Zone 2b; 4 m (13 ft.); climbing, red, recurrent.

'John Davis'*** Zone 3; 2.5 m (8 ft.); climbing; medium pink, with buds like miniature hybrid tea blooms; recurrent.

Parkland roses

'Adelaide Hoodless'*** Zone 3; 1 m+ (3 ft.+); medium red; recurrent.

'Cuthbert Grant'**** Zone 3b; 1 m (3 ft.); dark red, hybrid tea type blooms; recurrent.

'Morden Amorette'*** Zone 3; 50 cm (18 in.); carmine to rose flowers produce almost continuously if you remove the old blooms.

'Morden Blush'*** Zone 2b; 1 m (3 ft.); pale pink to creamy white flowers are freely produced and recurrent; flower colour depends on the temperature.

'Morden Fireglow'**** Zone 2b; 70 cm (28 in.); bright scarlet flowers; recurrent.

ROSE OF SHARON *Hibiscus syriacus****
Height: 3 m (10 ft.) Zone 6

This is a good plant for the mixed border or as a specimen on the lawn. It flowers in late summer with large, cup-shaped blooms in red, white, or mauve. There are many named forms but the majority of nurseries seem to sell by colour in single or double forms. Don't plant in either very wet or very dry soils.

SASKATOON *Amelanchier*****
Saskatoon *A. alnifolia*
Height: 2–6 m (6–20 ft.) Zone 2b

This is a shrub for most seasons. White flowers smother the branches in early spring, the fruit is edible and can be used for jams and preserves (some named forms have been selected for their fruit), and in the fall the leaves turn a brilliant orange.

Shadblow, serviceberry *A. canadensis*****
Height: 5–8 m (16–26 ft.) Zone 4

Similar to the last in attributes except that the fruit is not as tasty uncooked and the fall colour is redder.

SEA BUCKTHORN *Hippophae rhamnoides****
Height: 4 m (13 ft.) Zone 2b H

Sea buckthorn is an excellent background plant grown mainly for its winter fruit which is bright orange. Its narrow silver leaves make a good foil for other shrubs in summer. The male and female flowers are on separate plants and to be sure of fruit you should have one male for every five or six female plants, especially in hedges. (The male plants have long pointed buds; the females, small rounded ones.) This is a good choice of hedging for roadsides because the plants are salt tolerant. They grow best in poor sandy soils.

SMOKETREE *Cotinus coggygria****
Height: 5 m (16 ft.) Zone 5

The flowers on smoketree are yellow and hidden by the foliage, but there are hairs on the stalks that expand after blooming is finished to give the smoke effect. There is also a good yellow fall colour, less pronounced in the purple-leaved forms. '**Royal Purple**' has dark burgundy leaves and red, not pink, smoke.

SNOWBALL—see Viburnum.

SNOWBERRY *Symphoricarpos albus***
Height: 2 m (6 ft.) Zone 2

A somewhat straggly shrub that is grown for its winter effect. The small flowers are white with a pink tinge; the fruit is cherry-sized, white, and persists late into the winter. The fruit gets lost against a snowy background so this shrub is best in regions where snow does not last all winter.

The closely related **Coralberry**, or **Indian Currant**, *S. orbiculatus*, (zone 2b) is probably a better choice for most of us. It has raspberry-like clusters of berries that turn red and show up against the snow.

SPINDLETREE—see Euonymus.

SPIREA *Spiraea*
Bumalda spirea *S.* x *bumalda*
Height: 1 m and 1.5 m (3 ft. and 5 ft.) Zone 2b H

This plant is hardly ever offered for sale but the named forms of it are some of the best small shrubs. They grow best in full sun but will take partial shade providing you are willing to sacrifice the fall colour of the foliage. Flowers are pink, and blooming starts in midsummer and continues up to frost.

'Anthony Waterer' and **'Froebelli'***** are similar, differing only in height, but **'Goldflame'****** is very distinctive. The new leaves are a pale wine-red, turning yellow as they age and eventually changing to green. The plant seems to continue to produce new foliage all summer so this three-tone effect is always present. Like 'Anthony Waterer' it grows about 1 m (3 ft.) high but the flowers don't stand out as well against the multi-coloured foliage. They all make good informal hedges.

Goldmound spirea
S. japonica 'Goldmound'****
Height: 1 m (3 ft.) Zone 3b H

An introduction from Perron's Nursery in Montreal, this is similar to 'Goldflame' except that the leaves are yellow and then green. The flowers are more conspicuous and it, too, makes a good hedge.

Halward's silver spirea *S. nipponica* 'Halward's Silver'****
Height: 1 m (3 ft.) Zone 4

Named for Ray Halward, the late propagator at the Royal Botanic Gardens in Hamilton, who introduced this shrub, Halward's Silver spirea is a compact plant ideal for small gardens. Masses of white flowers cover the plant in June.

Bridalwreath *S.* x *vanhouttei***
Height: 2 m (6 ft.) Zone 4

The common name of this shrub has always intrigued me; I never associate brides with wreaths. It is a very free-flowering plant with arching branches smothered in flat-topped clusters of white flowers. It tended to be over-planted in the '50s and '60s and you will find many mature plants in gardens of older subdivisions.

SPRUCE *Picea*
Norway spruce *P. abies*
Zone 2b

Although the Norway spruce itself is really too tall and spreading to be suitable for suburban gardens, the cultivar **'Nidiformis'***** (bird's nest spruce) is, and is readily available. It forms a spreading, compact plant up to 1 m (3 ft.) tall, often with a hollowed-out top that gives it its common name. A more upright form is **'Ohlendorfii'*****, still slow-growing but reaching 2.5 m (8 ft.) in time.

Dwarf Alberta spruce *P. glauca* 'Conica'***
Height: 4 m (13 ft.) in 30 years Zone 2

This pale green plant makes a very good foundation evergreen, if you must have evergreens in the foundation planting. Its slow rate of growth—5 to 10 cm (2 to 4 in.) per year—means it will not need replacing every few years. Watch out for mites in the summer, especially on the side facing the house, which gets the reflected heat. They suck the juices from the needles, causing them to turn a copper colour, then brown, then dead. At the first sign of damage spray with a strong fan of water to wash them off, and repeat daily.

TRAVELLER'S JOY—see Clematis.

TRUMPET VINE *Campsis radicans****
Height: vine to 20 m (65 ft.) Zone 5b

While this plant will survive in Ottawa, it does get severely cut back in hard winters. It should be grown on a trellis, fence, or dead tree stump since its growth is rampant and it can kill a living tree. The orange flowers appear in summer and are up to 10 cm (4 in.) long in clusters of 4 to 6.

VIBURNUM *Viburnum*
Fragrant snowball *V. x carlcephalum*****
Height: 2 m (6 ft.) Zone 6 ●

The viburnums as a group are very useful shrubs. They are mostly early-flowering but have attractive fruit that brings birds into the garden and generally have good fall colour in the copper, purple, and bronzy tones. In addition, most grow and flower well in light to moderate shade. The common name tells you about the main attributes of this species.

Arrowwood *V. dentatum*****
Height: 4 m (13 ft.) Zone 4 H ●●●

This was presumably used by Native people as a source of straight canes for arrow making. It flowers in June with flat heads of white flowers. The fruit is black and the fall colour is red. Its upright growth makes it a good choice for hedging.

Wayfaring tree *V. lantana****
Height: 5 m (16 ft.) Zone 2b ●

A more rounded shrub that is good on dry soils. The fruit is yellow, changes to red and, finally, becomes black. All three colours may be present in the same fruit cluster at once.

European high bush-cranberry *V. opulus****
Height: 4 m (13 ft.) Zone 2b ●

Don't let the common name fool you—they are not cranberries on bushes. Like all viburnums, the fruit can be eaten, but you would have to be pretty hungry. This shrub will thrive in wet soils as well as in regular gardens. In May it produces flat flower heads with an especially showy outer ring. The fruit is bright red and gives the shrub its common name. '**Compactum**' only gets half as tall and is good for hedging.

European snowball, Guelder rose *V. opulus* 'Roseum'***
Height: 4 m (13 ft.) Zone 2b ●

Seeing the previous listing and this shrub side by side you wouldn't think they were so closely related. The flowers on this are in globes and are infertile, so no fruit is set. The blooms start out a green shade and then turn white, persisting for several weeks. This shrub does suffer from an aphid that feeds on the leaves, causing them to curl under and become deformed. Spray with insecticidal soap or just about any other insecticide. Aphids are easy to control if a close watch is kept for new infestations, but they return just as quickly.

High bush-cranberry *V. trilobum****
Height: 4 m (13 ft.) Zone 2 ●●

Another shrub that gets its common name from the persistent fruit. It tends to get tall and lanky with time, but it can be cut down and will sprout again from the base. The fruit is reputed to be edible but it doesn't suit my taste buds. There is a dwarf form that is probably more suitable for smaller properties.

VIRGINIA CREEPER *Parthenocissus*
Virginia creeper *P. quinquefolia****
Height: vine to 15 m (50 ft.) Zone 2b

A vigorous climber that will grow up to 3 m (10 ft.) a year. It can also be used as a ground cover but will climb anything it encounters in its wanderings. The new leaves have a pinkish tinge, turn green, and then become purple-red in the fall. It is one of the first plants to change colour. This species has five leaflets on a stalk; on Boston ivy, the leaves are three-lobed, more like a maple. Virginia creeper is really tough, but the young plant can be confusing. I recommended them for a certain situation and some weeks later got a call that everything was growing well except the Virginia creeper. On inspection, I found they had been planted upside-down. We replanted them and they were producing new shoots a week later. I know of no other shrub that could stand having its roots exposed for weeks without dying.

Boston ivy *P. tricuspidata****
Height: vine to 12 m (40 ft.) Zone 5b

This is the ivy commonly found on old buildings. '**Veitchii**', which is the most readily available, has smaller leaves that are pinkish when young.

The leaves of both species can be made

unsightly by the grape flea beetle that chews many tiny holes in the leaves. Virginia creeper is particularly prone to attack. Try dusting with rotenone in early spring as the buds are beginning to open, as this is when the adults are emerging from the soil after winter. If you can control this first generation, the damage will be negligible.

VIRGIN'S BOWER—see Clematis.

WAYFARINGTREE—see Viburnum.

WEIGELA *Weigela florida*
Height: 1–3 m (3–10 ft.) Zone 5 (most)
Useful late spring-flowering shrubs with bright red to pink flowers. They often rebloom in late summer or early fall. These are the easiest to find.
'**Bristol Ruby**'*** Bright red flowers; upright growth to 2 m (6 ft.).
'**Pink Princess**'*** Hardier (zone 4) and more compact at 1.5 m (5 ft.).
'**Variegata**'*** The leaves are edged with pale yellow; the flowers are rose pink.
There is a series named after dances ('Minuet', 'Tango', etc.) introduced from Ottawa. They are compact and hardy to zone 4.

WILLOW *Salix*
Arctic Willow *S. purpurea* 'Gracilis'***
Height: 1.5 m (5 ft.) Zone 4 H
A hedging plant that is as attractive in winter as summer. The twigs are a bright yellow when young so you should cut this back almost to the ground every couple of years, providing you only want a dwarf hedge.

WINTERCREEPER—see Euonymus.

WISTERIA *Wisteria*
Japanese wisteria *W. floribunda****
Height: vine to 10 m (33 ft.) Zone 5b
Spectacular climbing vines that will twine happily over a trellis or arbour. On a wall they need very firm supports since the plants become heavy and woody with age. Spring flowers are a violet-blue in hanging clusters up to 30 cm (1 ft.) long.
'**Lawrence**'***, found growing in Lawrence Street, Brantford, in 1970, has proven to be hardy in Ottawa (northern zone 5) and flowers most years. It has survived -39.5°C (-39°F)—just.

YEW *Taxus*
Japanese yew *T. cuspidata****
Height: up to 4 m (13 ft.) Zone 4 ●●●
The most common forms of Japanese yew are listed as "spreading" or "upright." How they are pruned when young determines the form and shape of the mature plant. The dwarf form 'Nana', grows to only 2 m (6 ft.). All yews are good for shady sites and are most commonly used for foundation planting on the north side of the house. They suffer badly from wind-burn during the winter. The wind dries out the needles and because the ground is frozen, the plant cannot take up more moisture. Wrap them in burlap in late fall to reduce the flow of air over the branches.
Hybrid yew *T. x media*
Height: up to 2.5 m (8 ft.) Zone 5 or 6 ●●●
Plants in this group are hybrids between the Japanese and English yews. There are several named forms that differ in habit.
'**Brownii**'**** Slow-growing shrub with vase-shaped dark green needles.
'**Densiformis**'*** A dense, spreading cultivar that makes a good low hedge.
'**Hicksii**'*** An upright selection that gets 3 m (10 ft.) high.

YUCCA *Yucca*
Adam's needle *Y. filamentosa****
Height: 1 m (3 ft.) Zone 4
An exotic-looking plant that would appear more at home in a desert setting than on a suburban front lawn. The leaves form a rosette at ground level, each tipped with a sharp thorn.

In the variety '**Golden Sword**'*** the leaves have a yellow centre.

Spanish bayonet *Y. glauca****
Height: 1 m (3 ft.) Zone 3

Similar to Adam's needle in habit, this plant is hardier, growing in the Rockies as far north as Alberta.

Both these shrubs demand a well-drained, sandy soil to grow well. Once established, these shrubs will reward you with towering spikes of waxy white flowers on stems up to 2.5 m (8 ft.) tall.

CARE OF MATURE SHRUBS

Most trees are grown in lawns, but shrubs are often grown in borders or as a foundation planting, where they don't benefit from fertilizer applied to the lawn and need their own supply. In early spring, as soon as the soil is dry enough to walk on without it sticking to your shoes, give your shrubs a top-dressing of a balanced fertilizer such as 6-9-6 or 7-7-7. Avoid one with high nitrogen as this may promote growth at the expense of flowers. Scratch this lightly into the surface with a rake; the rain will wash it down into the root zone. If you are feeding acid-loving plants like azaleas or pieris, be sure to use an acid-based fertilizer. Using regular fertilizers will gradually turn the soil alkaline.

Sooner or later, all shrubs will need pruning (see the next chapter for details), and, late fall, once the leaves have fallen and the branch structure is easily seen, is a good time to look over your shrubs and decide what, if anything, should be removed. Most shrubs are spring-flowering and so it doesn't make sense to prune them in the fall; you are better to enjoy the flowers first. Tie a piece of bright ribbon or wool onto branches you plan to cut out, then, once flowering is over, you will easily see which to prune.

Keep an eye open for pests and diseases during the growing season and take the appropriate action (see Chapter 14). Problems are much easier to deal with when they first start, rather than leaving them until they have got a good hold. Often, just clipping off an insect-infested branch or picking off a few leaves with spots is enough to nip the outbreak in the bud, as it were.

SHRUBS LISTED BY ZONE

Find the zone you live in (see page 11 for the zone map): these are the shrubs you can safely plant.

ZONE 1B
Russian virgin's bower.

ZONE 2A: The above, plus
Alpine currant; bearberry; big-petal clematis; Clavey's dwarf honeysuckle; common lilac; creeping juniper; Dropmore Scarlet honeysuckle; dwarf Alberta spruce; golden currant; high bush-cranberry; Manchu cherry; Peking cotoneaster; Preston lilac; Siberian peashrub; snowberry; tatarian dogwood; tatarian honeysuckle; Ural false spirea.

ZONE 2B: All the above, plus
American lilac; Annabelle hydrangea; bumulda spirea; coralberry; European high bush-cranberry; European snowball; flowering almond; mock orange (some); mugho pine; ninebark; Norway spruce; rose (some); rose daphne; Saskatoon; sea buckthorn; Virginia creeper; wayfaring tree; Zabel's honeysuckle.

ZONE 3A: All the above, plus
American elder; bristlecone pine; cinquefoil; common cedar; Eastern red cedar; European elder; Japanese spurge; periwinkle; red osier dogwood; Spanish bayonet; virgin's bower; winged euonymus.

ZONE 3B: All the above, plus
Goldmound spirea; large-flowered clematis; Northern Gold forsythia; peegee hydrangea; purple-leaved sand cherry.

ZONE 4A: All the above, plus
Adam's needle; alpine clematis; arctic willow; arrowwood; bearberry cotoneaster; bridal-wreath spirea; February daphne; Halward's Silver spirea; heather; Japanese yew; kolomik-ta vine; Ottawa forsythia; rhododendron (some); scarlet clematis; shadblow.

ZONE 4B: All the above, plus
Cranberry cotoneaster; Sawara falsecypress.

ZONE 5A: All the above, plus
Azalea; beautybush; Blue Star juniper; Chinese juniper; climbing hydrangea; cross-leaved heath; Dutchman's pipe; Goldflame honey-suckle; Harry Lauder's walking stick; hybrid yew (some); Japanese angelica tree; Japanese kerria; Oregon grape; smoketree; spring heath; star magnolia; weigela.

ZONE 5B: All the above, plus
Boston ivy; butterfly bush; double kerria; flow-ering quince; Japanese maple; Japanese pieris; Japanese wisteria; trumpet vine.

ZONE 6A: All the above, plus
Cornelian cherry; firethorn; fragrant snowball; Hall's honeysuckle; Lynwood forsythia; rose of sharon; Scotch broom; slender deutzia; winter-creeper.

SUGGESTED READING

Manual of Woody Landscape Plants. Michael A. Dirr. Stipes Publishing Co. (4th edition), 1990.

Landscape Plants for Eastern North America. Harrison L. Flint. Wiley & Interscience (2nd edition), 1996.

These two books are as useful for shrubs as for trees.

Gardening With Trees and Shrubs. Trevor Cole. Whitecap Books, 1996.

This gives a lot more details of care and selection than I could fit in here.

Shrubs. Roger Phillips and Martyn Rix. Random House, 1989.

A British book with coloured photographs of almost 2,000 shrubs. Some we can't grow, but a good lot will thrive here.

Flowering Shrubs and Small Trees. Isabel Zucker. Grove Weidenfeld, 1990.

One of the best books on shrubs, at last revised, updated, and reprinted with colour pictures, not the black and white of the origi-nal edition.

Clematis. Christopher Lloyd and Tom Bennett. Capability's Books, 1989.

Full of information about the culture of clematis.

Making the Most of Clematis. Raymond J. Evison. John Markham, 1995.

Coloured pictures of ways to use clematis in the garden.

Pruning

6
chapter

Pruning is one of those garden tasks that many people seem loath to tackle. They are not sure when to cut, what to cut, or how to cut, but few people even consider the most important factor: why to cut. Let us first look at the reasons for pruning.

1. Disease control. This is the most important reason for pruning and overrides all other considerations. If you see disease or pest infestations on your plant that you cannot control by normal means, and that are going to be harmful to the plant, you should prune them out regardless of the time of year.

While this sounds drastic, there are actually few occasions when this situation will arise. There are a couple of diseases that will spread fairly rapidly and kill your tree or shrub if not dealt with quickly, and I can think of one pest that you may be better to prune out when the infestation starts rather than trying to use chemicals. The diseases are black knot, a fungus disease that attacks plums and cherries

(both ornamental and orchard types) and fire blight, a bacterial disease that can attack many members of the rose family, but particularly mountain ash. They are best controlled by pruning out the diseased wood as soon as it is noticed. Sterilize the tools between each cut with rubbing alcohol to avoid reinfecting the branch, and destroy all infected material as quickly as possible. Scale insects, which may attack a wide range of plants, are difficult to eradicate with garden sprays. If you can catch the pest when it first appears, prune out all affected twigs to prevent it spreading.

2. Safety. There are two aspects to safety pruning. The obvious one is the removal of dead and dying limbs that may fall and cause damage. If these are high in a large tree, you are better to call in a firm of tree surgeons. It would be ironic to fall out of a tree you were pruning for safety reasons. This type of pruning would normally be done while the tree was dormant, but if the limbs are dead, it could be done at any time. The other safety pruning is for the safety of your family and guests. Once young trees are established, which would normally be two years after planting, you can start to gradually remove the lower branches so that you can walk round the tree without having to duck. It will take several years, since you must balance top growth with lower limb removal. It will also depend on the type of tree you choose. A crab apple for example, many of which have a naturally open crown, may never get large enough. Upright trees, with their branches growing parallel to the main trunk, are seldom trimmed to give a clear stem either. Trees and shrubs planted close to the front path and driveway should be inspected annually to make sure they are not posing a hazard to visitors.

3. Effect. You prune to change the shape of a tree or shrub, to keep it within certain limits of growth or to direct growth the way you want it to go. A shade tree on your back lawn may grow more on one side than the other because of shade from an adjacent building. Pruning can help to keep the shape of the tree symmetrical. A storm may damage a branch on your tree and leave a hole in the canopy. Pruning to encourage a new shoot to develop and grow into the gap can, in time, correct this problem.

4. Flowering. The majority of the woody plants in our gardens are chosen for their flowers. Hopefully they have other attributes, such as fruit or coloured bark, but flowers are the main concern. We therefore need to prune to get the best display of flowers possible. With trees, this involves reducing the number of branches or opening up the centre of the tree to let light in. I hope it is obvious that a tree such as a linden, with a definite central shoot (leader), should not have this leader removed to let in more light. I was recently asked to advise on restoring an overgrown crab apple that no longer flowered. I doubt if it had been pruned for at least 10 years, and the whole

crown of the tree was a mass of crossing branches competing for light. Shrubs in particular need regular pruning to encourage flowering, but the frequency depends on the rate of growth. It would be nice if I could tell you to prune every third year, but some shrubs need pruning every year and some every tenth year.

Whether you are pruning a 15-m (50-ft.) oak or a 2-m (7-ft.) viburnum, before you remove any branch, ask yourself "Why am I removing this particular branch?" If you can't answer with one of the four reasons above, then the branch should stay. So many people prune because their neighbour is doing it and because they think the plant needs it.

 # WHEN TO CUT

The correct time to prune a tree is while the plant is not under stress (except for disease control, as mentioned above). With the majority of species, late February to early March is a good time, when it is not too cold to work outside, but the plants are still dormant. Those trees that have a heavy sap-flow in spring, such as birch and maple, should be pruned earlier than this, from late fall to midwinter, to give the cuts a chance to dry before the sap flows. A certain amount of bleeding of the sap is not harmful, but excessive amounts can weaken the tree. The worst time to prune is immediately after the leaves unfurl, when the plant's reserves of food are at their lowest.

Flowering shrubs produce their blooms in two distinct ways. Those flowering in the early part of the year make their buds the previous fall. These buds overwinter and develop into flowers in the spring or early summer. Such shrubs are pruned as soon as they have finished flowering so that the plants have time to make new growth (and flower buds) before winter. Shrubs that bloom later, in midsummer to fall, make their flower buds on the current year's growth and can be pruned late in fall or, most usually, early in the spring.

"When" can mean from what age and how often, as well as the time of year.

Trees need pruning annually while young, as this is when the basic shape of the tree is being formed. As the tree matures, less frequent pruning will be required and a fully grown tree will need attention only every four or five years. Even then, there may be no need to actually prune anything, but you should inspect the tree to spot potential problem areas. With shrubs, the reverse is true; young shrubs need little pruning, apart from a possible removal of broken branches at planting time. As the shrubs get older and growth increases, they will need pruning more often and more thoroughly.

The exception to the "older needs less" rule for trees is apple trees. Here the production of fruit is most important. The trees are cut back hard each winter for two reasons: to reduce the number of flowers, thus growing larger fruit; and to promote the type of growth leading to a good formation of flower buds late in the season to bloom the following year. Apples can be classified into two groups: tip bearers, which have the apples on the ends of the branches, and spur bearers, which have the fruit on short side branches called spurs. Any good book on pruning will give you line drawings of how to prune the two different types. Unfortunately, the tree in your garden never looks in the least like the drawings in the book. When we moved into our present home, there were two unnamed apple trees in the yard. One was obviously a spur type, and pruning this has been relatively easy. Even with the aid of about six books on pruning, I still haven't decided which type the other tree is.

Crab apples are dealt with somewhat differently since the flower is all-important, and fruit production is secondary. They flower in spring on buds produced the previous year, and should be pruned after flowering. The pruning should not be as severe as for apples and should be finished by midsummer so the wood and flower buds have time to mature for the following spring.

WHAT TO CUT— TREES

Many trees produce what are known as water shoots. These are thin branches growing vertically up through the tree, often arising from the top of almost horizontal branches. They are especially obvious on crab apple varieties that have a spreading habit, and can grow up to 2 m (6 ft.) in their first summer. If left, these water shoots will lead to a cluttered tree with a very shaded centre and a resulting loss of bloom and fruit. They should be removed at the base ideally in the summer as they develop, since their growth uses energy the tree should be putting into fruit and bud production. This is an easy task—easy to decide and easy to do—but already your tree will look better. Pruning after flowering, as suggested above, will reduce the production of both water shoots and suckers.

Walk around the tree and look at the branch structure. You have to decide if this is a tree with a leader or one with an open habit. Figure 6–1 may help you make this decision. On trees with a leader, follow it carefully up the tree and make sure that it has not been broken at some time and developed into two competing shoots. If this was the case, one must be removed. Leave the one that most closely follows the line of the tree and cut the other off. Pines that lose their tops in storms will often grow a ring of new shoots from the tier of branches just below the break. If allowed to grow they will make the tree top-heavy, so just the straightest one should be left. If you can select this in its first year of growth, tie a cane to the top of the tree and then loosely tie the

FIGURE 6-1 A tree with a leader branch structure (left) and one with an open habit (right).

new shoot to this cane so that it grows straight. Undo the ties after the first winter so that the new shoot will not be constricted during spring growth.

If you have an upright tree with a leader (such as oaks, lindens, and spruce), the side branches should radiate evenly, more or less at right angles from the stem (seen from above) and should be evenly spaced. Think of each branch as having its own territory and its own lighting supply. Remove any shoots growing at odd angles which, in time, will enter the territory of another branch. Also remove any that are growing immediately above (or below) another branch and not getting their share of the light. In this case it doesn't matter which branch you remove, but try to leave the one that best fits the even spacing of the tree structure.

On an open habit tree (like crab apples, amur maple, and hawthorn), look for branches growing back into the centre of the tree, those crossing another branch causing shading, or, even worse, those crossing and rubbing on another branch. This is an invitation

to disease. Try to keep the centre of the tree open, with a framework of branches, not a thicket.

Often there is a situation in which two branches are competing for the same space and one must go, but it doesn't really matter which one. I always use the angle that the stem leaves the trunk as the final word. The closer to 90 degrees the angle between the trunk and branch is, the stronger the branch will be and the less likely it is to break in storms. As the angle narrows, the union becomes progressively weaker. This is typified by a tree that has lost its leader and developed two shoots in a narrow "Y." This is a very weak joint and will probably split down the centre some day.

Remember, if you remove the end shoot on a branch, the side shoots will grow. On plants with a thin spot, or on spruce and pines you want to make thicker, removing the growing tip will cause them to thicken up. Conversely, removing the side shoots and leaving the tip will push all the energy into creating a long shoot, useful if you had damage to a tree and are trying to direct a new shoot to fill a hole.

Plate 9 *By planting different types of clematis, you can have bloom for most of the summer.*
Upper: *'Francis Rivis' alpine clematis* — *May*
Centre: *'Duchess of Albany' scarlet clematis* – *July to frost*
Lower: *'Polish Spirit' virgin's bower* — *June–July*

Plate 10 *Hardy geraniums come in many forms and are becoming increasingly popular. These three are*
Upper: 'Spessart' bigroot geranium
Centre: 'Ballerina' grayleaf geranium
Lower: 'Biokova' Cambridge geranium

Plate 11   *These three plants are good for moist shade, under shrubs, or in the edge of woods.*
Upper: Yellow barrenwort
Centre: Japanese painted fern
Lower: 'Ruby Veil' foliage coralbell

Plate 12 Upper: *Golden hakonechloa is attractive from spring onwards, but the seed spikes are not showy.*
Centre: *Northern sea oat is grown for its display of seed heads in the fall.*
Lower: *Gardener's garters spreads slowly but has striped foliage and midsummer flower spikes.*

Plate 13 *'Fireglow' Griffiths spurge (upper) and 'Hewitt's Double' meadow-rue bring color to the perennial border in early summer.*

Plate 14 Upper: 'Golden Glow' coneflower is an old favorite.
Centre: 'Barnsley' mallow makes a shrub-like plant but is somewhat tender.
Lower: 'Bravado' purple coneflower spreads easily from seed if you
don't deadhead.
All three flower towards the end of summer.

Plate 15 Upper: *Bidens, seen here with tricolor sage, is a good annual for edging or planters.*
Lower: *The tobacco known as Only-the-Lonely is an imposing annual with a strong evening fragrance.*

Plate 16 Upper: *A mixed border of annuals, perennials, and shrubs.*
Lower: *The delicate, tall flower heads of* Verbena bonariensis *allow you
to see beyond them.*

WHAT TO CUT— SHRUBS

With the exception of hedges, shrubs should not be lightly sheared. All you do by giving shrubs a haircut is remove possible flowers for the following year. If your shrub is getting too large and overgrown, it needs some of the old wood completely removed, to allow new growth to come up from the base and take over. This is known as renewal pruning.

With fast-growing shrubs, such as mock orange and honeysuckle, you will probably need to do some pruning each year. For the majority of shrubs—viburnums, forsythia, and the like—every two or three years should suffice. On slow-growing shrubs, such as lilac, major pruning will not be needed more than once every five years.

Renewal pruning is very easy. Look at your overgrown shrub and make a rough count of the number of shoots. Prune out one-third of the shoots just above ground level. If you do this immediately after flowering, you will get new growth from the base. Later in the summer thin these new shoots to the strongest, leaving about as many as the old shoots you originally took out. In other words, if your shrub had thirty shoots and you pruned out ten, leave the ten strongest new shoots to replace them (Figure 6–2 A and B).

The second season, the shoots that are left will flower and the new shoots will continue to grow. Once the flowering has finished cut out another third of the old shoots and, later, thin out the new growth as before (Figure 6–2 C). By the third year, the new shoots that grew in year one should start to flower, and the last of the old branches should be removed after flowering (Figure 6–2 D). You will then have renewed all the branches, and the shrub can probably be left for two or three years before starting to prune again.

If you have mature plants that are not really overgrown, you can do the same sort of thing but on a longer cycle. You can either take out just two or three of the oldest branches each year, or you can remove a third or a quarter of the old branches every couple of years. Either way it should take you six or eight years to rejuvenate all of the shrub. Remember, this method of pruning is for spring-flowering shrubs that flower on the wood produced the previous summer.

Shrubs that flower late in the season, such as butterfly bush and hydrangea, should be pruned while dormant, because the flowers are produced on the current season's growth. Cut them back in late winter or early spring— almost to the ground if you want them to stay relatively small, and about halfway if you need them to grow tall.

There is one other type of pruning that you should do on some shrubs. If berry production is not important, it helps to remove the old flowers shortly after blooming is finished so

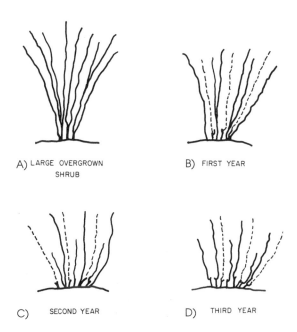

A) LARGE OVERGROWN SHRUB

B) FIRST YEAR

C) SECOND YEAR

D) THIRD YEAR

FIGURE 6-2 Renewal Pruning: This systematic approach to pruning will keep shrubs healthy and control their size.

that the plant does not put energy into seed production. This is particularly true with lilacs. Once the flowers have faded, remove the old spikes just above the pair of leaves below the flower. The energy that would have gone into seed formation will then go into the buds which have the embryo flowers for the next spring. The blossoms will be larger as a result.

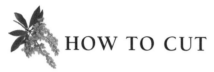

HOW TO CUT

If you are taking off small branches, up to about the thickness of your finger, use a pair of pruning shears. Cut cleanly without twisting the pruners. Wood varies greatly in hardness, and what you can manage to cut with regular pruners on hydrangea, for example, would be impossible on honeysuckle.

If you cannot cut with normal hand pressure, then the wood is either too thick or too hard and you need the next stage of pruners, known as loppers. Loppers are like overgrown pruners on long wooden or metal handles and you can cut wood up to 4 cm (1½ in.) thick with them. HINT: When shopping for loppers, open and close them with considerable force several times in the store to make sure they will not allow your knuckles to bang together. When cutting a tough branch, it will often give suddenly and you can really hurt yourself if the handles are badly aligned.

To cut branches larger than loppers can handle, you need a pruning saw. This may be straight with coarse teeth on one side and fine on the other, or slightly curved with the teeth on the inside edge. The thing that makes pruning saws special is the way their teeth point backwards so that you do most of the cutting on the pull stroke, rather than on the push. If you are working from the top of a ladder you will realize the importance of this; the pull stroke pulls you closer to the tree, the

push stroke pushes you (and the ladder) away. You can also get loppers and pruning saws that fit on top of a long pole so that you can prune up into a tree without climbing.

The latest type of pruning saw is based on Japanese bonsai pruners. The teeth don't have a kerf—the slight alternating outward bend. Instead, the whole blade tapers slightly from the teeth to the back. They are made of very hard steel and stay sharp for ages, which is just as well since they are difficult to sharpen. The best thing is the super-fine cut they give. The cut surface looks almost as if it has been sanded smooth, resulting in fewer ledges for fungus spores to anchor themselves on.

Any branch large enough to need sawing should be removed as shown in Figure 6–3. First, undercut the branch a little way out from the trunk (A), sawing about one-third of the way through. Next cut down from the top (B) outside the first cut, and the branch will fall off, leaving a short stub. If you don't undercut the branch first, you will saw about three-quarters of the way through and the branch will break and tear a strip of bark right down the side of the tree.

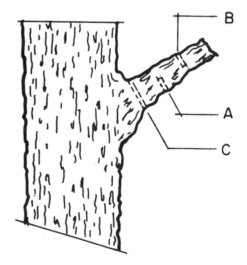

FIGURE 6–3 This three-cut method of branch removal avoids tearing and discourages disease.

Look closely at the branch where it comes out of the trunk. You should see a sort of ring of bark round the branch. This is called the collar and if you can't see it on your tree, look at some other trees to locate it before you make the final cut. Recent research has shown that if you cut the branch stub off immediately outside this collar (C), healing may be slightly slower but the chance of getting disease into the trunk is definitely less. Research has also shown that using black wound paint does no good at all and may even be harmful to the tree. I know that it makes you feel better to put a dressing on the wound you have just made on the tree, but in actual fact you are probably sealing in spores of several fungi that can cause rotting.

PRUNING OLDER TREES

So far, most of what I have written has been about newly planted or quite young plants. After all, these are the formative years and a good beginning is essential. If you live in an older home with established trees, be aware that the pruning of mature trees is a job for an expert. Any pruning that means going more than a couple of metres (over six feet) above the ground should be left to a professional tree company. This includes the removal of large limbs and any bracing or cabling that may be required to make a tree safe. Professional tree people have insurance to cover dropping a branch on a neighbour's car, safety equipment to ensure that they don't fall, and compensation in case they do. I will never forget watching a neighbour taking down a large tree at the end of his laneway. He used no safety belts and was operating a chain saw with one hand while his children ran about underneath. I had to go into the back garden where I couldn't watch this scenario for tragedy.

Sometimes, existing mature trees are left in place on a new subdivision. Unfortunately, these old trees often have a short life. The construction of the subdivision means there have been substantial changes in the water table, roots on the tree may have been cut, changes in grading may have buried or exposed roots, and some of the root area may be covered with blacktop. While not wishing to spread gloom and doom, this often happens because the developers do not understand the needs of trees. It can take several years for the full effects of maltreatment to become obvious, by which time the developer has long gone. If you are considering buying a new home with original trees close by, you may want to check with the builder on the precautions taken to protect these trees.

PRUNING EVERGREENS

The majority of mature evergreens need little regular pruning except for shearing, in the case of cedar hedges, or the removal of dead branches on tall-growing pines and spruce. This dying of the lower branches is natural and is caused by the shade cast by the branches higher up the tree. There are, however, a couple of special cases where pruning is regularly required.

Mugho pines can be kept smaller if you prune the "candles" (new growth) each spring. The time to trim them is when they have finished their growth but before the needles start to open out. Reduce by about three-quarters, using a pair of pruning shears or your thumb and finger. The following year there will be several new shoots on each of the old candles, making the shrub both more dwarf and denser.

Spreading junipers can quickly grow beyond their allotted space, especially if wide-growing varieties were chosen in the first place. Keeping them within bounds, without leaving a lot of unsightly cut ends showing, takes a bit of cunning. Look back along the branch you want to shorten until you find a small shoot growing on the top of the branch. Cut the main stem off underneath this shoot, which will then become the growing tip for that branch and will hide the cut end below it. As this shoot is now receiving all the nutrition that was previously going into the part you removed, it will grow quite fast and will itself probably need cutting back in a year or two. The moral of this is that you should shorten spreading junipers well inside their growing space. If they are growing over the path, don't just trim them to the path edge; go back into the shrub and give them some room to grow again.

Young pines and spruce can be lightly sheared (or hand pinched) to make them thicken out providing you don't trim back into the hard wood below the level of the greenery. Unlike most deciduous trees, the branches will seldom produce new shoots if the growing parts are removed.

Cedar hedges will regrow in time—although if you trim the sides back into the wood they will take a long time and then may not green up all over. Cedar hedges that have become too tall can be pruned down to about two-thirds of their height. A 3-m (9-ft.) hedge can be cut down to about 2 m (6 ft.) without killing it. It will look like hell for a year or two but will eventually green up and start to grow again.

SUGGESTED READING

Pruning Made Easy. Lewis Hill. Storey Communications, 1997.
A good basic book that covers all the essentials.

The Pruning of Trees, Shrubs and Conifers. George E. Brown. Timber Press, 1996.
An old standard revised and reprinted.

Arboriculture. Richard W. Harris. Prentice-Hall, 1983.
One of the best textbooks, with an in-depth review of pruning.

Roses
7
chapter

Although I wrote briefly about shrub roses in Chapter 5, those are not the plants most people think of when you say the word *roses*. To the majority, whether gardeners or not, roses are red, fragrant, beautiful, and cost the earth on Mother's Day. They are also the one plant most gardeners want to grow. Before you dash out and buy up every rose in sight, discover a little about the different types of roses and the ways you can use them in the landscape. This chapter is about the roses that are not really hardy in much of our region. Except in the warmest parts of the Niagara Peninsula they will need a little assistance to come through the winter undamaged. They fall into four groups: **bush roses**, so named to distinguish them from the hardy shrub roses mentioned in the chapter on shrubs; **miniature roses**, an increasingly popular group; **patio roses**, larger than miniature roses but still small; and **climbing roses**, used to cover walls and trellises.

BUSH ROSES

The modern bush rose has come a long way from its ancestors, which also gave rise to many of the shrub roses we grow today. The native European roses had been collected and selected for hundreds of years, and it was not until the start of trade with China that things changed. The Chinese had an even longer tradition of plant breeding, and with the introduction of plants from there, the European rosarians had a whole new lot of plants to try. These gave rise to the Chinas, a group of roses that are still to be found in specialists' catalogues. Also introduced at this time were the tea-scented roses, which apparently smelled like dried tea. Eventually these were crossed with some of the old European hybrids and the results were what has since become the most famous group of roses—**hybrid tea roses**.

Hybrid tea roses are characterized by having

a single flower on a stem and usually a pointed bud which opens into a bloom that has 20 to 70 petals. They grow on bushes up to 1 m (3 ft.) high, although in more favourable climates they will grow twice as tall. There are literally hundreds of different-named cultivars in a wide range of colours, although the "blue" roses you will see advertised are actually a pinkish-mauve, not a true blue. They are probably the least hardy of the bush roses.

Another group of roses developed about this time was the **polyantha**, which has small flowers in numerous clusters. They have fallen out of favour but a few are still seen in the specialist nurseries. Their claim to fame is being crossed with the hybrid tea roses to give rise to the next group, the **Floribunda roses.** Floribundas have several flowers on each stem, sometimes as few as 7, or as many as 60. The buds may be pointed or oval and the flowers are like small hybrid teas, like miniatures of the old cabbage roses, or single, like some of the species. The plants are similar in size to hybrid teas but are somewhat hardier. If you are looking for colour, rather than cutting, these are the roses for you. They come in the same wide colour range as the hybrid teas but because of the multiple blooms, they give a better display.

The next logical step was to cross the hybrid teas with the floribunda roses. This was done in 1955, and the resulting roses are known as **Grandiflora roses**. This cross combined the best qualities from both parents: several blooms to a stem but large individual flowers; long stems for cutting plus the free flowering of the floribundas. There is not such a wide choice of varieties but they are well worth growing. They seem to grow slightly more vigorously than the hybrid tea type.

As well as the bush form of all these roses, many varieties are available grafted onto the top of a straight stem, which may be up to 1.5 m (5 ft.) tall. These are known as tree or standard roses and make a wonderful accent plant or centrepiece for a rose bed. They are

generally the large-flowered hybrid tea type but floribunda roses are also offered. They need extra special care in cold areas to bring them through the winter—see the section on winter protection on page 125.

 # MINIATURE ROSES

These are becoming the favourite roses of a great many people. Because of their dwarf growth they are easy to protect for winter. In fact, in regions with a good snowfall, they don't need protecting at all; the snow will do the job for you. In a recent 10-year period, 1,349 roses of all types—including climbers, shrub and bush roses—were registered with the American Rose Society. Of these, 254, or almost 19%, were miniatures, a proof of their popularity. In 1989, miniature roses were voted All-America Rose Selection winners for the first time ever.

One of the best things about miniatures is that they can be any kind of rose you like. If you favour hybrid tea roses, you can find miniatures with HT-shaped blooms and form. The same with floribunda, grandiflora, climbing, and cascading roses. They are all closely replicated somewhere in the wide range of miniature roses.

Miniature roses grow 25 to 50 cm (10 to 20 in.) tall and are perfect for tiny gardens. They flower freely and can be cut for flower arrangements. Some nurseries are now offering microminiatures which are even smaller and grow only 10 to 15 cm (4 to 6 in.) high.

If you grow plants indoors under fluorescent lights during the winter, then miniature roses are for you. If dug and potted in the fall, they will continue to bloom all winter, given enough light. Grow several plants and take them into the living area of the house one at a time. If you change them around frequently, so that they are only away from the bright lights for a couple of days at a time, they will keep on blooming. Buds are formed only in good light, so a plant kept for too long in an area of low light intensity will stop flowering.

PATIO ROSES

This relatively new group of roses is based on the larger miniatures, but is slightly bushier. There does not seem to be a clear-cut distinction in height; some of the larger miniatures are taller than some patio roses. Like the miniatures, this group can have flowers of many different forms, from single-flowered to cluster, and from a single row of petals to a fully double flower. As the name suggests, their main use is for growing in containers or beds flanking the patio, to bring colour and fragrance. Like the miniature roses, they can be grown indoors under fluorescent lights in winter. If you grow them in containers, bury the containers in the garden in fall (or bring them indoors) to help insulate the roots from the cold.

CLIMBING ROSES

Second only to clematis in popularity as a wall covering, climbing roses are fairly easy to grow but they do need some special winter care. You will have to tie the roses to some form of trellis or system of wires since they do not twine like a clematis.

There are two different forms of climbing roses and their pruning needs are totally different. **Climbers** are in the majority and, unless you go to one of the specialist nurseries, you may not be able to find anything else. Climbers flower on the new wood, the growth that is made in the spring, and so they are cut back by about one-third in early spring—

unless they have been killed even more than this by winter cold. Cut back the leader to a strong new shoot about one-third of the way down the stem. Also remove any dead, diseased, or spindly growth. In summer, once the main flush of flowers has finished, trim back each flowering stem to two buds.

Ramblers flower on the old wood, the growth produced the previous season, and they should be pruned immediately after they have finished flowering so that the new growth has time to set buds before winter. Prune young canes (branches) back by about one-third, but remove old canes almost to ground level to encourage new growth from the base. This is just our old friend renewal pruning (see page 113) in a new disguise. In general, ramblers grow taller than climbers. They are best for covering an archway, but their flowers are smaller and they don't bloom over such a long period.

The choice of varieties is much smaller with climbers and by far the most common one is 'Blaze'. Personally, I prefer 'Dublin Bay' which is a brighter red, is a slightly stronger grower, and flowers more freely later in the summer. The best pale pink is probably 'New Dawn' with 'America' being my choice for a darker shade. If I lived in the Niagara region I would grow 'Golden Showers' for a yellow, but this is quite tender and, even with protection, may not survive in Toronto. 'Royal Sunset' has done well in Ottawa but is not easy to find in catalogues. For a white I would plant either 'Ilse Krohn' or 'Swan Lake'. The most famous rambler is 'Dorothy Perkins', a pink, but this is almost impossible to find, as indeed are most ramblers.

In recent years some new climbing roses have been introduced, first by the Central Experimental Farm in Ottawa and later by the research station at L'Assomption, Quebec. Named after Canadian explorers, these do not need winter protection. Look for 'John Cabot', a fragrant, medium-red rose that grows up to

3 m (10 ft.) tall; **'William Baffin'** with clusters of up to 30 fragrant red flowers. This also grows to 3 m (10 ft.). **'John Davis'** is a light pink rose growing 2.5 m (8 ft.) tall that is slightly fragrant and has buds like miniature hybrid tea blossoms. The latest introduction is **'Captain Samuel Holland'**, with clusters of rich pink, semi-double flowers on trailing stems that grow almost 2 m (6 ft.) long. Like all these hardy climbers, it is resistant to blackspot and mildew.

HOW TO GROW

Growing roses is easy; growing prize-winning roses is more difficult. In our climate, growing roses to survive the winter cold and the summer heat is where the skill really lies. So let us look at this business of rose growing from the very beginning.

Roses like a fairly heavy soil, and if your garden is on a light, sandy soil you will either have to amend it or grow something different. They are heavy feeders, which isn't very surprising when you think how much they grow and how many flowers they produce in one season. Because of this they need the kind of soil that acts as a storehouse for plant foods and moisture, a soil with a high clay content. At the same time, roses will not grow in a cold wet soil, so very heavy clay is not suitable either. They need this mythical soil that every avid gardener dreams of, a good clay loam. If you have a yen to grow roses and your soil isn't suitable, you can replace it, but since roses have a deep root system, you should excavate a good two spits deep, about 60 cm (24 in).

Roses must have good light, preferably full sunshine, but certainly no more than a couple of hours of shade morning or evening. If you try to grow them in more shade than this, they will grow but will not bloom. They should also be where the air is moving, out in the open,

not surrounded on three sides by buildings that restrict the air flow. Roses are prone to a large number of diseases and trying to grow them in a poor site is asking for trouble.

Because you may need to work between your roses to mound soil around them for winter protection, don't crowd too many into a small space. Allow 60 to 75 cm (2 to 2 ½ ft.) between plants for bush roses—half this for miniatures. If you have a large blank wall you want to cover in climbers, space them at least a metre (yard) apart.

WHERE TO BUY

When it comes to buying roses you have three choices. You can get them in building supply stores or supermarkets, etc.; you can visit your local nursery or garden centre; or you can order them by mail from a nursery specializing in roses. Each has its advantages.

The chain store or supermarket rose is generally bare-root inside a plastic bag with a picture of the rose printed on it. Providing you remember that these should not be bought once the shoots have started to grow, they are usually good plants of older varieties, for a reasonable price. Some stores also offer roses packed in cardboard boxes. These are only half the depth of the plastic bags and the roots have been severely pruned to make them fit. These plants are not a good buy, whatever their price.

Garden centres and nurseries will also usually have some prepackaged roses. Since these outlets often have cold storage, the plants should be less likely to have started growing, but this is not always the case.

More and more garden centres are selling potted roses. One local nursery explained to me that when they were selling just prepackaged roses they had a lot of complaints about plants that didn't grow. Now that they are selling potted roses that are already established, the buyers realize it must be their own fault if the plants die. At a garden centre the choice of plants is generally greater than at a chain store, there will be newer varieties, and they will generally cost more.

If you get bitten with the rose-growing bug, or see some new variety in a public garden that you must have, then you will probably have to turn to one of the specialist rose nurseries. There are a couple of these in eastern Canada, although many of the large nurseries with many outlets have their own exclusives and a few of the newer introductions.

Buying from the expert ensures the plant you get will be true to name, well-grown in a similar climate (not shipped in from Oregon), delivered at the right planting time and guaranteed to grow. They operate by mail order and, while the plants may cost a few pennies more, this is the best way to get some of the newer varieties. For the really new introductions you will have to import from the breeders in the U.S., Europe, or New Zealand.

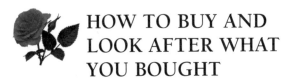

HOW TO BUY AND LOOK AFTER WHAT YOU BOUGHT

The roses that you buy in spring are dug the previous fall and kept in cold storage over winter. To prevent them from drying out, the stems are dipped in a green wax before storage. This wax hides the buds and makes it impossible to inspect the stems properly when you buy prepackaged. It is easy to peel off small pieces so that a couple of buds can be found. If these buds are brown or black and shriveled looking, that cane is probably dead. If the buds are already growing they will have pushed the wax off for you, and you will know not to pick these plants. The buds should be a pink to red or yellowish-green colour, plump but not yet growing. The bud colour is often—but not always—an indication of flower colour. Red-flowered varieties tend to have pink to red buds, white and yellow varieties tend to have green, but this is not written in stone.

The potted roses that you find in garden centres often haven't been potted for long and do not have a good root system inside the pot. If you try to remove the pot too forcibly at planting time, the soil mix will fall away and you will be left with a bare-root plant that has already started to grow. Try to pick plants that have only just started to produce leaves, as early in the season as you can. Or alternatively, leave it fairly late in spring so that the rose bush will have made a lot of roots inside the pot, which will hold the soil ball together.

It may happen that you are wandering round a store or garden centre and give in to an impulse to buy some prepackaged roses. It is only when you get home that you realize that you didn't mean to buy them yet, the bed isn't prepared, and, in fact, you don't even know where the bed is to go! Apart from reminding you that roses need full sun, I can't help you with the bed location. I can, however, help with advice on storing the roses until you are ready to plant them properly.

If you have a vegetable garden or a flower bed that will be filled with annuals later in the season, then your problems are solved. In a vacant spot, dig a trench, banking the excavated soil on one side to form a wall as in Figure 7–1 A. The length of the trench depends on the number of roses you have to deal with; allow about 20 cm (8 in.) for each plant. Unpack the roses a couple at a time and lay them in the trench with the roots down and the tops leaning against the bank (Figure 7–1 B). Dig a second trench alongside the first and turn the soil onto the roots to cover them (Figure 7–1 C). This is known as heeling-in and is only a temporary measure, so you don't need to worry about the roots being straight down or the plants being at the right depth. Lightly tread the soil you just turned to bring

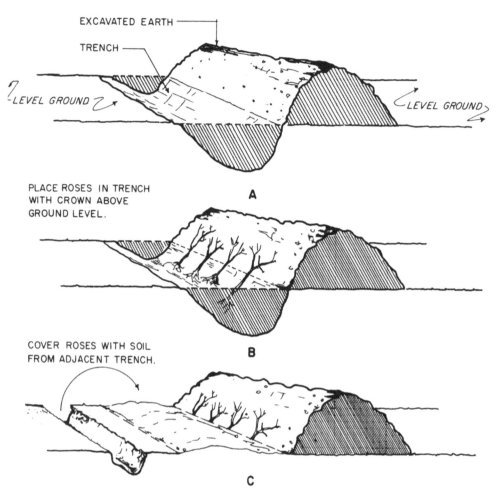

EXCAVATED EARTH

TRENCH

LEVEL GROUND

LEVEL GROUND

PLACE ROSES IN TRENCH
WITH CROWN ABOVE
GROUND LEVEL.

A

COVER ROSES WITH SOIL
FROM ADJACENT TRENCH.

B

C

FIGURE 7-1 "Heeling-in" is a temporary measure designed to keep prepackaged roses happy until planting.

it into contact with the plants and stop them drying out. Water them if the soil is dry, and as needed until planting time; remember that loose soil will dry out faster than the surrounding land. They can be left like this for several weeks if you bought early in the season. They can also be stored in a fridge, basement cold-storage room, or a root cellar should you be lucky enough to have one. They should not be left in their bags sitting on the patio in full sun. In early spring, while the weather is still cool, they could be left in a garage or carport out of direct sunlight for a few days, if absolutely necessary.

If you bought potted roses, leave them in the sun but make sure that you water them. Feel the soil each day and as soon as it is dry to about 5 cm (2 in.), water the pot until water runs out the holes in the base. How often this needs doing depends on the size of the plant, the number of roots, the wind, the temperature, and several other factors that make it impossible to, say, water every Wednesday.

If you ordered your roses from a mail-order nursery and they arrive before you are ready, heel them in as described above or store them in a cool place. You should aim at getting bare-root (which includes prepackaged) roses planted before the buds start to break. Container-grown plants can be planted at any time, even in full flower, as long as you are careful not to disturb the roots. Remember to break the rim off paper-fibre pots below ground level to stop them acting as a wick and allowing moisture to evaporate into the air.

 ## PLANTING

Roses love company. Because they need special treatment in the fall, they are best planted together without other plants, but if you only want to grow a couple of roses, they can be planted in a mixed border with other shrubs, perennials, and annuals. The following two paragraphs refer to bare-root bush roses and miniatures being planted in the spring.

The evening before you are ready to plant, unpack all your bare-root roses and put them to soak in a tub (or several buckets) full of water. We have found that a 12-hour soak greatly reduces the number of plants that don't thrive. Next morning, move one plant into a pailful of water or diluted plant-starter fertilizer, and carry it out to the planting area. The basic rules of planting still apply; the hole should be large enough to take the roots without crowding them; there should be no manure or fertilizer in contact with the roots; and the soil should not be specially prepared for each hole, only for the entire bed. There are, however, one or two special things that apply only to roses. Once you have dug the hole, especially if you are working on your own, make a mound of soil in the centre of the hole and, taking the plant out of the water, sit it on the top of the mound. Lay a piece of wood across the hole to mark ground level and make sure the graft union—where the rose branches come out of the roots—is below ground level by about 2.5 to 5 cm (1 to 2 in.). If you need to adjust the height of the mound, pop the rose back in the water to prevent the roots drying.

If you have someone to help you with the planting, the mound is not essential, but it does help to spread the roots evenly through the planting hole, rather than having them crowded together in the middle. If directions on the bag tell you to plant with the graft union 2.5 cm (1 in.) above ground level, ignore them. That is intended for warmer climates than ours. Somewhere there must be a line that separates the above ground from the below ground, but I have yet to discover where it is. Fill the hole and firm the soil in the normal way and gently pour the bucket of water into the depression that you left to water it in. Once the water has drained away, mound the soil up around the plant to almost cover the canes. This mounding protects the important basal buds from drying and freezing if the weather turns cold. It can also help to keep the buds cool and delay their growth while the bush makes roots if the weather is hot. Refill the bucket with water and go get the next rose to plant.

In colder parts of the country (zone 5 or below) it is worth the extra effort of deep planting. Dig a hole about 45 cm (18 in.) deep and set the rose in this so that the graft union is 10 cm (4 in.) below ground level. If necessary, set the rose bush at an angle so that the roots are not buried too deeply. Fill in over the roots but leave a depression around the neck of the plant. Fill this with a coarse sand or fine gravel. The first summer, leave a depression around each bush so that the union is only about 5 cm (2 in.) below the soil. In winter, mound the roses as described in "Winter Protection," but the following spring only remove the mulch to the original soil level. If the top of the plant is killed by the winter cold, the extra length of stem below ground will normally survive and send up new growth. The sand or gravel around the plant makes it easier for the new shoots to push their way through.

If you bought your roses in pots, plant them

like potted shrubs (but make sure the graft union is below ground level) and only mound them up if it is early in the season. If you left it until the roses were in full growth before you planted them, mounding will not be needed and would actually harm the plant.

Remove the mounds after a couple of weeks unless there are still cold-weather warnings. The plant should be rooted out into the soil and able to support some top growth by then. Now comes the time to prune.

This first pruning is most important because it develops the frame of the bush for future years. Unlike shrubs, with which you should only thin out any weak growth, roses are cut back almost to ground level the first spring. Once you have removed the soil mound, start by clipping off any thin shoots so as to leave just the main branches that are thicker than a pencil. Starting at the base of the cane, count the buds up the stem, noting which way the shoot from that bud will grow. You need an outward-facing bud that is three or four buds up from the base. Prune on a slanting cut, just above this bud, as shown in Figure 7–2. Try not to leave a stub of shoot above the bud because this will only die and be a potential source of infection; at the same time, don't cut so close to the bud that you risk bruising it.

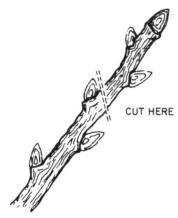

CUT HERE

FIGURE 7–2 In pruning rose bushes, care must be taken to avoid bruising buds, therby increasing the risk of infection.

Do this on each shoot, looking each time for an outside bud so that as the shoots grow, the centre of the plant remains open. In subsequent years do not prune as low—you can leave five or six buds—but the method remains the same.

FERTILIZING

Do not feed newly planted roses until the new growth is at least 5 cm (2 in.) long, but after this you should feed regularly throughout the growing season. Every fertilizer company makes its own special rose food, and no two formulations are the same. Somewhere in the 24-14-14 range seems to be the average. Follow the directions on the bag for amounts. It is best applied as a soluble feed, watered into the ground around each plant. Like fertilizing the lawn, you can either feed little and often or give more at less frequent intervals. Little and often gives the best results but is a lot more work. The basic feeding schedule should be mid-May, late June, and late July with the high nitrogen fertilizer, and a further feeding in mid-August with a high phosphate fertilizer such as 10-30-20 or 10-52-10 (the plant starter). Organic gardeners should use a mixture of fish meal, blood meal, rock phosphate, and greensand applied monthly until the end of July. On established rose beds, a top-dressing of well-rotted cow manure at least 5 cm (2 in.) thick should be applied in spring as soon as the winter protection is removed.

CUTTING

One of the joys of growing roses is cutting some for the house, or entering them in the local flower show. Do remember, the longer stem you cut, the more time it will be before you get another flower on that shoot. Every leaf has a bud at the point where the leaf stalk meets the stem. If anything happens to the growing tip of the stem, the buds in the upper leaves will start to develop and take over the growth of that shoot. As the plant gets taller, the buds in the leaves near the base become progressively more dormant. If you cut a rose with a long stem, you are removing the active buds and forcing some of these dormant buds to wake up and take over the growth of that shoot, which could take some time. Also, flowers tend to be carried at about the same level all over the plant, so not only has a dormant bud got to become active, it also has to grow up to the same height as the other shoots to produce a flower. So don't cut long-stemmed roses when all you need is flowers for a table arrangement.

This is especially true towards the end of the season, from August onwards. New growth produced then will not have time to mature and harden up before winter. If you cut deep into the plant you are asking to have a considerable amount of winter-kill the following spring. When trimming off faded blooms, cut down to the first leaf with five leaflets.

 WATERING

There is a great similarity between lawns and roses. As we have already seen, roses benefit from frequent feedings, just like lawns, and similarly, roses need about 2.5 cm (1 in.) of water each week during the growing season. The use of a rain gauge, located somewhere in the rose bed or close to individual plants, is a great help in knowing when nature needs a hand. A mulch of something like wood chips, 5 to 7.5 cm (2 to 3 in.) deep, really helps to conserve moisture and cut down on the need to water.

Because of certain diseases that favour wet foliage, it is not a good idea to water roses overhead with an oscillating sprinkler or similar equipment. If you are growing only roses in a bed, lay down soaker hoses at the start of the season and connect them up in turn. Put them with the holes pointing down so that the water soaks into the soil rather than spraying up to wet the leaves. With roses grown in a mixed bed, make a saucer-shaped ring of soil around each plant and fill this depression several times using a hose with a water breaker on the end to prevent erosion. It is impossible to measure how much water you are actually adding, but experience will soon tell you if you need to have the soakers running for one hour or two.

By using one of the automatic diluting devices, you can combine feeding your plants with the watering. The easiest is the kind that attaches between the tap and the hose. A thin tube goes into a concentrated mix of soluble fertilizer, mixed at 16 times the normal strength. When the water is turned on, this concentrate is sucked up the thin tube and diluted to the right strength when mixed with the water.

 WINTER PROTECTION

In all of our region some form of winter protection will be needed to bring bush roses through the winter. Obviously, they will need greater pampering in North Bay than Niagara, but the same principles apply. Stop watering your roses in mid-August, because this will help to slow down their growth and make them ready for winter. Not being native plants, roses do not respond to the shortening days in the way that most other plants do, and they try to keep on growing and flowering. If the fall is very dry, give the plants a good watering in late October or early November just before you expect the soil to freeze. Cut the plants back slightly, removing unopened flower buds and any very long shoots that would be broken by winter gales.

Rake up all the fallen leaves and, if necessary, pick the remaining foliage off the bushes. Put these leaves in the garbage, not on the compost heap, because they may have spores of blackspot disease on them. Mound up soil around the base of each plant, as high as you can, but certainly to a minimum of 20 cm (8 in.). If your roses are planted close together, digging this from between the plants would expose or damage the roots, so bring it in from somewhere else, such as a bed in the vegetable garden, or use peat moss. If you use peat moss, cover it with burlap or evergreen boughs to prevent it blowing away. A 100-L bag (4 cu. ft.) will cover about 10 plants.

If your roses are all in one bed, you can surround the bed with snow fencing and pile leaves or straw on top, but let the ground freeze first or you will have trouble with mice. The better the insulating layer over your rose plants, the less winter-kill there will be. If you live in a region where snow comes early and stays all winter, try to shovel a good layer of snow over the bushes as soon as possible. This is the best protection you can give them. Gardeners in the warmer parts where midwinter thaws can be expected will have more difficulty bringing roses through the winter, even though the minimum temperature may not be as low.

Climbers should be taken down from their trellis (wear leather work gloves) and laid on the ground. If you have difficulty bending the canes down, pick a warm day when the canes are more flexible or take them off the trellis and let them hang for a week before tying down. Their own weight will bend them. HINT: Tent pegs hammered into the soil in pairs on either side of the canes make it easy to rope them down and prevent them springing back. Cover them with straw and burlap or with "A" frame boards. Put some mouse bait inside as well to stop mice from

eating all the buds over winter.

Tree roses are difficult. Except in the Niagara region you will need to dig them up and bury them for the winter. Some gardeners dig a trench beside the tree and dig up the roots on the other side. They find they can bend the plant over, with some of its roots still intact, and bury it in the trench. Again, cover with straw and burlap if possible. Burying them against the house foundations is also effective as the soil is a few degrees warmer there.

In the spring, once the snow melts and the soil thaws, don't be in a rush to uncover your roses. The buds in the centre of the soil mound have been well protected and are quite tender. If you suddenly expose them to sharp frosts, they could be killed. Remove the mound over three or four weekends, taking a little off each time to allow the exposed canes to acclimatize. This way, if there is a sudden cold snap you can leave the plant with some of the protection still in place for an extra week or two.

Once the covering soil or peat is all gone, leave the canes alone, even if they seem quite dead. Don't be in a rush to chop off all the old dead wood. It is amazing how often seemingly dead canes will break into growth. If you did a good job of protecting your roses, and they come through the winter with very little dieback, then you can prune them back to about five or six buds as described earlier. If it was a hard winter and there is a lot of winter-kill, you may end up pruning back almost to ground level.

There is one other way worth considering; treat roses like geraniums and just leave them in the garden in the fall without any protection at all. Occasionally they will surprise you and survive the winter anyway. If you bought prepackaged roses on sale, they were probably not much more expensive than geraniums and any survivors can be considered a bonus.

SUCKERS

Buds of the named varieties of bush roses are grafted onto seedlings of a rose species that provides the roots. Because of this, sometimes a shoot will grow from below the graft union. This is known as a sucker. Since these get first choice of the available foods, they grow quickly and, if left, will eventually take over, killing the desired variety. However, just to confuse things, in this part of the world the graft union is below ground level and shoots of the named form sometimes grow from beneath the soil.

There are three ways that will help you decide if the underground shoot on your rose is a sucker or a good guy. Most of the named varieties of roses have five leaflets to each leaf and the rootstocks have seven. Leaves of desirable roses have a few quite large teeth around the edges; those of the suckers normally have many very fine teeth. Thorns on good roses are large, recurved and infrequent (although the number of thorns varies greatly from one variety to another); thorns on the rootstock are thin, straight and numerous.

Because there are several different species used as rootstock, and because the individual varieties of roses differ so much, it is impossible to say that all suckers have seven leaflets and all the good guys five, but if any two of the three differences mentioned above occur on one shoot, it is probably a sucker.

Suckers should be cut off where they arise on the rootstock. Cutting them off just below ground level will only result in a thicket of new shoots coming up. Pulling them off will probably tear the stem and it is generally an injury that gave rise to the sucker in the first place. Use a trowel and carefully dig down alongside the stem to the base of the sucker and cut it off where it starts.

PESTS AND DISEASES

Because of their popularity, roses are grown far more than they would occur in the wild; thus all the problems that can occur with roses become magnified since they have a ready supply of host plants. Many of the pests and diseases also attack other plants and they are dealt with in the final chapter. Here I am concerned with problems that are specific to roses.

BLACKSPOT: This is probably the most important disease of roses. It attacks the leaves, causing small black spots with a yellow margin. In a bad attack the spots can run together, turning most of the leaf surface black. Eventually the leaves turn yellow and fall. This disease overwinters on fallen foliage and on the canes, so good sanitation in the fall will do much to stop reinfection next spring. The spores are spread up the plant by rain (or irrigation) droplets splashing on infected leaves—hence the need for care when watering. The disease starts on the lowest leaves and moves upwards and I have seen plants that have just a few leaves left on the top in very severe cases.

Control is by sanitation as mentioned, by hand-picking the infected leaves as soon as noticed, and by mulching. Spray with lime-sulphur in early spring, as soon as you remove the winter protection, to kill any spores that overwintered on the canes. It may help to spray the soil surface between the plants as well. The fungicide (fungus killer) benomyl is reputed to control blackspot. Some growers swear by it; others swear at it. You can also use an all-purpose rose spray, adding some insecticidal soap as a spreader, and making sure you cover the underside of the leaves. You will need to spray at least twice a month throughout the growing season for good control.

ROSE WILT: A virus disease that causes a single shoot or the entire plant to collapse and die. This and rose mosaic, which causes yellow streaks in the leaves, are spread by sucking insects or by garden tools. There is no control. Dig up and trash infected plants.

CROWN GALL: While this disease does attack other plants it is relatively common on roses. It is a bacterial disease that lives in the soil and causes the base of the stems to become swollen, rough and brown. Plants become stunted, with distorted leaves and flowers, and eventually die. There is no control. Don't plant roses in the same spot for three years; better yet, replace the soil completely.

MILDEW: Different strains of mildew attack a great number of plants. See the last chapter for description and control.

LEAFCUTTER BEES: This pest seems to favour roses, although it does also attack other plants. The adults cut small circular notches from the edge of the leaves. They use this material to construct a nest for their young. Their work is very obvious on the rose bushes but, unless they cut the leaves on a stem you were planning to enter in a competition, it is seldom serious.

ROSE SLUG: This isn't really a slug but a sawfly larvae which mimics one. They eat one surface of the leaf, leaving it semi-transparent; a bad attack can defoliate a plant quickly. Later in the season the adult form attacks the leaves and eats them all, veins as well. Insecticidal soap will control them.

MOSSY ROSE GALL: This problem is more unsightly than dangerous, unless the attack is very bad and every shoot is infected. A small insect lays its eggs inside the stem. When it hatches, the grub puts out a chemical that causes the plant cells to multiply and form a mossy-looking ball. Prune it out as soon as you notice it to stop the pest from completing its life cycle.

There are many other pests that feed on roses as well as other plants. See the final chapter for control of aphids, leafhoppers, thrips, weevils, tarnished plant bugs, Japanese beetles, spider mites, and slugs.

SUGGESTED READING

Rose Gardening on the Prairies. George W. Shewchuk. Lone Pine, 1988.

I would put this at the top of my list for an easy-to-understand book on roses. The author grew over 350 different roses in Edmonton.

Roses. Roger Phillips and Martyn Rix. Random House, 1988.

Like their book on shrubs, this is a picture book of roses of all kinds. Use it with catalogues to put pictures to the names.

Roses for Canadian Gardens. Robert Osborne. Key Porter Books, 1991.

A good, well-illustrated book on the culture, propagation and selection of roses. What a pity this Canadian book uses U.S. hardiness zones.

Tender Roses for Tough Climates. Douglas Green. Houghton Mifflin (Chapters), 1996.
Lois Hole's Rose Favorites. Lois Hole. Lone Pine, 1997.

Two books by Canadian authors—especially for harsh climates.

Easy Roses for North American Gardens. Tom Christopher. Reader's Digest, 1999.

How to know which are the best roses for your climate. I was the Canadian consultant for this.

Plate 17 Upper: *The rose is everyone's favorite flower, but not easy to grow in Canada. This is a hybrid tea type called Flaming Peace.*
Lower: *Floribunda roses have clusters of flowers. This spray of Rumba has 55 blooms and buds.*

Plate 18 Upper: *Sometimes grandiflora roses are hard to tell from hybrid teas. This is Montezuma.*
Lower: *Irish Beauty, another floribunda, only has about six flowers per stem.*

Plate 19 Upper: *Climbing roses can be spectacular, but may need special winter care. The most popular one is Blaze.*
Lower: *John Cabot is a new variety from Agriculture Canada that is hardy and doesn't need winter protection.*

Plate 20 *A well-designed perennial bed will give color from early spring until freeze-up.*

Plate 21 Upper: *Peonies are probably the most popular of all perennials. Single peonies have one row of overlapping petals.*
Center: *Japanese types are similar but have frilly centers.*
Lower: *The double forms are the most popular and easiest to find.*

Plate 22 Upper: *Irises come in a range of heights, with the dwarf forms like Dixie Pixie flowering first.*
Lower: *Tall bearded irises come in many colors, almost everything except bright red. This is Dazzling Gold.*

Plate 23 Upper: *The most popular of modern daylilies is Stella de Oro, a dwarf variety that flowers all summer. It makes a good ground cover.*
Lower: *New varieties, such as Turned On, are a lot different from the old orange roadside lily.*

Plate 24 Upper: *Astilbe is a good choice for moist, shady sites. They come in white, pink, or red shades. This is a German variety called Irrlicht.*
Lower: *Siberian irises also grow best in damp soils but need full sun. This variety is called Ego.*

Perennials

chapter 8

My dictionary gives the botanical definition of *perennial* as "living more than two years." This definition includes woody plants, like trees and shrubs, and bulbs, such as tulips and daffodils—not what is generally meant by the term. Some books use the term *herbaceous perennials*, and this is a lot closer to the mark since *herbaceous* means dying back to the ground each winter. It is still not truly accurate for the plants that we commonly refer to as perennials, since some of these (such as moss phlox) remain evergreen all winter. However you define them, they are extremely popular at the present time, with supply only just keeping up with demand and more and more choices available every year.

Traditionally, perennials have been grown in special borders, usually with a wall or hedge behind them. This stems from the origins of using perennials, when they were cultivated for their medicinal use, not their decorative value; the days when the barbers were surgeons because they had the sharp tools and the monasteries were the source of medicinal knowledge. Plants, many believed, were put on earth for the benefit of humankind, and if a plant looked like a part of the body it was obviously put here to cure that part. Common names of plants, and often their Latin names, reflected this thinking. Lungwort—Latin name *Pulmonaria*—looked like diseased lungs so an infusion of its dried leaves was used to treat consumption. Similarly, the European form of our native liverleaf—*Hepatica*—looked like the liver and was used to treat disorders of it.

In the monastery gardens it was important to have fresh herbs available for the longest time, so they were often planted in an enclosed garden where the walls would collect and reflect the sun's heat. In time, herbs fell out of favour or were replaced by more effective cures, but those plants that had beauty were retained for decorative purposes. And so began the perennial border.

In England, in the late 1940s, there was a nurseryman, Alan Bloom, who has probably done more to popularize perennials than anyone else. His nursery was strictly wholesale but he had large display beds where he would take prospective customers to show them the plants and write down their orders. Eventually, he ran out of walls and hedges to display his plants against and one day was suddenly struck by an idea. Why did perennials always have to have a backdrop? Why couldn't they be grown in beds that you could walk around? Thus was born the idea of island beds.

Nowadays perennials are grown in just about every conceivable situation: in traditional types of borders, in island beds, as low hedges, and as specimen clumps on the lawn, but mostly they are used in mixed borders with shrubs, bulbs, and annuals. It is rare to find a garden without at least one clump of peony, iris, or daylily.

SOIL AND SITE

No matter what your garden type—sand or clay soil, wet or dry site, shady or sunny location—you can find perennials to grow there. Naturally, if you have a good, well drained soil, lightly shaded for part of the day, you will have a much greater choice of plants than with a hot, dry, sand pile. But even on the sand pile there are plants that will survive and grow for you. It therefore follows that the more you can do to improve your soil the greater the range of plants you can grow. As your soil improves year by year, so you will be able to replace some of the dry-soil perennials with more desirable ones.

The one thing to remember when growing any plants that are going to be in situ for several years, be they trees, shrubs, bulbs, or perennials, is that you must take the time to prepare the bed thoroughly. Be extra careful that you remove every piece of the major perennial weeds. Recite these names as you go to sleep at night and learn to recognize their roots in the soil.

COUCHGRASS: This is a rampant creeping grass with fairly tough underground runners. In light soils you can often pull up yards of it, but in heavy soils it breaks off. Use a fork to dig this out—a spade just cuts it up into lengths. The worst thing you can do is rototill it; that cuts it into a multitude of pieces, each of which grows. It is also known as quackgrass, twitch and other less polite names.

CANADA THISTLE: I am not sure why poor Canada has been blamed for this weed since it is native to Europe and only naturalized here. It, too, spreads by underground stems but not nearly as aggressively as couchgrass. Its roots go down very deep and regular digging will only remove the top so that one shoot becomes several.

CREEPING BINDWEED: A relative of the morning glory, this has thin, wiggly, white roots that break very easily. It is usually fairly shallow-rooted but even the smallest piece left in the soil will grow.

MARES TAIL: Most commonly found on poorly drained soils, mares tail, like Canada thistle, is very deep-rooted. This is a very ancient plant and similar species have existed since the time of the dinosaurs. Do not be in a hurry to put in permanent plants if you have this in your soil. It may take a year or more before you can be sure it is killed.

These weeds can all be controlled with glyphosate. I keep a small spray bottle of it mixed ready during the summer (although the makers recommend that you mix it fresh, it doesn't seem to lose its effectiveness when stored diluted). With care, you can spray small patches of persistent weeds if they appear between your plants, as long as you don't get it on the leaves of the desirable plants. You may need to give several treatments, three or four weeks apart, to kill these persistent weeds.

There are also a couple of invasive so-called ornamental plants, sometimes grown in gardens by the unenlightened. These should be considered as noxious as the previous weeds when preparing soil for a perennial border.

BISHOP'S WEED or **GOUT WEED** was mentioned under ground covers in Chapter 3. It is most invasive and great care should be taken to make sure it has been killed before replanting a border. It may take several applications of weed killer to finally eradicate it.

CREEPING or **CHIMNEY BELL-FLOWER** is almost as bad. It has brittle, white roots that grow a new shoot from the smallest piece. I have known this to grow under a concrete path—solid concrete, not patio slabs—and come up the other side. It too may take several applications of glyphosate to eventually kill it. See page 42 for a fuller description.

Beware of planting in beds that are close to shallow-rooted trees, particularly maples. The special bed that you make, with its improved soil, will quickly be filled with roots from this type of tree. They will take all the moisture and your plants will suffer. Unless you are prepared to dig down a metre (3 ft.) or more, and put in a physical barrier such as heavy-duty plastic sheeting, simply cutting off the roots at the edge of the bed will not stop the invasion for more than a few weeks.

I cannot emphasize too strongly that you must match your plants to the situation in your garden. It is no good trying to grow peonies and irises in the shade of a building, hedge, or trees. They will grow, sort of, but you will be most unlikely to ever see any blooms. Also shun areas that get flooded in winter. Spring runoff that flows away is not harmful but sites where a January thaw will leave standing water should be avoided. Even though the plants are dormant, the roots still need some oxygen; a thick layer of ice over the ground prevents the movement of air into the soil and the plants will die.

PLANNING

One of the beauties of perennial plants is that if you don't like what you see one summer, you can change things around in the fall until you get it to your satisfaction. Nevertheless it is probably a good idea to have a basic plan that you can work towards. No matter how marvelous a plant sounds in a gardening book, try not to pin yourself down to specific cultivars of plants unless you are willing to put in a great deal of time tracking down sources. If you live near a good source of perennials, you can be much more adventurous than someone who lives in a small town with one conservative garden centre and who has to rely on mail order.

This is particularly so with the major groups of perennials—things like peonies, irises, daylilies, phlox, or Oriental poppies—where there are many, many named forms available. You could spend several summers searching for a specific variety, when it has probably already been dropped from the catalogue to make room for the "new improved" forms.

Planning is a winter operation, the sort of thing to do when you are not rushed, while you can sit with gardening books and check up on the plants you may be able to grow.

Make a list of each plant's height, time of flowering, flower colour, and special points, as follows.

PEONY	1–1.25 m	June	white, pink, red	different types, single, double, Japanese
IRIS	15 cm–1.25 m	May–June	range of colours but not bright red	dwarfs flower first with tulips
IRIS, SIBERIAN	1.25 m	late June	blue, white	likes wet soils but will grow in normal
POPPY	1–1.25 m	July	pink, red	dies down after flowering

Keep this list beside you as you start to consider the details of your proposed bed. If this is a mixed bed, with shrubs and annuals as well, you probably have the shrub locations already marked and it is a case of choosing perennials that will tone with them, probably flower at different times, and, if they are on the north or east side, will take shade for part of the day.

If your border is to be just flowers, a mixture of perennials and annuals, then you should plan it on paper first. Make it as wide as possible, since narrow borders are difficult to plan and rarely give a satisfactory display. On another sheet of squared paper, make a scale drawing of your proposed bed. Use a large enough scale that you can mark individual plants. Divide the bed into blocks something like Figure 8–1. This is the traditional way of marking out perennial beds, both on paper and on the ground. Make the individual bays large enough to take several plants, about 1.5 m (5 ft.) long or deep. Large, bold perennials, such as globe knapweed, can be left as individual plants but generally you should plant in groups of 3, 5, or 7 for best effect.

Then comes the fun part—trying to visualize the border as it will look at different seasons and juggling the plants on your original list to give a good effect. Remember, you have to take into account the time of flowering and the height as well as the colour. You don't want to end up with all the spring flowers at one end of the border, or all the red plants in one

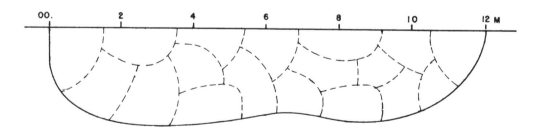

FIGURE 8–1 The traditional method of planning a perennial bed—drawing to scale large enough to mark individual plants.

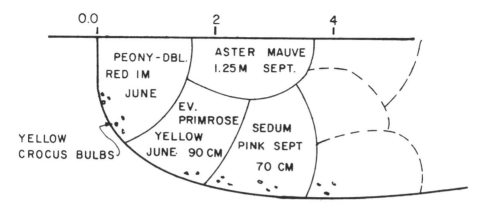

FIGURE 8-2 The colour, flowering time, and height of each flower should be noted on the layout.

place. Tall plants should normally be at the back, but you may want to put them in front of an earlier-flowering plant that dies down and leaves a patch of bare soil.

The texture of the foliage is also very important. Most perennials are only in flower for two or three weeks; the rest of the time it is the leaves that give interesting effects. Try to arrange plants with bold, solid foliage next to those with a fine texture. Contrast leaves of one colour against those of a different tone: blue-green with yellow, dark green against bronze. This will emphasize the texture of the groupings.

Don't forget that if you leave a few pockets for annuals, they should blend or tone with the perennials around them. These pockets can often be used for spring bulbs, tulips and daffodils especially, planted far enough apart that the annuals can be planted between them. Aim at having two or three different plants in each location eventually. Dwarf, early-flowering bulbs, like spring squill and crocus, should be spread throughout the width of the border, not be confined to the front edge. They will come up and give colour before the perennials have started into growth, and their dying foliage will be hidden by the perennials later. Later-flowering bulbs, like tulips, daffodils, flowering onions, and crown imperials, are generally taller and should be planted farther

back between the clumps of perennials that will be growing when the bulbs flower. As gardens get smaller, we need to pack in more plants to make the most of the available space.

You will find that making a list of basic perennials when you are doing the planning invaluable. Having decided to put a border phlox in a particular spot, you can refer back to the list to see what colours are available as you fill in the other plants around it, and change your original choice if it would clash. But colour is such a personal thing: what may seem a terrible combination to me, in your opinion may be glorious. There are no rules to say that two colours should never be placed together.

The only thing that remains to be done on paper is to decide how many plants you need. If you write the colour, flowering time, and height on the plan, as in Figure 8–2, this will help. Your plants should be about half to three-quarters of their eventual height apart. (Low, wide-spreading plants that you would use for front edging do not follow this rule of thumb. Plant them about 30 cm [12 in.] apart). You will find suggested planting distances in the plant descriptions later in this chapter. Mark the actual planting positions on the plan, but remember that the plants will grow over the edge of your lines, so don't plant close to the line on both sides—see Figure 8–3.

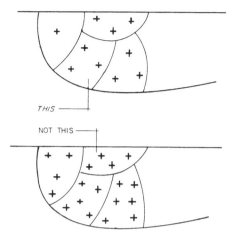

THIS ⎯

NOT THIS ⎯

FIGURE 8-3 Flowers will spread. Do not place them near the edge of the "bays" in your layout.

Make yourself a plant list from the plan and put it away safely. In fact, make several and put them in different places; you may find one when you need it. A good tip is to look for a flower colour rather than a specific variety when you shop. It is much easier to find a red daylily that grows about 75 cm (30 in.) tall than it is to find 'Firestorm'.

 PLANTING

With a few exceptions, perennials can be planted in spring or fall. There is generally a greater choice of plants in the spring, but this is the only reason for planting then. Providing you don't leave it late in the fall when the plants won't have time to make new roots before winter comes, they move just as well as in spring. Ideally, perennials that flower in spring and summer are planted in fall, while those that bloom from September onwards are planted in spring. This way, when you are dividing existing plants, you don't have to cut them down in mid-bloom. The main exceptions are peonies, irises, and Oriental poppies. They are all moved during the summer since they need lots of time to become established before winter. Oriental poppies die down after flowering and then make new leaves in fall which remain over winter. They can only be moved during their dormant period. If irises, peonies, or Oriental poppies are on your plan, plant annuals in their spots until these plants can be moved. Dwarf snapdragons would be good; they are often gone to seed by mid-August anyway.

The majority of perennials are planted like miniature shrubs. Make sure the hole is large enough, don't plant them too deep, and water them well. Most nursery-grown plants are now sold in pots and are simplicity itself to plant. Again, the only exceptions are peonies and irises and they are planted as follows.

Peonies are best moved in mid-August so that their fleshy roots have time to grow before winter. If you look where the roots and stems join, you will see some large pinkish buds. These must go at least 2.5 cm (1 in.) but not more than 7.5 cm (3 in.) below the surface of the soil (Figure 8–4). If they are shallower or deeper than this the plant will grow but won't flower. This is the source of the old wives' tale about peonies taking seven years to come back into bloom when they are moved.

Irises are moved slightly later than peonies, but still long before the rest of the perennials. These are the German or flag irises that have a thick stem, called a rhizome, on the surface of

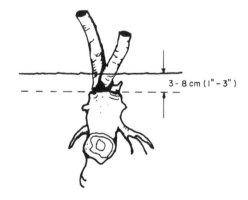

3 - 8 cm (I" – 3")

FIGURE 8-4 Peonies must be planted to just the right depth if they are to flower.

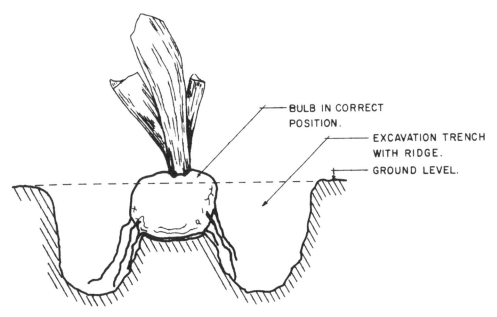

FIGURE 8-5 Iris bulbs are planted with the roots trailing down either side of a ridge, as shown.

the soil. They will normally arrive on your doorstep with the leaves removed down to about 15 cm (6 in.) long and the roots trimmed back. They often have the name of the variety written on the fan of leaves. Dig a hole in the normal way and then, with your hands, make a ridge of soil across the centre of the hole, almost back up to ground level. Sit the iris rhizome on this ridge with the roots going down either side, so that, when the hole is filled, the top of the rhizome will be showing above the soil (Figure 8–5). Fill in around the roots, and unless you have a very heavy clay (which irises don't like anyway), firm the soil around the roots very well.

 ## SUMMER CARE

Aside from the obvious jobs that need doing, such as weeding and removing spent flower heads (usually called dead-heading), there are a couple of tasks that are specific to perennials. One of these will make itself

known if you neglect it, the other is more obtuse but just as important.

The advent of island beds, mentioned earlier in this chapter, led to a radical change in the nature of perennial plants. When borders were planned with a backdrop, the plants could be given support from behind. If you can only walk along one side of a border it is easy to hide the canes and ties behind the plants. However, once island beds came into vogue and you could walk all round the bed, it became much more difficult to hide stakes and canes. As a result, plant breeders started selecting plants that were more stiff in their habit and had less need of support. Also, with the expanding urban population, gardens became smaller and the size of the beds was reduced comparatively. Plants that grow 2 m (6 ft.) or more do not fit into small gardens like they do in large estates and so the demand for these tall plants, which need support, has shrunk to almost nothing.

Staking and tying is a task that shouldn't be neglected, however, on the assumption that modern perennials don't need it. While many will stand straight and tall, a few are still going to need a little help. One of the mainstays of the perennial border, the peony, looks much better if you push three or four canes in round it and run a string around to stop the leaves from drooping all over the nearby plants. One year's experience will tell you which plants need to be given a little assistance to remain upright citizens rather than sleeping partners.

Mark these plants, if necessary, by leaving one cane in place over winter, and put in the supports as soon as growth begins in spring. It is much easier to tie a plant if the canes are already in place and you don't have to struggle with droopy stems at the same time. Tie little and often is a good rule. String is cheap and nothing looks worse than a plant that has flopped over and been gathered up and after tying, looks like a bag of straw tied around the middle. If you use four or five canes to a plant, it is a good idea to put cross-ties from cane to cane over the plant before it grows tall. The plant will grow up through them and they will help to support it. The outside string can be added once the plant has become tall enough. Soft green string, available in the larger garden centres, blends in with the plants and is almost invisible. The stretchy flat plastic tie gives too much for large plants and can break in a strong wind. Knitting wool made of one of the synthetic fibres works very well and can often be bought cheaply at end-of-line sales.

The other chore is one that the majority of gardeners neglect—keeping records. Keep a notebook for jotting down the dates that plants come into flower—and finish. Note possible colour combinations, and any companions that shouldn't be together. Mark the plants that will need to be staked the following year and any that die down early and leave bare patches in the bed. No one can remember everything from one season to the next and the best way to remember is to write it down. All the best gardeners make notes of successes and failures. I use a little tape recorder and talk to myself as I tour the garden. I transcribe the tapes while sitting in the shade during the heat of the day.

It is also a good idea to take photographs of your garden, especially of areas that you are developing but are not sure about. Keep a monthly record at the very least; every two weeks would be better, especially in spring when bulbs come and go so quickly. Then in the winter, you can sit down and spread out the pictures and decide that, yes, there was a lack of colour in August, or there was too much yellow in July, and plan the changes to correct the problem.

One other small task that should not be overlooked is to give a light top-dressing of general fertilizer in midsummer. If you have an abundance of compost, spread a 5- to 10-cm (2- to 4-in.) top-dressing between the plants. If not, apply a 6-9-6 or 7-7-7 fertilizer at about a handful to each square metre (yard). This is enough to see that you have put fertilizer on; not so much it looks as though it had snowed.

WHAT TO DO IN FALL

Early-flowering perennials will have finished their growth cycle in September, but those that don't flower until the fall can generally take quite a bit of frost and will continue to give colour for several more weeks. I generally wait until late fall and deal with all the plants at the same time, but you can cut back the early-flowering ones before this if it's more convenient.

Those plants with woody stems—phlox, asters, and the like—should be cut down with a pair of pruning shears or sharp hedging shears (if you use hedge shears it is easier if you have help to hold the top of the plant together). Cut the stems about 25 cm (9 in.) above the ground. I always like to leave a good long stub since this helps to hold insulating snow in place. In spring, I go over the beds again and cut them down to ground level. Don't use these cut stems as a mulch between the plants. There is probably seed on the late bloomers; this attracts mice and once they have eaten the seed, they will dig down and start on the dormant buds. These woody stems do not compost well either, unless you can put them through a shredder, and will take a couple of years to break down.

The tops from plants with soft leaves, such as irises and daylilies, can be put on the compost providing they are not diseased. Cut these plants down almost to ground level. Their leaves will be killed by winter anyway and they will make new foliage next spring. Irises can be cut with a sharp knife, slicing upwards from either side of the fan of leaves, but daylilies really need a sharp pair of shears and three hands to do the task efficiently.

If you planted anything very late, or are trying something that you suspect is of borderline hardiness, you will need to protect it for the winter. If you can get straw, a good layer piled on top and held in place with branches will do the trick (if you can't get branches, knock in tent pegs around the heap and criss-cross garden twine). If you can't get straw, use a pile of leaves with netting or plastic sheeting over them to keep them from blowing away.

There are a few plants, mostly used along the front of the border, which keep their leaves all winter. These shouldn't be cut down in fall, of course. If the leaves still look green when everything else is turning brown, that plant is probably evergreen. If in doubt, don't cut it out.

IN SPRINGTIME

As the snow melts and exposes the plants, inspect them every couple of days, looking for any that have been frost-heaved. If you find anything with its roots showing, push it back into the soil immediately. As soon as the ground is dry enough to walk on without sticking to your boots, give a light top-dressing of fertilizer using the same rate and formula as at midsummer. If possible, gently fork over the bed, using just the tips of the prongs and going down only 5 to 10 cm (2 to 4 in.). This breaks up the crust caused by the winter rains and snow, allowing oxygen to penetrate into the soil, ready for root activity to begin. At the same time, it works the fertilizer into the surface so that it will be washed down into the root zone. Be careful that you don't go too close to the crown of the plant, where you might injure developing buds, and be especially careful where you have clumps of bulbs, since their shoots will be just below the surface.

NEW PLANTS FROM OLD

Although most perennial plants will survive for many years, they do not live forever, and there will come a time when the clumps are so large that something has to be done. How often this will be depends on the individual species. Some, like blanket-flower, need dividing every three years. Others, like peonies, can go for 10 or 20 years without harm. You have the choice of three methods of renewal.

1. Split just those plants that are becoming overcrowded. This means you seldom disturb peonies, but it is difficult to improve the texture of the whole bed.

2. Lift everything out on a regular basis, every five or six years, improve the soil, divide the plants and replant. This is probably the best method (especially if you can work around the peonies), but it is a lot of work.

3. A combination of 1 and 2, in which you lift everything less frequently, but divide the more aggressive plants more often. Plants that have a tendency to spread can be kept in check

for a few years by digging around them annually in late April or early May, and then forking out the traveling shoots.

If you are just wanting an extra piece of a plant to give to a friend or fill a gap in your own garden, you can cut a wedge-shaped piece out of an existing clump with a sharp spade, but once the plant has become large and dead in the centre and is outgrowing its allotted space, major rejuvenation is called for. As a rough rule of thumb, plants that bloom in the spring should be divided in fall, plants that bloom in fall should be divided in spring, and any you are not sure about should also be divided in spring.

With the exception of peonies and poppies, which have fleshy, brittle roots, and iris rhizomes, most perennials have a fibrous root system with many fine roots. These can be divided as follows.

Dig the plants up by spading around the clump, about 10 cm (6 in.) outside the stalks. This will cut off most of the extended roots, but the plant will soon make new ones. Lift the root ball out of the soil and drop it a few times to shake a lot of the soil off. Don't try to be gentle with the plant or you will never be able to subdue it. When you have most of the soil off, stick two garden forks into the middle of the clump, back to back, and push and pull on the handles until the clump splits in half. Depending on the size of the clump to start with, you may have to repeat this several times to make the pieces small enough to handle. Once you have them to a size you can lift with one hand, pull them apart to give pieces with five or six of the old stems. This is the right size to replant. The other 70 or 80 pieces you can give away to friends or sell to enemies. You can also chop the large clumps into smaller pieces with a sharp spade, but this chops through the roots as well, rather than teasing them apart. Use young pieces from the outside of the old clump to replant and throw the worn-out centre away.

Plants with brittle roots are treated in much the same way except that you aren't as rough with them. Use a pointed stick to get the soil out from between the major roots and a sharp hand axe to divide them. Perennials with woody roots, such as old hostas, will divide easier with an axe than a spade, providing you can hit the same place twice when chopping them apart.

HARDINESS

Because most perennials die down to ground level in the fall, they are not as easy to assign hardiness ratings to as woody plants. They are much more subject to things like microclimates, wind patterns, and snow drifts, and a plant that dies for you may grow perfectly well just a few houses away. An area that gets early snow that persists all winter can probably grow a much wider range of plants than a region that gets a midwinter thaw. If the warming trend that we seem to be in continues, it will be interesting to see what plants can be grown in a few years' time. Most of the plants in the following list *should* be hardy to zone 4 at least (any known exceptions are noted) and if your local garden centre sells it, it should be okay for you.

WHAT SHALL I PLANT?

The number of perennials available these days never fails to amaze me. Plants that were hardly ever seen just five years ago are now quite common. The following list contains basic perennials, plants that should grow for you in spite of all you do to them. In some instances, when the choice of varieties is large, I have simply indicated the available colour range; when the choice is more limited, I have given the names of the best forms. If the plant is easy to grow from seed it is noted with "S" and shade tolerance is marked with the ◖ symbol, as in previous chapters.

ANEMONE, WINDFLOWER *Anemone*

There are a large number of anemones, some of which are more suited to the rock garden and others to the woodland walk. One native species, *A. canadensis*, is quite common on roadsides in late spring. They get the common name of windflower from the way in which the flowers of some species move in the slightest breeze. In exposed gardens the flowers may be killed by sharp frosts before they have fully opened.

Japanese anemone *A. x hybrida*
Blooms: Sept.–Oct. Height: 90–150 cm (3–5 ft.) Spacing: 60 cm (2 ft.) apart ◖

The best form is a white usually called **'Honorine Joubert'** but there are also a number of pink-flowered varieties such as **'Queen Charlotte'** and **'September Charm'**. The flowers are cup-shaped with a golden centre and last for several weeks.

ASTER, MICHAELMAS DAISY *Aster*

Asters are a slightly neglected group of plants in North America because people tend to take them for granted. It was the European plant explorers who took these back home and European gardeners who selected most of the named varieties we grow today. The flowers are daisy-like in pastel shades.

New England aster *A. novae-angliae*
Blooms: Sept.–Oct. Height: 90–150 cm (3–5 ft.) Spacing: 60 cm (2 ft.) apart

This is the common large-flowered aster of our roadsides, slightly improved. The best forms are probably **'Harrington's Pink'** and **'Lye End Beauty'**, both pale pink.

New York aster *A. novi-belgii*
Blooms: Sept.–Oct. Height: up to 150 cm (5 ft.) Spacing: 30–90 cm (1–3 ft.) apart

A more refined aster than the last, and one

that has been used frequently to produce new forms. The named varieties vary greatly in height and there are probably a hundred or more different ones, but you will be lucky to find more than two or three in any garden centre. My own favourite is **'Winston Churchill'**, a red that grows about 90 cm (3 ft.) tall. There are numerous dwarf forms suitable for edging of which **'Professor Anton Kippenburg'** (pink) and **'Snow Cushion'** should be easy to find. The New England and New York asters are valuable for their late flowering.

They are rather susceptible to mildew in late summer, so try not to plant them where they are sheltered from passing breezes and divide frequently (every third or fourth year) to keep the clumps small.

ASTILBE *Astilbe hybrids*
Blooms: June–July Height: 60–90 cm (2–3 ft.) Spacing: 45 cm (18 in.) apart ◖◖◖

The ferny foliage and feathery plumes of flowers on astilbes make them a must for the shady garden, where they thrive in moist soils. They will also take sun and drier ground but will not be as lush. Flowers are red, pink, or white and many of the best varieties were developed in Germany and have names like **'Bonn'**, **'Rheinland'**, and **'Koblenz'**. They are a good choice beside a garden pool.

BABY'S BREATH *Gypsophila paniculata*
Blooms: June–Aug. Height: 90 cm (3 ft.) Spacing: 90 cm (3 ft.) apart

Indispensible to flower arrangers for both fresh and dried bouquets. Like peonies, baby's breath does not like to be disturbed, so try to work around it when renovating, or grow it in a special place with other flowers for cutting.

The species itself has single white flowers but the more desirable forms are **'Bristol Fairy'** and **'Perfecta'**, which are double. There are also pale pink forms available such as **'Rosenschlier'** ('Rosy Veil'), and the low-growing **'Viette's Dwarf'**.

BALLOONFLOWER *Platycodon grandiflora*
Blooms: July-Aug.   Height: 60 cm (2 ft.)
Spacing: 45 cm (18 in.) apart S ●

The flower buds, before they open, look like inflated balloons. The new growth is late to emerge so be careful not to damage it with early hoeing. Soft grey-green leaves set off the blue, pink, or white flowers. Good as a cut flower, but it must be planted with the crown 2.5 cm (1 in.) below ground level to succeed. The variety '**Apoyama**' is more dwarf and suitable for the front of the bed.

BARRENWORT *Epimedium*
A group of shade-loving perennials that make good ground covers in a woodland situation, being able to compete with the tree roots. They will take morning and evening sun but not that of midday. Grow them in a woodsy soil, rich in humus, that will hold moisture. New foliage is often tinged pink, and turns a good yellow in fall. Flowers are small, but shaped like those of columbines.
Red barrenwort *E. x rubrum*
Blooms: spring Height: 20–30 cm (8–12 in.)
Spacing: 30 cm (12 in.) apart ●●●●

Red-tinged foliage and crimson flowers in clusters of up to 20 just above the foliage.
Yellow barrenwort *E. x versicolor* 'Sulphureum'
Blooms: spring   Height: 30 cm (12 in.)
Spacing: 30 cm (12 in.) apart ●●●●

Bright green foliage mottled with red when young, and yellow flowers. This species will survive in dry shade.
White barrenwort *E. x youngianum* 'Niveum'
Blooms: spring Height: 15–20 cm (6–8 in.)
Spacing: 20 cm (8 in.) ●●●●

The red-tinged foliage turns red in fall. White flowers, without spurs, in clusters of up to 8.

BEARDTONGUE *Penstemon hybrids*
Blooms: June–Aug. Height: 60–120 cm (2–4 ft.) Spacing: 45 cm (18 in.) apart S

Beardtongues are a North American genus that grow well in sandy soils. They are mostly native to the prairies and Rocky Mountains but several of the species and many hybrids grow well here. The species are rarely found in nurseries and are available as seed from the American Penstemon Society.

'**Husker Red**' is a 75-cm (30-in.) red-leaved cultivar with white flowers that thrives in well-drained soil. Several other named hybrids can be grown from seed and will overwinter, although they may only live for three or four years.

BELLFLOWER *Campanula*
A large number of different bellflowers can be grown in the perennial border, and there are almost as many suitable for the rock garden. A few are very invasive and should be avoided.
Clustered bellflower *C. glomerata*
Blooms: June–July Height: 60 cm (2 ft.)
Spacing: 45 cm (18 in.) apart ●

Stiff, upright growth with the blue or mauve flowers clustered on top of the stem. '**Joan Elliott**' is a particularly good form.
Creeping bellflower *C. rapunculoides*
Blooms: July Height: up to 150 cm (5 ft.)

This is one of the bad guys and should be used with great caution. It is most invasive. The plant has tall slender spikes of mauvish flowers growing from a rosette of basal leaves that are wedge-shaped with toothed margins. Leaves on the flower stems are long and without stalks—just so you know what to avoid.
Milky bellflower *C. lactiflora*
Blooms: June–Aug. Height: 90–120 cm (3–4 ft.) Spacing: 60 cm (2 ft.) apart ●

A free-flowering species with several named forms in shades of pink, blue, and mauve. '**Loddon Anna**' is pink and '**Pouffe**' is a dwarf blue growing about 30 cm (12 in.) tall.
Peach-leaved bellflower *C. persicifolia*
Blooms: July–Aug. Height: 30–90 cm (1–3 ft.)
Spacing: 30–60 cm (1–2 ft.) apart S ●

The species is a good cut flower and easy to grow from seed; the seedlings will vary slightly in colour from pale to deep blue, and there is a white form that will come true. The named forms must be purchased—or begged from a neighbour. Look for the double varieties, especially '**Telham Beauty**', which I used to grow as a cut flower for market in my youth.

BERGAMOT *Monarda hybrids*
Blooms: June–Sept. Height: 90 cm (3 ft.) Spacing: 60 cm (2 ft.) apart ●

Many of the bergamots we grow in the garden are the result of crosses between the two native species. They have aromatic foliage and are useful in potpourri—and this is the plant that gives the distinctive flavour to Earl Grey tea. They suffer badly from mildew in most summers and should not be allowed to grow into big clumps that have poor air circulation. If you divide them every couple of years, the mildew will not be as bad. There are many good varieties in a range of colours: '**Cambridge Scarlet**', '**Gardenview Scarlet**', and '**Adam**' are red; '**Marshall's Delight**' and '**Beauty of Cobham**' are pink; '**Blue Stocking**' and '**Prairie Night**' are purple and '**Snow Maiden**' is white.

BLACK SNAKEROOT—see Bugbane.

BLADDERCHERRY—see Chinese lantern.

BLANKETFLOWER *Gaillardia* hybrids
Blooms: June–Aug. Height: 15–90 cm (6–36 in.) Spacing: 15–45 cm (6–18 in.) apart S

Short-lived, blanketflowers should be divided every couple of years to keep them growing well. They are bright yellow to red with daisy-like flowers. Some seed strains, like '**Portola**', are available and easy, but most named forms, such as '**Baby Cole**', 15 cm (6 in.), and '**Goblin**', 60 cm (24 in.), are increased by division.

BLAZINGSTAR *Liatris*
Another species from the prairies that has become very popular in the last few years. They are now being grown commercially as cut flowers since they last very well in water. The flower spikes are unusual because they open from the top downwards.
Spike gayfeather *L. spicata*
Blooms: Sept. Height: 90 cm (3 ft.) Spacing: 60 cm (2 ft.) apart S

This is the best species for home gardens unless you have a very dry, sandy soil, where the Kansas gayfeather may prove better. Flowers are a reddish-mauve but there is also a white form. A new, slightly shorter strain called '**Floristan**' is available as seed.

BLEEDINGHEART *Dicentra*
Three different species of bleedinghearts have a place in almost every garden, providing you have some shade, as in under shrubs.
Common bleedingheart, Dutchman's breeches *D. spectabilis*
Blooms: May Height: 90 cm (3 ft.) Spacing: 90 cm (3 ft.)

This one needs full sun, and my plants always die down in midsummer so I have to plant something in front to screen the bare spot they leave. Some other people tell me that their plants don't do this, so there must be two forms of the plant. Pink arching sprays of little bleeding hearts (or the breeches of Dutchmen, depending on your imagination). There is also a very beautiful white form.
Plume bleedingheart *D. eximea*
Blooms: May–Aug. Height: 45 cm (18 in.) Spacing: 30 cm (12 in.) apart S ●

Not as readily available as the next, but it has brighter flowers and takes more sun. A white-flowered form is quite often sold.
Western bleedingheart *D. formosa*
Blooms: May–July Height: 30 cm (12 in.) Spacing: 20 cm (8 in.) apart ●●

This one is similar to the last species, with the same fernlike leaves, but it spreads slowly by underground runners if in shady conditions. The species is a pale pink, but named varieties are brighter; **'Adrian Bloom'** is red and **'Bountiful'** is bright pink and longer flowering.

BUGBANE, BLACK SNAKEROOT *Cimicifuga racemosa*
Blooms: Aug.–Sept.   Height: 2 m (7 ft.) Spacing: 120 cm (4 ft.) apart ●●

The odour of the flowers is reputed to banish bugs, which gave this plant its common name. The height given is for the flower spikes, which are like slender white candles. The foliage grows only about 90 cm (3 ft.) tall.
C. simplex
Blooms: Sept.–Oct.   Height: 100 cm (3 ft.) Spacing: 60 cm (2 ft.) apart ●●●

Later flowering and occasionally caught by an early hard frost in Ottawa. The purple form 'Atropurpurea' is tinted a chocolate purple all over, contrasting well with the white flowers.

BUGLEWEED *Ajuga reptans*
Blooms: May–June   Height: 10 cm (4 in.) Spacing: 20 cm (8 in.) apart ●●

The species has green leaves with a bronzy tint and will grow in shade or sun. It can be invasive, spreading by runners, and will become a weed in lawns, if planted close by. The named forms are much preferable, although not as hardy. They tend to revert back to green, and reversions should be trimmed out as soon as they appear. **'Gaiety'**, which has leaves splashed with cream and pink, is sold in many nurseries. It needs full sun to grow well and makes an excellent ground cover that will take being walked on. The flowers are light blue and contrast well with the foliage.

CATMINT *Nepeta*
Catnip is a member of this family, but unless you have cats you want to send to feline heaven, it is not showy enough for border space.

Catmint   *N. faassenii* (but may be sold as *N. mussinii*)
Blooms: July Height: 30 cm (12 in.) Spacing: 30 cm (12 in.) apart

Silvery leaves and spikes of lavender flowers are a very nice contrast to some of the more flamboyant summer perennials. It spreads fairly fast and you may want to plant this in a bottomless container to control its spread. The leaves are scented but don't turn cats on.
Large-flowered catmint   *N. grandiflora*
Blooms: June–Aug.   Height: 60 cm (2 ft.) Spacing: 45 cm (18 in.) apart

The leaves on this species are much greener but the flowers are more showy, especially in the variety **'Blue Beauty'**. It is a good border plant that makes a nice contrast to the reds and yellows of companion plants.

CHINESE LANTERN, BLADDERCHERRY *Physalis alkekengi*
Blooms: July and October Height: 30 cm (12 in.) S

This is listed here purely as a warning. This plant is most invasive and unless you are big on dried flower arrangements, *do not plant this in your garden*. It is grown for the orange inflated seed pod. Buy a bunch on the local market in fall if you would like some for winter decoration, but don't throw it on the compost in spring, in case the seeds survive.

COLUMBINE *Aquilegia hybrids*
Blooms: May–Aug. Height: 60–75 cm (24–30 in.) Spacing: 30 cm (12 in.) apart S ●

There are a large number of species columbines that are beautiful and grow well in the garden, but the ones you are most likely to come across are the long-spurred hybrids. Columbines have no morals and they cross-pollinate very easily. Since bees do the pollinating the plants must be grown in strict isolation to be sure of getting pure seed. Chilling the seed to below 5°C (41°F) for 30 days will improve germination.

'**McKana Giants**' and '**Mrs. Scott-Elliott**' are two long-spurred mixtures, '**Crimson Star**' is bright red and white. An old double-flowered variety that has become popular again is '**Nora Barlow**'. This one will come true from seed and the flowers are double reddish-mauve and without spurs. Columbines are a good plant to attract hummingbirds into your garden.

CONEFLOWER *Rudbeckia laciniata*
Blooms: July–Sept. Height: 90 cm–2 m (3–6 ft.) Spacing: 90 cm (3 ft.) apart

Bright yellow flowers on an upright plant that seldom needs staking. This is another old-timer that marks old homesites. Several dwarfer varieties, such as '**Goldquelle**', have double flowers, but the old-fashioned tall double is '**Golden Glow**'.

CORALBELLS *Heuchera* hybrids
Bloom: May–June Height: 45–60 cm (18–24 in.) Spacing: 30 cm (12 in.) apart ●●●

Ideal plants for moist shade, although they will grow in sun or drier conditions. The flowers are light and airy, from white to red in colour, and make good cut flowers. There are many named forms with diverse parentage including '**Bressingham**', pink; '**Garnet**', rose; '**Plui de Feu**', crimson; and '**Snowflakes**', white.

New varieties grown for their attractive foliage are becoming popular. The first of these was '**Palace Purple**', which has purple, maple-like leaves, but newer varieties have mottled leaves of purple, brown and red. They often have showy flowers. '**Pewter Moon**' has silvered brownish leaves and pale pink flowers, while those of '**Ruby Veil**' are a metallic grey with darker veins.

DAYLILY *Hemerocallis* hybrids
Blooms: July–Sept. Height: 30–120 cm (1–4 ft.) Spacing: 20-60 cm (8-24 in.) apart ●

If you only know the orange daylily that grows wild on the roadsides, then you are in for a big surprise. Modern daylilies have come a long way in the last few years and they now bloom in a wide range of colours from almost white, through cream, yellow, and pink, to bright red. Flowers may be single or double, almost circular or with strap-like petals, and some varieties are strongly fragrant. Many modern hybrids both flower for longer periods and open their individual flowers for a longer time; while each flower still only lasts a day, they no longer close about 6 p.m. Every catalogue I pick up has varieties I have never heard of before and the number of named forms must run into the thousands.

When you look at catalogues you will notice that daylilies are listed as diploid or tetraploid, referring to the number of chromosomes in each cell. In general, the tetraploid varieties have larger flowers with thicker petals, and are better able to withstand summer storms undamaged, but my wife still prefers diploids. You will also find daylilies listed as dormant, semi-evergreen, or evergreen, referring to the amount the foliage dies down in winter. The evergreen varieties require warmer winter temperatures and only a few of these will survive this far north. I have grown semi-evergreen varieties in Ottawa without problems, but most of the varieties grown here are dormant forms.

Daylilies are tough. They will grow in almost any situation and soil but flower best in full sun. They can be moved at any time, even during the growing season if necessary. Because of their spreading root system, they make a good ground cover and are valuable for stopping erosion on banks.

DEADNETTLE, YELLOW ARCHANGEL *Lamium*
These are low plants that make excellent ground covers that will stand up to considerable foot traffic. They tend to spread out of

bounds both by runners and seed, but are easy to pull out.

Spotted deadnettle *L. maculatum*
Blooms: spring, with some bloom into fall Height: 10–15 cm (4–6 in.) Spacing: 30 cm+ (12 in.+) apart sun to ◖◗

An attractive—but somwhat invasive—plant with hairy leaves marked with silver in the centre. '**Beacon Silver**' has reddish-pink flowers and '**White Nancy**' is similar but in white.

Yellow archangel *L. galeobdolon*
Blooms: spring Height: 25–45 cm (10–18 in.) Spacing: 45 cm (18 in.) apart ◖◗

Often put into its own species but now included in Lamium. The yellow flowers are in whirls and the leaves are slightly marked. In '**Hermann's Pride**', the foliage is attractively marked with silvery veins.

DELPHINIUM *Delphinium* hybrids

Blooms: June and August Height: 45–200 cm (18 in.–7 ft.) Spacing: 30–90 cm (1–3 ft.) apart S

These are a must for every garden with perennials. The dwarf forms, such as '**Connecticut Yankees**', are easy from seed if you freeze the seed for seven days first (sow it and stick the pots in the freezer for a week). Named forms are usually grown from cuttings, but the Pacific Giant Series with names like '**King Arthur**', '**Blue Jay**', and '**Galahad**', and some of the taller kinds, like '**Blackmore and Langdon**' mix, can easily be raised from seed.

On an established clump, cutting off some of the new shoots, to leave only three or four, will give you giant flower spikes. Once the spike is finished, cut it down to the first pair of leaves below the flowers and fertilize the plant. Several smaller spikes will usually grow from further down the stem.

DROPWORT—see Meadowsweet.

DUTCHMAN'S BREECHES
—see Bleedingheart.

EVENING PRIMROSE *Oenothera*

Originally given its common name because many species open at night, the forms commonly grown are open all day as well.

Evening primrose *O. fruticosa youngii* (may be *O. tetragona* in nurseries)
Blooms: June Height: 30–60 cm (1–2 ft.) Spacing: 30 cm (1 ft.) apart

Grown for its brilliant yellow flowers, this plant also turns a good red in the fall with a touch of frost. It spreads quite fast but is very easy to divide. It is a good plant to practise on if you are unsure how to go about it.

FALSE DRAGONHEAD, OBEDIENT PLANT *Physostegia virginiana*

Blooms: Aug.–Sept. Height: 90–120 cm (3–4 ft.) Spacing: 60 cm (2 ft.) apart ●

I like the second common name best since the flowers can be pushed to one side of the spike and will stay there, making it great for flower arrangers. The species has mauvish flowers but '**Summer Spire**' is pink and '**Summer Snow**', white. There is a form with green and white leaves which is attractive even when out of flower.

FOXGLOVE *Digitalis* hybrids

Blooms: June–July Height: 90–150 cm (3–5 ft.) Spacing: 60 cm (2 ft.) apart S ◖◗

Strictly, these are biennials which flower the second year from seed and then die. Look for '**Giant Shirley**' and '**Excelsior**' in seed catalogues. There are some interesting small-flowered species such as the rusty foxglove (*D. ferruginea*) and the yellow foxglove (*D. grandiflora*), which are readily available and are true perennials.

GASPLANT *Dictamnus albus*

Blooms: June–July Height: 90 cm (3 ft.) Spacing: 60 cm (2 ft.) apart S ●

An interesting plant with dark glossy leaves and white or pink flowers. The seed pods dry well for winter arrangements. The common name comes from a volatile gas given off by the flower stalks, which can be ignited on a still evening without harming the plant—if that's the way you get your jollies!

GERANIUM *Geranium*

Not to be confused with the summer annuals (that are really *Pelargonium*), the true geraniums are hardy, attractive plants, with deeply divided leaves, that flower for a long period. Many of them make good ground covers. They have become very popular in recent years, with more and more species and varieties becoming available.

Bigroot geranium *G. macrorrhizum*
Blooms: June Height: 35 cm (14 in.) Spacing: up to 90 cm (3 ft.) apart ●●

The easiest geranium to identify, the scent of its crushed leaves is unmistakable. This makes a good ground cover that smothers weeds. It propagates from root cuttings, and every time I move a plant, a new one springs up again in the old site from pieces of root. The species has magenta flowers but there are white, pink, and red named forms.

Bloody cranesbill *G. sanguineum*
Blooms: May–June Height: 15 cm (6 in.) Spacing: 45 cm (18 in.) apart ●

A low-growing ground cover, suitable for the rock garden, that will occasionally rebloom in the fall. The bright magenta shade of the flowers is a hard colour to combine with other plants, but named forms are white or pink. The foliage turns crimson in fall.

Cambridge geranium *G. x cantabrigiensis*
Blooms: June Height: 30 cm (12 in.) Spacing: 60 cm (24 in.) apart

A mound-forming plant with bright green leaves with a slight scent. The flowers are bright pink in the variety **'Cambridge'** and white tinged with pink in **'Biokova'**.

Grayleaf geranium *G. cinereum*
Blooms: June Height: 15–30 cm (6–12 in.) Spacing: 30 cm (12 in.) apart ●●

When in bloom, this plant covers itself with pinkish flowers, hiding the foliage. **'Ballerina'** is a pale pink and grows only about half the size given.

'Johnson's Blue'
Blooms: June–Aug. Height: 60 cm (24 in.) Spacing: 60 cm (24 in.) apart

This hybrid does not set seed and so continues to flower for a long time. It a rather sprawling plant, and I have seen it growing up through the lower branches of a shrub, a good combination. The bright blue flowers have a purplish centre.

Meadow cranesbill *G. pratense*
Blooms: June–July Height: 75–100 cm (2½–3 ft.) Spacing: 75 cm (2 ½ ft.) apart

This is one parent of the previous hybrid and has blue flowers with red veins. It makes a good border plant in full sun, but needs a little support to stop it flopping. There are several named forms in different colours, such as **'Mrs. Kendall Clark'**, with pale blue flowers with white veins.

Oxford geranium *G. x oxonianum*
Blooms: June–July Height: 60–90 cm (2–3 ft.) Spacing: 45–60 cm (1 ½–2 ft.) apart

This hybrid is not sterile and several named forms exist. The first was **'Claridge Druce'**, named for the former curator of the University Botanic Garden, Oxford, where this plant was discovered. It has bright pink flowers, while those of **'A.T. Johnson'** are a silvery pink.

GLOBEFLOWER *Trollius* hybrids
Blooms: May and Sept. Height: 60–90 cm (2–3 ft.) Spacing: 60 cm (2 ft.) apart ●

Looking like double buttercups, globeflowers often flower again in the fall. They are equally at home in wet or dry soil. Look for the pale yellow **'Canary Bird'**, bright yellow **'Goldquelle'** and orange *T. ledebouri*.

GLOBE THISTLE *Echinops*
Blooms: July–Sept. Height: 90–120 cm (3–4 ft.) Spacing: 90 cm (3 ft.) apart

This is a very showy plant that rarely needs staking. The leaves are bluish and prickly, and the blue flowers are in globular heads that dry well. It is a fast-growing plant with a deep root system, and you should be prepared to divide it about every third spring. '**Taplow Blue**' is probably the best variety with the brightest flowers.

GOAT'S BEARD *Aruncus dioicus* (may be *A. sylvester* in nurseries)
Blooms: June–July Height: 90–120 cm (3–4 ft.) Spacing: 90 cm (3 ft.) apart ●●

A wide-spreading plant that needs a lot of room once it matures, goat's beard has plumes of creamy flowers that don't remind me in the least of its common name. It also grows well in wet soils or semi-shade.

HELEN'S FLOWER—see Sneezeweed.

HOSTA *Hosta* hybrids
Blooms: May–Sept. Height: 15–120 cm (6 in.–4 ft.) Spacing: 15–120 cm (6 in.–4 ft.) apart ●●–●●●●●

Grown for their foliage, hostas, also known as plantain lilies and funkia are the number-one plant for shade. There are hundreds of named forms and several species, and all are worth a place in the garden. Some are tiny and suited to a shady spot in the rock garden, others are huge and make an accent plant on their own. The leaves may be any shade of green, from almost blue to nearly yellow. They can be variegated on the edges or in the centre with white, cream, yellow, or a contrasting green, and the leaves can be smooth, ruffled, or crinkled. Flowers can be an added attraction on some varieties and are nicely scented in a few. While best in shade, the near-yellows will take a lot of sun, and a species with narrow leaves, the lance-leaved plantain lily, will take full sun.

They make a perfect ground cover for a shady place, although you can't walk on them. In case you hadn't guessed from the above, they are one of my favourite plants.

ICE PLANT—see Showy Stonecrop.

IRIS *Iris*
One of the mainstays of the spring and early summer garden, irises come in several different types and there are hundreds of named forms.
Dwarf bearded iris
Blooms: April–May Height: 10–30 cm (4–12 in.) Spacing: 15 cm (6 in.) apart

Dwarf irises go well with bulbs for giving early spring colour along the edges of garden beds. There is a great range of colour, but the bloom season does not last long. They are classified by their height and time of bloom and by planting different groups they can be in flower for several weeks. Many are deliciously scented (if you can bend that low) with a honey, spicy, or chocolate fragrance.
Tall bearded iris
Blooms: June Height: 60–90 cm (2–3 ft.) Spacing: 30 cm (1 ft.) apart

Irises are one of the most popular of all perennials and come in an amazing range of colours and combinations. Some varieties rebloom in the fall if given a feed of 5-10-10 fertilizer after the first flush of flowers. If your garden is on heavy clay soil, irises will not do well for you. The rhizomes need a well-drained soil with good aeration.

There are two problems specific to irises: borer and soft rot. Borers tunnel into the fleshy underground stem (rhizome) and cause the leaves to yellow and wilt. A bad attack will kill the plants. Once the borers are in the plant, it can only be controlled by drenching the bed with dimethoate. Preventative measures include good sanitation to remove old foliage and overwintering eggs and frequent sprays with pyrethrum from the time the leaves start to grow until they are 15 cm (6 in.) tall.

The soft rot is often introduced by the borers. Rhizomes that are buried or are growing in wet soil also suffer more. There is no cure and it can live for many years in the soil. The leaves rot at the base and fall over and the rhizome becomes soft and foul-smelling. One you have smelled this, you will always recognize it.

Siberian iris
Blooms: June–July Height: 90–120 cm (3–4 ft.) Spacing: 90 cm (3 ft.) apart ◖

Siberian irises bloom just after the tall bearded type. They don't have rhizomes and so are not subject to borers or soft rot. Flowers are smaller and not in as wide a colour range but they are well worth a place in any garden and thrive especially well in wet areas.

JAPANESE PAINTED FERN *Athyrium niponicum pictum*
Foliage: all summer Height: 30 cm (12 in.) Spacing: 15 cm (6 in.) apart ●●●

A very pretty small fern for the front of a shady border in humus-rich soil. They can take some sun, preferably at either end of the day, providing the soil remains moist. The fronds are a silvery green with a pinkish tinge, especially when young. It grew slowly for me until I moved it to a new bed with lots of humus, then it took off!

KANSAS GAYFEATHER—see Blazingstar.

KNAPWEED *Centaurea*
Tough plants that grow best in dry soils, knapweeds make good cut flowers, both fresh and dried. There are several native species of *Centaurea* and once you have seen the garden forms, you will easily recognize them.

Globe knapweed *C. macrocephala*
Blooms: June–July Height: 120 cm (4 ft.) Spacing: 90 cm (3 ft.) apart S

This is the giant of the family with a stiff habit of growth and doesn't need staking. Flowers are bright yellow and the seed heads make good winter decoration.

Mountain bluet *C. montana*
Blooms: May–Aug. Height: 60 cm (2 ft.) Spacing: 45 cm (18 in.) apart

Looking like a large annual cornflower, mountain bluet's main attraction is its long flowering period.

Persian centaurea *C. dealbata*
Blooms: June–Sept. Height: 60 cm (2 ft.) Spacing: 45 cm (18 in.) apart

Similar flowers to *C. montana*, but in pink and mauve shades. **'John Coutts'** has the brightest pink flowers. Foliage is silvery on the underside.

KNOTWEED *Fallopia japonica*
(also known as *Polygonum cuspidatum*)
Blooms: Aug.–Sept. Height: 180–240 cm (6–8 ft.) apart

Sold as Japanese knotweed, Chinese bamboo, and Japanese bamboo, this plant should be avoided like the plague. It is attractive in flower but very, very invasive. There is no place for this in *any* suburban garden.

LAMB'S EARS *Stachys byzantina*
Blooms: spring Height: 45 cm (18 in.) Spacing: 30 cm (12 in.) apart

A valuable edging plant with grey, woolly foliage. Don't plant it too close to the edge or it will flop over the lawn. The pink flowers are not attractive and should be removed. Try to find the variety **'Silver Carpet'**, which is flowerless. My favourite edging varieties are **'Countess Helen von Stein'**, with larger, greyish, almost circular leaves and very few flowers, and **'Primrose Heron'**, which has lemon-tinted foliage in spring.

LEOPARD'S BANE *Doronicum caucasicum*
Blooms: May Height: 45–60 cm (18–24 in.) Spacing: 45 cm (18 in.) apart

Bright yellow daisy-like blooms cover this plant in spring. It always looks as though it is dying in early summer because the leaves wilt in the hot sun, but it recovers each night and doesn't seem to be harmed. The plants go dormant by midsummer and leave a bare patch in the planting.

LOOSESTRIFE *Lysimachia* and *Lythrum*

Two unrelated plants share the common name of loosestrife. They are even in different plant families. Both, however, should be used with caution.

Gooseneck loosestrife *Lysimachia clethroides*
Blooms: late summer Height: 60–90 cm (2–3 ft.) Spacing: 90 cm (3 ft.) apart

An attractive, but somewhat invasive plant with long, arching spikes of white flowers.

Yellow loosestrife *Lysimachia punctata*
Blooms: June–July Height: 75 cm (30 in.) Spacing: 45 cm (18 in.) apart ◖

In rich soils this plant can become invasive and spread rapidly by underground runners. Yellow flowers are in whorls between the leaves.

Purple loosestrife *Lythrum*
Blooms: July–Sept. Height: 60–120 cm (2–4 ft.) Spacing: 60 cm (2 ft.) apart

The cultivation of this species, which is taking over so much of our native wetlands, is now banned in several areas. In view of its invasive nature, its cultivation should not be encouraged—although, with the millions of plants already growing wild, I sometimes wonder if the few we grow in our gardens make much difference.

LUPIN *Lupinus* hybrids

Blooms: June–July Height: 120 cm (4 ft.) Spacing: 60 cm (2 ft.) apart S

Lupins, in mixed colours, are readily available in most garden centres in spring; they are easy to grow from seed providing you gently file the hard seed coat to allow water to penetrate. Lupins do best in cool climates, but if they like your garden they will thrive and flower well; if not, they will die out when the hot weather arrives. Remove the seed heads after flowering to get a second crop of blooms.

MALLOW *Lavatera* hybrids

Blooms: July–Sept. Height: 2 m (6 ft.) Spacing: 2 m (6 ft.) apart

Looking like small hibiscus, these free-flowering, shrub-like plants are good for the back of a border. '**Barnsley**' has pale pink flowers with a darker centre, while '**Burgundy Wine**' is darker pink with dark veins. These have not survived long in my zone 5 garden.

MALTESE CROSS *Lychnis chalcedonica*

Blooms: July–Aug. Height: 60 cm (2 ft.) Spacing: 45 cm (18 in.) apart S

Easily identified by its four-petaled flowers, the brilliant red of Maltese cross is eye-catching, but it is also a hard colour to place with other flowers. Try it next to pale yellows or blues. There are also white and pink forms that are occasionally available. Closely related is **rose campion** (*L. coronaria*), with leaves covered with silver hairs. This can be invasive since it grows readily from seed.

MEADOW-RUE *Thalictrum aquilegifolium*

Blooms: May–June Height: 90 cm (3 ft.) Spacing: 60 cm (2 ft.) apart ●●

This is the most available species. It has mauve or white flowers and the variety '**Thundercloud**' is the brightest. There is also a yellow species, flowering at the same time. '**Hewitt's Double**', a variety of *T. delavayi*, has bright mauve, fully double flowers for a long time in summer. Plant this in a hollow about 15 cm (6 in.) deep and fill the hollow slowly over the first two summers. All the meadow-rues like either shade during the heat of the day or a wet soil if in full sun.

MEADOWSWEET *Filipendula*

According to most books, these do best in a moist, shady location, but they have grown well in my sunny, dry garden. They look rather like astilbes when in flower.

Dropwort *F. vulgaris* (but may be sold as *F. hexapetala*)

Blooms: July–Aug. Height: 60–90 cm (2–3 ft.) Spacing: 45 cm (18 in.) apart S ●●

The leaves are much divided and it looks rather fernlike when not in flower, but upright spikes of small, fragrant, cream blooms soon make you realize it cannot be a fern. It can be increased from pieces of root, so if you move it to a new location it may reappear in the old one.

Queen-of-the-Prairie *F. rubra*
Blooms: June Height: 120 cm (4 ft.) Spacing: 60 cm (2 ft.) apart S ●●

While the leaves of this are still divided, they look nothing at all like the previous plant. The flower spikes are pinkish, rather than cream, and look like cotton candy.

MOSS PINK—see Phlox.

MUM *Dendranthema (Chrysanthemum)* **hybrids**
Blooms: Aug.–Oct. Height: 75–90 cm (2 ¹/₂–3 ft.) Spacing: 60 cm (2 ft.) apart

These fall-flowering mums add so much to the late garden display. They are on the tender side and will often winter-kill in zone 5b and colder unless either protected by snow or planted close to the house. Hardiness varies greatly from one variety to the next with an old pink one called **'Orchid Helen'** being the toughest. Many people are happy to treat them like annuals and buy new plants each spring. If you buy small plants, remove the tips from each shoot several times during the early summer, making the last pinch in July, to produce a bushy plant that will have lots of flower buds.

OBEDIENT PLANT—see False Dragonhead.

ORIENTAL POPPY *Papaver orientale*
Blooms: May–June Height: 60–90 cm (2–3 ft.) Spacing: 60 cm (2 ft.) apart S

As mentioned in the introduction to this chapter, Oriental poppies are one of the plants that should be moved in late summer. They produce evergreen leaves in fall, bloom in early summer, and then die down for a while. This is the time to move them. Because they die down it is best to plant them singly, so the gap they leave in the bed is not too large, and to place a later-blooming plant in front of them to hide the bare spot. Flowers can be up to 20 cm (8 in.) across and the colours range from white through pink to dark red. There are many named forms and the bright red variety **'Allegro'** comes true from seed.

ORNAMENTAL GRASSES
Blooms: summer and fall Height: 15 cm–2 m (6 in.–6 ft.) Spacing: 15 cm–1.5 m (6 in–4 ¹/₂ ft.) apart

It is amazing how the interest in ornamental grasses has developed during the last few years. Grown mainly for their showy seed heads, many grasses are attractive throughout the entire growing season. **Japanese blood grass** (*Imperata cylindrica* 'Rubra'), with its red foliage and stems, and the **golden variegated hakonechloa** (*Hakonechloa macra* 'Aureola') make a good combination in light shade all summer. In fall and winter the waving plumes of grasses like feather reed grass (*Calamagrostis acutiflora* 'Karl Foerster') and the many forms of Chinese silver grass (*Miscanthus sinensis*) add interest. Choose clump-forming grasses and beware of the invasive grasses like blue wild rye (*Elymus glaucus*) that spread by underground runners; they're good for a container, but not for the border.

PEONY *Paeonia* **hybrids**
Blooms: June Height: 90 cm (3 ft.) Spacing: 75 cm (2 ¹/₂ ft.) apart

If I had to pick the all-time favourite perennial it would have to be the peony. Almost every old garden you look at has at least one clump and you can often tell where there was once a farmhouse by the presence of a lilac bush and a peony. Peonies are another plant that needs transplanting at a special time, but, providing you plant them at the correct depth, they will bloom for years. As the flower buds grow, they exude a sweet sap, which the ants collect. This is why you will often see ants running round on the unopened buds, but they don't do any harm. To get bigger flowers, remove all the buds on a stem *except* the top one, as soon as they are large enough to see. If you leave it until the buds are half developed, it won't make much difference.

There are three main types of flowers: **single**, with a row of overlapping petals; **Japanese**, with the same petal structure but more frilly centres; and **double**, where the centre of the flower is a mass of petals. Many of the varieties that are still popular have been around for close to a hundred years; newer is not always better—especially with peonies.

Another type of peony has become more available recently; thanks to tissue culture, **tree peonies** no longer cost an arm and a leg. These have greyish foliage and hugh flowers in pastel shades. They have a woody base and will form a small shrub in mild climates. Mine get cut back to soil level most years, but still produce spectacular blooms.

PERENNIAL SWEET PEA *Lathyrus latifolius*

Blooms: July–Sept. Height: climber to 2.4 m (8 ft.) Spacing: 60 cm (2 ft.) apart S

This is the perennial form of the well-known annual sweet pea, although the flowers are not as large and are without perfume. It needs something to climb on but is excellent for a boundary fence or a trellis. They are easy to grow from seed and you will get plants that flower in a range of pink and mauve shades.

PERSIAN CENTAURIA—see Knapweed.

PHLOX *Phlox*

There are two different types of phlox commonly grown in gardens. One is a dwarf plant often used as edging; the other is much taller.

Moss phlox, moss pink *P. subulata*
Blooms: April–May Height: 10–15 cm (4–6 in.) Spacing: 30 cm (12 in.) apart

Forming a bright green mat for most of the year, in spring it is literally covered with red, pink, white or blue flowers. It makes a good ground cover and will take light foot traffic.

Summer phlox *P. paniculata*
Blooms: July–Aug. Height: 45–120 cm (18 in.–4 ft.) Spacing: 45 cm (18 in.) apart ●

Their beautiful fragrance makes phlox worthy of a place in any garden. Add ease of cultivation and a wide range of colours and you can see why they are so popular. They are very adaptable as far as site and soil go and will take shade for part of the day. Like bergamot, they suffer badly from mildew. Divide them often to keep the clumps small, and plant them in an area with good air circulation.

PLUME POPPY *Macleaya cordata*

Blooms: June–Aug. Height: 1.8–2.4 cm (6–8 ft.)

Any time a friend tells you they have this great perennial that you must have, accept it graciously but inspect it carefully when you get home. If the roots are orange where they broke off, take my advice and don't plant it. As a small plant, plume poppy is nice, with leaves that are pale green above and silvery below and clouds of tiny yellow flowers. Unfortunately, it only stays small for one season and then proceeds to take over the garden. Which is probably why your so-called friend gave it to you in the first place.

PRIMROSE *Primula*

If your garden is shady and the soil is not too heavy, do give primroses a try. The ones listed here are easy and they may tempt you to try some others that need a bit more t.l.c. but are worth the trouble.

Drumstick primrose *P. denticulata*
Blooms: April–May Height: 30 cm (12 in.) Spacing: 20 cm (8 in.) apart S ●●

One of the first to flower, and in a mild winter in southern Ontario they will start to bloom in March. The flowers show colour while they are still down in the rosette of leaves and then elongate to give the "drumstick" effect. Flowers are in shades of mauve and pink, or white.

Polyanthus *P. polyantha*
Blooms: April–May Height: 15–25 cm (6–9 in.) Spacing: 15 cm (6 in.) apart S ●●●

These have a great range of colours; it is one of the few plants that flowers in bright yellow, red, and blue, plus all the pastel shades. They are spring-flowering, with more flowers in the fall if you are lucky, and they are usually available from the garden centre in flower. In late winter you may find them in the supermarket, sold as house plants. Keep the plants watered once the flowers have finished and plant them out later to bloom again the next year.

Siebold's primrose *P. sieboldii*
Blooms: May Height: 25 cm (9 in.) Spacing: 15 cm (6 in.) apart ●●

Flowering later than the first two, this Japanese species has flowers that are pale pink, sometimes splashed with white. It can take more sun than the others but is better in shade. It spreads slowly by underground stems, and if it didn't die down in July, it would be a super ground cover.

PURPLE ANGELICA *Angelica gigas*
Blooms: late summer Height: 1–2 m (3–6 ft.) Spacing: 1.2 m (4 ft.) apart S

A striking plant that grabs attention. Large compound leaves up to 40 cm (16 in.) long, dark red stems, and rich purple heads of flower like Queen Anne's lace. It is often only biennial, dying after flowering, but if you remove the old flowers to prevent seed forming, it will often grow again.

PURPLE CONEFLOWER *Echinacea purpurea*
Blooms: summer to fall Height: 1.5 m (5 ft.) Spacing: 45 cm (18 in.) apart S

Much touted for its medicinal properties, this plant has become widely grown for its showy purple flowers. The named forms, such as '**Bravado**' and '**Magnus**', are brighter and larger. There are also white varieties, but they all seed freely and can become a weed.

PYRETHRUM *Tanacetum coccineum*
Blooms: June–July Height: 60–90 cm (2–3 ft.) Spacing: 45 cm (18 in.) apart

I could never figure out how pyrethrums and chrysanthemums were in the same family—they don't look a bit alike—but botanists have now moved these to a different one, so I am happy. Pyrethrums come in white, pink, and red, with single or double flowers, but they are not hardy north of zone 5.

QUEEN OF THE MEADOW—see Meadowsweet.

RED-HOT-POKER *Kniphofia* hybrids
Blooms: July–Aug. Height: 90–150 cm (3–5 ft.) Spacing: 90 cm (3 ft.) apart

Modern hybrids of red-hot-poker are not necessarily red, but yellow-hot-poker sounds strange. They are a striking plant and should be used with caution—too many can be overpowering. They are slightly tender, and in zone 5a and colder will definitely need a mulch in fall to bring them through the winter.

ROSE CAMPION—see Maltese cross.

RUSSIAN SAGE *Perovskia atriplicifolia*
Blooms: late summer Height: 1.2 m (4 ft.) Spacing: 1 m (3 ft.) apart

This is really a dwarf shrub but it is usually included in perennials since it fits well in a sunny, well-drained border. When in bloom, the fragrant grey foliage is lost in the violet-blue flowers that last for weeks. Cut back to about 15 cm (6 in.) in spring when the buds plump up.

SAGE *Salvia nemorosa*

Blooms: June–Aug. Height: 45–90 cm (18–36 in.) Spacing: 45 cm (18 in.) apart S

Related to the bright red annual, salvia, and the culinary herb, perennial sage is a useful addition for its blue, long-lasting flowers. The best form is a German hybrid called '**East Friesland**', which needs a well-drained soil and is reliably hardy only to zone 6.

SEA HOLLY *Eryngium amethystinum*

Blooms: July–Sept. Height: 45 cm (18 in.) Spacing: 45 cm (18 in.) apart

Looking rather like a small globe thistle, sea holly is easily identified by the young growth, which has a steel-blue colour. The leaves are prickly and may also be blue. The stems can be air-dried for winter decoration but remember to leave some stems to feed the roots for next year.

SHASTA DAISY *Leucanthemum* x *superbum*

Blooms: June–Aug. Height: 90 cm (3 ft.) Spacing: 60 cm (2 ft.) apart S

Shasta daisies are really hybrids between several species and they may be listed as *Chrysanthemum maximum* in catalogues. Single forms look rather like the wild ox-eyed daisy, only bigger, up to 15 cm (6 in.) across. Double forms are also available. The shasta daisies in general are not very hardy, only to about 5b, but '**Silver Princess**'—also called '**Little Miss Muffet**'—is hardy to zone 4b.

SHOWY STONECROP, ICE PLANT *Sedum spectabile*

Blooms: Sept.–Oct. Height: 45–60 cm (18–24 in.) Spacing: 45 cm (18 in.) apart

There are a great many stonecrops, most of which are small and better suited to the rock garden. The showy stonecrop has flat heads of pink to red flowers and grey-green fleshy leaves. '**Autumn Joy**' and '**Meteor**' are brighter and are invaluable for their late colour in the garden.

SILVER MOUND—see Wormwood.

SNEEZEWEED, HELEN'S FLOWER *Helenium autumnale*

Blooms: July–Sept. Height: 60–120 cm (2–4 ft.) Spacing: 60 cm (2 ft.) apart

A rather straggly native that has given us some good named varieties. This plant must be staked from early in the season or it will sprawl all over the place. Flowers range from a bright yellow to a dark mahogany. Look for '**Copper Spray**', '**Butterpat**', and '**Gypsy**'.

SPEEDWELL *Veronica*

One of the best plants for blue flowers in midsummer. They are best in the centre to front of the border and provide a good foil for difficult colours like Maltese cross.

Hungarian speedwell *V. latifolia*

Blooms: June–July Height: 30–45 cm (1–1 ½ ft.) Spacing: 30 cm (1 ft.) apart ●

This species has the most brilliant blue flowers, especially '**Crater Lake Blue**'.

Spiked speedwell *V. spicata*

Blooms: July–Aug. Height: 30–45 cm (1–1 ½ ft.) Spacing: 30 cm (1 ft.) apart ●

Not such a brilliant colour but a less floppy habit of growth. There are several named forms in blue, pink, or white such as '**Barcarolle**' and '**Minuet**'.

Woolly speedwell *V. incana*

Blooms: June–July Height: 45 cm (18 in.) Spacing: 30 cm (12 in.) apart S

This is an ideal edging plant, forming mats of grey foliage with slender spikes of blue or pink flowers. It is good for dry, sandy soils.

SPIDERWORT *Tradescantia* hybrids

Blooms: June–Sept. Height: 60 cm (24 in.) Spacing: 45 cm (18 in.) apart

This plant is named after John Tradescant the elder, who was gardener to Charles I of England and who was responsible for the introduction of many North American plants into England. This species was introduced from Virginia. It gets its common name from the coiled stamens in the centre of the flower that look a bit like a spider. Modern varieties come in all shades of blue, white, mauve, and carmine. They tend to seed readily, especially in clumps of other species, and unless you are careful to pull out unwanted seedlings while small, they can be the devil to remove. 'Pauline' is mauve, 'James C. Wegulin' is pale blue, and 'Osprey' is white with a blue centre.

SPURGE *Euphorbia species*

Related to the Christmas poinsettia, it is the showy bracts that give colour, not the flowers.

Cushion spurge *E. polychroma*
Blooms: spring   Height: 40 cm (16 in.) Spacing: 60 cm (24 in.) apart

A mound-forming plant with bright, lemon-yellow flowers from spring to early summer. Foliage turns coppery in the fall.

Griffiths spurge *E. griffithii*
Blooms: June–July   Height: 2 m (6 ft.) Spacing: 1 m (3 ft.) apart

Spreading slowly by underground stems, this plant makes a good display with its orange-copper blooms, but needs a little support to keep it upright. 'Fireglow' is brighter than the species.

TICKSEED *Coreopsis*

Bright yellow, daisylike flowers on plants that are short-lived and should be divided every couple of years.

Large-flowered tickseed *C. grandiflora*
Blooms: June–Sept.   Height: 20–90 cm (8–36 in.) Spacing: 15–30 cm (6–12 in.) apart

There are several good hybrids of this species, but they must be dead-headed regularly to get a long season of bloom. 'Goldfink' is 20 cm (8 in.) and 'Mayfield Giant' is 80 cm (30 in.).

Thread-leaved tickseed *C. verticillata*
Blooms: July–Sept. Height: 45–60 cm (18–24 in.) Spacing: 45 cm (18 in.) apart

Looking at these two plants, you wouldn't

suspect they were so closely related. This plant has very fine, filmy leaves which become hidden by the small golden flowers. 'Moonbeam' is a light yellow form worth searching for.

WINDFLOWER—see Anemone.

WORMWOOD, SILVER MOUND *Artemesia schmidtiana*
Foliage: all summer Height: 30 cm (12 in.) Spacing: 30 cm (12 in.) apart

Grown for its fine silver leaves, the cultivar name, 'Silver Mound', has become a common name as well. It does have small yellow flowers late in the summer, but they are not conspicuous. If your plant gets straggly by late July, cut it back almost to the ground and it will put up more new growth and become, once more, a silver mound. 'Powis Castle', a hybrid, is taller and more open in habit, with feathery foliage on a 60-cm (24-in.) plant.

Western mugwort *A. ludoviciana*
Foliage: all summer Height: 1.2 m (4 ft.) Spacing: 60 cm (2 ft.) apart

Still silvery, but with broader leaves, these are good choices to give foliage contrast in the border. Look for 'Silver Queen' and 'Valerie Finnis'.

YARROW *Achillea*

These are good plants for poor soils; hot, dry sites will curb their somewhat rambunctious nature and keep them from taking over. Don't plant the common yarrow if you have a rich soil!

Common yarrow *A. millefolium*
Blooms: June–Sept.   Height: 60 cm (2 ft.) Spacing: 45 cm (18 in.) apart S ●

The species itself is white-flowered and it can become a bad weed, especially in lawns. Some of the red-flowered named forms such as 'Cerice Queen' and 'Fire King' are more restrained. In recent years there have been several new, dwarf forms of what would seem to be common yarrow introduced at high prices. They may grow well in Europe with its cooler summers, but in Canada the colours bleach out of the flowers in a couple of days during the hot days of July and August, leaving them an unattractive buff shade.

Dwarf yarrow *A.* x 'Taygetea'
Blooms: June–Sept. Height: 45 cm (18 in.) Spacing: 30 cm (12 in.) apart

This is also a hybrid between the common yarrow and another species, but it is one of the best small plants. The pale yellow flowers are produced continually throughout the summer and dry well for the winter. The foliage is a silvery green and the plant spreads slowly to form a mat.

Fernleaf yarrow *A. filipendulina*
Blooms: July–Sept. Height: 90–150 cm (3–5 ft.) Spacing: 60–90 cm (2–3 ft.) apart

Like the last species, this has its flowers in flat heads, but here they are yellow and larger, up to 15 cm (6 in.) across. While the plants are stiff, they should be given a restraining tie to prevent them blowing over in a strong wind. 'Gold Plate' has the largest flowers; 'Coronation Gold' has flowers half the size, but is much more free-flowering. The flowers on this also air-dry well and keep their colour if dried out of bright light.

Sneezewort yarrow *A. ptarmica*
Blooms: June–Aug. Height: 90 cm (3 ft.) Spacing: 60 cm (2 ft.) apart

This species has masses of small, white, globe-shaped heads of flowers. It cuts well for arrangements and can also be dried. 'The Pearl' is the most common form.

SUGGESTED READING

Taylor's Guide to Perennials. Norman Taylor (with additions by various authors). Houghton Mifflin, 1986.

Perennials, How to Select, Grow and Enjoy. Pamela Harper and Frederick McGourty. Berkley Publishing, 1985.

Successful Perennial Gardening. Lewis and Nancy Hill. Storey Communications, 1988.

These are three basic books with coloured pictures and descriptions of a wide range of perennials and basic growing practices.

Herbaceous Perennial Plants. Allan M. Armitage. Varsity Press Inc., 1989.

This book goes into the details of perennials, describing many cultivars and the conditions they require.

Designing with Perennials. Pamela J. Harper. Macmillan, 1991.

This book delves into the intricacies of design, use, and colour combinations.

Gardening with Perennials, Month by Month. Joseph Hudak. Timber Press, 1993.

A revision of a classic that is invaluable for ensuring a succession of bloom.

Tough Plants for Tough Places. Peter Loewer. Rodale Press, 1992.

The Undaunted Garden. Lauren Springer. Fulcrum Press, 1994.

These two books concentrate on growing good plants in difficult conditions.

Perennials. Roger Phillips and Martyn Rix. Random House, 1991.

A two-volume picture set covering early and late flowering species respectively. This is most useful for identifying unknown perennials.

Annuals

9 chapter

Much as I love perennial plants, and my garden is full of shrubs and herbaceous perennials, I must admit that when it comes to a long-lasting colourful display, you can't beat annuals. No other type of plant will flower for weeks on end with the minimum of maintenance, will survive and bloom in the poorest of soils, or will adapt to such a wide range of situations.

There are annuals suitable for sun, semi-shade, and full shade; for use as cut flowers, ground covers, and temporary hedges; for replacing specimen shrubs; for filling window boxes, planters or hanging baskets; for following bulbs and hiding their foliage as they die down and, of course, for giving colour to the pockets you left for them in your mixed border. They range in height from 5 cm (2 in.) to 2.5 m (8 ft.); there are often large differences among varieties within the same species, so be sure you get a suitable height when you buy.

A large proportion of modern annuals are F$_1$ hybrids. This means they are the result of crossing variety "A" with variety "B." This crossing often has to be done by hand, which is why these seeds are a little more expensive. The results of this cross are larger flowers, greater vigour, and more intense colours. The disadvantage is that if you collect seed from these plants, you will get mostly plants "A" and "B" and only a small percentage of the hybrid. Look at the labels when you buy the plants or seed packet to see if they are F$_1$ hybrids or not.

As you look through the catalogues to decide what to plant, look for a shield logo or the words *All-America Selection winner*. The AAS is a non-profit organization dedicated to promoting plants raised from seed. Each year trial grounds across North America evaluate new annuals and vegetables sent in by breeders and report back to AAS headquarters. Those that rate highly are awarded a medal and can be expected to be superior. (See page 168 for their website.)

SOIL PREPARATION

Growing annuals successfully depends to a large extent on good soil preparation. The soil should have been dug before planting, either the previous fall or in spring, not just a couple of days before you plant. Digging opens up the soil, letting air in and improving the drainage, but it also leaves large air spaces in the soil. Allow enough time for the soil to settle before you plant. Roots growing into air pockets will dry out and die.

Take this opportunity to improve the soil by adding compost, leaf mould, aged manure, or peat moss. Remember that peat moss is not the best choice on heavy clay, since it retains water and the main problem with clay soil is its wetness. On other soils peat is great, *providing* you wet it before you dig it in. If you add dry peat, it removes moisture from the soil without becoming really wet itself.

When you buy peat moss, always check the bags and pick one without holes. Carry it to where you need to use it, carefully cut along the top seams, and add water with the hose until the bottom of the bag bulges out—the water runs through at first. By the next morning the water will have been absorbed by the peat and more water can be added. It will probably take three or four days to wet the peat right through, and you will then see why you carried the bag to where you needed to use it. The only way to move it now is with a front-end loader!

As you spread this wet peat on the garden, ready to dig it in, try not to puncture the plastic bag the peat is in. These bags are most useful in the garden. In the fall they are great for carrying leaves—much more convenient than a wheelbarrow as the leaves don't blow back over the garden. During the summer they can be used instead of a wheelbarrow to collect weeds or hedge clippings. Once they get worn, open them out; the heavy-duty plastic is great for spreading on the lawn when you are lifting and dividing perennials, for instance. Once you are done, it is easy to tip the soil back onto the bed, rather than having to rake it up off the lawn. When the bags get too holey for even this job, use them to line the leaf composter described in Chapter 1.

If you have only small pockets to plant and proper digging isn't possible, try to at least fork the patches over to loosen the soil—it will make planting so much easier. Add fertilizer to all these areas unless you have just dug in compost or manure. Use an all-purpose 6-9-6 or 7-7-7, blend at a handful per square metre (yard), then rake the areas level; this will work the fertilizer into the surface at the same time.

SHOPPING LIST

Plan your garden before you go shopping. Measure the areas you have designated for annuals and write down their sizes. Sit down with a seed catalogue or book on annuals and decide what you are going to plant where. Single colours give a better visual effect than mixed groups of the same species, although using just two shades can be very effective. Visit your local parks and public gardens to get ideas for plant combinations. Take a notebook with you to jot down plants that you see. Try to go midweek when there are staff on duty who can tell you the names of plants not labeled. Make sure you get the variety name as well as the species; when you get to the garden centre, knowing it is a salvia won't help you to find the specific variety that looked just the right height. Make careful notes and put them in a safe place for next spring.

Practise crop rotation. It really helps to reduce the pest and disease problems if you grow a different annual in a given spot each year. There are annuals other than petunias, and you should try not to grow the same plant for four years. There is a wealth of annuals to choose from, and you could easily go ten years without repeating your bedding.

Most homeowners plant annuals much too close together. If the plants are crowded they soon start shading one another and don't reach their full potential. The majority of annuals can be 35 cm (14 in.) apart, which works out to 8 per square metre (7 per square yard). Geraniums can be 40 to 45 cm (16 to 18 in.) apart, while small plants like pinks and dwarf marigolds should be 30 cm (12 in.) apart. Most annuals come in packs of six, so you can round the numbers up or down slightly when making out a list of the plants you need and the quantities to buy. Geraniums and some of the other larger plants that are grown in pots are sold singly.

It is a good idea to keep your shopping list flexible. While you list the desired varieties, also note the heights you need. Then, if, for example, the marigold you wanted is not available, you can at least get a substitute of the right size. Although you planned your garden in meticulous detail, try to get a small pack of something you have never tried before. You can always fit a few more annuals somewhere and growing a plant is far better than reading about it.

If garden centres started selling eggs and bacon, or coats and furniture, there would be an outcry, but it seems that any chain or grocery store can open a so-called garden department with impunity. There are two drawbacks to shopping in non-garden centres: there are no knowledgeable staff to help you make your choice of plants, and if the plants die it is difficult to get replacements because the garden department is long gone. While annuals are unlikely to die, providing they are watered, many of these fly-by-night operations are also selling trees, shrubs, and perennials.

There is a race among sellers of bedding plants to see who can have their plants on sale the earliest. Every year they seem to appear in the stores at an earlier date. Soon they will be on display at Valentine's! One garden centre owner admitted that he was glad when there was a late frost because all the people who had bought their plants early and planted them out were back for a second lot. You, as an informed shopper, are caught in a no-win situation. If you plant out early, you risk having the plants killed by frost; if you leave it until the right time to plant, the selection is much less. The answer is to buy the plants soon after they arrive at the stores, but don't actually plant them until all danger of frost is past.

When contemplating the massed display of annuals on sale, how do you decide which pack to actually buy? Look for the ones that are just showing colour in the flower buds. Plants in full flower take longer to become established when they are planted. Pick up the flats and look at them from the side. Are the plants nice and bushy or are they spindly, with only a single stem and one bud on the top? Are the plants in individual cell packs or planted six to a container? Individual cells grow better because they have little root disturbance at planting time. Are the leaves droopy even if the soil is wet? This can be a sign of insufficient care by the staff if many plants are affected. Next, tip a plant out of its pack and look at the roots. The root ball should have lots of roots with soil showing between them; a ball filled with roots usually indicates that the plant has been growing for too long and is probably starved. Is the soil wet to the base of the pot? If only the top is wet, they have been "splash" watered, a common failing with inexperienced staff. And you thought you were just going to pop to the garden centre and pick up a few annuals!

BRINGING BABY HOME

I always distrust the hardiness of plants I buy from a garden centre as I have seen too many flats brought straight from the greenhouse and sold. Make a point of hardening-off the plants you buy to acclimatize them to conditions in the real world. When you get the plants home, put them on the patio or row them up along the wall of the house in full sun. They should be in full sun all the time, except for those you bought for a shady place. That evening, when the temperature starts to drop, either put the plants in a garage or rig up some sort of shelter over the flats. If there is a frost forecast it would be a good idea to move the plants to a cool basement for the night. You could also leave the plants outside in front of a basement window. If you cover them, then open the window; warmth from the house will keep them frost-free.

The next morning, once any frost has melted, bring the plants out again or remove the covers and allow them to grow in the light. Repeat this procedure each night and morning, gradually shortening the time that the plants spend indoors until, by the 24th of May weekend—the traditional time to plant annuals—they are staying out all night. In other words, treat them like teenagers.

During this time, don't forget to water as needed. "As needed" may be twice a day if the plants are large, the sun is bright and there is a strong breeze. You should also feed them with a 20-20-20 soluble fertilizer every other week, or every week if the plants start turning a pale yellow. Try not to wet the foliage just before dark; it makes it more susceptible to disease; if the plants are dry, water just the soil.

Young plants are like babies, hence the title of this section, and unless there is someone home to take care of their needs during the day, you are probably better to forgo buying early for the best selection and not get your plants until you are ready to put them in the ground. It is no savings to buy the plants early and then kill them off yourself.

PLANTING

Depending on where you live, the 24th of May long weekend may or may not be the best time to plant. Since this date does not actually fall on a weekend most years, the long weekend can be almost a week before the date. Let the weather be your guide to planting, not the calendar, and don't let the fact that all your neighbours have planted their annuals stampede you into doing the same. He who plants last laughs longest, sometimes.

When the weather warms up and the forecasts are no longer predicting "chance of frost in low-lying areas," this is the time to plant. Early in the evening of the day before you plant, water everything thoroughly, whether it needs it or not. The ideal conditions are a cloudy day with rain forecast for later, but failing that, try to plant early in the day so you can water before the sun gets too hot.

Carry the flats out and put them on the grass in front of their respective areas, just to be sure you have something for everywhere. If the plants are in cell packs or individual pots, push them out of the pack from below or turn the pot upside-down and tap around the rim with the handle of your trowel until the plant slides out (dry plants are much harder to remove from the pot than wet ones). Spread the plants out over an area, spacing them evenly. Unless the flower bed is long and narrow, the plants should be randomly spaced, with just the front row in a straight line. A narrow bed looks best if the plants are in rows. Random planting is much more forgiving, and being a plant or two short doesn't matter; you can spread the ones you have a little farther apart.

Lay out only one part at a time since the plants dry quickly when their roots are exposed to the air. In a large bed with several different varieties, you may be able to mark it out like a perennial bed and lay out one variety at a time. With a trowel, dig a hole deep enough to take the root ball, put the plant in place, push soil back around it and firm the soil down with your fingers. There should be a very slight depression around the plant to collect water when you are done. Annuals are tough and forgiving but I doubt if they would have forgiven one planting method I witnessed. A shallow hole was dug, with only a quarter of the root ball below ground level, then soil was pulled up around the plant and patted into place, making a nice mound that would shed the rain away from the plant. I never had the heart to go and see the plantings later in the summer.

If the plants you bought were in small flats, with several plants in the same block of soil, then you have to separate them before planting. This can be done in two ways—you can get an old knife and cut them into single plants, or you can pull them apart. Cutting is neater and ensures that each plant gets the same portion of the old soil, but I always feel that pulling is better since you tend to get longer roots. You will probably need a larger hole to plant flat-grown annuals because the roots are more widespread.

Once you have finished planting an area, water the plants with a plant-starter fertilizer (one with a formula something like 10-52-10) but try not to get it on the leaves, especially if the sun is shining, or it may burn them. I always like to spray the plants with a once-over of plain water after feeding, so there is no danger of them being burnt.

If you are on a really tight budget, you may want to think about growing annuals from seed. This is quite easy indoors but you must have big window sills to fill with plants, or a fluorescent light set-up to grow them under.

There are many annuals that will give a good display if you sow them outdoors in the spring. These are mostly tough and they can be sown before the danger of frost is gone; they will not germinate until the soil temperature is right. Direct-sown annuals will not give you the length of display you will get from planted ones, obviously, but they will flower well and there are some that don't like being disturbed and grow much better this way. If you decide to try this, don't scatter the seed over an area; sow it in rows a few centimetres (inches) apart. You will have to hand-weed at least once, as the weed seeds will germinate just as readily as the flowers. It is much easier to tell which ones to weed out if you can see rows of seedlings all looking the same.

 ## SUMMER CARE

Weeds are the biggest enemy of newly planted annuals. Until the plants become established and start to grow, vigorous weeds can germinate and quickly start to smother them. Weeds competing for light and moisture can severely reduce the growth and flowering of the annuals you so lovingly planted. As soon as you see weeds germinating between your annuals, get out the scuffle hoe and "off with their heads." It only takes a few minutes but it can save you hours of work removing large weeds by hand.

The other main summer job is dead-heading—removing the old flower heads to keep new flowers coming. Depending on your temperament, this can be a weekly task or an ongoing occupation. Some gardeners make a point of going round once a week to remove the old flowers, others pick, pick, pick every time they walk round the garden. As long as the job is done, either way is good.

We all look at our plants and admire the colourful display they are providing, but from time to time you should look at them critically. Are they putting on a first-class show? How do they compare with plants down the street? Are the leaves a good colour? If not, is the problem nutrition or pests? Until the soil is built up to a rich loam, you may have to give an additional feed or two during the summer to keep the plants growing well. A 5-10-10 granular feed is ideal, but the general-purpose 6-9-6 or 7-7-7 mentioned earlier will also do. Just avoid a high-nitrogen fertilizer, which would promote too much growth. Most annuals are relatively pest- and disease-free, but they can be attacked. Specific problems are mentioned in the plant list, while the identification and control of pests is covered in Chapter 14.

WHAT SHALL I PLANT?

The following list of annuals focuses on the ones that are found in almost every garden centre, plus a few of my personal favourites that are a little harder to find or that will grow well from direct-sown seed. All those that can be sown outside and still give a fairly long flowering period are marked with an S. The ● sign indicates those that will take shade. Many varieties of annuals are available in a range of individual colours, with a common name, for example, 'Ultra Red', 'Ultra White', 'Ultra Blue' petunias. These are referred to as a series.

AFRICAN DAISY *Osteospermum*
Height: 30–45 cm (12–18 in.) Spacing: 30 cm (12 in.) apart

The 1999 AAS winning '**Passion Mix**' has a blend of rose, pink, purple, and white 6-cm (2 ½-in.) daisylike flowers. Grow in well-drained soil and full sun. They flower best in cooler weather and are remarkably frost tolerant.

ALYSSUM, SWEET ALYSSUM *Lobularia maritima*
Height: 15 cm (6 in.) Spacing: 35 cm (14 in.) apart S ●

A very easy plant that flowers all summer long and is sweetly scented. It can be transplanted from nursery plants or sown direct and makes a good ground cover. It often self-sows and the seeds will overwinter and come up the following spring. White is the most common colour and the new variety '**Snow Crystals**' is outstanding. There are also forms that have coloured flowers, such as the **Wonderland Series**.

ASTER, CHINA ASTER *Callistephus chinensis*
Height: 30–75 cm (12–30 in) Spacing: 20–35 cm (8–14 in.) apart

Plant asters for a display in late summer. They are excellent for cutting and come in a wide range of colours. They do suffer from a couple of very specific diseases—aster wilt and aster yellows. Buy wilt-resistant varieties and pull up and trash any plants that don't seem to be perfectly healthy. These diseases are spread by sap-sucking insects like aphids and leaf hoppers and can also overwinter in the soil, so crop rotation is a must. Don't let these negative comments put you off growing asters, but be warned these diseases may occur. There is a wide range of heights, so be sure the ones you buy will be the correct size when they grow.

BACOPA *Sutera cordata*
Height: 30 cm (12 in.) Spacing: 30 cm (12 in)

A low, trailing plant, grown from cuttings, that is excellent in hanging baskets or window boxes or as a ground cover. '**Snowflake**' is pure white, while '**Pink Domino**' (also called '**Mauve Mist**') is a pale mauve.

Plate 25 Upper: *The best plant for shade is hosta. They are grown mainly for their foliage. This is a form of the wavy-leaved hosta.*
Lower: *Annuals are well suited for use in containers and can be grown in locations where permanent plants would not survive.*

Plate 26 Upper: *Geraniums are one of the most popular bedding plants. A mix of two pale colors can be eye catching.*
Lower: *Some forms of geranium are best suited to hanging baskets, providing you are home to water them.*

Plate 27 Upper: *Some forms of tuberous begonias are pendulous and are ideal for window boxes or planters.*
Lower: *Wax begonias are a good choice for shady situations. Their foliage may be green or bronze.*

Plate 28 Upper: *This dwarf tulip from Iran (Tulipa urumiensis) is one of the first bulbs
to flower. It will naturalize itself and spreads slowly.*
Lower: *The double form of our native bloodroot flowers for a long time. It
increases slowly and is not often listed in catalogues.*

Plate 29 *You can create a better display by planting different bulbs close together, rather than spreading them across the flower bed.*

Plate 30 Upper: *There are several similar, giant flowering onions that bloom in late spring. They will survive for many years.*
Lower: *The blue flowering onion blooms in summer.*

Plate 31 Upper: *The false autumn crocus (Colchicum) may have single or double flowers. This variety is called Waterlily. The leaves come up in spring.*
Lower: *Some species of true crocus also bloom in the fall. The flowers last for weeks, opening on sunny days and staying closed in bad weather.*

Plate 32 Upper: *Companion planting is fine in theory. This mix of pansies and lettuce looks good.*
Lower: *When the lettuce is large enough to cut it leaves big gaps in the design.*

BEGONIA *Begonia*

There are two different kinds of begonia that are commonly used as annual bedding plants.
Tuberous begonias *B. x tuberhybrida*
Height: 30 cm (12 in.) Spacing: 30 cm (12 in.) apart ●●●

Modern tuberous begonias such as the **Nonstop Series** are often grown from seed and make such a small tuber they are almost impossible to save. They have large flowers up to 10 cm (4 in.) across and come in colours from white and yellow through a range of pinks and salmon to bright red and orange. **'Pinup Flame'**, a 1999 AAS winner, has bright apricot petals flushed with orange. It does well in planters. These tuberous begonias will take full sun, but grow better in some shade.
Wax begonias *B. semperflorens*
Height: 20–40 cm (8–16 in.) Spacing: 25 cm (10 in.) apart ●●●

This type of begonia has a mass of small flowers in shades of white, pink, and red. The **Cocktail** series has bronze leaves while **Ambassador** has green. They can be lifted in the fall before there is danger of frost, potted and brought indoors. They make good house plants if given bright winter light. Outdoors, they require a shaded position.

BIDENS *Bidens ferulifera*
Height: 75 cm (30 in.) Spacing: 60 cm (24 in.) apart

Another low, spreading plant. The size given is its spread. Masses of small, bright yellow, zinnia-like flowers all summer long with light green lacy foliage. Great for edging or planters.

BUSY LIZZY—see Patience plant.

CALIFORNIA POPPY *Eschscholzia californica*
Height: 25 cm (10 in.) S

A charming little annual that dislikes being transplanted; sow it where you want it to flower. It needs full sun and a dryish soil.

Foliage is a greyish-green and lacy, and the flowers are bright red, yellow, and orange, and fluted in the variety **'Ballerina'**.

CASTOR OIL PLANT *Ricinus communis*
Height: 2–4 m (6–12 ft.) Spacing: 1.2 m (4 ft.) apart

The first year we moved into one home, I used this as a very effective temporary tree while deciding which permanent tree to buy. At the end of the summer I had to use an axe to cut it down. It makes a very bold statement in the landscape and should be used with restraint in small sites. One is usually enough. Leaves may be either green or bronze and are the reason for growing this plant. Flowers are small and the fruit is toxic when ripe. If you have young children, the seed pods are easy to remove but rarely ripen in our short growing season.

CHINA ASTER—see Aster.

COCKSCOMB, FEATHER CELOSIA *Celosia*

Although they look quite different, these two plants are closely related.
Cockscomb *C. cristata*
Height: 15–20 cm (6–8 in.) and 60–100 cm (20–40 in.) Spacing: 20 cm (8 in.) and 35 cm (14 in.) apart ●

Available in both short and tall forms, cockscombs have brightly coloured crest-like flowers that are a real conversation piece. Be especially careful to harden off these plants. If they get a sudden chill they stop growing and any flowers already formed fail to develop. A good red is the 1997 AAS winner **'Prestige Scarlet'**.
Feather celosia *C. cristata* var. *plumosa*
Height: 25–40 cm (10–16 in.) and 80–100 cm (30–40 in.) Spacing: 30 cm (12 in.) and 35 cm (14 in.) apart ●●

Feathery plumes of flowers in pink, red, orange, and yellow shades. These are more popular than the cockscombs and flower more freely. The flowers can be air-dried for winter decoration. **'Pink Castle'** is a 1990 AAS winner.

COSMOS *Cosmos*
Height: 60–120 cm (24–48 in.) Spacing: 35 cm (14 in.) apart S

Fairly stiff, upright plants with feathery foliage, cosmos have pink, white, red, or orange flowers. They can be used for a temporary hedge. If sown direct they should be in flower by early August. **'Sunny Red'** is actually orange and was an AAS winner for 1986; **'Cosmic Orange'** was a 2000 winner.

DAHLIA *Dahlia*
Height: 30–90 cm (12–36 in.) Spacing: 45 cm (18 in.) apart

There are several strains of dahlia that can be raised from seed to flower the first summer. They are low-growing, with small flowers in a wide range of colours. Buy plants in individual pots and harden them off properly. They will form tubers during the summer, which can be stored in the same way as the large-flowered hybrids (see Chapter 10).

DUSTY MILLER *Senecio* and *Tanacetum*
Height: 20–25 cm (8–10 in.) Spacing: 30 cm (12 in.) apart ●

Dusty miller is a common name used to cover several different silver-leaved plants. They are used for contrast and as edging. Some have wide leaves; others have finely cut foliage. Remove flower stems as they appear—the blooms are not decorative.

FAN FLOWER *Scaevola aemula*
Height: 30–45 cm (12–18 in.) Spacing: 35 cm (14 in.) apart

This Australian native is grown from cuttings, and plants are available in spring. The blue flowers look like small fans. A spreading plant that's good for planters and baskets. It blends well with licorice plant.

FEATHER CELOSIA—see Cockscomb.

FLOSSFLOWER *Ageratum houstonianum*
Height: 15–30 cm (6–12 in.) Spacing: 30 cm (12 in.) apart ●

One of the best dwarf carpeting annuals. Use it en masse with occasional tall, contrasting plants dotted through, or as an edging. It comes in shades of blue or white. It is, however, a strange blue—it always looks pink in photographs.

FLOWERING TOBACCO *Nicotiana* x *sanderae*
Height: 30–50 cm (12–20 in.) Spacing: 35 cm (14 in.) apart ●●●

The new flowering tobaccos are equally at home in sun or shade. They don't have the perfume of the older, taller kind but the flowers are open all day long, not just in the evening. **'Merlin'** and **'Domino'** are two of the best strains.

Known as **only-the-lonely** for some reason, *N. sylvestris* is an imposing plant, growing up to 2 m (6 ft.) tall with huge leaves up to 60 cm (2 ft.) long. It has long, tubular, white flowers with a very strong perfume. One plant strategically placed scents my patio each evening. It self-seeds readily but is easy to weed out.

FOUR O'CLOCK, MARVEL OF PERU *Mirabilis jalapa*
Height: 60 cm (2 ft.) Spacing: 35 cm (14 in.) apart

An undervalued annual that gives a good display of flowers in a variety of colours. The flowers open in late afternoon, hence one of the common names, but they last all the following day. It forms tubers that can be stored like dahlias. The resulting plants are twice the size given above and bloom profusely. It really opened my eyes to the value of this plant when I started to save the tubers.

GAZANIA *Gazania ringens*
Height: 15–20 cm (6–8 in.) Spacing: 35 cm (14 in.) apart

This South African plant has recently come into prominence. The flowers are daisy-like, in yellow and orange shades, often with a contrasting dark band around the petals. Plants are surprisingly cold tolerant and will carry on blooming well into the fall. They need full sun.

GERANIUM *Pelargonium* x *hortorum*
Height: 30–45 cm (12–18 in.) Spacing: 35–45 cm (14–18 in.) apart ●●

Everybody loves geraniums, and no wonder—they are bright and full of flower for months on end. It is a challenge to bring them through the winter—they often become tall and spindly. Most of the geraniums sold now are grown from seed; in the past they were all overwintered under glass as cuttings. Seed geraniums have fewer disease problems. Look for the '**Pinto**', '**Orbit**', and '**Multibloom**' series. In hot, muggy weather the flowers are attacked by a fungus that causes them to turn black. Pick off all the affected blooms (slide your fingers down the flower stalk and snap it off where it grows from the main stem) and spray the plants with an all-purpose fungicide, or live with poor blooms until the weather cools off.

LICORICE PLANT *Helichrysum petiolare*
Height: 50 cm (20 in.) Spacing: 35 cm (14 in.) apart

Another plant that has become readily available, its grey foliage acts as a foil to bright flowers. It is a spreading plant grown from cuttings; use it as an edging ground cover, or in planters. '**Limelight**' has leaves with a yellow tint.

MADAGASCAR PERIWINKLE—see Vinca.

MARIGOLD *Tagetes*
Height: 15–90 cm (6–36 in.) Spacing: 20–35 cm (8–14 in.) apart S

Marigolds used to be dwarf French with small flowers or tall African with large flowers. Now, however, there is a whole range of heights and flower sizes. Check the label very carefully before you buy, to ensure getting the size you need. Marigolds are very versatile. The rock-garden types form green mounds of ferny foliage studded with little yellow stars. Dwarf types may have single or double flowers on compact plants and make a good contrast to geraniums or salvias. Tall varieties can be used as a temporary hedge or as specimen plants through a contrasting carpet. Failure to bloom is often caused by leafhoppers feeding on the developing buds. Ragged blooms are caused by earwigs eating the petals at night (see Chapter 14).

MARVEL OF PERU—see Four o'clock.

MOSS ROSE *Portulaca grandiflora*
Height: 10–20 cm (4–8 in.) Spacing: 20 cm (8 in.) apart S

Plants for hot, dry, sunny locations. They come in a bright array of colours but flowers open only when the sun shines. It will often self-seed. Look for '**Sundial Peach**', a 1999 AAS winner. New varieties of purslane (*P. oleracea*) have smaller flowers in more muted colours but are good for really dry soils and planters in full sun. These are grown from cuttings, not from seed.

NASTURTIUM *Tropaeolum majus*
Height: 15–30 cm (6–12 in.) Spacing: 35 cm (14 in.) apart S

Nasturtium is so easy to grow from seed. Soak the seeds overnight in warm water and then sow them individually where you want them to flower. Grow in full sun to enjoy a profusion of yellow, orange, or red blooms. Both the flowers and leaves are edible and they brighten up any salad, adding a hot, sharp taste. Watch for aphids—usually the black form—which can rapidly defoliate the plants.

A new type of nasturtium is now becoming widely available. Grown from cuttings and available in spring as plants, these have double flowers in bright colours and a trailing habit that makes them good for planters.

NIGHT-SCENTED STOCK *Matthiola bicornis*
Height: 15–45 cm (6–18 in.) Spacing: 45 cm (18 in.) apart S ●●

I could never see why my wife insisted on sowing this each spring. The scent was nice but the plant never grew very well or produced much bloom. Then one spring, up came a mass of self-sown seedlings. That summer, as we sat on the patio in the evenings, we were bathed in a most glorious perfume that even wafted out to the street. I was converted. Sow this in place, putting little pinches of seed between shrubs and other plants. The flowers are very drab during the day but open in the evening to release their heady scent. Allow this to go to seed in the fall to give you next year's plants. (Don't bother with this if you have air conditioning and spend your summer evenings indoors.)

ONLY-THE-LONELY—see Flowering tobacco.

ORNAMENTAL GRASSES
Height: 30 cm–1.5 m (1–5 ft.) Spacing: 30–60 cm (1–2 ft.) apart

In addition to the perennial grasses in Chapter 8, there are some ornamental grasses that are annuals. **Quaking grass** (*Briza maxima*) has pendulous seed heads that move in the slightest breeze. **Job's tears** (*Coix lacrymae*) has small, round, tear-shaped seed pods. **Fountain grass** (*Pennisetum setaceum*) is one of the joys of a fall border with its feathery plumes of seed. The variety '**Purpureum**' has stems and seeds tinged reddish-purple. All can be cut and air-dried for winter decorations.

PAINTED NETTLE *Coleus* x *hybridus*
Height: 20–60 cm (8–24 in.) Spacing: 30–35 cm (12–14 in.) apart ●●●●

A plant for sun or shade, although some colours may bleach in bright sunlight. This is grown for the leaves, which may be anywhere from a dark, dark red, to pink, cream, yellow, or green, or any combination of these. Leaves may be solid colours, be edged in a different colour, or be a mixture of many hues.

They may be cut into branched fingers like the **Saber Series** or entire like the **Rainbow Series**. Easy to root from cuttings, they can be brought indoors in the fall and grown on a bright window sill. Pick the flowers off, if any develop, as they are not very attractive.

PANSY *Viola* x *wittrockiana*
Height: 15–20 cm (6–8 in.) Spacing: 30 cm (12 in.) apart ●●

Although pansies don't flower as well during the heat of the summer, they are still worth a place in the garden for their spring and fall display. They need shade; plant them under tall shrubs where they will get light shade, but not in areas of heavy shade. Don't remove them with the rest of the annuals in fall; pansies will often overwinter and bloom again the following spring and can be dug out when you plant the new annuals. In warm regions, they may be available in the fall. In this case don't remove them after the spring flowering as they will bloom all summer. Look for the dark orange '**Padparadja**', a 1991 AAS winner or the '**Majestic**' or '**Imperial**' strains in various colours.

PATIENCE PLANT, BUSY LIZZY *Impatiens walleriana*
Height: 15–60 cm (6–24 in.) Spacing: 35 cm (14 in.) apart ●●●

Light shade is a must for patience plant. It will shrivel and die if planted in the sun. The colours are pastel shades of pink, red, mauve, and white, often with a contrasting star of colour. The paler colours seem to glow, especially at dusk, and these were a "must" when we had a shady garden. Like painted nettle, they are easy to grow from cuttings and can be wintered indoors. A different type of patience plant, the New Guinea hybrids, will take brighter conditions; about half sun is ideal. A seed strain called 'Tango' won an AAS award in 1989 but most are raised from cuttings and are grown for their marbled foliage as well as their bright flowers.

PETUNIA *Petunia* x *hybrida*
Height: 30–45 cm (12–18 in.) Spacing: 35 cm (14 in.) apart ●●●

Canada's favourite annual, the petunia is deservedly popular for its reliability to produce an outstanding show under all sorts of conditions. Grow them in beds, borders, baskets, and boxes; in bright shade or sun, they unfailingly put on a great display. This is everyman's annual—petunias will thrive for even the brownest of thumbs.

There are two main types of petunia. **Multiflora** has many small flowers about 6 cm (2 ½ in.) across; **grandiflora** has fewer but larger flowers, up to 10 cm (4 in.) wide. Both types are available with single or double flowers—but to me the doubles never seem to bloom as well. Many petunias have won AAS medals over the years but my favourite is the 1995 winner 'Purple Wave', which forms a carpet of blooms hugging the ground. The **Supercascade Series** has been specially developed for use in containers and hanging baskets.

Plants can get very tall and floppy by early August if grown in a rich soil. If this happens, shear the tops off to about half the height. Within a couple of weeks the plants will be back in flower and looking great again.

Two new classes of petunia that are ideal for planters and hanging baskets have appeared recently. Both are grown from cuttings, rather than from seed. 'Million

Bells' have tiny flowers and much smaller leaves than regular petunias and make compact, trailing plants. They are not really petunias but belong to the genus *Calibrachoa*, although the flowers are petunia-like. The 'Surfinia' types are true petunias but with masses of small flowers on a trailing plant. A basket of pink 'Surfinia' and blue fan flower is a stunning combination.

PINKS *Dianthus chinensis*
Height: 20–30 cm (8–12 in.) Spacing: 25 cm (10 in.) apart

Bright and cheerful plants as long as you dead-head regularly. They lack the fragrance of carnations or the perennial pinks but are good as cut flowers for small arrangements. Red, pink, white, and two-toned flowers are the most common. 'Melody Pink', with sprays of 2.5-cm (1-in.) pink blooms, was a 2000 AAS winner.

SCARLET SAGE *Salvia splendens*
Height: 30–75 cm (12–30 in.) Spacing: 25–35 cm (10–14 in.) apart

This is another plant that varies greatly in height from one variety to another. Much of the colour comes from the bracts (modified leaves) just below the flower, which persist long after the flowers have fallen. New varieties in other colours don't seem to be as free-flowering as the red forms.

A related sage, *S. farinacea*, has blue or white flowers on thin stems growing 60 cm or more (24 in.+). The blue form, called 'Victoria', is frost-tolerant and the flowers dry well.

An All-American winner, *S. coccinia* 'Lady in Red' is almost a perennial. This Texas native may overwinter in milder regions. It grows up to 90 m (3 ft.) tall and the carmine flowers are attractive to hummingbirds and butterflies.

SNAPDRAGON *Antirrhinum majus*
Height: 15–30 cm (6–12 in.) and 75 cm (30 in.)
Spacing: 30 cm (12 in.) and 45 cm (18 in.)
apart

The dwarf snaps are good bedding plants, while the tall ones are better for cut flowers. When the dwarf types start to go out of flower, shear the old spikes off, give the plants a feed with liquid fertilizer, and they will swiftly push up new flower spikes. These are the "bunny rabbits" that children love to play with, but new forms, such as '**Madam Butterfly**', have open-faced flowers, not "bunnies." Be warned if you have young children; they may be disappointed by the lack of "snap."

SUNFLOWER *Helianthus annuus*
Height: 60 cm–3 m (2–9 ft.) Spacing: 35 cm (14 in.) apart S

The dwarfer kinds, such as '**Zebulon**' and '**Teddy Bear**', can be used as bedding, but large varieties are best grown singly from seed sown in place. '**Soraya**', a 2000 AAS winner, has orange petals and a chocolate-brown centre; it makes a good cut flower. Like many sunflowers, the pollen can stain permanently if it gets on fabric; some new varieties are now advertised as being pollen-free. If you like to see birds in the garden, these tall varieties will bring the goldfinches and blue jays once the seed ripens in fall.

SWEET ALYSSUM—see Alyssum.

SWEET POTATO *Ipomoea batatas*
Height: 90 cm (3 ft.) Spacing: 60 cm (2 ft.) apart

Although they do produce edible potatoes, the ornamental forms of sweet potato are grown for their foliage, rather than their fruit. A climber in warm climates, they tend to form mounds here when grown in an open border, but will trail over the edge of a large planter. '**Blackie**' has purple-black foliage, and that of '**Terrace Lime**' is yellow-green.

TOBACCO—see Flowering tobacco.

TUBEROUS BEGONIA—see Begonia.

VERBENA *Verbena* x *hybrida*
Height: 30–45 cm (12–18 in.) Spacing: 35 cm (14 in.) apart ●

Not grown as much as it should be, but those who try it are converted. Useful for hot, dry places, it also does well in window boxes and planters. Flowers are blue, red, pink, and purple, often with a white eye. The 1993 AAS winner '**Imagination**' makes a good ground cover especially on dry soils. It has lacy foliage and a profusion of violet-blue flowers.

A new class of verbena, grown from cuttings, is getting rave reviews. '**Tapien**' and '**Temari**' strains have finer foliage and make spreading to semi-upright plants that are good for edging or containers. They are very frost-resistant and were still in bloom (just) in November in my garden.

One other verbena I wouldn't be without is the species *V. bonariensis*. Easily grown from seed, it reaches 2 m (6 ft.) in height but with thin, wiry stems topped with clusters of mauve-blue flowers. A few plants, dotted through a border, give height without being overpowering.

VINCA, MADAGASCAR PERIWINKLE *Catharanthus roseus*
Height: 30–40 cm (12–16 in.) Spacing: 30 cm (12 in.) apart

Super flowering annuals for hot, sunny locations where they will cover themselves in flower all summer long. Look for the **Cooler Series** in pastel colours, often with a darker eye, and '**Stardust Orchid**' (AAS, 2000), orchid-pink with a white eye and glossy, dark green leaves.

WAX BEGONIA—see Begonia.

ZINNIA *Zinnia elegans*
Height: 15–120 cm (6–48 in.) Spacing: 20–35 cm (8–14 in.) apart S ●

An almost foolproof annual, zinnias are great for cut flowers as well as for giving bright colour in the garden. New dwarf forms with large flowers, such as the '**Peter Pan**' series, have done much to increase the popularity of this plant. '**Crystal White**' is a 1997 AAS winner that, like all zinnias, is drought resistant. The short varieties can be used for planters and window boxes; the taller ones make good hedges. They will also flower in light shade. Flowers come in red, pink, orange, yellow, and a near white. This is also one of the few plants that has green flowers—the variety '**Envy**'.

ANNUAL CLIMBERS

Most gardeners are familiar with perennial and woody climbers such as clematis, honeysuckle, and Virginia creeper, but there are several very good annuals that also climb. Because they have to cram all their growth into a single season, these are vigorous plants. Use them to hide a fence while a woody climber gets established, or to provide rapid vertical colour in a small garden. They are ideal for balcony gardens where perennial vines may not survive, giving a quick screen that is gone before the gales of winter strike. Many can be sown directly where you want them to flower, or you can start them in single pots on a sunny window sill a few weeks before your last frost date.

CANARY CREEPER *Tropaeolum peregrinum*
Height: 2.5–4 m (8–12 ft.) Spacing: 30 cm (12 in.) apart

A fast-growing vine with masses of small yellow flowers and pale green foliage. The flowers have two large upper petals that stand out like wings and smaller ones beneath form the body of the canary bird.

CHILEAN GLORY VINE *Eccremocarpus scaber*
Height: 2–3 m (6–9 ft.) Spacing: 20 cm (8 in.) apart

Start these indoors (or buy plants) to get a long season of bloom. The flowers are 2.5-cm (1-in.) tubes in bright colours from yellow to dark red. Look for '**Tresco Mixed**'.

CUP AND SAUCER VINE *Cobaea scandens*
Height: 3–4 m (9–12 ft.) Spacing: 30 cm (12 in.) apart

Bell-shaped flowers open a creamy yellow and turn purple as they mature. Each flower sits on a green, saucerlike ruff of foliage, hence the common name.

HYACINTH BEAN *Lablab purpurea*
Height: 3–6 m (10–20 ft.) Spacing: 20 cm (8 in.) apart

This may still be listed by its old name of *Dolichos lablab*. It is a vigorous climber that has spikes of purple flowers and broad, flat, shiny, purple pods of beans that add to the display. It needs a strong trellis to take its weight. '**Ruby Moon**' is the brightest coloured selection.

MORNING GLORY *Ipomoea tricolor*
Height: 3–4 m (9–12 ft.) Spacing: 20 cm (8 in.) apart

Do not be too kind to morning glories. Plant them in poor soil without additional compost or fertilizer or you will get lots of growth but few flowers. '**Heavenly Blue**' is a pale sky-blue with a white throat; '**Pearly Gates**' is pure white.

ORNAMENTAL GOURDS *Cucurbita pepo*
Height: 2–3 m (6–9 ft.) Spacing: 30 cm (12 in.) apart

These come in a variety of shapes and colours and are often listed in the vegetable part of seed catalogues, although they are not edible. When laden with fruit, the plants are heavy, so be sure to grow them on a strong trellis. When ripened and thoroughly dry, the fruit can be used for winter decoration indoors.

POTATO VINE, STAR OF BETHLEHEM, *Solanum jasminoides*
Height: 3–6 m (9–18 ft.) Spacing: 30 cm (12 in.) apart

Buy these as plants, which are grown from cuttings. These are a good choice for containers as they will spread outwards and trail over the edge as well as climb. The white, starry flowers have prominent yellow stamens and are produced in clusters. There is also a form with variegated leaves, but it is not as vigorous.

SCARLET RUNNER BEAN *Phaseolus coccineus*
Height: 3–5 m (9–15 ft.) Spacing: 20 cm (8 in.) apart

Here is another vine you will often find hiding in the vegetable section. Showy, bright red flowers attract hummingbirds and give long edible beans. Pick them young and often to keep the plants flowering. This is my favourite bean, both fresh and frozen.

STAR OF BETHLEHEM—see Potato vine.

SWEET PEA *Lathyrus odoratus*
Height: 2–3 m (6–9 ft.) Spacing: 15 cm (6 in.) apart

Sweet peas need sowing early, before the soil warms up. Sow them as soon as the soil is dry enough to work so they can germinate and grow while the soil is cool. They can then withstand the summer heat better. There are hundreds of named varieties with large, fragrant flowers, but some of the old-fashioned varieties, like '**Matucana**' and '**Painted Lady**', which have smaller flowers, have the best scent and are wonderful as cut flowers. Be warned that dwarf sweet peas, like '**Knee-Hi**' and '**Bijou**', are bushy and do not climb.

SUGGESTED READING

Annuals. Derek Fell. Michael Friedman, 1996.
Taylor's Guide to Annuals. Norman Taylor (with additions by various authors). Houghton Mifflin, 1986.

These two books have many coloured pictures which will help you get to know the plants.

Amazing Annuals. Marjorie Mason Hogue, Firefly, 1999.

Very good information and pictures of many of the new plants now available, but a bit skimpy on the old standbys.

Annuals with Style. Michael A. Ruggiero and Tom Christopher. Taunton Press, 2000.

Lots of ideas for using annuals, complete descriptions of the individual species, and masses of good coloured pictures.

The All-America Selections website at *http://www.all-americaselections.org* has information, pictures and sources for the award-winning annuals and vegetables.

The majority of gardening books divide bulbs into spring-flowering and summer-flowering. I can never tell where spring ends and summer begins and prefer to divide them into hardy bulbs that can be left in the ground through the winter, and tender bulbs that are best dug in the fall and stored over winter. True, there are still a few borderline cases that are hardy in Niagara but tender in North Bay, but if in doubt, lift most and just leave a few to test if they freeze or survive.

In the gardening world, the term *bulb* is used very broadly to cover true bulbs, corms, tubers and sometimes rhizomes, but the differences between them needn't worry you. Bulbs are best grown in groups and the size of the group will generally depend on the price of the bulb—100 crocuses or three lilies. Many of them die down for part of the growing season. These can be combined with other plants that will fill the space while the bulbs are resting.

Lovely as tulips and daffodils are, they are finished flowering by June and their foliage has gone by July or early August. If you rely on them to fill your flower bed, you will have a very fleeting display, but if you plant them between clumps of summer- and fall-blooming perennials, or overplant them with annuals, you will have a display that lasts for several months.

 **SOIL AND FERTILIZER**

Because bulbs have to crowd their growth cycle into a short time, it is essential that they be planted in rich soil that will enable the bulb to build itself again. Let's look at a typical bulb to see why this is important. If you cut an onion in half lengthways, you will see a typical bulb cross-section. You can see the swollen leaf-bases that make up the onion scales and, right in the centre, if you use a good hand lens and a little imagination, you can see the embryo flower bud that would have produced a flower had you planted this bulb. When a bulb grows, the leaf-bases provide the food that fuels the emergence of the roots, leaves, and flower. These leaves in turn manufacture food that is stored in their bases to form a new bulb. If your soil is poor, the leaves will not be able to produce much food and the bulb they form will be small, probably without an embryo flower.

Soil should be well drained. Few bulbs will grow well in a wet location. A large number of bulbs in the wild grow on hillsides and meadows at the base of mountain ranges, where they get abundant moisture in early spring from the melting snow and then are in semi-drought conditions for the rest of the summer. You can see this for yourself in the bulbs we grow. Crocuses, which complete their growth cycle in a few weeks, came originally from a more arid region than daffodils, whose foliage may linger on into August. Even the summer-flowering bulbs that obviously have developed in regions with an adequate summer rainfall, don't grow well in a heavy soil that is either wet or baked solid.

The bulb you buy and plant has its flower already formed inside it. No additional fertilizer is going to affect the size of the flower that first year, but the treatment you give once growth starts determines what the flower will be like in the years to come. If possible, dig in compost or other rich humus to the entire area before planting. Otherwise, fork in a low-nitrogen fertilizer such as 5-10-10 at a handful to the square metre (yard)—gardening is not a very exact science. In early spring, when the shoots start to push through the soil repeat this application taking care not to get it on the foliage. If you don't like using granular fertilizers, use a mix of 1 part bone meal and 3 parts weathered wood ash at half this rate.

HOW TO PLANT

In general, the larger the bulb, the deeper it goes. In the plant lists in this chapter, the recommended planting depth is given after the height of the plant. This is the depth to the *bottom* of the bulb, the depth you need to make the hole. Failure to plant at the right depth will lead to poor growth, although bulbs are quite accommodating. A public park superintendent came to me one spring with some poor-looking tulips, stunted, with short stems and twisted leaves, to find out what was wrong. This was only happening at one end of the bed. Was it the soil? I suggested that the bed had been planted late in the day, possibly on a Friday, and his workers were getting tired. The planting depth gradually got less and less across the bed and the samples he brought me were only about 10 cm (4 in.) deep. You could look across the bed and see the height of the flowers getting lower from one end to the other.

Hardy bulbs are planted as early as possible in the fall—with a few exceptions that will be noted. Many bulbs have to make roots before winter comes or they won't grow. If you leave it too late, the soil may be too cold and will keep the bulbs dormant. Spring-flowering bulbs must be planted in the fall. At least once each winter I get a call from someone who "didn't get around to planting and they are still in the fridge. Can I plant them in April?" Sure, if you like, but you are probably wasting your time. I always qualify this with a "probably" since I know one person whose tulips did bloom after spring planting, but in theory they won't.

If you have to plant late for some reason (my usual reason is sale bulbs that I can't resist), mulch them with leaves or straw to keep the frost out of the ground for as long as possible.

Tender bulbs should not be planted until danger of frost is past, or at least until the ground has warmed up. Keen gardeners will plant some of their gladioli early to extend the blooming season but they are willing to cover the new shoots if there is a frost warning. Late spring frosts are seldom hard enough to penetrate into the soil and it will take the shoots about two weeks to break the surface while the soil is still cool. In the fall, leave them for one or two frosts to kill the foliage, but dig before the soil gets cold.

If you have just a few bulbs of a variety, space them out where you want them to bloom and plant them with a trowel (more about spacing later). The bulb planter that is offered in some catalogues is good for the smaller bulbs but not deep enough for tulips and daffodils. If you have a lot of bulbs to go in one area, excavate with a spade to the proper depth, space the bulbs in the bottom of the hole, and fill in. You can get a multilayer planting by choosing three or four types of bulbs that flower at different times and require different depths. Try lilies at the bottom (summer), tulips next (late spring), and crocuses and blue onion mixed on top (early spring and summer) for a bulb cocktail.

When you plant the small, hardy bulbs, such as crocuses, they should go about 10 cm (4 in.) apart. This leaves them room to grow and multiply but still gives a good display the first year. With the larger bulbs, like tulips and daffodils, you have two choices. You can plant them about 15 cm (6 in.) apart, which gives a good splash of colour but makes them hard to hide when not in flower, or you can plant them about 35 cm (14 in.) apart so that you can interplant with annuals once the bulbs have finished flowering. This doesn't have to be an either/or choice; you can combine the two depending on the situation. Between clumps of perennials, the bulbs could be close together, but in gaps left for annuals, they can go farther apart so these spaces can do double duty.

The most popular tender bulbs are gladioli. Since the size of these varies greatly, with some

old bulbs reaching 10 cm (4 in.) across, you should space them from edge to edge, rather than centre to centre. Leave 10 cm (4 in.) between small bulbs and 15 cm (6 in.) between large ones. Like all bulbs, glads look best in groups of a single colour. Three is the minimum to plant; five or more make a better show. The effectiveness of the display increases twice as fast as the number of bulbs planted.

 ## HARDY BULBS

Hardy bulbs are, as the name suggests, hardy. They *do not need to be lifted* after flowering and can stay in the ground ready for next fall. Forgive me for stating the obvious, but every spring I get phone calls from people wanting to know how to store their tulips for the summer, to plant again in the fall.

The most popular spring-flowering bulbs are tulips and daffodils and the bulk of those planted are hybrids. Since they will not come true from seed, you should remove the seed pods. This is a pleasant task and one that can be done as you stroll round the garden seeing what else is coming into flower. The seed pods on tulips are edible (but those on daffs are poisonous) and I never had any problems keeping them dead-headed—my teenage son used to pick and eat them as soon as the petals fell. While I wouldn't encourage young children to eat plants from the flower garden, it is easy to teach older children which ones are safe. Don't remove the flower stalk along with the seed pods; tests carried out in Holland show the old stems contribute considerably to feeding the new bulb.

Allow the rest of the foliage to die down naturally. Cutting it off reduces the food stored in the bulb. Tulip stems will come away at the neck of the bulb with a gentle tug when they are ready. If you have to give a good yank, they have not finished feeding. Many old books suggest you tie daffodil foliage in a knot to make it tidy. While this looks nice, it seriously reduces the food supply to the bulb. With all bulbs, leave the foliage until it is brown and dry and falls away naturally.

Most hardy bulbs will multiply if you can give them the right conditions, although this is not always easy. As mentioned, some live on dry mountain slopes that get meltwater in spring, bake all summer, and then get some autumn rain to start root production again. Conditions like this are hard to duplicate in the average garden. However, the commonly planted bulbs are quite happy in our conditions and will generally multiply and last for many years. Daffodils, crocuses, grape hyacinths, lilies, and some of the small tulips are all at home here. Eventually, they will run out of room to grow and start crowding each other. When this happens the flowers get smaller and the leaves become a pale green. This tells you it is time to lift and divide them, and replant them in some fresh soil.

Leave clumps you want to divide until the foliage starts to die down so the bulbs are built up as much as possible, or mark their location carefully by pushing markers into the soil around the clump and leave them until early fall. Lift them with a fork and shake off most of the soil, then pull the bulbs apart into small groups, or even individual bulbs. Most bulbs grow in clusters and you will easily recognize what should be pulled apart and what should be left joined. Replant in fresh locations or share the surplus with friends. The flowers will still be small the next year since they were formed this year, but they will return to normal after that.

Hybrid tulips are the main exception to this rule. They seldom increase and continue to bloom for many years. Generally, after four or five years the bulbs are worn out and all you get is a lot of single leaves with the odd small flower. These should be dug up and composted. The weather conditions in eastern Canada are not right for tulips to have a long life. They like a long cool spring, not our "blink and you miss it" kind. The soil gets too warm for them and, instead of building up a new large bulb, they fragment into several smaller bulbs. After a few years of this, the bulbs are no longer flowering size.

Some bulbs can be planted in the lawn, where they multiply, a process known as *naturalization*. The sod is lifted and the bulbs planted underneath. They will push their way up through the grass in the spring. When I lift and divide clumps of bulbs, I replant the big ones and naturalize the small ones in a strip of grass along the driveway. I use a bulb planter and make a row of holes, laying the soil plugs alongside them. Then a bulb is dropped down each hole and the plugs replaced. I usually have two or three species to mix together and, over the years, have planted well over a thousand bulbs in this strip. The bulbs have multiplied and are starting to make a colourful display each spring. Almost all the smaller flowering bulbs are suitable, crocus, squill, grape hyacinths, glory of the snow, and the smaller-species tulips.

There are a couple of things to remember; you can't mow these areas until the bulb foliage has started to die down, and you can't use any weed killers while there are any leaves on the bulbs.

If you buy pots of flowering bulbs to brighten the house in winter, with the exception of **'Paperwhite'** and **'Soleil d'Or'** these can be planted in the garden later, providing you don't neglect them. Once the flowers have finished, continue to water the pots as needed and keep them in a bright window. In early spring, gradually start to withhold water to encourage the bulbs to go dormant. When danger of frost is past, put the pots outside and lay them on their sides. When the bulbs are completely dormant, tip them out of the pots, clean off the soil and either plant them immediately or store them in a paper bag until early fall, then plant them like newly purchased bulbs. They may not flower well the following spring, but should bloom properly after that. You cannot force bulbs successfully for two years running but you can plant them out.

WHAT SHALL I PLANT?

The following list, like previous listings, denotes shade with the ◗ symbol.

ANEMONE *Anemone*
Small spring- and early summer-flowering tubers that look like pieces of dried leather when you buy them. Soak them overnight in warm water to plump them up. You can usually see the dormant buds which tells you which way up to plant. If in doubt, plant them on their sides so the shoots and roots only have to turn 90 degrees to grow in the right direction.

Greek anemone *A. blanda*
Blooms: early spring Height: 10 cm (4 in.) Depth: 5–7 cm (2–3 in.) ◗◗

A pretty plant with ferny leaves and blue, pink, or white blooms. If given midday shade it will self-seed and increase slowly.

Poppy anemone *A. coronaria*
Blooms: late spring to summer Height: 30–45 cm (12–18 in.) Depth: 10 cm (4 in.) ◗◗

This is a borderline plant that will survive the winter in warm regions, but is best planted in spring and lifted in the fall where winters are very cold. The two common forms are '**De Caen**' with single flowers, and '**St. Brigid**' with double. Both come in a wide range of velvety colours and are excellent cut flowers.

There are two other spring-flowering anemones that are occasionally available (usually on sale tables at garden clubs): the white-flowered **wood anemone** (*A. nemorosa*) and the yellow **buttercup anemone** (*A. ranunculoides*). Both grow from thin, brown rhizomes,

which should be planted just below the soil surface under shrubs.

BLOODROOT *Sanguinaria canadensis*
Blooms: spring Height: 20 cm (8 in.) Depth: 10 cm (4 in.) ●●●

The common bloodroot is a native woodland plant that will grow well in the garden as long as it is in shade. If you ever see the double form on sale, grab it, for it is a most desirable plant. The flowers are made up of many rows of petals and, unlike their wild parent, they last for weeks. Providing you have light shade, such as under shrubs, this plant is a must.

BLUEBELL *Hyacinthoides hispanica*
Blooms: late spring Height: 40 cm (16 in.) Depth: 10 cm (4 in.)

While the English bluebell does not seem to grow well in our climate, the Spanish bluebell thrives. This produces its flowers all around the stem, rather than on only one side, and comes in blue, pink, or white. '**Excelsior**' is blue but has a darker stripe on each petal.

BLUE ONION—see Flowering onion.

BULGARIAN ONION—see Flowering onion.

CHECKERED LILY—see Fritillary.

CHINESE CHIVES—see Flowering onion.

CHIVES—see Flowering onion.

CROCUS *Crocus*
There are three main groups of crocuses, two of them are common, while the third deserves to be better known.

Small-flowered crocus *C. chrysanthus* and other species
Blooms: very early spring Height: 10 cm (4 in.) Depth: 10 cm (4 in.)

These are usually about the first bulbs to

flower. Plant a group in a spot that catches the early sun, where you know the snow melts first. They will often push up through the snow and flower before it melts. There are many different species and a few hybrids that fall into this group. Some of the earliest are **'Snow Bunting'**, **'Golden Bunch'**, **'Lady Killer'**, and **'Whitewell Purple'**.

Large-flowered crocus *C. vernus*
Blooms: spring Height: 15 cm (6 in.) Depth: 10 cm (4 in.)

This group is more popular than the small-flowered ones, but doesn't have their charm. They are very reliable and will flower for years if divided occasionally. They are also relatively inexpensive, so you can plant them by the hundreds to make a real splash of colour. These are good for planting in the lawn because they die down very quickly. **'Remembrance'**, **'Pickwick'**, **'Peter Pan'**, and **'Vanguard'** are all good varieties.

Autumn crocus *C. speciosus, C. sativus* and other species
Blooms: autumn Height: 15 cm (6 in.) Depth: 10 cm (4 in.) ◖

They're not well known but are often available from the specialty nurseries and mail-order catalogues. They have to be planted in late summer and will flower that fall. The leaves appear in spring and die down by early summer. These enjoy a little shade, especially at midday. They are not as hardy as the spring crocuses and don't thrive in such a wide range of soils but do give them a try. I have been growing *C. speciosus* and some of its varieties for at least 10 years and they are multiplying well and bloom every fall. After a hard frost the flowers look dead but a warm day sees them stand up and open out again. *C. sativus*, the source of saffron, is not as hardy and even against the house wall has not lived for more than a couple of years.

CROWN IMPERIAL—see Fritillary.

DAFFODIL *Narcissus*
Blooms: spring Height: 15–60 cm (6–24 in.)
Depth: 25 cm (10 in.); but species only 10–15 cm (4–6 in.) ●●

If I could only grow one spring bulb in my garden, it would have to be a daffodil. However, trying to decide just which daffodil to choose would keep me awake for many a night. There are many different classes of daffs, and strictly speaking, *daffodil* refers to only the large trumpet narcissus, but most people call them all daffodil.

Daffs must be planted early in the fall, to make roots before winter comes. They are accommodating as regards site and will grow in sun or part shade and in most soils except heavy clay. They look wonderful when naturalized, but because their foliage doesn't die down until summer, this treatment is best for a park-like setting. In average garden soil they will multiply slowly but surely. I now have three clumps of approximately 40 bulbs, each from one bulb of **'Ice Follies'** received as a bonus about 25 years ago.

There are so many named varieties on the market that trying to pick out the best is impossible. Remember that daffodils don't have to be yellow. They can be white, pink, or fawn in trumpet or perianth (the name given to the ring of petals behind the trumpet). The three main groups that you are going to find in every garden centre are **trumpet**, **large cup**, and **small cup**, with the trumpet (cup) shorter in each. Also worth trying are the *triandrus* group, such as **'Thalia'** and **'Hawera'**, with up to six flowers per stem; the *cyclamineus*, like **'Peeping Tom'**, where the perianth is bent in the opposite direction to the cup; jonquils (*jonquilla*) such as **'Baby Moon'**, with white flowers in pairs; and **poet's narcissus**, like **'Actea'**, with the cups usually rimmed in scarlet. A couple of my favourites don't fit into any of these groups but are free-flowering dwarf varieties that make a splash of colour. **'Jumblie'** is bright yellow, with several stems per bulb, each stem having three flowers. **'Tête-à-Tête'** usually has two back-to-back flowers on each stem, and is golden yellow with a darker cup.

Daffodils are hardy to about -35°C (-31°F), and probably below that with a reliable snow cover. Many old established plantings were nearly all killed in Ottawa one winter when the temperature went down to -39°C (-38°F). Two popular varieties, **'Paperwhite'** and **'Soleil d'Or'**, are sold for indoor forcing only and are not hardy even in Niagara.

DOG'S-TOOTH VIOLET—see Trout lily.

DRUMSTICK ONION—see Flowering onion.

FALSE AUTUMN CROCUS *Colchicum autumnale*
Blooms: early fall   Height: 20 cm (8 in.)
Depth: 15 cm (6 in.) ◖◗

Looking like very large crocuses, the false autumn crocus is both hardier and easier to grow than the true autumn crocus. The leaves appear in the spring but they are not very attractive, being a dull green and up to 10 cm (6 in.) wide. Flowers are a lilac-pink but there is also a white form. **'Waterlily'** has double flowers.

FLOWERING ONION *Allium*
There are a great number of onions that are suitable for the garden. They range from tiny species suitable for the rock garden to giants that will grow close to 2 m (6 ft.) high. These are the most common ones.

Blue onion *A. caeruleum*
Blooms: summer   Height: 60 cm (24 in.)
Depth: 10 cm (4 in.)

This is one of my favourites in this group with bright blue globes of flower on thin stems. It is most effective if interplanted with daffodils so that it can come up through the foliage as it begins to die down, or under a mat of moss phlox to give summer interest.

Bulgarian onion *Nectaroscordum siculum* var. *bulgaricum*
Blooms: late spring Height: 1–1.2 m (3–4 ft.)
Depth: 20 cm (8 in.)

This used to be called *Allium bulgaricum*. It doesn't look much like an onion and I can see why it was changed, but did botanists have to give it such an unpronounceable name? The flowers are pink bells, tipped with green, that appear in arching clusters at the top of the stems. It is an interesting plant that causes many comments in my garden.

Chinese chives *A. tuberosum*
Blooms: late summer Height: 75 cm (30 in.)
Depth: 10 cm (4 in.)

You are most likely to find a pot of this in the herb section of your garden centre, rather than as a dry bulb. While the foliage is a garlic-flavored chive, the white heads of flowers make it worth a place in the flower garden. Be sure to dead-head the flowers as they start to fade. This species sets lots of seed that germinate well, especially amid other perennials.

Chives *A. schoenoprasum*
Blooms: early summer Height: 60 cm (24 in.)
Depth: 10 cm (4 in.)

Again, I always feel that the flowers are too nice to have them lost in the herb garden. If you remove the flowers as soon as they finish, chives will often rebloom later. Grow it from seed or buy plants.

Drumstick onion *A. sphaerocephalum*
Blooms: summer   Height: 75 cm (30 in.)
Depth: 10 cm (4 in.)

This is similar to the blue onion but with maroon flowers; a mix of the two gives a nice effect. The flower heads are more oval than round and dry well for winter arrangements.

Giant onion *A. giganteum*
Blooms: early summer Height: up to 1.5 m (5 ft.) Depth: 25 cm (10 in.)

There are several onions with dense round heads of bright mauve flowers that differ slightly in height and flowering time. The giant onion is the tallest but *A. aflatunense* flowers earlier. Try a mixed planting of the two. These die down soon after flowering and can leave a big hole in your planting unless you have a later-flowering plant in front to hide the bare spot. Another way is to dot them through the bed so they make a sea of purple when in flower but only leave small bare patches when they go dormant.

Golden garlic *A. moly*
Blooms: summer   Height: 30 cm (12 in.)
Depth: 10 cm (4 in.)

This is a very showy plant but it does tend to be a bit invasive. Be sure to remove the flower heads as soon as the flowers fade to stop it seeding. A good plant to mix with something low and spring-flowering, like moss phlox.

Star of Persia *A. christophii*
Blooms: late spring   Height: 90 cm (36 in.)
Depth: 25 cm (10 in.)

Like the giant onion, the flower head on this plant is a large globe, but the individual flowers are very different. The blooms are paler, with a sheen, and the individual petals are pointed, giving a star effect. A very striking bloom that can be cut and dried for winter use.

FOXTAIL LILY *Eremurus*
Blooms: summer   Height: up to 2.5 m (8 ft.)
Depth: 30 cm (12 in.)

A plant to use in moderation, as it can be overpowering en masse. The roots are thick, fleshy, and widespread. The first time I saw one I was reminded of a baby octopus. Plant it on a bed of sand and put a layer of sand over the root area after planting. Also, put a support in place when you plant to avoid damaging the roots later. Mulch well for the winter and don't be in a hurry to remove it in spring. Some varieties start growing early; their shoots can be killed by a late frost.

FRITILLARY *Fritillaria*
Up to a few years ago, only the first two fritillaries were ever seen in catalogues, but now there are several other species available.

Checkered lily *F. meleagris*
Blooms:; late spring   Height: 45 cm (18 in.)
Depth: 10 cm (4 in.) ●●●

This has long been a favourite of mine, but then I always did like the offbeat plants. Flowers are solitary bells, often heavily marked with a purple or maroon netting, on thin stems. They grow best in filtered shade, under shrubs for example, and will seed themselves if conditions are right.

Crown imperial *F. imperialis*
Blooms: spring   Height: 120 cm (48 in.)
Depth: 20 cm (8 in.)

An amazing plant, the crown imperial almost grows before your eyes. I swear it shoots up a hand-span each day. The bulbs are large with a hollow centre and smell faintly of skunk—as does the foliage—so it is not bothered by mice or squirrels. Flowers are yellow, orange, or red clusters of bells on top of the stems. As soon as flowering is over the plants start to die down. The area where they grow should be mulched heavily with rich compost after planting and each fall, to ensure plenty of food for the bulb. Otherwise they tend to flower every other year.

Persian fritillary *F. persica*
Blooms: spring   Height: 1 m (3 ft.)   Depth: 20 cm (8 in.)

Plant these in full sun and good soil. They are easy-to-please plants that will send up their stiff shoots without fail. The top third of each stem bears greenish-maroon bells that are most attractive, followed by angular, papery seed pods. The flowers of '**Adiyaman**' are a brownish-purple, which sounds dull, but isn't.

GLORY OF THE SNOW *Chionodoxa luciliae*
Blooms: early spring   Height: 10–15 cm (4–6 in.)   Depth: 10 cm (4 in.) ●●●

Bright blue star-shaped flowers appear almost as soon as the snow melts. They will self-seed and form a carpet of blooms, especially under shrubs, but will also grow in full sun.

GOLDEN GARLIC—see Flowering onion.

GRAPE HYACINTH *Muscari armeniacum*
Blooms: spring Height: 15–20 cm (6–8 in.)
Depth: 10 cm (4 in.) ●

This is the most common of several *Muscari* species available. The flowers are blue bells in dense spikes. There is also a white form. They will seed freely and the clumps should be lifted in July and replanted immediately. Grape hyacinths put up their new foliage in the fall and it overwinters beneath the snow, so they should always be planted in early fall.

HYACINTH *Hyacinthus orientalis*
Blooms: spring Height: 20–30 cm (8–12 in.)
Depth: 15 cm (6 in.)

Usually grown as indoor forced bulbs, hyacinths may be planted directly into the garden, in which case the second size bulbs 15–18 cm (6–7 in.) are large enough. They are not as hardy as many other bulbs and will occasionally be killed in zone 5 but the singles are hardier than the double forms. Flowers are sweetly scented and come in blue, pink, white, and a creamy yellow. Bulbs that have been forced for use indoors can be planted in the garden once danger of frost is past and will generally flower after a year's rest.

IRIS *Iris*
There are several bulbous irises that are good additions to the spring garden. They take up little room and give a colourful show.
Danford's iris *I. danfordiae*
Blooms: early spring Height: 10 cm (4 in.)
Depth: 15 cm (6 in.)

This often pushes its way through the soil before the snow has melted and the bright yellow flowers open amid the last of the drifts. The narrow, triangular leaves come up as the flowers begin to fade and grow about 20 cm (8 in.) tall. A closely related species, *I. histrioides* 'Major', flowers a few days later and has blue blossoms. The two make a good mixed planting.

Netted iris *I. reticulata*
Blooms: spring Height: 20–30 cm (8–12 in.)
Depth: 15 cm (6 in.)

Similar to the last species, but later to flower, there are several named forms of the netted iris. '**Cantab**' is a pale blue and '**Harmony**' is violet.

LILY *Lilium*
Blooms: summer Height: 30–180 cm (1–6 ft.)
Depth: 25 cm (10 in.) ●●●

Where can I start writing about lilies? If you look at the price of them in catalogues, they may seem outrageous, but the pleasure they give makes them good value. Plant in threes, about 15 cm (6 in.) apart, and within a couple of years you will have 8 or 10 flower spikes. Plant in light shade if possible, especially at midday. Lilies will not grow well in a wet heavy soil, preferring one rich in humus, moist but well drained.

Like daffodils, lilies have been classified into various groups, depending on their parentage. The **trumpet** lilies have long flowers in clusters on the top of generally tall stems. '**Black Dragon**' (white with a dark purple outside) and '**Pink Perfection**' are typical of this group. **Oriental hybrids** are very variable and may have trumpet, bowl-shaped, or flat, fragrant flowers. '**Imperial Gold**' is white with a yellow stripe in the centre of each petal, and '**Journey's End**' is bright pink edged with white. The most popular group is the **Asiatic hybrids**, and the bright orange '**Enchantment**' is probably the best known of these. Flowers may face up, out, or down, and in general the plants are shorter than the other hybrids and will stand direct sun better.

The European lily beetle has become a serious pest in many parts, although it seems very localized. The bright red beetle is highly visible but even so, it is usually the disappearing foliage that alerts us. Both the adults and the brownish grubs have ravenous appetites and can defoliate a clump of lilies in a few days.

THE NEW ONTARIO GARDENER

Pyrethrin will give a quick control, but will not kill the eggs. Drenching the plants with dimethoate will give a long-term control as it is absorbed through the roots and makes the plant toxic.

SNOWDROP *Galanthus nivalis*
Blooms: early spring Height: 10 cm (4 in.)
Depth: 8 cm (3 in.) ◗

Another harbinger of spring, snowdrops will bloom in the late snow. They move best while they are still growing, but naturally you cannot buy them like this. There is also a double form available (for twice the price) but, unless you are willing to lie down on the cold, wet ground to peer into the flowers, I fail to see any advantage in buying it.

SNOWFLAKE *Leucojum*
There are two different snowflakes commonly available, and both make a good addition to the garden.

Spring snowflake *L. vernum*
Blooms: early spring Height: 30 cm (12 in.)
Depth: 10 cm (4 in.)

Single white bells tipped with green appear before the leaves, as soon as the snow melts. They look like giant snowdrops and flower just a little later.

Summer snowflake *L. aestivum*
Blooms: late spring Height: 45–60 cm (18–24 in.) Depth: 10 cm (4 in.)

The flowers are similar to those of spring snowflake but are creamy white and there are up to eight per stem.

SQUILL *Scilla sibirica*
Blooms: spring Height: 10–15 cm (4–6 in.)
Depth: 10 cm (4 in.) ◗

Deep blue flowers in clusters of three to five are usually busy with bees collecting nectar. I am amazed that the bees come on days when the temperature is just above freezing, but they arrive just as squill start to bloom. These will seed themselves and multiply slowly but reliably.

STRIPED SQUILL *Puschkinia scilloides*
Blooms: early spring Height: 15–20 cm (6–8 in) Depth: 10 cm (4 in.) ◗

Small heads of sweetly scented, very pale blue, open flowers, with a darker stripe down each petal are freely produced. *P. scilloide* var. *libanotica* has white flowers.

TRILLIUM *Trillium*
Blooms: spring Height: 40 cm (16 in.) Depth: 15 cm (6 in.)

The common white trillium, *T. grandiflorum*, the floral emblem of Ontario, is well-known and makes a good addition to a woodland garden. The bulbs are often available from specialist nurseries. Once they're well established in the garden the plants will seed happily, although seed is difficult to germinate indoors. Double-flowered forms, and various other strange mutations, are very occasionally offered at prices that match their rarity. There are several other native trilliums that are worth buying if you ever see them in catalogues. The **purple trillium** (*T. erectum*) has nodding flowers on a long stem above the foliage. **Toadshade** (*T. sessile*) has dark red flowers sitting on grey-green spotted leaves. All of these are hardy to zone 4b at least. The **yellow trillium** (*T. luteum*) is more tender and will survive only in zone 6. It has yellow, cup-shaped flowers above pale green foliage.

TROUT LILY, DOG'S-TOOTH VIOLET *Erythronium*
Blooms: spring Height: 10–15 cm (4–6 in.)
Depth: 10 cm (4 in.)

This bulb comes in several colours and is a good choice for growing under shrubs. The native trout lily (*E. americanum*) is yellow and dwarf. The hybrid '**Pagoda**' is a brighter yellow, taller, and later-flowering. Native to Europe, dog's tooth violet (*E. dens-canis*) is pink, but there are several named forms, such as '**Lilac Wonder**', '**Purple King**', and '**Snowflake**'.

TULIP *Tulipa*

On the west coast, where spring is a leisurely process, the hybrid tulips will bloom in succession for weeks on end. Here, I am sorry to relate, the season is compressed into a two or three week period. I must admit that I am not a great lover of the tall tulips. The massed beds of stately blooms, swaying in the breeze, don't turn me on. I am much more attracted to the small species and rock garden types; I feel they are more in keeping with small city gardens.

Garden tulips

Blooms: spring Height: 30–90 cm (12–36 in.) Depth: 25 cm (10 in.) ●

The planting depth for tulips is often given as 20 cm (8 in.) but if you can get them down deeper, they will last longer. Within reason, the deeper you plant, the longer it will be before they need replacing; 30 to 35 cm (12 to 14 in.) is not excessive if you are planting a group with a spade, although it is a bit deep to dig with a trowel.

There are thousands of named varieties of tulip and these have been classified into various groups, depending on the flower shape and flowering time, by the Netherland Flower Bulb Institute, whose members produce the bulk of the world's tulips. The first to flower are the **single** and **double early** group, followed by the **triumph** and **Darwin hybrid** types at midseason. Late tulips are the **Darwin**, **lily-flowered**, **single** and **double late**, and the **parrot** type with their streaked petals.

Dwarf tulips

Blooms: early spring Height: 15–25 cm (6–10 in.) Depth: 15 cm (6 in.) ●●

These are ideal for use at the front of a border or between shrubs in the foundation planting. Two groups of tulips can be planted to give blooms that are bright and cheerful. The **waterlily tulip** (*T. kaufmanniana*) has pale flowers with bright outer petals; many cultivars are named after composers, such as '**Johann Strauss**' and '**Verdi**'. The foliage on **Greig's**

tulip (*T. greigii*) is striped with dark purple, making it attractive when the flowers are finished, and the blooms, in bright reds and yellows, stand out. My favourite is '**Cape Cod**'.

There are several easy-to-grow **species tulips** that will multiply or self-seed. *T. linifolia* has narrow, grasslike leaves, flat on the ground, and scarlet flowers; *T. tarda* is yellow with a white edge to the petals, while *T. urumiensis* is bright yellow with crinkled leaves. These charming tulips all deserve to be better known.

WINTER ACONITE *Eranthis hyemalis*

Blooms: early spring Height: 5–10 cm (2–4 in.) Depth: 10 cm (4 in.) ●●

Here's another flower I always look for as a sign spring will soon come; the bright yellow blossoms sit on a ruff of finely divided leaves. Soak the bulbs in warm water for several hours before planting to fill them out. In a suitable location in light shade, where they will not dry out in summer, winter aconites will seed themselves and multiply.

 # TENDER BULBS

These will not generally survive the winter outdoors, although the borderline between hardy and tender is tenuous, and one of the hardy bulbs is also included here for areas where it will not overwinter. The location in the garden can also make a difference to a bulb's survival. I have had gladioli survive two winters when planted close to the house wall, but I would not recommend leaving them outside.

AFRICAN BLUE LILY *Agapanthus africanus*

Blooms: late summer Height: 40–120 cm (16–48 in.) Depth: 5 cm (2 in) (top of crown)

This is not really a bulb—it has fleshy roots—but it is usually sold in packs with bulbs in spring. Leaves are straplike and the blue or white flowers are clustered on the end of long stems. This is a good container plant and should be stored over winter in its pot at just above freezing. Mature plants may overwinter outside with good snow cover; they have come through two winters so far in my Ottawa garden, and several winters in Patrick Lima's garden on the Bruce Peninsula, when mulched heavily with peastone. Most of the named forms are tall, but 'Lilliput' is short and deep blue.

BEGONIA *Begonia* x *tuberhybrida*
Blooms: all summer   Height: 45–75 cm (18–30 in.) Depth: 5 cm (2 in.) ●●●

Although these can be raised from seed (see Chapter 9) the fancy forms with picotee edges or ruffled petals must be grown from tubers. In March, plant the tuber in a pot of peat moss or soilless compost, with the concave side up, placing the tuber just on the surface. Water and keep in a bright light once growth starts. As the days lengthen, reduce the light intensity, as these plants need shade in the summer. Plant them out when all danger of frost is past. In fall, allow one good frost to kill the tops and seal the stems but dig before there is any danger of the tubers freezing. Store in dry vermiculite or peat at 7 to 15°C (45 to 60°F).

CALLA LILY *Zantedeschia*
Blooms: midsummer Height: 60 cm (24 in.) Depth: 8 cm (3 in.)

There are three different species of calla available, in white, pink, and yellow, and many new hybrids in a range of colours. They should be started early (like begonias) but need full sun to grow well. Plant them in a rich soil that will retain water, as they won't thrive in light, dry soils. Store at the same temperature as begonias but in slightly moist peat, and check them during the winter. If the tubers seem shriveled, water lightly. If you start them in clay pots, they can be plunged into a wet area beside a pool (sink the pot down to its rim) and then left in the pot when you bring them indoors to dry for winter.

CANNA LILY *Canna* x *generalis*
Blooms: all summer Height: 60–150 cm (2–5 ft.) Depth: 8 cm (3 in.)

Spectacular, towering spikes of flowers that arise from tropical-looking green or bronze leaves make cannas a showpiece in the garden. They are best started like begonias, as planting them directly in the ground will shorten the flowering period. Lift when frost has blackened the leaves and air-dry for a few hours (but take care not to freeze the tubers). Clean most of the soil off but don't wash them, then store in dry sand or peat at 5°C (41°F). Flowers can be red, yellow, pink, or two-toned. 'Praetoria' has orange flowers and green and yellow striped foliage; 'Stuttgart' has pink and orange flowers and leaves splashed with white.

DAHLIA *Dahlia*
Blooms: late summer   Height: 45–150 cm (18–60 in.) Depth: 30 cm (12 in.)

Between them, the culture of dahlias and gladioli could fill a book this size and all I can hope to do here is provide a few pointers. If you are buying dahlias for the first time, they can be planted out shortly before the danger of frost is past, providing they don't have shoots that will be above ground. Plant in a good, well-drained, rich soil and give plenty of water during the growing season. If you are growing the large-flowered type, they will need some form of support before summer is over, so put a suitable stake in the hole at planting time. In fall, after a couple of good frosts, dig the plants and turn them upside-down to drain the stems, then move them to a warm basement and dry the entire plant for a couple of weeks. In heavy soil, store with all the soil attached, but in light soil that falls off the tubers, store in dry vermiculite at 5 to 13°C (41 to 55°F). Inspect occasionally during the winter and water if the tubers are shrinking.

GLADIOLUS *Gladiolus*
Blooms: mid- to late summer Height: 90–200 cm (3–7 ft.) Depth: 10–15 cm (4–6 in.)

There is room in every garden for a few glads. Even if you don't try to store them they are well worth their price, either as cut flowers or just to brighten the borders. If you have a supply of bulbs, plant them out in succession, every two weeks, starting just before the date of the last frost, to get a sequence of bloom. Don't forget there are early-, midseason-, and late-flowering varieties, which take about 70, 80, and 90 days respectively from planting to blooming. This is for large bulbs—5 cm (2 in.) or more across—smaller bulbs will take up to 10 days longer but still give good flower spikes. Plant in full sun in almost any soil so long as it is well drained. While glads need lots of water to grow well, they will not stand wet feet.

Lift in the fall and cut the stem off about 10 cm (4 in.) above the corm. Keep the different varieties separate if possible (an aid when planting next spring) and put in a warm room for a couple of weeks. Then clean the bulbs, removing the old stem, which should just break away; if not, leave it a little longer. Also remove the old corm, which is attached to the base of the one you dug. Dust the bulbs with a general-purpose insect dust to kill **thrips**, which would feed on the bulbs all winter, and store in a dry place at 5 to 10°C (41 to 50°F).

MONTBRETIA *Crocosmia* x *crocosmiiflora*
Blooms: late summer Height: 60 cm (24 in.) Depth: 8–10 cm (3–4 in.)

Spikes of orange-to-red or yellow flowers arise from grassy foliage. These bulbs do not like being disturbed, so start them in a pot, about 10 cm (4 in.) apart, and plunge them in the garden. In fall, lift the pot, allow to dry, and overwinter at 5°C (41°F). The dark red 'Lucifer' has overwintered in my Ottawa garden and in Aurora.

PEACOCK ORCHID, PEACOCK LILY *Gladiolus (Acidanthera) murieliae*
Blooms: late summer Height: 60–90 cm (24–36 in.) Depth: 10 cm (4 in.)

Botanists now classify this as *Gladiolus*, but I think it will be *Acidanthera* in catalogues for a few years yet. It produces elegant stems of nodding white flowers with a chocolate-maroon throat and a delightful scent. Treat them just like glads but make sure you plant them early or they may not have time to flower before frost. In areas with a short growing season, start them in pots. They are easy to increase from the small cormels (baby corms) produced in abundance around the large ones.

PINEAPPLE LILY *Eucomis bicolor*
Blooms: summer Height: 30–60 cm (12–24 in.) Depth: 20 cm (8 in.)

From a rosette of broad, straplike leaves, arises a flowering stem crowned with a cluster of leaves like the top of a pineapple. The greenish-yellow flowers, each petal edged in red, open on the upper third of the flower spike. This does well in the border or in a container. Store at 5°C (41°F) for the winter.

POPPY ANEMONE *Anemone coronaria*
This bulb was already covered in the section, hardy bulbs, but it is not reliably hardy below zone 6a. Store in dry vermiculite or peat moss at 7 to 13°C (45 to 55°F).

SHELLFLOWER, TIGER FLOWER *Tigridia pavonia*
Blooms: summer Height: 60 cm (24 in.) Depth: 15 cm (6 in.) ●●

Brightly coloured, almost triangular flowers dance on thin wiry stems. The individual blooms are short-lived, but each stem produces several flowers that open in sequence. Dry in a warm room after digging and then store at 10 to 15°C (50 to 59°F). Don't divide the clumps of bulbs if you can help it—they grow better in close company.

SUMMER HYACINTH *Galtonia candicans*
Blooms: late summer Height: 1–1.2 m (3–4 ft.) Depth: 20 cm (8 in.)

Another good plant for a sunny border. The spikes of slightly fragrant, white flowers appear in late summer and last for several weeks. This may overwinter outside if well mulched, or you can lift it after frost and store at 5°C (41°F).

TUBEROSE *Polianthes tuberosa*
Blooms: late summer Height: 90 cm (36 in.) Depth: 10 cm (4 in.)

An extremely fragrant plant—just a couple will scent a whole garden—but it often flowers too late for use here. Try starting the plants indoors in spring, like tuberous begonias, or dig the plants in fall before danger of frost and bring them inside to flower. Actually, I find the perfume overpowering in my dining room—but don't tell my wife.

SUGGESTED READING

The Bulb Book. Martyn Rix and Roger Phillips. Pan Books, 1981.

A beautiful book with wonderful colour pictures of bulbs, many growing in their native habitat which is a great help in deciding what conditions they require.

Taylors Guide to Bulbs. Norman Taylor (with additions by various authors). Houghton Mifflin, 1986.

Both have lots of pictures and a helpful text.

Daffodils for American Gardens. Brent and Becky Heath. Elliott & Clark, 1995.

This will make you want to plant more and more daffs.

Let's Grow Lilies. Virginia Howie. North American Lily Society, 1978.

Gardener's Guide to Growing Lilies. Michael Jefferson-Brown. Timber Press, 1995.

The first is an easy-to-understand book with lots of how-to drawings; the second equally easy but in greater depth.

Rock Gardens
11
chapter

There is an old English saying, "Never build a rock garden bigger than your spouse can weed." There is an element of truth in this because, apart from lawns, rock gardens are the most labour intensive form of gardening there is. At the same time, they are probably the most rewarding, and certainly the most challenging. Rock gardens can vary in size from a miniature mountain range needing a small army of gardeners to maintain it, to a small trough garden containing just a couple of choice pieces of rock and a few equally choice plants.

Rock gardening can be an absorbing hobby and is the ideal choice for people with an interest in gardening but only a small garden. Unlike growing annuals or perennial plants, in a rock garden, you'd normally grow a single plant of each species. You can grow a lot of different plants in a small space because the rocks tend to contain the soil, allowing you to customize each planting space to the needs of a particular plant. Large rocks can provide shade for some plants, while nearby another plant can grow happily in full sun. The potential number of plants you can grow is enormous, and as your knowledge of plants and their needs grows, so does the range of plants available to you.

I first got hooked on rock gardening while a student at the Royal Botanic Gardens, Kew, in England. I spent six months rebuilding one end of the huge rock garden there and have built some form of rock garden at almost every house I have lived in ever since.

WHAT IS A ROCK GARDEN PLANT?

When rock gardening first became popular, around the turn of the last century, most of the plant collecting was done in the mountains of Europe, especially the Alps, so rock garden plants became known as *alpines*. These days, rock plants come from the Alps, the Himalayas, the Rockies, and mountain ranges the world over, but they are still known as alpines and the two terms are used interchangeably in this chapter. Alpines can also come from low elevations providing they are subject to the harsh growing conditions found high in the mountains. Many of our choicest, and more difficult, plants come from the Arctic and subarctic. If you visit northwestern Newfoundland you will find typical arctic flora growing at just above sea-level.

As a rough guide, plants normally considered suitable for the rock garden are low growing, usually trailing or forming a mound, and generally not more than about 20 cm (8 in.) tall. There are a few commonly grown plants that are taller than this, but they are usually light and airy in habit; also, dwarf shrubs and conifers are not restricted to this height limit. Some of the really choice plants form compact small hummocks, known as *buns*. This gave rise to the bumper sticker "Rock gardeners have nice buns!" Alpines are mainly species that could be found growing in the wild, but dwarf forms of garden plants are also suitable.

Because of their short growing season, most rock garden plants are spring-flowering, and even a small rock garden should be a picture from early spring until well into June. There are lots of plants that flower later in the season, but in the average rock garden the main display will be in spring. If your rock garden is lacking in colour in July and August, it is permissible to plant annuals to improve the display. No, not petunias, but moss rose, verbena, and vinca would not look out of place.

LOCATION, LOCATION, LOCATION

In nature, most alpines grow beyond the tree line where the light is bright, nights are cool, water from melting snow may be available below the surface, winters are cold, and the growing season is short. Our gardens meet few of these conditions and yet we can grow a surprising number of different plants.

Winter is generally no problem—in fact, we can grow plants in Ontario that are difficult in the damp winters of Britain or B.C.—it is the humid heat of summer that kills our plants. Most alpines need a lot of light, and need to be grown in full sun, although dappled shade from distant trees at midday is okay. The aspect of your rock garden can have an influence on how well your plants survive. If you go out on a summer's day and hold your hand up to the sun, your palm will quickly get warm. If you turn your hand so your fingers are pointing to the sun, your palm is still in full light, but it is much cooler. In the same way, if you slope your rock garden towards the north, it will still get full light but the heat will be reduced.

CONSTRUCTION

Hopefully your rock garden will be in place for many years, so it makes sense to start with a clean site. All that I wrote about eliminating perennial weeds in Chapter 8 applies doubly here. A clump of couch grass in a perennial border can be dealt with by moving a few plants; in a rock garden it becomes a major renovation, and most alpines don't take kindly to being dug up.

Most rock gardens in public parks and gardens are made of large pieces of rock, set in layers, with the grain of the rock running parallel, and the plants growing in the soil pockets between the layers. This was the way the rock garden at Kew was formed, and the way I had built all my rock gardens. Then I went up into the mountains in Colorado. There are no strata lines in nature! Pieces of rock, ranging in size from a house to a pea, lie jumbled higgledy-piggledy where they have fallen off the mountain face. The plants grow in between them, often on the lee side where they are sheltered from the wind and where snow tends to collect in winter.

I came back from the mountains convinced that my style of rock garden was all wrong, although the plants were happy enough. My present rock garden is a combination of the two: formal rows of rocks to form the shape, with a jumble of rock pieces in the centre. If you have access to quantities of rock and a back strong enough to lift them, build a formal rock garden; if not, a minimal garden will grow good plants, providing the drainage is good. To get an idea of the way to construct a rock garden, visit the gardens at Montreal Botanical Garden, the Central Experimental Farm in Ottawa or Edwards Gardens in Toronto. The rock garden at the Royal Botanical Gardens, Hamilton, is not a very good example of construction because this was originally a quarry.

You will need some rocks to form the basic shape and keep the soil mix from spilling out across the lawn. These should be buried at least half their height in the soil and must be firmed in place. Walk on each rock after you have set it in place to be sure it is stable. These rocks form the basis of your garden and must not move when you step on them. If your basic soil is heavy clay, do not attempt to excavate a hole; it will only fill up with water. Build upwards so the water can drain away.

 ## SOIL

Every book on rock gardening has its own recipe for the perfect soil mix for a rock garden. I will just say that the most important factor is good drainage. In the mountains, plants grow in a very gritty soil, composed of broken rock fragments, with very little humus. Their roots go deep and spread wide to find the available nutrients. If you turn a rock over on a hot day, you'll find the soil under it is moist; the roots of alpine plants grow close to the underside of rocks and rock fragments, to take advantage of this moisture.

When I built my present rock garden, I broke up a lot of house bricks into walnut-sized and smaller pieces. I did the same with the pieces of rock too small to use in construction. These were mixed with a quantity of pea gravel and coarse sand. I excavated the site to a spit deep, spread a good layer of the rock-mix over the subsoil and forked it in. As I replaced the topsoil, which was very sandy to start with, I added more of the crushed rock, so the resulting mixture was very well drained. It is a terrible soil to try to plant in, but once in place, the plants grow well.

Some friends of ours, when building their rock garden, would drive into the country looking for rock cuts. They would take a dustpan and brush to sweep up the rock pieces and dust, tipping them into a pail. Over the summer they collected a large quantity, which they added to their garden to improve drainage. Their only worry was what they would say if a police car drove by: "Well, you see, officer, we were just tidying up the countryside."

Most alpines grow well in soils that are neutral to slightly alkaline, and since limestone is one of the predominant rocks used in construction, this is just as well. Some prefer an acidic soil and it is comparatively easy to make part of the garden with granite and fill it with an acid-based mix. Just don't put it at the bottom of an alkaline slope where it will get all the runoff.

 ## WHERE TO GET PLANTS

Most garden centres carry a few common rock garden plants in spring, and the selection at some of the larger ones is quite good. To find more than the basic plants you will have to go to one of the specialist nurseries. There are a number of these in Ontario and western Quebec and some of them sell by mail. You can also grow alpines from seed and the larger seed catalogues, such as Thompson and Morgan, list a fair selection of species.

Once you get bitten by the rock gardening bug, you should join one of the rock garden societies. The North American Rock Garden Society has a large international membership and many local chapters, including the Ontario Rock Garden Society, based in the Toronto-Hamilton area, and the Ottawa Valley Rock Garden Society for the eastern end of the province. For information on these societies, go to *http://www.nargs.org*. For the local societies click on *Chapters*, then on the society name. This will give you the date, time and location of upcoming meetings, and a contact phone number or e-mail address.

Society meetings usually feature a guest speaker or a hands-on workshop, but they also give you the opportunity to discuss your problems with more knowledgeable gardeners, who are more than willing to show off their expertise and help a novice. Membership also entitles you to take part in plant sales where members donate both common and rare plants that are sold at a reasonable price, and in the seed exchanges. Seed is the only way you are going to be able to obtain some of the choicest species, which never appear in specialist nursery catalogues. The number of potential alpine plants is huge and even the 5,000+ entries in the North American Rock Garden Society seed list only scratch the surface.

In the high mountains, the snows melt late and come early, giving the plants a short growing season. Most alpines flower in spring, giving them time to ripen and disperse their seed. If the seeds germinated as soon as they were shed, the resulting seedlings would not be large enough to survive the winter, so many seeds have a built-in delay mechanism that has

to be unlocked by a period of cold. Keep this in mind when you sow seeds—if you sow too late there will not be sufficient cold to break down the inhibitors, and seeds will not grow that spring. A very few have what is called a *double dormancy*. This means they need two cold treatments before the seed will start into growth. Never throw out ungerminated pots of seed for at least two years, and preferably not for three.

Sow the seeds in one of the soil-less mixes, with about 50% of perlite or turface (a sports field conditioner made of fired clay particles), added to improve the drainage. Moisten the mix the previous day; it is very difficult to make it damp once it is in a pot because it floats. Fill the pots and firm gently, then sprinkle a little fine chicken grit (available at feed stores) on the surface. Sow the seeds on the surface and tap the pot gently to settle the seeds between the pieces of grit. Label each pot as you sow it. Soak the pots by standing them in water until the surface changes colour. Let them drain, place them in a flat, and keep the pots in the house for a couple of days to give the seeds time to absorb water. Then put a clear plastic dome over the flat and put it out in the cold. If you don't have a dome cover, slip the flat into a plastic bag but try to stand a piece of wood upright in the centre to keep the plastic from resting on the pots.

When warm weather comes, inspect the flat every day and remove the pots as they germinate. Ungerminated pots should be left in the covered flat. Water them as needed, and keep them out of direct sunlight. Hopefully, these will germinate after a second winter outdoors.

Keep the germinated pots moist, but not standing in water, and place them in bright light. Once the seedlings are large enough to handle, transplant them to individual pots or line them out in a flat. Grow them until they're large enough to plant out in the rock garden—or take them to a plant sale.

WHAT SHALL I PLANT?

The following list is made up of generally widely available plants that are easy to grow, with a few favourites I couldn't leave out. These all have have common names but many alpine plants don't—they aren't common— and once you get involved in rock gardening you will find that botanical names are not so frightening after all. By the time you have made a list of seeds to order, made labels for the seed pots and again for plants in the garden, the names seem like old friends. Since most alpines are planted as single specimens, the listings give the height and spread, rather than height and planting distance. Those that are easy to raise from seed are indicated by "S".

ALPINE ASTER *Aster alpinus*
Blooms: summer Height: 20–30 cm (8–12 in.) Spread: 15–20 cm (6–8 in.) S

This is easy to grow from seed but plants may vary both in size and in colour, from almost pink to a blue-mauve. It grows well in regular soil, so if you have room, plant out a row of seedlings and select the ones with best form and colour.

AUBRIETA *Aubrieta* hybrids
Blooms: spring Height: 15 cm (6 in.) Spread: 35 cm (14 in.)

A trailing plant that grows well in a crevice or hanging down a rock face. The flowers vary from pink to red to mauve, depending on the variety. It was named for Claude Aubriet, a French botanical artist, but we usually pronounce it au-BREE-sha. The species can be grown from seed, but the named forms, propagated from cuttings, have brighter colours. After flowering, cut the plant back hard to promote new growth that will flower the following spring. This also stops it from getting too big and bare in the middle.

AURICULA *Primula auricula*
Blooms: spring Height: 15 cm (6 in.) Spread: 15 cm (6 in.)

The majority of primroses prefer an acidic soil, either shaded or very moist; auriculas are different. This species grows in limestone rock crevices in full sun, and the various named forms, which are commonly available, like the same conditions. Flowers are in many colours, often banded with a darker shade, and the leaves are leathery and covered with a whitish meal called *farina*.

BASKET OF GOLD *Alyssum saxatile*
Blooms: spring Height: 15 cm (6 in.) Spread: 35 cm (14 in.) S

This bright yellow trailer flowers at the same time as aubrieta, and the two grow well together. This can be invasive, spreading freely by seed, so try to shear off the flowers as soon as they fade. It should be cut back after flowering in the same way as aubrieta. Several other species of alyssum are worth growing and not so invasive; they may be available occasionally from specialist nurseries.

BEARDTONGUE *Penstemon* species
Blooms: summer Height: 5–20 cm (2–8 in.) Spread: 20–30 cm (8–12 in.) S

A native North American species that occurs mainly in the west. The easiest is the dwarf form of the hairy penstemon, *P. hirsutus* 'Pygmaeus', which is native to Ontario and has white bell-shaped flowers flushed with pink at the base. Many of the western species will form low mats with pink, mauve, or blue flowers.

BELLFLOWER *Campanula* species
A very useful group of upright or trailing plants that flower in summer and add late colour. The flowers are usually blue and are bell-shaped, as the common name suggests.
Carpathian bellflower *C. carpatica*
Blooms: July–Aug. Height: 15 cm (6 in.) Spread: 15–30 cm (6–12 in.) S

A variable species that is available in many named forms, differing mostly in the shade of blue. Many of the varieties are trailing, but the two most readily available, **'Blue Clips'** and **'White Clips'**, are mound-shaped.

Fairies' thimbles *C. cochlearifolia*
Blooms: summer to fall Height: 5–7 cm (2–3 in.) Spread: infinite

A delightful, tiny plant that spreads slowly by underground runners but seldom becomes invasive. It is a good choice for a trough garden. The small, nodding bells are held above the bright green foliage on wiry stems. There are a few named forms in pale blue and white.

Italian bellflower *C. garganica*
Blooms: late summer Height: 15 cm (6 in.) Spread: 30 cm (12 in.) S

A good, free-flowering trailing plant with ivy-shaped leaves and violet-blue blossoms on arching stems.

Harebell, bluebell of Scotland *C. rotundifolia*
Blooms: summer Height: 15–30 cm (6–12 in.) Spread: 10–15 cm (4–6 in.) S

A circumpolar plant, this seems to vary in height depending on the richness of the soil. At high elevations in Colorado it is quite dwarf, but on heavy clay in Alberta it grows much taller. Only the basal rosette of leaves are round; those on the flowering stems are lance-shaped.

There are a couple more bellflowers that are easy to find and worth growing, but they don't seem to have common names. *C. portenschlagiana* and *C. poscharskyana* are trailing plants, good for planting at the top of a rock where they can cascade over. Both flower in late summer but the latter is more rampant and has lavender-blue flowers, rather than clear blue.

BULBS

Many of the bulbs covered in the last chapter are suitable for the rock garden, especially species crocus, spring squill, dwarf narcissus and some of the species tulips. They are often the first plants to flower and can be planted close to young spreading plants so that, in time, they grow up through their foliage.

CANDYTUFT *Iberis sempervirens*
Blooms: spring Height: 20 cm (8 in.) Spread: 30 cm (12 in.)

This is a small sub-shrub with woody stems, so don't cut it back. The dark green foliage is hidden by the flat heads of white flowers each spring. **'Nana'** and **'Little Gem'** are smaller.

COLUMBINE *Aquilegia flabellata* **'Nana'**
Blooms: late spring Height: 10–15 cm (4–6 in.) Spread: 10–15 cm (4–6 in.) S

Comparatively large blue flowers are held above a rosette of greyish foliage and stand up well to bad weather. There is also a white-flowered form, **'Nana Alba'**. The native columbine, *A. canadensis*, has charming red and yellow flowers but is a little too tall for all but the largest rock garden. Some of the species from the Rocky Mountains, such as *A. saximontana*, grow only a few centimetres (1 to 2 in.) tall but you need experience to grow them successfully.

DRABA *Draba aizoides*
Blooms: early spring Height: 5–7 cm (2–3 in.) Spread: 5–7 cm (2–3 in.) S

Although this is sometimes called whitlow grass, draba is much easier to say. The plant forms a small rosette of pointed, dark green leaves and the bright yellow flowers are often the first to open in my garden. It spreads slowly by seed and forms a small mat in time. There are also white-flowered species, but these tend to be taller and less choice.

FLEABANE *Erigeron compositus*
Blooms: summer Height: 10 cm (4 in.) Spread: 7 cm (3 in.) S

A native species with small, white daisy-like flowers carried above mounded, dark green foliage. It self-seeds slightly but is not invasive. A Mexican species, *E. karvinskianus*, has flowers that change from white through pink to red as they age. This is a mat-forming species that does well in dry-stone paving. It may not be completely hardy but will self-seed.

GENTIAN *Gentiana*
Blooms: spring or fall Height: 7–15 cm (3–6 in.) Spread: 20–30 cm (8–12 in.)

Many gentians are plants for an experienced grower, but there are a couple that are not too difficult given a well-drained soil. The trumpet gentian, *G. acaulis*, has pale green, pointed leaves in tight rosettes. The intense blue (gentian blue), cup-shaped flowers stand upright above the foliage in spring. The fall-flowering *G. septemfida* has prostrate stems with clusters of blue flowers at the end.

HEN AND CHICKS *Sempervivum* species and hybrids
Season: spring to fall Height: 2–10 cm (1–4 in.) Spread: 5–30 cm (2–12 in.)

Hen and chicks are not grown for their flowers, but for the mats of tight rosettes they form. The parent plants that flower die soon after, but by then have budded off "chicks" all around themselves. There are surprising differences in colour and form among the various named forms, and visitors are always intrigued by a bank of more than 80 named varieties in my garden.

IRIS *Iris* species and hybrids
Blooms: spring Height: 10–20 cm (4–8 in.) Spread: 20–30 cm (8–12 in.)

Some of the short bearded irises covered in Chapter 8 are good in the rock garden. Look for varieties classed as Miniature Dwarf Bearded (MDB), as these are the smallest. The bulbous irises listed in Chapter 10 are also suitable, as are some of the species, such as crested iris (*I. cristata*), with mauve-blue flowers.

LEWISIA *Lewisia cotyledon*
Blooms: early summer Height: 15 cm (6 in.) Spread: 20 cm (8 in.) S

A few years ago, I would not have dreamed of putting this plant in a book for inexperienced rock gardeners, but modern hybrids seem to be much tougher and are often available at local garden centres. The plants form a rosette of leathery leaves from which grows a stalk of apricot, pink, yellow or red flowers. Lewisias need a well drained but rich soil and should be planted on a slope so that water cannot lie in their crown to cause rot.

MOSS CAMPION *Silene acaulis*
Blooms: spring Height: 5 cm (2 in.) Spread: 15–30 cm (6–12 in.) S

This is one of the "nice buns" mentioned earlier. It forms a tight mound of almost grassy foliage and has pink starry flowers in early spring. They are not very free-flowering in cultivation but a well-grown plant makes other rock gardeners jealous, even without flowers.

PASQUE FLOWER *Pulsatilla vulgaris*
Blooms: spring Height: 45 cm (18 in.) Spread: 30 cm (12 in.) S

Only the flowers reach the height indicated above; the plant makes a low mound with finely cut, pale green foliage. The flowers, in pink, red, mauve or white, are up to 7 cm (3 in.) across and are followed by fluffy seed heads that are almost as attractive as the flowers.

PEARLWORT, SCOTCH MOSS *Sagina subulata*
Blooms: early summer Height: 1 cm ($^1/_2$ in.) Spread: 20–30 cm (8–10 in.)

This forms a bright green carpet studded with white, starlike flowers in summer. It makes a good ground cover but doesn't take heavy foot traffic. The golden form, **'Aurea'**, is the one most often available.

PHLOX *Phlox* **species**
Blooms: spring Height: 10–15 cm (4–6 in.)
Spread: 15–30 cm (6–12 in.)

The common moss phlox, mentioned in Chapter 8, is a bit too rampageous for all but a large rock garden. There are several native western species that are more refined and occasionally available at large garden centres. Look for named varieties of *P. douglasii* and *P. procumbens*.

PINKS *Dianthus* **species**
Pinks are a large family that includes carnations, sweet williams, the annual China pinks, and many dwarf forms suitable for the rock garden. Some of these make really tight buns and are attractive in flower or out.
Alpine pink *D. alpinus*
Blooms: early summer Height: 5–7 cm (2–3 in.) Spread: 10–15 cm (4–6 in.) S

Plants grown from seed vary in their flower colour, from deep rose to white, and in the tightness of their foliage. Either buy a plant in flower or plant out a row of seedlings to choose the best one. No fragrance.
Cheddar pink *D. gratianopolitanus*
Blooms: summer Height: 10 cm (4 in.)
Spread: 30 cm (12 in.) S

Fragrant, single flowers in pink or red shades. There are several named forms to pick from.
Maiden pink *D. deltoides*
Blooms: late summer Height: 20 cm (8 in.)
Spread: 25 cm (10 in.) S

The species has a more open habit with grassy foliage, but some of the named selections, like '**Flashing Light**', are more mounded and smaller.

ROCKBREAK *Saxifraga* **hybrids**
Blooms: spring to summer Height: 10–20 cm (4–8 in.) Spread: 10–25 cm (4–10 in.)

This is a very complex group of plants that is divided into several sections botanically. Some have soft foliage and form creeping mats;

others are stiff rosettes of silvery leaves. There are hundreds of named forms, some of which are difficult to grow, but those offered in local garden centres are, hopefully, the easy ones. Flowers can be white, pink, or yellow and most hybrids prefer an alkaline soil with limestone chips added.

ROCK CRESS *Arabis alpina caucasica*
Blooms: spring Height: 15 cm (6 in.) Spread: 45 cm (18 in.)

A rather rampant grower that is covered in pure white flowers in spring. It forms a carpet of growth that will trail well over a rock edge. Treat this the same as aubrieta and cut it back after flowering. There is also a double-flowered variety, a pink form, and a variety with variegated foliage that is slower-growing.

ROCK JASMINE *Androsace sarmentosa*
Blooms: early summer Height: 10 cm (4 in.)
Spread: 25 cm (10 in.)

This is the easiest-to-grow member of a large genus. It forms small rosettes 2 to 5 cm (1 to 2 in.) across that grow on the ends of wiry stems. The pink flowers grow in dense heads, like those of some primroses, to which it is related. Plants seem to grow best where they have narrow rock crevices to root into.

SCOTCH MOSS—see Pearlwort.

SEA THRIFT *Armeria maritima*
Blooms: summer Height: 20 cm (8 in.)
Spread: 25 cm (10 in.) S

This forms low mounds of grassy foliage with taller stems carrying globelike heads of pink flowers. There are several named varieties in different shades; '**Vindictive**' is a dark pink.

STONECROP *Sedum* **species**
A large group of plants, many of which are garden thugs and should not be planted. The weedy ones root easily from the smallest piece and most have brittle stems so they spread

easily. The golden stonecrop (*S. acre*) will grow in almost no soil and can spread into lawns; it's pretty in flower but not desirable.

'Cape Blanco' stonecrop *S. spathulifolium 'Cape Blanco'*
Blooms: summer   Height: 10 cm (4 in.) Spread: 20 cm (8 in.)

Found on Cape Blanco in Southern Oregon, this will not survive over winter in zone 5. The flowers are yellow, but it is grown for the grey foliage with overlapping, scaly leaves forming dense rosettes.

Kamschatka stonecrop *S. kamschaticum*
Blooms: early summer Height: 15 cm (6 in.) Spread: 25 cm (10 in.)

A fairly restrained species with yellow flowers on the end of arching stems. The variety '**Variegatum**', with white-edged leaves, is prettier when not in flower.

Siebolds stonecrop *S sieboldii*
Blooms: late summer Height: 15 cm (6 in.) Spread: 25 cm (10 in.)

An attractive species with grey, flat leaves and pink flowers, It cascades gently over a rock face and grows slowly.

'Vera Jameson' stonecrop *S. 'Vera Jameson'*
Blooms: late summer Height: 20 cm (8 in.) Spread: 25 cm (10 in.)

An attractive hybrid with arching stems and bronzy-purple foliage. The heads of pink flowers are not very showy but the overall effect is good.

THYME *Thymus*
Blooms: summer Height: 1–5 cm (1–2 in.) Spread: 15–30 cm (6–12 in.)

Both lemon-scented thyme and mother-of-thyme have some named forms that are slow-growing or do not get too large. Look for '**Silver Queen**', a lemon-scented variety, and '**Minor**' and '**Elfin**' in the regular thyme.

WHITLOW GRASS—see Draba.

WOOLLY YARROW *Achillea tomentosa*
Blooms: summer Height: 10–15 cm (4–6 in.) Spread: 30 cm (12 in.)

The bright yellow flowers are in heads up to 7 cm (3 in.) across, and the compact mats of silvery, hairy foliage are attractive even when there are no flowers. The variety '**Aurea**' has brighter, more golden flowers.

 # SUGGESTED READING

Rock Gardens: A Firefly Gardeners Guide. Katherine Ferguson (editor). Firefly Books, 1996.
Rock Gardens. New York Botanic Gardens Staff. Crown, 1997.
Two basic books for the beginner.

Rock Gardening. Laura L. and H. Lincoln Foster. Timber Press, 1982.
Written by a former president of the North American Rock Garden Society, this is an in-depth look at rock gardens and their plants.

There are also many books on individual genera, such as campanulas, dianthus and saxifrages that you may want to consult as your interest grows.

Plate 33 Upper: *Chilean glory vine climbs with tendrils and a light frame is enough.*
Lower: *Hyacinth bean is a vigorous twiner and needs a strong support.*

Plate 34 Upper: *'Pagoda' dog-tooth violet flower in late spring after the crocus are finished.*
Lower: *Spring snowflake looks like a giant snowdrop but is later into bloom.*

Plate 35 *The bulbs we grow came from many countries originally.*
          Upper: Spanish bluebells will thrive where the English one is not hardy.
          Centre: Bulgarian onion is not very showy, but is eye-catching.
          Lower left and right: Persian fritillary is attractive in flower and seed.

Plate 36 *Tender bulbs can add an exotic touch.*
Upper: Canna lily has many new varieties. Here are 'Stuttgardt' (back)
and 'Praetoria' (front).
Centre: Montbretia will survive winters in southern Ontario.
Lower: Pineapple lily also does well as a container plant.

Plate 37 *Three basic, easy rock garden plants:*
          Upper: *'Hartswood Purple' aubrieta*
          Centre: *Basket of gold — the lemon flowered form*
          Lower: *The variegated form of rock cress.*

Plate 38 Upper: *The trumpet gentian is one of the easiest of this species.*
Lower: *New lewisia hybrids are not difficult to grow. Plant them in a crevice.*

Plate 39 Upper: *A planter with a variegated sedge and 'Kent Beauty' oregano.*
Lower: *Licorice plant and fan flower in an urn-shaped planter.*

Plate 40 *Lettuce are quick to mature and equally quick to bolt once the weather warms up.*

Container Gardening

12 chapter

Small can be great. Whether you garden on an apartment balcony or an acreage, growing plants in containers will add interest and colour. In a tiny rowhouse garden or balcony, planters and window boxes might be all you have room for, while in a larger garden, plants in pots can be a movable, changeable source of seasonal colour or act as a focal point to distract the eye from an unsightly view.

Gardening on a small patio or balcony calls for a particular mind-set. You need to think of how to make the most of the available space and pinpoint what you want from your garden. If you only use containers you will have a portable garden that you can change from year to year and can rearrange at any time. Make good use of space by gardening vertically, using climbing vines that take up little ground space to cover the walls with foliage and flowers. Annual vines can even be grown in containers.

Start by assessing the factors you can't change, since these will determine what you can do.

- What is the aspect of your potential garden? Is it in full sun, full shade, part shade? If the latter, what time of day does it get sun? Make a rough sketch of the area and note the amount of light, where it falls and at what time of day. If the garden is in full sun, will surrounding walls reflect heat in summer? If so, should you consider covering the walls or providing shade?
- What about water? Will rain fall on the area or is it shielded by an overhang? Is there a tap you can use or will water have to be brought from inside the house?
- Will wind be a factor, and if so, is there anything you can do to deflect it?

How do you want your garden to look? Try to develop a theme; it could be Spanish, wickerware, or ultra-modern, but there should be something to tie the various elements together. In a very small garden or on a balcony, it may be possible to change the theme from year to year by using different planters and slipcovers for furniture cushions.

A small water feature can add extra interest. A half whisky barrel can be fitted with a special liner, or you can buy preformed fibreglass pools designed for small spaces. Add a submersible pump and a fountain head and you have sound and movement in the garden. (On a windy balcony, use a head that forms a dome of water or you will be constantly refilling the pool.) In a shallow pool, all you really need is a group of stones to hide the pump, but in a deeper pool you can add some small water plants and replace them each year. Fish are not a good idea in small pools that have to be emptied for winter; they are too difficult to bring through the winter indoors.

 ## CONTAINERS

Containers these days are not always what they seem. Modern plastics do such a good job of imitating traditional materials that it is often hard to tell the real from the false—until you pick them up. Although plastic containers may look like pottery or antique lead, they are lightweight and, even when full of plants, may not be a good choice for a very windy location where they could blow over.

Many modern containers are now self-watering—they have a reservoir below the planting level and some sort of wicking system that helps to keep the planter evenly moist, providing you remember to fill the reservoir. If you are using dark-coloured plastic containers, try to find ones that have double walls. Dark colours heat up more in sunlight and the double walls help keep the soil cool.

Most garden centres carry containers in a bewildering range of styles, shapes, and materials. They can be made of glazed earthenware, terra cotta, concrete, wood, fibreglass, or plastic, with plain or decorated exteriors. Unless you are using them purely for their decorative value, be sure to pick ones that are deep enough to hold a good volume of soil. Also, check that the drainage holes are large enough, or numerous enough, to allow surplus water to run away freely. On balconies, where weight may be a consideration, try to avoid containers that are heavy before they are filled with soil.

 ## SOIL

The type of growing mix you use in containers will depend on where your garden is located. Planters for a patio or ground-level garden need a different mix from that used for a high-rise balcony. On balconies, weight is a consideration and you should use one of the soilless, peat-based mixes. These are comparatively light in weight but do have some drawbacks. Unlike soil, they do not store nutrients and you will have to feed your plants more often. Also they are very difficult to wet, and if you use them straight from the bag, most of the water will run straight through without soaking in.

A couple of days before you intend to plant your container, place the appropriate amount of soilless mix in a bucket or bowl and add hot water. This will be absorbed overnight, and you can feel the mix the next day to see if you need to add more. If it is too wet, mix in more of the dry mix; this is why I suggest you do this at least two days before you want to use it. Soilless mixes have some fertilizer included, but it won't keep your plants growing well for more than a few weeks. If you can find one of the slow-release fertilizers designed to be mixed with soil, you can add this to the soilless mix before planting. This will save you having to fertilize for the first couple of months at least. You can also get water-retaining granules to mix with your soil, or soilless mix. These have the ability to absorb large quantities of water and then release it slowly. To be honest, I didn't find they reduced the need for watering an appreciable amount when I tried them.

For containers where weight is not a factor, use a mix of sterilized (or pasteurized) soil, bagged sheep manure, peat moss, and horticultural sand, in a 3-2-1-1 ratio. Squeeze a handful of the resulting mix and see how easily it crumbles afterwards. If it stays as a lump, the soil had a high clay content, so add another part of sand to improve the drainage. (Horticultural sand is also known as washed river sand. It is sand with all the very fine particles removed.)

 ## FILLING THE CONTAINER

The night before you intend to plant, thoroughly water the plants you will be using. This makes them easier to remove from their pots; more importantly, if they're planted dry, it's difficult to moisten them later. If you are using one of the self-watering planters, the rest of this paragraph does not apply to you. Unless you are growing bog plants, good drainage is essential in your containers. Start by putting a good layer of coarse gravel, small stones or pieces of broken flower pot on the bottom of the container. Cover this with some form of roughage to keep the soil from washing down into the drainage material. This can be coarse peat, partly decayed leaves, or a piece of old carpet. If you are making several planters, it is worth buying a single length of sod and cutting this into pieces to place grass-side-down over the drainage.

With a large planter, move it into position at this stage, as it may be too heavy to move once it is full of soil and plants. Half-fill the container with your soil (or soilless) mix and firm it down gently. Remember, good drainage is essential, so don't pack the mix down too hard, just firm it enough to remove air pockets. Take the largest plant for that container and remove it from its pot, then adjust the soil level so the top of the root ball is 3 to 5 cm (1 to 2 in.) below the container rim. This depth allows you to add enough water to soak the entire container later. If you fill the container to the correct level first, and then scoop out holes for the plants, the planter will end up overfull.

Place the largest pot in position, then unpot the remaining plants. If needed, add soil mix to bring the tops of the remaining root balls up to the level of the first one, then fill in around the plants, firming the soil between the roots. When you are done, water the container using a plant-starter fertilizer (one with a high middle number) to stimulate the plants to make new roots. If possible, keep the containers in light shade for a couple of days while the plants get acclimatized to their new home. If you don't have any shade, drape an old sheer drape or a piece of floating row cover over the container to shield plants from the direct sun.

It pays to raise the planter off the ground. This improves the drainage, air-prunes any roots that manage to grow out of the drainage hole, and makes it more difficult for pests like slugs and earwigs to find your plants. Keeping the base of the container dry also slows down the unsightly green mould that grows on terra cotta pots. To raise the pot, use three flat stones of equal size or pottery feet available at the larger garden centres. You may want to move your planters around, and you can also get small wheeled platforms to sit the containers on.

PLANT CARE

Once the plants are established and growing well it is amazing how much water they can use. Because the roots are growing in a limited space, they form a dense mass and, being unable to penetrate deep into the soil in search of moisture, they depend on you to supply their needs. A lush planter in full sun, or on a breezy balcony, may need watering twice a day. When you water, add enough that you can see it running out of the bottom of the planter—another good reason for having your planters raised off the ground. At ground level, all this water doesn't matter, but balcony gardeners may need to take precautions to prevent the excess water dripping onto the balcony below. You may need to place your planters on some form of tray to catch the surplus and allow it to evaporate.

Naturally, all this water running through the soil quickly washes out the available nutrients. Even if you added some of the slow-release granules when you mixed the soil, you will have to start fertilizing before long. Watch your plants; they will tell you when they are beginning to suffer. Look for smaller leaves, yellowing or paleness in the new foliage, and a slowing of flower production and growth in general.

The easiest way to fertilize planters is with water-soluble fertilizers—after all, you have to water anyway. Use a balanced fertilizer such as 6-9-6 or 7-7-7. If all you can find is 20-20-20, use it at half the recommended strength. These soluble fertilizers are quick-acting since they are in a form that is readily available to the plants and don't have to be broken down first by bacteria in the soil. You will probably need to fertilize your planters about every ten days for a soilless mix and every two to three weeks for a soil-based mix. Organic gardeners can use fish emulsion (if they don't mind the smell) or liquid seaweed, but these are not as quick-acting and often come in much lower concentrations, like 2-1-1, and have to be used more frequently.

To keep them flowering well, just as with plants in any garden, remove the old flowers as they fade to stop the plants from setting seed. Keep an eye open for pests and diseases and take action at the first sign of trouble (see Chapter 14).

The most popular use of containers is to grow a mixture of flowering plants. Most will be trailing or bushy forms, but you may want a plant that will give some height. If this is the plant known as "spike" (*Dracaena indivisa*) you have nothing to worry about, but most other upright plants have a tendency to flop and will need some support. Since planters are usually seen from one side, it is easy to hide a thin bamboo cane behind a tall plant and tie it in place with some green garden twine.

If you are growing climbers, they will need something to climb. In most cases, it is not a good idea to put a trellis into the container along with the plants. When the climbers get large, they tend to be top-heavy and blow over in even a moderate wind. It is much better to fasten the trellis into a wall, or, on a balcony, to the rail. You can, however, use one of the obelisks that are now readily available. Usually made of thin metal rods or tough plastic, they are ideal for most annual climbers, although you may need to thread some extra strings or tie the plants up to get them started.

Different plants climb in different ways; some twine their entire stem round the support, other use their leaves and curl the leaf-stalks or leaf tips round the trellis, others modify some of the leaves to form special tendrils that twine or have suction-cup-like tips.

To some extent, the way they climb determines what type of support you must provide. A plant that has twining leaf stalks, for example, cannot climb a trellis made of thick strips of wood, while one that climbs by twining the entire stem would be able to. Do not mount a trellis flat against the wall; there won't be room for plants to twine between them. Instead, mount it on blocks that hold it out a few centimetres (an inch or two). If you are growing a permanent vine that needs cutting back each spring, as some clematis do, it is helpful to hinge the trellis at the bottom so it can be lowered, making it easy to remove the previous year's stems. Mount the spacer blocks on the trellis itself and hold it upright with a couple of hooks and eyes.

 ## WHAT CAN I GROW?

In winter, a hardy plant growing in the garden has most of its roots well below the surface of the soil; while they may become frozen, they are not as cold as the soil surface. The soil in a container, because it is exposed to cold air all around, freezes harder and plants have to be super-hardy to survive. Don't try to overwinter plants that are of borderline hardiness; pick those you know are tough. HINT: Use catalogues from nurseries on the prairies to find out what perennials can take low temperatures. Grow trees and shrubs that are about two zones hardier than where you live.

By far the most popular plants for containers are **annuals**. Their bright colours, ease of growth, availability, and wide range of suitable varieties make them most people's first choice. And they make it easy to change the look of your garden from one year to the next; you can have a hot-looking red and yellow garden one year, and a cool pink and blue the next. Annuals come in so many forms—trailing, upright, bushy, spreading, and climbing—that they can fill just about every need. Because they are only growing for a summer, it is easy to dispose of the growing mix at the end of the season and start afresh each spring. It also means that if you come across a combination of plants that you really like, you can repeat it

year after year without having to worry about pest and disease build-up.

Popular annuals are described in Chapter 9; the following selections are particularly good for growing in containers and window boxes: Alyssum, especially the Basket Series; bacopa, good trailing habit; wax begonia, great for shade; bidens, a big plant, so don't crowd it; celosia, both the dwarf cockscombs and the feather type; dusty miller, a good accent plant for the middle; fan flower, only available as plants, not seed; geranium, especially the ivy-leaved types; licorice plant, grey foliage that contrasts well with bright flowers; nasturtium, especially the variegated 'Alaska' and the new varieties grown from cuttings; ornamental grasses, such as fountain grass, which makes a centrepiece in a large planter; patience plant, a good choice for shade; petunia, any of the Wave Series of multifloras or the Supercascade Series of grandifloras; verbena, especially many of the newer trailing varieties.

Perennials can fill a vital role in a permanent container garden, providing the foliage contrast that makes the vibrant colours of annuals stand out. In a shady corner, for instance, the big, bold leaves of hosta can act as a foil for the pale blooms of patience plant. Most perennials have a fairly limited flowering period, so try to use those that have attractive foliage when they are out of bloom, like peonies, ice plant, and meadowsweet. Ornamental grasses are also good container plants, with both attractive foliage and a good fall display. You can even grow the invasive ones in containers where they can't spread, but be warned, some can break the planter if they get too pot-bound. Just don't try to grow species that are of doubtful hardiness—they might not survive over winter in a container.

A few years ago, I was visiting some gardens on a local horticultural society garden tour. When I walked into one garden, my eyes were drawn to a clump of Japanese iris in full flower. As I had never seen these

197

growing in Ottawa, I rushed over. On close examination, the flowers proved to be silk. As the owner of the garden explained, with only a small flower bed, she wanted as good a show as possible, so when the Siberian iris finished flowering, she bought good-quality silk flowers to extend the display. The silk flowers lasted the summer, fading slowly in colour, and they certainly fooled me. This idea would have merit in many other small gardens.

Vigorous perennials will have to be moved to a larger container after a couple of years, whereas less vigorous ones will probably need repotting only every five years or so. Eventually their container will be as large as you want. From then on give them an annual top-dressing in spring. Remove the top few centimetres (1 to 2 in.) of soil from the container and replace it with a mix of half soil, half sheep manure.

Depending on where you garden, you may be able to enjoy the first touch of spring by planting a container with **spring bulbs**. Because the soil in a container freezes colder than soil in a garden, bulbs may not survive over winter. If you live in a high-rise and have a balcony garden, I would not recommend that you try them. In a townhouse courtyard, if you can move a planter into a sheltered corner and protect the exposed sides with some insulation or bales of straw, the hardiest bulbs, like grape hyacinths and crocus, should survive. They will not come through the winter unprotected in zone 5a, but will in warmer zones. These bulbs are inexpensive enough to experiment with, so give it a try. **Summer-flowering bulbs**, like lilies, are great container plants but must be lifted and stored over winter. Miniature gladioli are inexpensive, so can be grown and discarded. A small group will add height to a planter of annuals.

You can add permanence to your garden by growing **trees and shrubs** in containers. Choose species that will be in keeping with the scale of your garden, or be prepared to replace them once they get overlarge. Small trees, like the amur maple (page 78), make good container specimens, providing you have a large enough planter. Weeping trees can add an interesting effect to a small garden; try the weeping white mulberry (page 79) where space is adequate, but use Walker weeping peashrub (page 80) in a tiny garden. Both are very hardy and you can plant a few annuals at the base for summer colour.

Choose shrubs for their foliage, rather than just for their flowers; some of the new mounding spireas are excellent for this purpose, and they are very hardy. In warmer climates, try the foliage forms of wintercreeper (page 94). Many of the dwarf conifers, such as the dwarf Alberta spruce (page 104) and mugho pine (page 101) are tough enough to be grown in containers and add winter interest to a patio or balcony.

Your container garden does not have to be restricted to flowers—you can also include **vegetables**. Choose varieties appropriate to the depth of your planter (round or stubby carrots rather than long ones, for example). Salad crops do very well in spring and early summer. My daughter in Edmonton, where nights are cool, keeps herself in mesclun all summer long in two 35-cm (14-in.) square planters on her apartment balcony. Consider scarlet runner beans for a screen. They grow quickly, the flowers are attractive, and the beans are delicious if picked young.

 # WINDOW BOXES

These are really just another planter, except they are hung on a wall, or on the outside of a balcony railing. All that I have said previously about soil mixes, planting, and aftercare applies here. The main concern is to ensure the boxes are secure enough to hold their weight when they are newly watered.

Think safety! Many high-rises have restrictions on what can be used, or whether they are permitted at all, so check your lease carefully before starting.

WALLS DO NOT A PRISON MAKE

Many balconies have solid concrete walls at either end to provide a privacy screen, and townhouses often have some form of dividing fence for the same reason. These walls provide a great opportunity to add individuality to the garden. They offer a place to try vertical landscaping.

The most obvious way to do this is to grow climbers. These may be permanent, perennial plants, like clematis or Virginia creeper, or annuals such as canary creeper and cup and saucer vine. Whichever you choose, the structure on which they climb will need to be slightly away from the wall so the plant can twist around it.

Permanent vines will need a permanent structure—some form of trellis. Vines that climb by twisting their stems can climb the diagonal trellis available at most lumber supply stores. Those that climb by twining their leaf stalks need something thinner, a frame covered in large-mesh chicken wire perhaps. One idea for expanding the sense of space in your garden is to mount a large mirror in the wall and surround it with trellis and plants, creating the illusion that the wall is only a screen with more garden behind it.

An easy way to provide support for annual climbers is to mount two pieces of wood horizontally, at the top and bottom of the space. Hammer 3-cm (1 ½-in.) galvanized nails into these strips every 7 cm (3 in.), sinking the nails to about two-thirds of their length. Fasten strings to the nail heads at top and bottom. At the end of the season, simply cut the strings at either end and put them,

complete with the vine stems, out for yard-waste pick-up.

Another way to brighten a plain wall is to use wall sconces filled with plants. These are small, one-sided hanging baskets made of plastic or pottery. Garden centres also sell plastic sleeves that you fill with growing mix and plants. Some are rigid, with planting holes at intervals, while others are more like slender garbage bags with push-out planting slots. Many have built-in drip trays so you can hang them over a seating area—a good way to watch hummingbirds.

Another interesting wall feature is a small self-contained waterfall. These are made to hang on a wall and have a built-in submersible pump that pumps the water up to fall or trickle into the basin below. These come in several forms and may have a sheet of water falling from a ledge or a single stream, often spouting from the mouth of a cherub, frog, or gargoyle.

Other ways of adding interest to a blank wall include a vertical sundial (providing the wall is in the sun), various masks, decorative figures, sculptures and the like. In my youth, a flight of three flying ducks would have been obligatory, but thank goodness fashions change.

The advent of *xeriscaping*, low water-use gardening, has evolved special watering hoses. Instead of spraying out water along their entire length like a regular soaker hose would, the pipes are without holes. With a special tool, you make small holes where needed and insert a thin, flexible pipe with a small nozzle on the end. These are placed beside each of the plants you wish to water. Simply turning on the tap will water all your planters at once. To simplify things even more for those who forget to water or for vacation times, there are programmable units that will turn the water on at preset times. You can paint the main hose to match the wall so it is not intrusive.

 # SUGGESTED READING

Gardening off the Ground. Art C. Drysdale. Self-published, 1996.

The No-Garden Gardener. Jane Courtier. Reader's Digest, 1999.

The first deals with balcony gardening; the second with all types of restricted-space gardens.

The City and Town Gardener. Linda Yang. Random House, 1995.

A book by a New York garden writer who lives in an apartment.

The Edible Garden
13 chapter

No matter how small your garden, there is always room to grow some plants you can eat. Edible landscaping may be all the rage, but the concept is far from new; the French were practising this form of gardening many years ago and English cottage gardens carry on the tradition. If you don't have space for a separate vegetable garden, it is simple to grow a few early lettuce, a small patch of radish, or a climbing cucumber in with your flowers and shrubs.

Vegetables and fruit that you have grown yourself are a real taste treat. You don't have to restrict yourself to the easy-to-grow, quick-to-mature, tough-skins-to-travel-well varieties that commercial growers must use to stay competitive. You can grow the varieties that have soft skins that ripen over a period of time, the ones that are listed as being best for short-day regions, and the ones with flavour.

 ## SOIL AND SITE

Any soil that will grow shrubs or perennials will grow vegetables and fruit. The warnings about perennial weeds that I mentioned earlier apply equally to fruit and vegetables. If you are creating an area purely for food production, you would do well to consider slightly raised beds unless your soil is very sandy. These beds will dry out quicker and warm up faster in spring, so you will be able to get your crops planted sooner. Making the beds narrow enough to reach the centre from either side eliminates the need to step on the soil, and you can put the rows closer together, or you can even do away with rows altogether. The heavier the soil type, the more essential it is to avoid treading on it and damaging the soil structure.

Work towards producing a well-drained soil, with lots of humus in it. On sandy soils add manure, leaf mould, peat moss or compost; while on heavy clays add coarse sand and humus (manure and compost) as described in Chapter 1. On heavy soils especially, try to find the energy to double-dig the beds, working lots of organic material into the lower spit. You don't have to do all this in one season; you can do a bit at a time. Green manuring really helps to improve soils for vegetable growing.

If you can dig the garden in the fall, leaving it in rough chunks to overwinter, you will get a head start in spring and have crops up and ready weeks ahead of your neighbours. Do not add manure to your garden in spring, even if you dig it then. Many vegetables react negatively to the presence of fresh manure in the soil. You are better to add it as a mulch on top of the soil (but away from the stems of the plants) once the seedlings are germinated or the plants are established.

Locate your vegetable garden in full sun. Planting in the shade is, with a very few exceptions, a waste of time and liable to put you off growing your own food. Roots from nearby trees and hedges can quickly invade rich soil, so keep at least 1 m (3 ft.) away from a hedge and twice this from a tree. This problem is not quite as serious as with a perennial bed because digging the vegetable garden each year chops off invading roots and prevents them from becoming a major nuisance.

 **PLANNING**

If you are a novice at growing food, start small. Don't think you can suddenly become self-sufficient in one year, especially on an average suburban lot. Concentrate on a few easy-to-grow vegetables and herbs to begin with and expand your range when you gain experience and find out how much free time you have. Growing a few vegetables well is a great way to boost your self-confidence.

Try to concentrate on vegetables you (and your family) like, and ones that aren't readily available. With the growth in popularity of farmers' markets, it is now easy to find really fresh produce, but nothing is quite the same as vegetables straight from the garden. If space is limited, use it to grow the things you read about but can't buy: blue potatoes, white beets, asparagus peas, or summer leeks, for example.

Even if your proposed garden is tiny, try to have some sort of plan to work towards. If the plants end up in the wrong places, draw a new plan of the way it turned out so that next year you will be able to put different things in each spot, a process known as crop rotation. While this may seem silly when you are only growing lettuce, tomatoes, radishes, and a few herbs, many diseases will overwinter in the soil and planting your tomatoes in fresh soil each year, on a three- or four-year cycle, will do much to reduce disease problems.

The common vegetables can be put into several groups, each containing plants with similar likes, dislikes, and pests. Do not plant one member of a group in the place occupied by a different member of that group the previous year, and preferably not for the previous two years. The **tomato group** contains tomatoes, potatoes, peppers, and eggplants. The **root crop group** has carrots, beets, parsnips, parsley, Swiss chard, dill, and celery. The **squash group** includes cucumbers, squash, pumpkins, melons, watermelons, and zucchini. The **cabbage group** is made up of Brussels sprouts, broccoli, cauliflower, cabbage, kohlrabi, kale, and turnips. Onions, shallots, bunching onions, leeks, and garlic all belong to the **onion group**, while the various peas and beans, both bush and pole, belong to the **pea group**. **Corn** is best considered as a group on its own.

When you are selecting seed from a catalogue or the seed rack in your local garden centre, pay special attention to the *days to maturity*. This is the average number of days it will take the crop to mature, either from sowing or transplanting, whichever is the normal way to grow that particular plant. Providing you have a rough idea when your average first and last frosts occur, you can then be sure you have enough time to mature that crop. Most Canadian seed houses sell varieties that are suitable for our climate, but if you are buying from U.S. firms, their seed may be intended for more southerly gardens with much longer growing seasons.

You will almost certainly have to water at some stage, and it makes sense to recognize this and plan ahead. If you have a vegetable garden, as distinct from growing a few vegetables in with your flowers, it pays to lay down soaker hoses shortly after the seedlings come through. As with roses, put them with the holes facing down so that the water goes into the soil, rather than up into the air. You will use half as much water, since much of that sprayed upwards evaporates and never reaches the root zone at all. There are also several drip- and trickle-irrigation systems on the market with flexible watering tubes that can be curved to accommodate any planting scheme. These are worth checking out because they make efficient use of the water, putting it where it is needed, rather than wetting everything.

GETTING THEM GOING

A great many vegetables can be sown directly into the soil once it has dried out. Some germinate best in cold soil; others should be sown only when all danger of frost is past. Others are best planted as young plants, and a few can be grown both ways.

Most of the young plants you might need (tomatoes, peppers, and eggplants) need an early start and plenty of space so they're best suited to greenhouse production. Unless you have experience at raising seedlings indoors, buy them from a nursery.

Onion and leek seed is quite slow-growing and should be sown in pots about two months before the planting date. As the seedlings grow and get about 15 cm (6 in.) tall, clip them back halfway with a pair of scissors. This will help to produce sturdy seedlings and may have to be done several times before planting time. HINT: Onion seed is large enough to handle with tweezers and can be sown about 1 cm (½ in.) apart in pots. This will eliminate the need to transplant the seedlings into individual pots or cell-packs.

Lettuce is much faster-growing and sowing a few seeds indoors in mid-March will give you plants large enough to set out a month later. Make a second sowing in early April, and again in midmonth (and make an outdoor sowing then, too). Lettuce is cold tolerant and if you harden the seedlings off as described for annuals, you could start planting out by mid-April in southern Ontario, mid-May further north. HINT: By experimenting with planting under row covers or plastic containers with the bottoms cut out, such as windshield washer fluid jugs, you could get an even earlier crop.

When growing seedlings under lights, they must be up close to the tubes. Although the lights seem bright to our eyes, they are nowhere near the intensity of sunlight, and the brightness decreases rapidly as you move away from the tubes. The tops of the seedlings should be no more than 10 cm (4 in.) below the tubes for good growth. The light given off by a fluorescent tube decreases with age. Tubes in use on a regular basis should be replaced once a year, preferably in spring when you are ready to have seedlings growing under them.

PLANTING

There is nothing sacred about the 24th of May long weekend. You do not have to plant all your vegetables in one hectic burst of energy. Rather, spread the planting out over several weeks, starting as soon as the soil is dry enough to crumble. I am sure people don't believe me when I tell them we're picking such and such a vegetable early in the season. But then, my plants were probably established and growing before theirs were sown.

Some plants grow best in cool soil and should be planted early; others won't grow unless the soil is warm. (Here you can use a temporary cover of plastic to warm the soil quickly, as noted above.) This is detailed for each vegetable in the listings for this chapter.

Make yourself a measuring stick as an aid to planting and sowing seeds. I use an old broom handle marked off at 8-cm (3-in.) intervals with a permanent marker to help me space plants evenly. Vegetable plants grown in pots should be set just a little deeper—1 to 2 cm (½ to 1 in.)—than they were growing. Dig the hole with a trowel, set the plant in place, and fill in around it with soil. Firm the plant with your fingers to remove large air spaces, leaving a slight depression over the roots to collect water. When all are planted, water them in with a plant-starter fertilizer mixed according to the directions on the package. Never use more than the recommended amount; you could burn the roots and kill the plant. If you are growing plants that will need some support, such as tomatoes, put the canes or stakes in place at planting time. Leaving it until later will damage the roots. HINT: Old broken hockey sticks make great tomato stakes if you saw the broken end to a point.

When growing from seed, rake the seed bed with your garden rake to remove the stones and break up the large lumps of soil. The finer the seed you'll be sowing, the smaller the particles of soil should be.

Measure off from the last crop or end of the bed and put a popsicle stick at both ends of the row. If you have short rows you can use your measuring stick as an edge; otherwise you will have to make a garden line (use nylon or plastic string; it doesn't rot if you leave it out in the rain).

With the point of your trowel, make a shallow trench between the two markers, along the string or measuring stick. Sow the seed in this trench as thinly as possible. Gently push a little soil over the seeds and firm into place with your foot, touching the soil just enough to leave the impression of your shoe. A common mistake is to sow too deeply and too thickly. The seed should be about twice its diameter deep, which for small seed is just below the surface. You can water the seed providing you have a fine spray on your can or hose, and only use low pressure. Watering with coarse droplets or high pressure will wash out the seed you have so carefully planted. Remember, you are going to have to weed these seedlings later on and that is much simpler if they are in straight rows.

The *floating row covers*, such as Reemay, made of polypropylene, are excellent for getting young plants and seedlings off to an early start. The cover floats upwards as they grow but lets water and light through. Simply spread a sheet of the fabric loosely over the bed and weigh the outer edge down to keep it from blowing away. I dot small flower pots between the rows to lift the cover off the soil and keep it clean. A dirty fabric won't let as much light through. One word of warning; inspect your plants from time to time. One batch of peppers that we covered were alive with aphids when we finally removed the cover. With care, each sheet will last several seasons.

Plants such as pepper and eggplant should not be set out until the soil is really warm, but tomatoes will take cooler conditions (although not actual frost), and can be planted earlier.

You can get a good start on the season—and earlier fruit—if you protect the young plants. You can use bird feed bags as described on page 86, or a commercial device made from a circle of plastic tubes that you place over the plant and fill with water. The water holds the heat at night and keeps the plant warm. We have brought plants through nights when the temperature dropped to -5°C (23°F) without damage.

 # MULCHING

As mentioned, some plants grow best in cool soil. Obviously, as the weather warms up the soil is going to get warmer as well, so how are these poor plants that like it cool going to thrive? You can help keep the soil temperature lower by mulching the soil surface. This only works if you ignore that May 24 date and sow your crops when they need it. Peas and broad (fava) beans are especially sensitive to warm soil temperature and you will get a much better crop if you sow early, while the soil is cold, and mulch when the seeds have germinated and are a few centimetres (1 to 2 in.) tall.

Crops that prefer warm soil should not be mulched until the soil has had a chance to warm up. You can speed the soil warming by mulching with a plastic sheet. Clear sheets warm the soil up quickest but they allow the weeds to grow underneath; black plastic allows weeds to germinate but then kills the seedlings by keeping them in the dark. Remove this mulch before planting. A porous mulch applied between the plants in late June will help greatly to slow water evaporation from the soil and reduce the amount of irrigating you will have to do—a worthwhile consideration if summer water restrictions continue.

What you use for a mulch depends on what you have or can get locally. Straw works well but is a bit messy, blows around, and has to be raked off the soil before you can dig. If you have been collecting and composting leaves, these work great and can be dug in come the fall, but weed seeds will germinate in a compost mulch. Plastic sheeting does the job but doesn't look nice and it's a problem to keep it from blowing away. If your mower has a grass catcher, the clippings can be spread thinly after each mowing and will quickly dry and turn brown. Build them up in thin layers over several mowings rather than putting on a thick mulch. This way they don't start to decompose and heat up. Peat moss is often recommended, but I find it blows away unless you have a very sheltered garden. It also forms a crust that is almost impervious to rain. Cocoa husks and bark chips can be used if they are all that is available, but I would suggest them only as a last resort since you don't want them to get mixed into the soil. They are better between flowers and shrubs where appearance is more important and worth paying a high price for.

Even if you are only growing a few vegetables here and there through your flowers, they will produce better crops if you mulch the soil around each clump to keep the moisture level from fluctuating. Vegetables need a steady supply of moisture to grow well and produce good crops.

 # SUMMER CARE

The primary summer task, apart from cutting and eating your produce, is controlling weeds. If you mulched well, there should be few or no weeds except along the row where the mulch doesn't cover. If you leave weeds to grow they will take much of the moisture and nutrition that should be going to your crop plants. Also, weeds by definition are strong-growing plants, able to compete and win in most situations; they will grow faster than the desired seedlings and shade them, so that even if they survive the amount of food produced will be reduced greatly. While the seedlings are small, and you cannot mulch, use your scuffle hoe carefully, but regularly, between the rows. Done while the weedlings are small, it takes only a few minutes. Let the weeds gain control, and killing them becomes a major undertaking. You will need to hand-weed along the rows as well and this should be done once while the seedlings are small; the second time it can often be combined with the next task.

Unless the seeds are large and you can sow them individually, no matter how sparsely you sow the time will come when the young plants need thinning. If your original sowing was well spaced, thinning can wait until the young plants are large enough to be usable (baby carrots, small leaf lettuce, etc.). It is hard to make oneself pull out plants that have taken so much trouble to grow, but unless the spacing is sufficient, you will not get a good return for your efforts. Twenty large carrots will weigh a lot more than 50 or 60 crowded ones. Try to choose a day when rain is forecast, to help settle in the remaining plants. If necessary, water the rows thoroughly beforehand so the soil is moist and the seedlings pull out easily. Don't forget to remove any weeds along with the excess plants. Clean up after thinning and put any thinnings not intended for the kitchen on the compost heap.

Many vegetables benefit from an application of fertilizer during the growing season and often a good time to apply this is just after thinning. The actual fertilizer to use depends on the crop. Plants with edible roots need a different formulation to those grown for their fruit. The timing and type of fertilizer are given in the individual plant recommendations. When choosing between organic and chemical fertilizers, don't forget that many organic fertilizers need to be broken down by bacteria in the soil. This means they become available to the plant more slowly than granu-

lar or soluble chemical fertilizers, but the chances of burning plant roots are much less.

All that remains now is to pick your produce. While it seems silly to say so, this is a task that must be done. The whole reason for a plant to grow is to reproduce and set seed. If you let your plants ripen their seed, they will stop producing. Peas, for example, will continue to crop for several weeks as long as you pick the pods; once the peas ripen, the plant will stop making new flowers and the pea season is over. If you are going away on holiday, arrange for someone you can trust to gather all the vegetables as they are ready. We went to a garden conference one summer and arranged with friends to pick the garden while we were gone. When we came back just about everything had finished producing. Our friends hadn't wanted to seem greedy, so they hardly picked anything. This is why you need someone you can trust—trust to do as you asked. If you can't eat it, freeze it, preserve it, or turn it into wine—give it away. Anyone want a 5-kg (11-lb.) zucchini?

 # WHAT SHALL I GROW?

Because of the different sizes of vegetable varieties, it is not always possible to give spacing suggestions. Cabbage, for example, can be miniatures that you can pick up with one hand or giant drumhead types that may weigh 20 kg (44 lb.) or more. Check the directions on the seed packet or in the catalogue for the spacing requirements.

The descriptions that follow are arranged by planting time. If your soil is poor and you haven't yet built up the organic level, you may need to use some chemical fertilizer to grow good crops. The requirements for the common vegetables are included.

Side-dressing is the term used to describe the application of granular fertilizer on either side of a row of plants. Roughly calculate the amount of fertilizer needed for your row and sprinkle it evenly in a band about 15 cm (6 in.) wide down both sides of the row, taking care not to get it on the leaves of the plants. You can either hoe it lightly into the surface of the soil or water the rows to dissolve the fertilizer. The rates given are for granular fertilizer, not soluble feeds that are dissolved in water before application.

VEGETABLES FOR COOL SOIL

LETTUCE
Start from seed or grow from plants.

Lettuce is a short season crop. It's not in the ground for very long and can be tucked in between other plants or sown in small groups wherever it will fit. Start some indoors in March, ready to plant out as soon as the soil is dry. The seed needs both light and cool temperatures to germinate. Sow seed in the garden when you transplant your seedlings and every two weeks thereafter for a succession of salads. You will only need a few seeds every 15 cm (6 in.), which you can thin to one plant as the seedlings grow. Lettuce doesn't like hot weather and will usually bolt (form a flower spike) instead of making a head once the weather warms up. Side-dress the plants with a little 10-10-10 when the plants are growing strongly. Lettuce is mostly water and needs a regular supply to grow well. It does best on rich soils.

There are four types of lettuce, which mature at different rates. A sowing of some of each will give you lettuce over a long period. **Leaf lettuce** forms a cluster of leaves and matures quickly. '**Red Sails**' has leaves tinged a bronze colour and was an All-America winner. These are the best types for warm regions. **Boston lettuce** (also known as **butterhead**)

forms a loose head and matures next, '**Buttercrunch**' is fairly heat tolerant. **Cos** or **romaine lettuce** forms a tall plant and has very crisp leaves. This is the best-flavoured lettuce, for my money. '**Paris Island Cos**' is one of the most reliable varieties. The last to mature is the head lettuce. It forms the tight, crisp head typified by '**Iceberg**', although this variety does not grow as well here as '**Great Lakes**' or '**Minilakes**'.

MESCLUN
Start from seed.

The rather tired and wilted array of greens found in many supermarkets bears no relation to this crisp, tasty crop that is so easy to grow. Almost anything that can be eaten as a young plant can be included; mesclun is really a mix you can blend to suit your personal tastes. A good mix may include several different types of lettuce, arugula, endive, mustards, and possibly some of the Asian vegetables. Other mixes are composed of just lettuce of various types and colours. You can buy mixes ready made, or make up your own.

Sow this early, and thinly, in a band 5 to 10 cm (2 to 4 in.) wide. The length of the row depends on how much you like salad. The seedlings will be ready to harvest in about three weeks, but use them before they are 15 cm (6 in.) tall. With scissors, cut them off well above soil level and the plants will regrow. You will be able to get about three cuttings off each sowing, providing you keep the bed moist. It will also help if you give a half-strength liquid feed after each complete cut. To ensure a continuous supply, sow a short row every three weeks.

Like most salad crops, mesclun does not like heat and does best in spring and fall. If you can keep it well watered and provide some light shade, you will extend the cropping season. HINT: Don't throw out old window screens, they are good for providing small areas of shade.

RADISHES
Cabbage group. Start from seed.

Like lettuce, radishes can be dotted in wherever there is space. We usually make the first sowing along a sunny house wall as soon as the snow melts for our very first "fresh from the garden" crop. Radishes may be colours other than the red generally found in supermarkets. 'White Icicle' has roots up to 15 cm (6 in.) in length while 'Easter Egg' can be red, pink, purple, or white. Grow radishes fast, giving them lots of water, because poor growing conditions cause tough, hot roots. Sow a little, often.

CARROTS
Root group. Start from seed. Sow in rows or bands 35 cm (14 in.) apart and thin to 8 cm (3 in.).

Carrots grow best in loose, deep, sandy soils. If you have a heavy soil be especially careful not to tread on it after preparing the seed bed, and grow the short-rooted or round varieties. Often the seed will not seem to germinate because the seedlings cannot push their way through a packed clay soil. It helps to sow a little radish seed along the rows of carrots and parsnips, since these are strong enough to break through the crust and the carrots can then follow. You can leave the radishes until they are mature. Carrots grown on heavy or stony soils will tend to be forked and twisted when harvested.

If you love carrots, make successive sowings at three-week intervals until mid-July. Side-dress with 5-10-10 at 100 g (4 oz.) per 3 m (10 ft.) of row when the foliage is about 10 cm (4 in.) tall, and repeat at twice this height. For winter storage, lift in the fall and allow to air-dry just long enough to be able to rub off the excess soil, but do not wash them.

PARSNIPS
Root group. Start from seed. Sow and thin as for early carrots.

Not as well-known as they should be, parsnips have a nutty flavour and can be used in many of the ways you would treat potatoes. They are slow-growing and late sowings may not mature. Seed loses its viability fast and you should buy fresh seed each spring to be sure of good germination. Leave them in the ground until late fall, as the flavour improves greatly after a few frosts.

BEET
Root group. Start from seed. Sow and thin as for carrots. The seed is large enough to sow individually, 2.5 cm (1 in.) apart.

Beets are very cold-tolerant, and a few can even be started indoors and transplanted if you want to steal a march on the season. The "seeds" are actually small clusters of individual seeds and you will get several seedlings in each spot, which will need to be thinned. Make successive sowings at two- to three-week intervals until July for a continual supply of baby beets. Beets don't have to be red; you can also grow golden and white beets, and even one with alternating red and white rings, and they all taste different. We have found the cylindrical variety 'Formanova' especially easy to peel. 'Little Egypt' is fast-growing and gives us the first picking of baby beets.

SWISS CHARD
Root group. Start from seed. Sow in rows 40 cm (16 in.) apart; thin first to 10 cm (4 in.) and later to twice this.

The leaves can be used in place of spinach, although they taste different, and the thick leaf stalks can also be chopped into pieces and used as a vegetable. 'Bright Lights', an All-America Selections winner in 1998, comes in a variety of leaf and stem colours—purple, green, yellow, orange and red shades. It is worth growing in a perennial border for its fancy foliage, but it tastes good, too. The seedlings show colour when small, so you can be selective when thinning to get a good colour range. There is an all-yellow selection as well called **'Bright Yellow'**. Most of the colour disappears when the leaves are cooked.

SPINACH

Root group. Start from seed. Sow in rows 30 cm (12 in.) apart and thin to 10 cm (4 in.).

Spinach will not take hot weather and will germinate readily at 4°C (39°F), especially the variety **'America'**. Make successive sowings at three-week intervals. We have found that **'Tyee'** stands the heat well and crops into summer without bolting. It is a waste of time to sow past mid-May. In areas with a long fall, a second sowing in early September will generally mature enough to pick before winter. Pick individual leaves, rather than the whole plant, to extend the harvest for as long as possible.

PEAS

Pea group. Start from seed. Sow in a 15-cm-wide (6-in.) row, spacing the seed in a zigzag about 5 cm (2 in.) apart. The width between the rows depends on the height of the variety.

Sow as soon as the ground can be worked. Use your chop hoe to scrape out a shallow trench, about 2.5 cm (1 in.) deep and set out the seed by hand. Use dwarf varieties like **'Little Marvel'** unless you want to put up a trellis. They will spread about 60 cm (24 in.) across, so leave lots of room sideways. Side-dress with 5-10-10 when 15 to 20 cm (6 to 8 in.) tall, using 100 g (4 oz.) per 3 m (10 ft.) of row. You will get larger crops from the taller varieties but they need something to climb on. Netting with a 10-cm (4-in.) mesh enables you to pick both sides of the row at once, while chicken wire means you have to go up and down both sides. **Snow** peas and **edible pod** peas should also be considered, but they must be picked regularly to keep new pods forming. Pick snow peas when the individual peas can just be seen through the outer pod. Edible pod peas are left until the peas are well formed. **'Sugar Ann'** has given us the best and tastiest crops.

All peas and beans form a partnership with a soil bacterium that increases the amount of nitrogen available to them and thus improves their growth. This bacterium is available in culture form from many seedhouses. Look for **pea and bean inoculant** in the catalogues. In the fall, when cleaning up the pea and bean rows, cut the plants off at soil level, rather than pulling them up. This leaves the roots in the soil, where they will break down and release the stored nitrogen.

BROAD BEAN

Pea group. Start from seed. Sow about 5 cm (2 in.) deep and 10 cm (4 in.) apart in double rows 25 cm (10 in.) apart.

Also known as **fava bean**, this is a vegetable that you either love or hate. Sow as soon as you can—it is one bean that germinates best in a cold soil. Pinch out the growing tip of the plant as soon as the first pods are set to ensure filled pods. Strangely enough, this also seems to prevent attacks from black aphids which often feed on these plants. **'Windsor Longpod'**, **'Express'**, and **'Masterpiece Longpod'** have all given me good crops. If the weather co-operates, you can sometimes get a second crop in fall; cut the plants back to 15 cm (6 in.) once cropping is done, give a boost with 5-10-10 fertilizer, and keep well watered.

ONIONS

Onion group. Grow as sets or young plants.

A fertile, moist soil with good drainage is needed for successful onion growing. Work in plenty of good compost or manure in the fall; before planting in spring, rake in a dressing of 5-10-10 at 500 g (1 lb.) to each 7 m (20 ft.) of row. Keep the onion bed weed-free at all times as competition will severely reduce the crop. Onions have feeder roots close to the surface, so either use a scuffle hoe very shallowly while the weeds are small or hand-weed. A mulch of grass clippings works well to keep weeds down.

Perhaps the easiest way of growing good cooking onions is to plant sets. These are small dried onion bulbs which are readily available in the spring. Plant them 15 cm (6 in.) apart in a well-prepared bed, pushing each one half into the soil. Birds enjoy pulling them up and you should check the bed frequently at first and replant when needed. HINT: Cutting the dried "tail" off the top of the set makes them less attractive to birds.

The number of varieties available as sets is limited but a wide choice can be raised from seed started in a cool basement in early March, grown under fluorescent lights, and transplanted outdoors after hardening off. Spanish onions in particular need a long growing season and are rarely available as sets.

Pull off any flower heads as soon as they are noticed (more likely on onions raised from sets than those from seed) and in late summer, when about two-thirds of the tops fall over, bend them all down to encourage the bulbs to mature. Lift when the foliage turns brown and cure them in light shade, being careful to keep them dry at all times.

Multiplier onions, also known as **shallots**, are grown from small bulbs in the same way as sets, but spaced about 25 cm (10 in.) apart. Instead of forming a single larger bulb, each one multiplies to form a cluster of small bulbs. Harvest and dry in the same way as cooking onions. They are great for pickling.

Egyptian onions can also be grown from a small bulb or purchased as a rooted clump. They are more likely to be grown as a curiosity in the herb garden than in the vegetable garden. They start as a tight clump of typical onion foliage from which grow tall stems topped with clusters of small onions, called bulbils, which are very good in a stir-fry. If left, they fall to the ground and immediately take root and grow.

BUNCHING ONIONS

Onion group. Start from seed. Sow thinly in rows about 30 cm (12 in.) apart.

These are usually picked before they have time to form a bulb, but they will make a small one if left. The better seed catalogues will list varieties for spring sowing and others that will overwinter for early pulling. New on the market are varieties with pink, red, or purple onions. I tried '**Santa Claus**', which was advertised as having red stems, but I found it didn't colour up until the weather cooled off in the fall.

LEEKS

Onion group. Grow from plants.

One of the great vegetables of northern England, where they are grown to perfection and enormous size for the show table. Start seed indoors in late February or early March for plants to set out when the soil dries. Space plants about 10 cm (4 in.) apart. To develop the white, edible stem they must be blanched in some way, either by mounding soil around them or by planting them in a trench which you fill in as they grow.

Summer leeks are quicker to mature and can either be started indoors or sown outside as soon as the soil is workable. Sow them in rows 10 cm (4 in.) apart and thin to about 3 cm (1 in.) or plant them at this spacing. They do not need blanching and you can start to pull them when they are about finger thick. They never form large leeks but even though thin, they taste right. Look for '**Varna**' and '**King Richard**'.

GARLIC

Onion group. Grow from plants.

A very easy vegetable to grow from either an early spring or a fall planting. (The fall planting gives the larger bulbs.) Buy a couple of heads of garlic from the store, break them into individual cloves, and plant them 5 to 7 cm (2 to 3 in.) deep, about 10 cm (4 in.) apart. Lift in August just as the leaves begin to turn brown and you will have a large bulb on the base of each stem. To clean, peel the dirty outer skin away down to a clean white inner layer of skin. Peeling becomes much more difficult once the bulbs have dried and the best time to clean them is the day you lift them. Cure them for storage in the same way as cooking onions.

BROCCOLI
Cabbage group. From seed or plants. Sow seed indoors or set plants out 45 cm (18 in.) apart.

Sow broccoli seeds indoors under lights, for planting out in late April, or buy plants at the garden centre. Use early varieties, such as 'Premium Crop', at this time of year. Side-dress with 10-10-10 at 250 g (8 oz.) per 3 m (10 ft.) of row in midseason. Late varieties should be thinly sown directly in a seed bed around Victoria Day. Thin to a few centimetres (1 to 2 in.) apart and plant them in their final bed at about 60 cm (24 in.) apart once the seedlings have made sturdy young transplants.

CAULIFLOWER
Cabbage group. Plant as for broccoli.

Of all the cabbage group, cauliflower is the most difficult to grow. It does not stand up to frost as well as the other members of the tribe, yet it needs cool temperatures and will not form heads in hot weather. If the roots are allowed to become dry at any stage of growth, heading is also inhibited, so beware of buying transplants that show signs of wilting.

Start seed indoors about 6 to 8 weeks before the last expected frost date for spring crops, and plant out when frosts are unlikely (cover if there is a frost warning). For fall crops, sow outside in a seed bed in June and transplant when the seedlings are 10 to 12 cm (4 to 5 in.) tall. The distance between plants depends on the variety, but is generally about 45 cm (18 in.).

A new miniature variety called 'Garant' can be planted 15 cm (6 in.) apart and matures over a long period so you don't get a sudden glut of heads. One head is ideal for two people.

POTATOES
Tomato group. Grow from plants.

While it takes a lot of space to grow potatoes to feed your family for the winter, it takes little room to grow a few early roots so you can savour the taste of truly *new* potatoes or try unusual varieties, like 'All Blue' or 'Banana'. Plant them about 60 cm (24 in.) apart, using certified "seed" potatoes bought from a garden centre. There are several diseases carried on seed potatoes that can severely reduce the yield but certified seed is free of these. Supermarket potatoes are treated with a chemical to prevent them sprouting in the store, so don't plant these even if they have started to grow. The potatoes are actually formed on shoots that grow from the bottom leaves and turn down into the soil. Piling earth up around the shoots as they grow encourages more underground shoots to be formed, and gives you a bigger crop.

If you mound up your potatoes with straw or hay, rather than soil, the potatoes form on the surface of the soil and are both easy to gather and clean. You can slide your hand in under the straw and collect a few early ones without disturbing the plant.

JERUSALEM ARTICHOKE
Grow from plants.

Often used in place of potatoes, Jerusalem artichoke can also be eaten raw. Finely sliced, it adds crunch to a salad. The knobbly tubers are formed on the bottom of a very tall, sunflowerlike plant. Two tubers planted in spring 75 to 100 cm (30 to 36 in.) apart will probably give you as many artichokes as you will use over winter—store them like potatoes. The tubers are hardy and any you miss when lifting will come up next spring. 'Stampede' has smoother tubers, is shorter, and has earlier, chocolate-scented flowers.

VEGETABLES FOR WARM SOIL

GREEN AND WAX BEANS

Pea group. Start from seed. Sow in wide rows 60–75 cm (24–30 in.) apart, with the seed 7 cm (3 in.) apart.

Beans are sown from mid- to late May until the end of July. Seed sown before this, while the soil is still cold, may rot before it germinates. Side-dress with 5-10-5 when the plants are about 15 cm (6 in.) tall. Don't cultivate or pick following rain or early in the morning while the plants are wet with dew, as you may spread diseases. Pick the beans frequently to extend the cropping season.

POLE BEANS

Pea group. Start from seed. Sow along on a fence or to climb strings or poles.

I always think that these have a lot more flavour than the bush type, and they are certainly easier to pick. Prepare the planting site by working 250 g (½ lb.) of 5-10-5 per 8 m (25 ft). of row into the soil surface. Sow the seeds 5 cm (2 in.) apart and thin to 10 to 15 cm (4 to 6 in.) after germination. They must be given something to climb. Left to sprawl they will not produce good crops, and in small gardens a teepee of poles in the flower border works well. The first flowers don't seem to set fruit, but later ones do.

Side-dress with 5-10-5 at 50 g (2 oz.) per square metre (square yard) when flower buds form. HINT: Pole beans need lots of water to produce well, so lay down a soaker hose when the plants are young.

BRUSSELS SPROUTS

Cabbage group. From seed or plants. Set out plants 60–75 cm (24–30 in.) apart.

Sow the seed in a bed about May 24 and move the seedlings to their final location when they are about 15 cm (6 in.) tall, or buy plants at your local garden centre. Plant firmly

and keep well watered. Remove the lower leaves as they yellow and sprouts form, and give each plant a handful of 5-10-10 at this time. The sprouts taste better after a few frosts, but I don't recommend picking them while covered with ice unless you're trying out a new hand-warmer. HINT: Sprouts are slow-growing, so you can interplant and harvest a crop of lettuce or spinach before they need the room.

CABBAGE

Cabbage group. From seed or plants.

A good vegetable catalogue offers a bewildering choice of different types of cabbage: early to late; green, red, or white; savoy, Chinese, storage, or Kraut; the list seems endless. Read the descriptions carefully and decide which will best suit your needs. Either buy transplants or sow early varieties in mid-May. Transplant after about four weeks and they should mature before the hot weather. Sow late cabbage in mid-June, transplant as before, and they will mature in the fall. Storage cabbage is sown with the early varieties but takes much longer to mature. Whatever the type, give each plant a handful of 10-10-10 each month, sprinkled on the soil around the plant.

CORN

Corn group. Start from seed.

Corn is pollinated by the wind blowing pollen from plant to plant. It should therefore be planted in blocks of at least five plants each way, rather than in rows. Prepare the site by adding 500 g (1 lb.) of 10-10-10 to each 8 m (25 ft.) of row before planting. Sow four seeds per station, 30 cm (12 in.) apart, and thin to two plants after germination. Sowing in rows or smaller blocks will result in cobs that are not filled properly. Side-dress with 5-10-5, a small handful per clump when it's 15 to 20 cm (6 to 8 in.) tall.

Many of the newer varieties of corn are

sweeter than the old ones and keep their sweetness longer. As a result, most catalogues now identify the types of corn they sell as follows: **su** = normal sugar, the original sweet corn; **se** and **se+** = sugar enhanced, sweeter and more tender, with the sweetness lasting longer between picking and cooking; **sh2** = shrunken or supersweet (the "shrunken" refers to the dried kernels), extra sweet corn with prolonged sweetness that can last up to 10 days from picking. The **sh2** types must be grown at least 8 m (25 ft.) away from other types of corn to avoid cross-pollination, or you will get tough, starchy kernels in both types. Alternatively you can plant varieties with different maturity times, such as an early **se** and a late **sh2** so they are not flowering at the same time.

CUCUMBER
Squash group. From plants or seed.

Cucumbers come in both slicing and pickling varieties, so be sure you get the type you want if you are buying plants. You can start your own from seed by sowing them indoors about a month before your last frost date or by waiting for warm weather and sowing them directly into the garden. Plants outside need protection until cool nights are past; the semi-transparent containers for windshield-washer fluid make good covers if you cut the bottoms off. Both bush cucumbers and vining types are available. The bush types are good for small gardens but you can save space by growing the vining type up a trellis. If you are buying seed, look for varieties that are resistant to the many diseases that attack cukes. The variety name or description should be followed by a string of letters such as DM, CMV, ANTH, PM, ALS, or TLS; each refers to a specific disease, so the more the merrier. Avoid disturbing the roots when you plant. If the plants are in peat pots for example, don't attempt to remove the pots but slash the sides with a sharp knife before planting.

SQUASH
Squash group. From seeds or plants.

The various squash can be grown from seed sown directly into the garden, but for earlier fruit, start them indoors a couple of weeks before your last expected frost date. Squash are divided into summer types (including zucchini) that you eat young and tender, and winter varieties that you leave to mature almost until frost and then store indoors at about 15°C (60°F). Within these groups there are many different kinds to try and some varieties that can be used both ways.

Squash spread considerably and you should allow close to 3 m (10 ft.) of space for the largest winter squash and pumpkins, half that for smaller kinds and summer squash. Plant out after danger of frost is past and protect the seedlings as for cucumbers until the nights are consistently warm. Like cucumbers, new bush types and "space-saving" varieties are being introduced each year.

TOMATOES
Tomato group. Grow from plants. Set out plants 60 cm (24 in.) apart if supported, 90 cm (36 in.) if not.

Almost everyone who makes any pretense at gardening grows, or tries to grow, a tomato plant or two. There are two distinct types of tomato with entirely different growing habits. **Determinate** varieties have a built-in size regulator. They will grow just so many leaves and then stop, so the quantity of fruit they can produce is limited. These generally have a bushy habit and don't need much staking. **Indeterminate** varieties just keep on growing and producing fruit until the frost kills them.

There is probably a wider selection of tomatoes than any other vegetable and it will pay you to study descriptions in the catalogues. Pay particular attention to the "days to maturity"—how long it takes the plant to start producing ripe fruit—and choose short-season types. Varieties are available with red, pink, white, yellow, and orange fruit, while fruit size can range from cherry to beefsteak, where one slice can cover a hamburger. Height can also vary from the super dwarf 'Red Robin', small enough to ripen fruit on a kitchen window ledge, to 'Sweet 100' which I have had growing over 3 m (10 ft.) tall against a house wall. There are also different types for different purposes, from salad tomatoes to paste types grown especially for cooking.

When shopping for plants in a garden centre, look for those with a dark green colour and a short stocky stem. Try to pick plants that don't fall over when you remove them from the flat, although these are difficult to find. If you should have overgrown, floppy plants to deal with, pick off most of the lower leaves, leaving about half a dozen on top, then dig a deep, sloping hole and bury the bare stem of your plant below ground. This will quickly produce roots and the plant will benefit and grow faster. If you lay the plant down for a day or two before you plant it, the tip will turn up and make planting easier. Give each plant a handful of 5-10-5 monthly, sprinkling it over the root zone and watering it in.

If you only have room for a couple of plants, I would suggest you make one of them an early variety, such as 'Sub Arctic Maxi' or 'Alaska'. These varieties are very cold-tolerant and actually set fruit at low temperatures. We usually plant some out about five weeks before the last frost date, protect them with the circle of plastic tubes filled with water described on page 205, and start picking the first fruit in mid-June. Make a point to try a new variety of tomato each year. You will be surprised at how different they can be. The yellow and pink varieties tend to be low in acid and better for people with gastric problems.

Tomatoes can succumb to several diseases, so try to get varieties listed as V (verticillium), F (fusarium), N (nematode), and T (tobacco mosaic virus) resistant. Don't smoke when working near your tomatoes and always wash your hands before touching tomato plants if you have been smoking. Tobacco mosaic virus can be passed from smokers to tomatoes.

Sooner or later your plants will be affected by blossom end rot and blight, two troubles that most tomato growers experience. The cause of blossom end rot is still not fully understood, but it is tied in to the levels of calcium in the plant, which in turn is affected by the amount of water in the soil. A sudden wet spell following a drought can inhibit the plant's ability to take up calcium, leading to the lower end of the fruit becoming leathery and shrivelled. Mulching your plants to prevent excessive drying of the soil will help. It can also be caused by using a fertilizer with an equal amount of nitrogen and phosphorus (e.g., 10-10-10). Blight is a fungus disease that attacks the leaves, causing them to become shriveled and limp, with brownish blotches. It progresses up the plant and you can end up with a stem with no leaves in a bad attack. Luckily, the fruit is not affected (except that without leaves, no more are produced) and it ripens in the normal way. The disease overwinters on infected foliage left in the soil, so sanitation and crop rotation are the best ways to combat this.

GLOBE ARTICHOKE
Grow from plants. Space 1–1.2 m (3–4 ft.) apart.

Perennial farther south, these are worth growing if you have room. The introduction of varieties like 'Imperial Star' that will form buds the first summer has made this a vegetable I wouldn't be without. I plant out pot-grown seedlings and mulch between them, or intercrop with lettuce as an early mulch. They begin to crop in late summer and each plant will produce 6 to 8 mature globes before frost if given plenty of moisture.

VEGETABLES FOR HOT SOIL

EGGPLANT

Tomato group. Grow from plants. Space plants 60 cm (24 in.) apart.

Eggplants are always set out as plants. Our season is too short for direct-sown seed to produce a crop. They also hate cold soil and will drop any flowers they have and not make new ones for a long time if the soil temperature is low, so don't be in a rush to plant. Using a plastic mulch to warm the soil is very beneficial with eggplants. Cold winds are also detrimental, and if you can rig up a shelter to protect the plants from winds, your crop will be earlier and larger. HINT: When buying plants check the stems—they should be green, not woody.

PEPPER

Tomato group. Grow from plants. Space plants 30–45 cm (12–18 in.) apart, depending on variety.

Peppers may be hot or sweet; green, red, yellow, orange, or purple; round or tapering, but they all have one thing in common—they won't take cold weather. As with eggplants, don't hurry to plant them out. Wait until the soil and the nights are warm. Cold night temperatures cause peppers to abort their flower buds and in some seasons this can mean no peppers at all.

Being in the tomato family, the fruit of both peppers and eggplant can suffer from blossom end rot. It makes sense to mulch these in the same way you do tomatoes to reduce the fluctuations of soil moisture.

HARDY PLANTS

RHUBARB

Once it is established, rhubarb grows itself. The plants can get very large after a few years and one is enough for most families, unless they are real rhubarb fans. They are quite attractive and look at home in a mixed border when in flower, but if you're growing it for food, pull out the flower stems as soon as they appear. Rhubarb leaves contain oxalic acid which is poisonous if eaten in large quantities. I have never known anyone to eat rhubarb leaves, but when boiled in a stained saucepan, they do a wonderful job of cleaning it. To harvest rhubarb, grasp the stalk firmly and pull from the plant with a sharp tug. Cut off the leaf and place it at the base of the plant where it will rot down and help feed the clump. Because it may be growing in the same place for 20 years or more, deep soil preparation, making sure that there is good drainage below the plant, is essential. Rhubarb needs lots of water during the growing season and an annual mulch of good compost or manure. You can start to pick after the second winter.

ASPARAGUS

Although asparagus can be grown from seed, you can crop two years sooner by putting in plants. Allow lots of space, because you will not be satisfied with just a couple of roots. Twelve to fifteen roots per person is the usual recommendation, with 60 cm (24 in.) between plants. They are normally grown in a double row, 90 cm (36 in.) apart. This is another crop that will be in place for a couple of decades so good rich soil, free from perennial weeds, is essential. Plant in the spring using two-year-old crowns and mulch between the plants once the spears appear. You can make a light cutting the next spring, for no more than four weeks. Don't cut heavily until the third year after planting. When you cut, use a sharp knife and cut the spears below ground level, taking care not to damage any other shoots still below the soil. You can crop for six to eight weeks once the plants are mature, after which you must let the shoots grow and produce their fernlike foliage. Varieties like '**Jersey King**' and

'Jersey Knight' have predominantly male plants that give heavier crops for a longer period. You may be able to find them as transplants, but seed is readily available.

As soon as the soil is dry, it is beneficial to sprinkle a dressing of coarse salt on the soil surface at 1 kg (2 lb.) per 10 sq. m (100 sq. ft.). This old-time practice was thought to be a weed control, but research has shown that the salt enables the asparagus plants to resist crown rot—a serious disease of commercial plantings. Asparagus plants, native to the shores of the Mediterranean, are not affected.

Because asparagus starts to grow before the soil is warm, the bacteria aren't breaking down compost to release the nutrients, so it is beneficial to feed with a 5-10-10 fertilizer in early spring, applying 2 kg (4 lb.) to each 8 m (25 ft.) of row, and top-dress with a compost or manure mulch once cropping is over. Watch for red to brown beetles with black spots eating the leaves. These are asparagus beetles and they can rapidly defoliate your plants. Hand-pick or spray with rotenone to control them. In the fall, cut off the tops once they have been killed by frost.

HORSERADISH

Unless you are a real horseradish fanatic, you are wiser to buy this as roots or ready-prepared sauce. It is an invasive plant that will slowly colonize an increasingly large part of your garden. The roots grow very deep and are impossible to dig out. Like dandelion, horseradish will grow back from pieces of root left deep underground, and what was once a small clump becomes a thicket.

 # HERBS

Herbs may either be grown in their own special garden, or be mixed through the other flowers and vegetables. They should be fairly

close to the house so you can pop out and pick them fresh while in the middle of cooking.

BASIL
Tender annual. Start from seed.

Basil is extremely sensitive to cold, so don't sow until all danger of frost is past. It can be started indoors and then transplanted out after hardening off. This gives you good-sized plants earlier, but once the weather gets warm basil grows quickly anyway. Grow in full sun and pinch out the flower heads as they appear to keep the plants producing fresh leaves.

There are a number of different basils you might like to try. The common **sweet basil** is the type generally used for making pesto. It has leaves 5 to 7 cm (2 to 3 in.) long and grows 60 to 75 cm (24 to 30 in.) tall. The small-leaved varieties such as 'Spicy Globe' have a similar flavour but their leaves are only 1 to 2 cm (½ to 1 in.) long and the plant habit is dwarf and compact. **Lemon basil** grows about 60 cm (24 in.) tall and has a sharp lemony flavour; 'Sweet Dani', a 1998 All-America Selections winner, has a high oil content making it especially pungent. **Thai basil** has an anise-clove scent and is used in Asian cooking. 'Siam Queen', a 1997 AAS winner, has attractive compact flower spikes making it both ornamental and culinary. **Purple basils** can be grown in the flower border, and still be picked for kitchen use. The varieties with smoother leaves (like 'Osmin' and 'Red Rubin') have a better flavour than those with ruffled foliage. They make an interestingly coloured vinegar.

CHIVES
Hardy perennial. From seed or plants.

Grow chives in full sun or part shade, in either the flower garden or with your other herbs. It is a very hardy perennial that should be divided every two or three years and replanted in fresh soil. Old established plants don't produce the young leaves as freely. Clumps can be cut back almost to the ground during the summer and will quickly send up new growth to give you chives for the kitchen. Grow several small clumps and cut them back in rotation for a continual supply of fresh shoots.

If you have several clumps, lift and pot one in late fall. Leave it outside until it has had several hard frosts, and then bring it into the house. Placed on a bright window sill, it will give you fresh chives for most of the winter.

Garlic chives (also known as **Chinese chives**—see page 175) have flattened leaves and a garlic flavour. They can be used in place of regular chives in most dishes and are a good choice late in the season when regular chives are getting old.

CILANTRO

Annual. From seed or plants.

You can sow this like parsley, but it germinates more easily. Pick the leaves for use in cooking, and collect the seeds—they are sold as coriander. You may find cilantro in seed catalogues under that name. Make several sowings the first year; the plants should self-seed after this. It may be worth making a sowing in late fall to give a really early crop the following spring.

DILL

Hardy annual that self-seeds. Start from seed.

Sow dill in early spring in a rich, well-drained soil and full sun. It grows to almost a metre (3 ft.) with unmistakable feathery foliage that looks lovely grown with pink cosmos in the flower garden. Once you get this going in your garden you may never need to sow it again. If you leave a few flower heads to set seed, it will spread itself around and come up the following spring. The seedlings are unmistakable and you can leave them where they won't be in the way. Make successive sowings at first to keep young dill plants coming throughout the season. Later, it will spring up where you disturb the soil.

MINT

Hardy perennial. Grow from plants.

Although mint will grow almost anywhere, it does best in a moist, rich soil and partial shade. Mint is invaluable for enhancing the flavour of so many fresh vegetables. It does spread by underground runners and can take over if you aren't careful. Grow it in a large container, at least 60 cm (24 in.) deep with lots of drainage holes (or no bottom at all) and set this in the ground with a 10 cm (4 in.) rim above soil level. This will keep the mint from becoming a pest. There is a lot of difference in flavour among the various forms of mint, so taste and smell several to be sure of getting one with a flavour that pleases you.

OREGANO

Perennial. Grow from plants.

A necessary ingredient of many Mediterranean dishes. Look for the Greek strain of this herb. Grown in full sun it will reach 75 cm (30 in.) and should be cut back occasionally to encourage new growth with strong-flavoured leaves.

PARSLEY

Hardy, biennial.

Sow in early spring while the soil is still cool. Germination is slow and erratic, so be sure you mark both ends of the row; I am always getting hell for walking on the new parsley patch. Like mint, it grows best in rich soil and light shade, but it will survive almost anywhere. It will usually overwinter and can be used for a while, but once it goes to seed the flavour is not as good. Sow a short row each spring—the new plants will be ready by the time the old ones are starting to flower. The plain-leaved **Italian** type has more flavour than the curly kinds, but is not as attractive for a garnish. Parsley forms neat mounds 15 to 30 cm (6 to 12 in.) tall and looks good as an edging plant on mixed borders.

ROSEMARY

Tender perennial. Grow from plants.

Once you have tasted fresh rosemary, you will never be happy with the dried form again. This has to be overwintered indoors, preferably in a cool room with good windows or under fluorescent lights. Cuttings taken in August will root easily and often overwinter under lights better than the mature plants. It forms a small shrub about 45 cm (18 in.) tall and likes a light, sandy soil in full sun.

SAGE

Half-hardy perennial. From seed or plants.

The common garden sage is hardy to zone 5a, but the fancy-leaved forms, such as the purple, golden, and tricoloured sages, are not quite as tough and cannot be depended on to survive without good snow cover. It is easy to root from cuttings and grows well under fluorescent lights. In summer, grow it in full sun in poor, well-drained soil and cut it back each spring to preserve the bushy shape.

SUMMER SAVORY

Tender annual. Start from seed.

Summer savory is grown for use as a fresh or dried herb and needs a well-drained soil in full sun. Sow in early May so that the plants are established before the hot weather arrives. It has an open habit and will grow about 45 cm (18 in.) tall.

TARRAGON

Hardy perennial. Grow from plants.

Look for plants of the true French tarragon. This is the one with the flavour that is so lovely in chicken dishes. It can also be chopped into the salads you will make from your fresh produce, or it can be used to make a delicious vinegar, giving you the taste of summer year-round. French tarragon has a finer, shinier leaf than the Russian type. Grow it in full sun or part shade in a rich, well-drained soil where it will reach almost 1 m (3 ft.) in height. You will

often see tarragon seed offered in catalogues, but this is Russian tarragon, a much inferior beast and not worth growing.

THYME

Half-hardy perennial. From seed or plants.

The dwarf forms of thyme have been described under ground covers in Chapter 3, but the culinary thyme is a different species. It is taller and grows about 30 cm (12 in.) high which makes it much easier to cut and dry or freeze for later use. Start seed indoors in March and plant out into a light, well-drained soil in full sun once there is no danger of frost. You can direct-seed, but young plants are slow-growing and may not get large enough to be of use. Plants are not reliably hardy except in the mildest areas, and it is safest to consider them annuals and start fresh seed each year. Cut the plants back in midsummer to make them produce fresh foliage and prevent them from developing woody stems. Water frequently during dry weather.

 # SEED STORAGE

Like the annuals described in Chapter 9, many of the modern vegetables are F_1 hybrids and will not come true from seed. Many others are biennials and don't produce seed until the second year, by which time we have eaten them. However, the packets of seed that we buy often contain more seed than is needed for a single season, and correct storage will ensure they retain their viability for the coming year.

Reseal the packet once you have finished sowing by folding the top over and taping it closed. Place all the packets in a plastic container with an airtight lid.

Put a few of the packets containing drying chemicals that come with new binoculars, electronic equipment, and so on, in the container and close it properly. HINT: Drugstores get these packets in the bottles of prescription pills and if you talk nicely to your local pharmacist he or she may be willing to save you a few. If you make dried flower arrangements, the silica gel used to dry flowers will work equally well for storing seeds.

Store the container of seed in the refrigerator, but not in the freezer. Some seeds are killed by being frozen. You need to provide a cool, dry atmosphere to keep seeds properly.

The crystals inside the dri-pack absorb the moisture from the air and will occasionally require drying themselves. Some of the packs have a blue stripe, or blue crystals inside. When this turns pink it is time to recharge them. Either heat gently in the oven or place on a dark surface in full summer sun. The colour changes back to blue when they dry out. The lower the humidity in the storage area, the better the germination rate next year.

SUGGESTED READING

The Random House Book of Vegetables. Roger Phillips and Martyn Rix. Random House, 1993.
Pictures of vegetables and varieties with notes on cultivars. Use this with seed catalogues to see what you are ordering.

Vegetables From a Country Garden. Anstace and Larry Esmond-White. Lee Valley, 1993.
A revision of a long out of print book by the Canadian hosts of a popular PBS TV show.

The new Northern Gardener. Jennifer Bennett. Firefly Books, 1996.

The Harrowsmith Illustrated Book of Herbs. Patrick Lima. Camden House, 1986.
First published in 1982, this popular book has been updated to cover new ideas and varieties.

The Complete Book of Herbs. Lesley Bremness. Studio Books, 1994.
Just about everything you could consider to be an herb is included, plus recipes for using them.

The Random House Book of Herbs. Roger Phillips and Nicky Foy. Random House, 1990.
A companion volume to the one on vegetables, full of photos and information.

Pests
14
chapter

Efficient pest management is a state of mind; it needs planning from the beginning. Many of the things that I have been telling you in this book have been with that in view. A healthy soil grows strong healthy plants, which in turn have a greater disease resistance. A disease is something that affects the health of the plant and so an attack of aphids, which suck the sap and weaken the plant, can be considered in the same light as a bad case of mildew.

Adding organic matter to the soil will improve the structure, the water retention, and the drainage. This organic matter can come from compost, manures or green manuring as described in Chapter 1, or from a previous mulch you have dug into the soil. In addition, an organically rich soil is more likely to have beneficial fungi, known as *mycorrhiza*, that attach themselves to the roots, much as the nitrogen-fixing bacteria do on peas and beans, and, by improving the plants' nutrition, help

them fight off attacks.

Another way you can reduce the number of problems is by selecting plants for disease resistance. With annuals and vegetables you grow from seed, choose resistant varieties where possible. Even if you aren't growing your own plants, take a seed catalogue with you when you go to the garden centre, and if you have a choice of varieties, pick the one with the best rating for disease resistance. When deciding which trees and shrubs to plant, try to avoid the ones that are prone to a number of pest problems. In the garden centre, look over the plants and select those without broken branches, missing bark, or similar damage. Also try and match the plant with the site; a plant that needs full sun won't grow well in half shade and thus will be more liable to disease.

You can help a plant's resistance to problems by the way you grow it. Practise crop rotation with annuals and vegetables, where you are growing many plants of the same kind. Use an efficient irrigation system that puts the water where the plants need it—at the roots. A plant under stress from drought is a plant more likely to be attacked. There is more and more evidence that indicates many plants manufacture their own pest-inhibiting chemicals when they are growing well.

Try to avoid monoculture. Much as you may love roses, if your garden is full of them you can expect serious problems before very long. The more varied the plants you grow, the less likely it is that any one pest or disease will do much overall damage.

Many pests are specific to a particular plant, even though a related pest does the same damage on a different plant. For example, every year I get leaf miner damage on my columbines—but never on the birch tree in whose shade they grow, although this tree is very susceptible to leaf miners. That's because this particular miner is restricted to columbines and doesn't attack birch.

Using mulch whenever possible is another way of improving plant health. Mulch helps to conserve moisture, which helps to reduce drought stress, but, more important, it prevents many annual weeds from germinating and smothers some perennial ones. A lot of weeds act as host plants for pests and diseases just waiting to move onto your prized ornamentals, so by eliminating the weeds, you help reduce the chance of disease. Controlling weeds, by a combination of hoeing and mulching, will do a lot to cut down on pests entirely. Mulches also help prevent some of the insects that overwinter in the soil from emerging to lay their eggs on new plants.

Once you have built up your soil with organic matter, it will act as a reservoir for nutrients and your plants will grow well. Until that time, you may have to use some form of chemical fertilizer to keep your plants growing strongly and able to fight off disease. Plants that are stunted from a lack of nitrogen, or weak and spindly from an excess, are also disease prone.

Hygiene is probably the most important thing when it comes to combatting problems in the garden. A large number of diseases and quite a few pests overwinter on old flowers, fallen leaves, last year's stalks, and so on. Doing thorough clean-up in fall will save you time and worry in the summer ahead. If you suspect a plant is diseased, put it in the centre of the compost where the temperature will be highest. If you know it is diseased, put it in the garbage. Pests also congregate in piles of rubbish, heaps of garden stakes, etc. All provide an ideal overwintering environment.

THE FIVE-PRONGED ATTACK

So far I have been writing about ways to prevent troubles from visiting, but eventually troubles, like mothers-in-law, are bound to come, and this is how to deal with them.

1. Encourage natural predators in your garden. These may be microscopic predacious insects and mites or quite large animals and birds, but they all feed on pests that feed on plants.

The insects and mites that feed on other insects may do so directly, actually eating the bad guys, as in ladybugs and their larvae-eating aphids, or they may lay their eggs on either the eggs or a juvenile form of the host pest. Here the good egg hatches and devours the bad one. These are almost invisible killers and you may need a good hand lens to see the blackened eggs of whitefly that indicate they have been eaten by the grubs of *Encarsia* wasp.

If you think about it, you will realize that this type of control is not instantaneous. Until the pest is present, there is nothing for the parasite to feed on. Once the pest is there, it takes a while for the predator levels to build up enough to effect any control. And that control is never going to be total, so you have to accept that there will always be some pests present, but within acceptable limits.

Many birds feed on a wide range of animals, from mosquitoes to worms, and encouraging these birds can have a dramatic effect on the level of pests, as well as adding movement and song to the garden. Start at the planning stages by consciously including in your landscaping plants that provide food and shelter for birds. Many birds are omnivorous and eat both fruit and insects. Birds that shelter in your garden, either during the migration season or to nest, will usually feed while they are there.

Put up birdhouses for anything you can attract; even sparrows have to eat, while tree swallows will really go to town on the mosquitoes. (I know mosquitoes aren't plant pests, but a lack of them makes the garden more enjoyable.)

Feed the birds during the winter for two reasons. Having birds in the garden attracts other birds and in winter this may bring in chickadees and woodpeckers, both of which feed on eggs and overwintering insects on the bark of trees and shrubs. In early spring, the birds that overwinter with you will help attract the summer migrants, and these may stay to nest and feed.

Try to encourage larger animals, such as toads, bats, and (dare I say it?) snakes. These are all nocturnal and feed on the bugs the birds don't see. Toads and snakes will do a great job of keeping slug and snail populations down. While toads don't actually live in water, a very shallow pool will provide a place where they can go to soak. I use the base of a self-watering planter, about 30 cm across by 5 cm deep (12 by 2 in.), and place a couple of rocks for them to climb out on over the edge. Put up special boxes for bats to encourage them as well.

Snakes overwinter deep underground in a rocky place called a hibernaculum, where they congregate and curl up together to snooze the winter away. When rebuilding a section of his garden, a friend of mine noticed a snake entering a hole in a rock wall. He excavated a deep hole, filled it with large rocks and made a rock tunnel in a raised bed so the snakes could reach their hibernaculum. It worked, and he now has a good population of snakes keeping the slugs under control.

It is, I hope, obvious that if you are encouraging beneficial wildlife in your garden, you cannot go round spraying hither and yon with toxic chemicals.

2. Use *physical* controls. Where the pest is large, such as some of the caterpillars, it is easy to go round and actually pick them off and either tread on them or drop them in a can of soapy water. (If you are squeamish I am sure there is a small boy near you who would love to do this—an offer of a penny a piece will clean up the garden like magic.) A small attack of aphids can often be squashed against the plant, but check a few days later to make sure you got them all. Going round the garden at night with a flashlight will reveal an amazing number of slugs and other nocturnal pests that can be picked off and stomped on.

Many pests lend themselves to being trapped, especially those that are active at night. By providing the type of habitat they need for daytime shelter, you can often lure them into a situation in which you can deal with them on your terms. Slugs will collect on the undersides of pieces of board laid on the soil between plants and can be destroyed during the day. Earwigs will hide in rolls of newspaper, upside-down pots full of straw, or special traps, for collection in daylight.

Whitefly are chiefly a pest of indoor plants but they thrive outside during the summer and are very fond of tomatoes. They are attracted by bright yellow, and yellow boards covered with a sticky substance are sold as traps for them. These are intended to be hung near a greenhouse crop; when you use them outdoors they need an extra hole in the base so you can tie a string from the bottom to stop them swinging in the wind and getting stuck to everything.

Cutworms live in the soil and come out at night to chew through the stems of young plants at ground level. A barrier pushed 1 cm into the soil and standing 5 cm tall (about ¹/₂ in. into the soil, 2 in. above) will defeat their evil intentions. You can make the barriers from tinfoil folded double and curved into a circle, but I find that the cardboard frozen juice containers, with both ends removed and cut in half, are ideal.

If you have problems with slugs eating your baby lettuce (look for the slime trails on the ground early in the morning), surround the plants with sharp sand, coarse ashes, or diatomaceous earth (see below). These will all cut into the slug's bodies and either kill them or deter them.

The use of floating row covers to enclose young plants can both increase their rate of growth and prevent pests from getting to them (*if* you didn't have pests to start with). Mulches, especially solid forms like a plastic sheet, can stop the pests that overwinter in the soil and emerge in spring to feed on the new crop.

3. Use *natural* sprays. There are a few sprays made from naturally occurring substances (as distinct from the next group) that can be used in certain circumstances with great success. Generally these affect very specific pests and thus are the safest of all the sprays. They have very short persistence and must be sprayed onto the pest to control it.

All true soaps have some insecticidal property (but not detergents) and spraying your plants with a solution of any soap will control some insects. However, one chemical company, Safer Ltd., has carried out tests and isolated the fatty acids contained in soaps that are the most effective bug killers. They now market these as **insecticidal soaps**. These will control a wide range of insect pests (and also some of their predators) but are non-toxic to higher animals and break down rapidly.

There are several bacteria that attack certain stages of the insect life cycle and one of these, *Bacillus thuringiensis* (BT), has been isolated and cultured and is available as a spray. Sold under various trade names, this product will kill *only* the caterpillar stage of moths and butterflies, although this covers a wide range of leaf-eating pests. It does not work against many other common beetles and bugs that feed on plants. A different strain will control Colorado potato beetle.

In a similar vein, beneficial nematodes, mentioned on page 59, can be used to control certain soil-dwelling pests. Although they are mostly used against chinch bugs and white grubs in lawns, they will also control cutworms, some borers, root weevils, wireworms and the eggs of slugs and earwigs, or so the suppliers claim.

While trees and shrubs are dormant, you can spray with light oils to kill eggs and insects overwintering in crevices of the bark. Strangely enough, this is called **dormant oil**, and it must be applied before there is any sign of growth but when the temperature is above freezing.

Many books on organic gardening recommend the use of sprays made from the actual insect. For example, if you have a bad attack of asparagus beetle, you collect some and purée them in the kitchen blender. This purée is then diluted and sprayed onto the asparagus. I must admit I have never tried this. I couldn't look a milkshake in the eye again!

While it is not strictly a spray, **diatomaceous earth** is definitely natural. It is composed of the spiny bodies of tiny diatoms that lived millions of years ago. When dusted onto plants or the soil it cuts the soft bodies of many insects as they crawl across it, causing them to lose body fluids and die. It is non-selective and kills the predators as well if they walk on it.

Sulphur has long been used to prevent diseases gaining a hold, but it is messy to apply and corrosive on spray equipment. Adding lime to sulphur increases its effectiveness and allows it to kill recently germinated spores. Use this in summer on certain disease outbreaks. It is also used in winter, like dormant oil, to kill overwintering spores of fungal diseases. Providing the plant is dormant, these two sprays can be combined and applied as one. In summer, use lime-sulphur on its own, but not when the temperature is above 30°C (85°F).

Copper is another element long used in fungal disease control. It gained fame during the bad disease outbreaks that decimated the French wine industry in the late 1870s and the most commonly used form is known as **Bordeaux mixture**—although you are more likely to find it spelt Bordo!

Another common chemical with fungicidal properties is **baking soda**. This is reputedly good against blackspot on roses and against mildew on many plants. It is not persistent and must be reapplied after rain or overhead watering. Dissolve 5 mL (1 tsp.) of baking soda in a litre (quart) of water and add a few drops of insecticidal soap or dish detergent to help the spray spread across the foliage.

4. Use *botanical* sprays. These are made up of chemicals extracted from plants, or improved versions of these made in the laboratory. They are non-selective and will kill both pests and predators on contact, but since they break down quickly, their effect is minimal. Use them as contact sprays when you see you have a problem.

Pyrethrum is made from the powdered flower heads of a species of chrysanthemum and has an extremely low toxicity for warm-blooded animals. Recent research, however, indicates that it may be toxic to the polliwogs of frogs and toads. Most often available are the synthetic pyrethroids, such as **permethrin**, which are equally safe for users and their pets, but not for the bugs.

Rotenone is the powdered root of tropical trees in the pea family, chiefly *Derris*, and this powder is sometimes called by that name. While it has low toxicity to us, it is highly toxic to fish and should be used with great care near pools and streams.

One other product has a botanical base. Made from hops and malt, **beer** can be used with great success to control slugs. Shallow saucers of beer, sunk flush with the ground, will provide a deadly drink for them. While it is generally recommended only as a slug killer, one friend told me that she fished out 30 or 40 dead earwigs every morning, day after day.

5. Use *synthetic* chemicals. Occasionally, when all else fails, you may have to resort to using a factory-made chemical to save your plant or the crop. Try to use something that is short-lived and fairly specific to have the least effect on the rest of the insects and animals in your garden.

The names given are the common names of the chemical. Each company may have its own trade name. If in doubt, ask one of the staff, or look for the active ingredient listed somewhere on the container.

Chlorpyrifos is generally found in soil and lawn insecticides and is available as a spray or powder. It is quite persistent and fairly toxic but is useful for applying in places where earwigs might hide in regions where these are a problem.

Dimethoate is a **systemic** insecticide, which means it can be absorbed into the sap stream of the plant and will control pests you can't touch with a regular surface spray. It can be taken in through the leaf surface, through the roots, or, in a few cases, through the bark. It is quite persistent and toxic but is the only thing that will control leaf miners on large plants.

Diazinon is one of the most commonly used insecticides because it will control a wide range of pests. It breaks down quickly and can be used on food crops providing you allow the necessary time between spraying and eating. It also kills good insects, so use it with caution.

Malathion is another widely used pesticide that is much safer than diazinon for the user. It also will kill a wide range of insects, good and bad.

Methoxychlor is one of the safest of all the commonly used insecticides and should be effective against whitefly. It also kills many other pests.

Carbaryl is another broad-spectrum insecticide that is widely recommended. It is extremely toxic to bees and should never be used on or near plants in flower.

Thiram is a fungicide used mainly on seeds to protect them from soil-borne diseases. It is also included in many deer and rabbit repellents because of its bitter taste.

Captan is probably the most widely used fungicide, as a dust or spray. It is used for scab, leaf blotches and mildew. Although there is now some doubt about its safety, it is still registered for use.

Benomyl is a systemic fungicide that is taken into the plant and attacks the disease from within. It is used mostly for mildew and leaf spot control. It is highly toxic to earthworms, so use it sparingly as a spray and not as a soil drench.

Triforine is a powdery mildew control that can also be used against some rusts and leaf spots.

Many other fungicides are registered for home use but are only available in combination dusts and sprays, often called Home & Garden Dust or Garden Spray. Check the labels to find out what each one will control, and any plants that it should not be used on.

In the section that follows, I suggest chemicals to use, should it be necessary. Remember that all insecticides and fungicides, both botanical and synthetic, are poisonous. They should be kept under lock and key, out of reach of children, and never be stored in a container that could be mistaken for something else. Liquid formulations may lose

their effectiveness if allowed to freeze, so they are best brought into the house for the winter if you normally keep them in an unheated building. Once mixed, all insecticides should be used without delay. They lose their effectiveness if stored for any length of time. Mix only the quantity you need and use it all. Always read and follow the directions carefully. Never mix stronger solutions than recommended—you may kill your plants along with the pest.

How often you use a pesticide depends on how much pest damage you are willing to tolerate on your plants. If you are willing to cut the outer, chewed leaves off a cabbage, you may not need to spray at all. If, as happened to me last summer, you get a tremendous attack of Colorado potato beetle, you either have to spray or resign yourself to almost no crop. If you are a competitive gardener who tries to win all first prizes at the local show, your level of tolerance will be low; if you are a confirmed organic gardener, your tolerance level is probably quite high. Be observant and learn to recognize friend from foe in the garden so that if you spray you are sure you know what you are aiming to control, and why.

So far, I have said very little about diseases caused by fungi. Generally, the chemicals used to control them don't seem to have the harmful side effects that insecticides do, and there aren't the biological alternatives available. Many diseases and pests can be ignored. While they may be unsightly, they are not going to threaten the long-term health of your plant.

All chemicals are toxic to some extent and should be used with caution. Wear rubber gloves at all times when handling the concentrate, even for "safe" substances such as BT. Mix them outdoors where there is good air circulation, wear a dust mask if you are mixing wetable powders and wear long trousers and a long-sleeved shirt while spraying. If you are spraying one of the toxic chemicals onto trees, where the spray may drift back on you, wear protective goggles and hat as well. Wash thoroughly when you are finished. Never put concentrated insecticides in any other container and never use a sprayer that has previously been used for herbicides.

 # PESTS

The number of pests that may attack your plants is enormous and I could fill a book twice this size just writing about each one. Luckily for us, the number of different insects that you are likely to find on a regular basis is quite small. Those are covered here. With all the rest, what you need to note is the type of damage they are causing and you will have a good idea of how to control them. After all, it doesn't really matter if your leaves are being eaten by a spotted or a striped cucumber beetle, the control for most chewing insects is the same. Each listing is followed by control based on the methods from the five-pronged attack. The control method(s) I consider the best are in italic. If you follow this method of pest control, the use of toxic chemicals in the garden can be greatly reduced.

Aphid: Probably the commonest of all pests, they are also known as greenfly but may be pink, yellow, black, or almost colourless as well. There are many different species of aphid, each of which has a preferred group of plants that it feeds on. Thus, the often recommended practice of planting nasturtiums between your roses to attract the aphids doesn't really work. Roses are attacked by the green form while it is the black ones that like nasturtiums. During the summer, the female aphids produce live young, all females, which mature in a couple of weeks and in turn give birth to more females. It is only in the fall that males are produced and normal mating takes place. In most species they overwinter as eggs,

which hatch in spring—all females, naturally.

As you can guess, a population explosion doesn't take long but, luckily, there are several natural predators—ladybugs and certain hover flies being the chief ones. An immature ladybug will eat 25 aphids a day and an adult twice this so they are to be encouraged to stay around. Some firms sell ladybugs to release in the garden, but unless you have a large aphid population they will go off to seek food elsewhere. Aphids are also a principal food for many birds, such as chickadees, sparrows, orioles, and most warblers. They can collect up to 1,300 aphids per hour during the nesting season.

Best Control: • *Ladybugs.* • Squashing. • *Insecticidal soap.* • Rotenone.

Beetles: These are a large family of insects that can be both beneficial and pestiferous. The large black beetle you will see scurrying about when you move a piece of wood is a ground beetle, and it feeds on other insects, including some we don't want, and slugs. This is a good guy; don't tread on him. Lady beetles are another one to encourage in the garden. Beetles that feed on plants are a different matter (see Japanese beetle later in this listing as an example).

There are a great many beetles, such as Colorado beetle, rose chafer, and lily beetle that chew leaves, stems, fruit, or roots and that you may have to deal with.

Best Control: • *Hand-pick* when populations are small; rotate crops in the vegetable garden. • Spray with the crushed pest. • *Rotenone.* • Carbaryl.

Borer: A number of different borers attack several different trees; the locust (*Robinia*) has the most problems. Because the larvae are inside the trunk, they are difficult to deal with and are often not noticed for a long time. Look for little piles of sawdust on the ground or caught in crevices on the bark. Vine borers tunnel into the stems of cucumbers, squash, and melons, causing the plant to suddenly wilt, while corn borers feed on the outer parts of the plant at first and then eat their way into the stem where they overwinter.

Best Control: • Poke thin wires into tunnels on trees; slit squash vines and kill larvae, then mound soil over the wound to encourage rooting; clean up old corn stalks. • *BT injected into holes or stems.* • Rotenone. • Methoxychlor.

Caterpillar: These are the juvenile form of moths and butterflies and most feed on plants of some kind. Only a few are serious enough to need controling, but these include codling moth on apples, corn earworm, cutworms, cabbage worms, gypsy moth, tent caterpillars, and fall webworms. Most are surface-chewing insects and are first noticed when we see holes in the leaves. Many other insects chew holes, but caterpillars are well-known and easy to recognize.

Best Control: • Small wasps and hoverflies that lay their eggs on caterpillars. • Hand-pick the large ones, such as tomato horn worm. • *BT.* • Pyrethrum.

Centipede: Generally a light brown colour, with a slightly flattened body and one pair of legs per segment (if you can keep them still long enough to count). These are fast-moving hunters that live in the soil and eat many plant pests. *Do not kill them.* See also **Millipede.**

Cutworm: Really a caterpillar, cutworms live in the surface of the soil and emerge at night to feed on stems at ground level.

Best Control: • Parasitic wasps. • *Collars around each plant.* • BT. • Pyrethrum.

Earwig: I wish I could find an efficient way to kill earwigs. I would make a fortune. In some parts of the country they are the major pest, chewing everything in sight. I heard of one lady who sowed her carrots three times and then gave up. Each time the seedlings came up, they were eaten off at ground level by a squad of earwigs. About 2 cm long (almost 1 in.) they are a chestnut brown colour and have a pair of pincers on the back. They are incredibly tough and keep on running away even when almost cut in half. Feeding at night, they will eat most plants, although dahlias and marigolds seem to be their favourites. I find many during the day hiding in daylily flowers, but have not seen any chewed petals.

In fact, earwigs prefer a diet of plant remains and only eat most growing plants because their preferred food is not available. We have found that adding lots of compost increases the earwig population, but decreases the damage they do. I still don't like them, but I am learning to live with them.

Best Control: • Toads. • *Trapping.* • Insecticidal soaps (but you have to *find* the earwigs first). • Carbaryl (bait), chloropyrifos.

Flea beetles: Tiny insects, generally black, that feed on the leaves of many plants but especially members of the cabbage family. They cause shot-hole damage on the leaves and a bad attack will kill young plants in a matter of days. They are very active and are hard to control with botanical sprays, which have a very short persistence; as soon as you start to spray, the flea beetles all jump back into the soil.

Best Control: • *Use a solid mulch* between the plants to stop the beetles jumping onto the plants from the soil. • Insecticidal soap if you can get a contact. • Pyrethrum. • Diazinon granules mixed into the soil.

Gall insects: A great many different insects cause galls (swellings) to occur on many plants. These range from the green or red pimples found on maple leaves to the large mossy rose gall. Generally they don't kill the plant and natural predators will keep them from becoming an epidemic. Apart from pruning off any that occur as swellings on single stems, no control is needed, but use dormant oil to kill overwintering adults and, if leaf galls are a problem, be sure to clean up and dispose of fallen leaves.

Japanese beetle: This is a serious pest in the U.S. and is slowly spreading into Canada. The larvae live in the soil, feeding on roots, and look similar to white grubs; the adults, which are a metallic blue or green, eat the leaves of many plants, especially roses.
    Best Control: • Special traps baited with a scent capture the adults. Shake adults off flowers into a container and then kill them. • *Milky spore disease* is similar to BT and kills the larvae underground. • *Rotenone* for adults. • Methoxychlor if all else fails.

Leafhopper: Small green insects that move quickly and feed on the developing buds of many plants. A bad attack will stop the flower buds from developing altogether. Being small and green they are difficult to detect, but if you brush your hand over a plant you will see them leap away.
    Best Control: • Some wasps (not very effective). • Floating row covers on vegetables. • *Diatomaceous earth.* • Rotenone. • Malathion or methoxychlor.

Leaf miner: Several different insects lay their eggs on the stems or leaves of plants and when the larvae hatch they tunnel into the leaves and live between the upper and lower leaf surfaces. Some chew out a large room; others make a winding tunnel. Both are hard to control since the leaf surface stops any spray from making contact. Cedar hedges and specimen trees can be badly affected by cedar leaf miner, which causes the tips of the leaf fans to turn brown. If you notice damage, clip your hedge in early June and destroy the clippings to kill the young inside the leaves. Keep a close watch on

the plants and if you see numerous small grey moths in late June and July, spray frequently with pyrethrum to kill the adults before they have a chance to lay eggs.
    Best Control: • *Pick off infected leaves* and destroy where possible. • Spray or water the soil with a systemic insecticide such as dimethoate, which is taken into the sap and kills the insect inside the leaf. This is the only solution if the attack is very severe or on large trees (see Birch in Chapter 4).

Mice, voles: These can be a real nuisance in spring when their winter activities are revealed. They will often thrive under the snow. They make tunnels in the surface of the lawn and eat the bark off shrubs. If the soil isn't frozen, they tunnel down after perennial buds and spring bulbs. Their damage goes in cycles and depends to some extent on the snow cover available to hide them from hawks, owls, and foxes, all of which prey on rodents.
    Best Control: • Wildlife to feed on them. • Traps. • *Any of the special baits* placed inside a soft-drink can (with the opening enlarged slightly) so that pets and birds can't get at it.

Millipede: Generally a darker colour than the centipede, millipedes have two pairs of legs per body segment and are circular in cross section. They are slow-moving and tend to curl into a spring when discovered. They feed on decaying plant remains, but also on roots and stems of seedlings and will tunnel into potatoes, carrots, and other root crops. Infestations are seldom severe enough to need any type of chemical.
    Best Control: • Centipedes. • *Squash them or pull in half whenever found.* Set up hiding places as for slugs.

Mites: Closely related to spiders, mites are not insects, so insecticides do not kill them. While chiefly a pest of greenhouse crops, mites do attack several outdoor plants, causing the leaves to turn a pale bronzy-yellow colour. On spruce, particularly the dwarf Alberta spruce, the needles will turn brown and fall off. Mites are very tiny and you are unlikely to see them without a good hand lens but you may see the webs sheathing each stem in a bad attack. They are sometimes called red spider but may be yellow or transparent as well. Don't confuse them with the velvet spider, bright red and about $1/4$ cm ($1/8$ in.) across. These are beneficial.

Best Control: • Lacewings, predatory mites. • *Frequent spraying with water* washes the mites off and discourages them. • Insecticidal soap will help in summer; dormant oil kills overwintering adults. • Look for a **miticide** in a general-purpose spray.

Plant bugs: There are several bugs which feed on plants. They are often distinctly marked and/or shaped but not all bugs are harmful so be sure they are feeding on your plants before you deal with them. From experience I would consider the **tarnished plant bug** to be the one you are most likely to find. These are a brownish-yellow with black and yellow markings and both adults and young suck the sap from flowers and fruit. They also inject a chemical which causes the flowers to become distorted.

Best Control: • Predatory wasps. • Sanitation. • *Rotenone.* • Malathion.

Sawfly: These are chiefly pests of pine, mountain ash, and roses, and are the caterpillars of a type of fly, not a moth or butterfly, so they can't be controlled with BT. They do considerable damage in a short time and any small caterpillar with black dots should be viewed with alarm.

Best Control: • *Insecticidal soap.* • *Permethrin.* • Methoxychlor.

Scale insects: Mostly pests of trees, shrubs, and house plants, scale insects look like rough, corky patches on shoots and branches. Eggs,

laid under the female's body, hatch in early summer and the young crawl away to find their own feeding spot. They insert a feeding tube into the plant, cover themselves with a protective waxy coating, and settle down to feed. If left undisturbed, they build up to a heavy infestation that weakens the plant and turns the foliage a pale yellow-green.

Best Control: • Parasitic wasps and hover-flies. • Painting with a 50% alcohol solution (works best on small plants with minimal pests); prune out infected branches. • *Dormant oil in winter.* • *Spray with pyrethrins* in May and June to kill crawling young. • Same as pyrethrins but use carbaryl.

Slugs and snails: Members of the same family as escargot, our slugs and snails don't reach the giant size that they do on the west coast or farther south, I am glad to say. Even so, they can do a lot of damage if they are allowed free access to all the plants, especially to young seedlings and lettuce. They are night feeders, and a trip round the garden at night with a flashlight can be a revelation. You won't believe just how much livestock your garden is sheltering.

Best Control: • *Toads, snakes, and ground beetles* (the shiny black ones often seen scurrying away when you move a piece of wood). • Barriers of gritty substances around plants, traps. • *Beer.* • Metaldehyde slug baits.

Spruce budworm: While mainly a pest of forest plantations, ornamental spruce and fir can also be attacked. The budworm feeds on the new growth and eats all the new needles, leaving only the stem. Severe infestations will kill a tree.

Best Control: • *BT.* • Rotenone. • Carbaryl.

Squirrels: To a non-gardener, squirrels are cute. I call them tree rats. They will dig up bulbs, eat buds, reach out from a tree to nibble on your prize blooms, raid bird feeders and scare off the birds, and do considerable damage to young trees and shrubs by feeding on the shoots all winter. If only the neighbours didn't feed them! Trapping does little good; it only creates a vacuum and other squirrels move in. Also, you then have to release them somewhere else, somewhere that already has a squirrel problem.

Best Control: I don't think there is one. Small areas of newly planted bulbs can be protected with chicken wire, but this doesn't work once the bulbs grow. Plant lots of fritillaries (see Chapter 10); the squirrels don't seem to like them.

Thrip: Tiny insects that are seldom seen directly, although the results of their feeding are often obvious. They hide in flowers and the folded leaves of many plants and feed on new shoots and developing buds. They are particularly bad on gladioli, where they cause a silvery sheen on the leaves, and on daylilies where they streak the flowers.

Best Control: • Dust gladioli bulbs with sulphur or *carbaryl* before you store them, to kill overwintering adults. • Insecticidal soap. • Permethrin. • Malathion.

Weevils: A kind of beetle, there are several different species that attack various plants. The **black vine weevil**, also known as the **taxus weevil**, is a serious pest of yews, rhododendrons, and some other shrubs. The adults feed on the foliage while the larvae munch the roots, eventually killing the plant. As the adults cannot fly, inspect the roots of newly purchased yews, rhodos and azaleas carefully for larvae before planting; once in the soil they are difficult to kill.

Best Control: • Diatomaceous earth. • Parasitic nematodes (for larvae). • Malathion or *methoxychlor*.

Whitefly: As mentioned, these can be a serious indoor pest but they also get carried out-side, will multiply rapidly, and can fly in from neighbouring gardens. They feed on the underside of the leaf and if you knock against an infested plant, will rise up in a white cloud. Be sure to spray upwards to coat the undersides of each leaf.

Best Control: • Several wasp species. • *Sticky yellow cards* attract the adults. • Insecticidal soap. • *Resmethrin*. • Methoxychlor.

Wireworms: Similar to millipedes, wireworms are generally lighter in colour, and don't have the many legs. They tend to curl into a comma rather than a coil when disturbed. They feed on plant remains but also on potatoes and other root crops. Control as for millipedes.

DISEASES

While there are a multitude of diseases that attack plants, many are specific to one or two species. If they are a major problem for that plant, I wrote about them under the plant heading. Those that follow are general diseases, likely to be found on a range of different plants.

Anthracnose: Generally recognizable as sunken areas with a watery-looking surround, anthracnose can attack leaves, stems, or branches on a wide variety of plants. Many of the "leaf spots" that are so difficult to identify are caused by anthracnose.

Best Control: Prune off infected twigs, rake up leaves and dispose of them in the garbage. *Do not compost.* On infected trees and shrubs, spray with lime sulphur in late winter. In early spring use a copper-based fungicide just as the leaves start to unfurl, again when they are half open, and a third time when the foliage is fully open.

Botrytis: There are many different races of botrytis, each attacking a fairly narrow range of plants. It starts as small brown spots on leaves or stems and spreads rapidly, especially in wet or humid weather. It will often attack flowers (especially geraniums) and coat them in a grey fuzz.

Best Control: Spray with benomyl or captan.

Cankers: Cankers may be small and easy to confuse with galls, or large and slow-growing. They appear as dead, often sunken, areas on stems and branches and may be fungal in origin (like the black knot disease of cherries and plums), bacterial, or the result of mechanical injury such as careless mowing. If left untreated they will often spread into the wood and girdle it, killing that branch or the entire plant.

Best Control: Prune out the infected branch where possible. Inspect the cut surface to make sure it is free from discolouration; if not, prune again further down after sterilizing the pruners with rubbing alcohol or bleach.

Downy mildew: Found mainly on vegetables, downy mildew occurs mainly on the underside of the leaves, causing the upper surface to become a pale greenish-yellow. This is mostly a disease of cool, wet weather in spring or fall.

Best Control: Crop rotation; don't walk between wet plants; spray with maneb.

Powdery mildew: If your plants look like they have been dusted with talc, you probably have powdery mildew. This is a high-humidity disease and is most likely to occur in midsummer on a wide range of plants, but especially on roses, bergamot, phlox, begonias, and zinnias. With perennials, try to make sure there is a good air flow round the plants and divide often to keep the clumps small. This disease is wafted in on the air currents and there is not a lot you can do to prevent it. It is seldom fatal on roses or perennials but it will weaken the plants by causing premature leaf drop.

Best Control: Sanitation; benomyl spray.

Rusts: This disease gets its name from the rust-coloured spores produced on the leaf surface. Most rusts need two separate host plants to complete their life cycle and removing one of these will act as a control. Some rusts have economic repercussions, such as the one that grows on wheat and barberry, leading to a ban on growing barberries in Canada, and white pine rust, whose other host is currants. The most common rust is the one that alternates between cedars and junipers and members of the rose family, such as apples, hawthorn or serviceberry. Other plants infected by other rusts include hostas, mint, asters, and several ornamental grasses.

Best Control: Remove alternate host or prune off fruiting bodies in late winter (bright orange swellings on juniper). Spray with a copper-based fungicide in spring. Control weeds, as these are often the alternate host.

Verticillium: The major cause of wilts, this disease enters through the roots and plugs the vessels that carry water up the plant. It attacks many trees, such as catalpa and lindens, and a range of annuals including asters, dahlias, impatiens, phlox and snapdragons. Since it lives in the soil, it is almost impossible to control, so if you get unexplained wilting and suspect this is the cause, don't grow these annuals.

Best Control: None.

SUGGESTED READING

Rodale's Chemical-Free Yard and Garden. Anna Carr, Miranda Smith et al. Rodale Press, 1991.

The Gardener's Guide to Plant Diseases: Earth-safe Remedies. Barbara Pleasant. Storey Communications, 1995.

Two books on organic methods of pest control.

Deer Proofing Your Yard & Garden. Rhonda Massingham Hart. Storey Communications, 1997.

Deer are becoming a problem in many areas and this helps us know the best plants to grow to avoid the problem.

Handbook of Natural Insect and Disease Control. Barbara W. Ellis and Fern Marshall Bradley (editors). Rodale Press, 1996.

A book I find myself turning to again and again for common sense controls.

Common-sense Pest Control. William Olkowski, Sheila Darr and Helga Olkowski. Taunton Press, 1991.

A fairly technical book that includes insect lifecycles and covers non-garden pests such as ticks.

INDEX

Where there is more than one reference, any main reference appears in **boldface.**

Acclimatization, 66, 158
Acer, 100
Achillea, 153, 191
Acidanthera, 181
Aconite, winter, 179
Actinidia, 99
Adam's needle, 106
Aesculus, 74
African blue lily, 179
African daisy, 160
Agapanthus, 179
Ageratum, 162
Ajuga, 142
All-American Selection, 155
Allium, 175–76
Almond: double flowering, 74; flowering 90
Alpine aster, 187
Alpines, 184
Aluminum sulphate, 16
Alyssum, 160
Alyssum, 187
Amelanchier, 103
Androsace, 190
Anemone, buttercup, 173; Greek, 173; Japanese, 139; poppy, **173**, 181; wood, 173
Angelica, 151
Angelica-tree, 89
Annuals, **155–69**; buying, 157; climbers, 167–68; feeding, 158, 159, 160; for containers, 197, plate 25; growing from seed, 159; hardening off, 158; planning, 156–57; planting, 157, **158–59**; soil preparation, 156; suggested other reading, 168; summer care, 159–60
Anthracnose, 231
Antirrhinum, 166
Ants, 59, 150
Aphid, 105, 160, 221, **227**; honeysuckle, 96
Aquilegia, 142–43, 188
Arabis, 190
Aralia, 89
Arborvitae. *See* Cedar, eastern white, 73
Arctostaphylos, 89
Aristolochier, 94
Armeria, 190
Arrowwood. *See* Viburnum, 105
Artemesia, 153
Artichoke, globe, 214; Jerusalem, 211
Aruncus, 146
Ash, 71
Asparagus, 20, **215–16**
Aster: New England, 139; New York, 139; China, 160
Aster wilt, 160
Aster yellows, 160
Astilbe, 139, plate 24

Athyrium, 147
Aubrieta, 187, plate 37
Auricula, 187
Azalea, 89

Baby's breath, 139
Bacillus thuringiensis, 224, 226
Bacopa, 160
Bacteria, nitrogen fixing, 17–18, 221
Balled and burlapped plants, 68, 86; planting, 69–70
Balloonflower, 140
Bare root plants, 68, 69, 86; planting, 69–70, 86, 123
Barrenwort, 140, plate 11
Basil, 216
Basket of gold, 187, plate 37
Beans, 204; broad, 209; green and wax, 212; pole, 212; scarlet runner, 168
Bearberry, 89
Beardtongue, 140, 187
Beautybush, 90
Beech, 72
Beer, 225
Beet, 208
Beetles, **227**; Colorado potato, 224, 226, 227; European lily, 177; flea, 228; Japanese, 58, **229**
Begonia, 180; tuberous, 161, plate 27; wax, 161, plate 27
Bellflower: Carpathian, 187–88; clustered, 140; creeping, 131; fairies' thimbles, 188; harebell, 188; Italian, 188; milky, 140; peach-leaved, 140–41
Benomyl, 226
Bergamot, 141
Betula, 72
Bidens, 161, plate 15
Birch, 72
Birds in the garden, 199, 223, 227
Bishops weed, 62, 131
Black knot, 109
Black medick, 55
Black snakeroot. *See* Bugbane, 142
Blackspot, 127
Bladdercherry. *See* Chinese lantern, 142
Blanketflower, 141
Blazingstar, 141
Bleedingheart, 141–142
Blight, on tomato, 214
Bloodroot, 173, plate 28
Blossom end rot, 214
Bluebell, 173, plate 35
Bluet, mountain, 147
Borer, 227–28; birch, 72; iris, 146
Boston ivy, 89
Botanical names, about, 45–46
Botanical sprays, 225
Botrytis, 232
Box elder. *See* Manitoba maple, 78

Bridalwreath, 104
Broccoli, 211
Broom, 90
Brussels sprouts, 212
BT, 224, 226
Buckeye. *See* Chestnut, 74
Buckthorn, 73
Buddleja, 90
Bugbane, 142
Bugleweed, 142; plate 5
Bugs, plant, 230
Bulbs, 169–82; dividing, 172; for containers, **172–73**, 198; for rock gardens, 188; hardy, 169, 170, **171–73**; mulching, 170; naturalizing, 172; planting, 170–71; soil preparation for, 169–70; suggested other reading, 182; tender, 170–71, **179–82**
Busy Lizzy. *See* Patience plant, 164–65
Butterfly bush, **90**, 113

Cabbage, 212
Calibrating a spreader, 50
California poppy, 161
Caliper trees, 68, 69
Calla lily, 180
Callistephus, 160
Campanula, 140–41, 187–88
Campsis, 104
Canada thistle, 130
Canary creeper, 167
Candytuft, 188
Cankers, 232
Canna lily, 180, plate 36
Captan, 226
Caragana, 80, 100
Carbaryl, 59, 226
Carpinus, 76
Carrots, 208
Castor oil plant, 161
Catalpa, 73
Caterpillar, 223, **228**
Catharanthus, 166
Catmint, 142
Cauliflower, 211
Cedar: common, 90; eastern white, 73
Celosia, 161–62
Centaurea, 147
Centipede, 228
Cercidiphyllum, 77
Cercis canadensis, 81
Chaenomeles, 101
Chamaecyparis, 95
Chamomile, 61
Chemical safety, 54–55, 226–27
Cherry: Amur chokecherry, 73; double flowering almond, 74; European bird-cherry, 74; flowering almond, 90; Japanese flowering, 74; Manchu, 91; Nanking, 91; purple-leaved sand, 91; Shubert chokecherry, 74